Historicizing
Theory

Historicizing Theory

edited by

Peter C. Herman

STATE UNIVERSITY OF NEW YORK PRESS

Published by
State University of New York Press, Albany

For information, address State University of New York Press,
90 State Street, Suite 700, Albany, NY 12207

Production by Christine L. Hamel
Marketing by Michael Campochiaro

Library of Congress Cataloging-in-Publication Data

Historicizing theory / edited by Peter C. Herman.
    p. cm.
    Includes bibliographical references and index.
    ISBN 0-7914-5961-6 (alk. paper) — ISBN 0-7914-5962-4 (alk. paper : pbk.)
    1. Criticism—History—20th century. I. Herman, Peter C., 1958–

PN94.H58 2003
801'.95'0904—dc21

                                                                    2003052817

10 9 8 7 6 5 4 3 2 1

CONTENTS

ACKNOWLEDGMENTS

This book could not have happened without the essential help and encouragement from a small army of people upon whose kindness I rely. First and foremost, I am happy to publicly acknowledge my debt to Jeff Williams, without whose knowledge and insights I could not have edited this volume. James Peltz is, as always, the editor par excellence, and we all owe a debt to Christine Hamel, who presided over the book's publication. I am also very grateful to Bernard Gotfryd for allowing us to use his photo of Harold Bloom. Finally, I dedicate this book to my wife, Meryl, and my children, Alison and Jon, without whom nothing would mean anything at all.

INTRODUCTION

The Resistance to Historicizing Theory

PETER C. HERMAN

"Always historicize!" commanded Fredric Jameson at the start of *The Political Unconscious* (1981).[1] Yet curiously, this imperative, which I take to mean the investigation of the complex, reciprocal relations between texts and sociological, political, and/or economic events, has largely bypassed theory itself. Even though the last thirty years or so have witnessed a resurgence of historical studies, a resurgence largely predicated upon rejecting the New Critical paradigms of the verbal icon and discoverable, transhistorical meaning, the discussions surrounding theory and its career in the academy are more often than not surprisingly ahistorical.[2] Ironically, most metatheoretical work uncannily replicates the old History of Ideas approach, which views texts almost exclusively in relation to previous texts and only rarely in relation to the political or social events surrounding and informing them.

Frank Lentricchia's *After the New Criticism* (1980) exemplifies this phenomenon.[3] While Lentricchia begins his book by promising an "historical account of what has happened [in the United States] since the American New Critics passed out of favor" and describes his project as a "critique of various forces that have shaped contemporary thought about literature and the criticism of literature,"[4] what he actually gives the reader is something very different. By "historical account," Lentricchia evidently does *not* mean an account of theory's intersection with, say, the Sixties, the protests against the Vietnam War, or anything analogous. We are told that Northrop Frye published "his monumental book *[The Anatomy of Criticism]* in 1957,"[5] but nothing we are told about what outside circumstances surrounded and shaped Frye's work, how it might have arisen from, or intersected with, nascent Canadian nationalism or, perhaps more obviously, the Cold War. Instead, Lentricchia situates Frye's text strictly in relation to other examples of literary criticism, such as Frank Kermode's *Romantic Image,* and philosophical works by Ernst Cassirer and Susanne K. Langer.[6]

Similarly, Lentricchia begins his chapter, "History or the Abyss: Poststructuralism," with this sentence: [7]

> When in late October of 1966 over one hundred humanists and social scientists from the United States and eight other countries gathered at the Johns Hopkins Humanities Center to participate in a symposium called "The Languages of Criticism and the Sciences of Man," the reining avant-garde theoretical presences for literary critics in this country were Georges Poulet, to a lesser extent members of the "Geneva school" associated with him, and, in the distinct background, in uncertain relationship to the critics of consciousness, the forbidding philosophical analyses of Heidegger *(Being and Time),* Sartre *(Being and Nothingness),* and Merleau-Ponty *(The Phenomenology of Perception).*

Although Lentricchia situates this famous conference chronologically, he tells us nothing about what else was going on in the world circa 1966 that might have shaped the papers presented and their reception, for instance, the Vietnam War, the growing antiwar movement, the growing counterculture, the different cultural circumstances surrounding the European and American papers presented at this conference, and perhaps even the musical soundtrack to the Sixties by such groups as the Beatles and the Rolling Stones.[8]

Lentricchia's project, however, is not exploring how deconstruction overlaps with, or arises from, a particular set of social or political events, but how Paul de Man's or Jacques Derrida's ideas relate to the previous ideas of Claude Lévi-Strauss, Northrop Frye, Roland Barthes, E. D. Hirsch, or Meyer Abrams. The ahistoricism of Lentricchia's argument particularly reveals itself when he writes that "Sometime in the early 1970s we awoke from the dogmatic slumber of our phenomenological sleep to find that a new presence had taken absolute hold over our avant-garde critical imagination: Jacques Derrida,"[9] or when he states that Derrida published his astounding essay, "Structure, Sign, and Play," in 1968.[10] Although he promises the reader an "historical account," Lentricchia makes no attempt to link Derrida's thought to the student uproars in France that culminated in May '68, or the protests over the Vietnam War, or Algeria, or the widespread dissatisfaction with Western culture that permeated the 1960s and a good part of the 1970s.[11]

The lack of historical texture in Lentricchia's *After the New Criticism* represents less a failing by its author (the book is superb and rightly elevated Lentricchia to the rank of an "academostar") and more an example of an approach to understanding theory that continues to dominate contemporary critical discourse. For example, both Jonathan Culler's *On Deconstruction* (1982) and Christopher Norris's *Deconstruction* (1982) continue the tradition of situating deconstruction within the context of continental philosophy to the exclusion of investigating how Derrida might have been consciously or unconsciously influenced by the political and social events surrounding the writing of his seminal works,[12] and one finds this uninterest in history in much more recent treatments of deconstruction (and French theory in general) as well.[13]

Perhaps because the New Historicism rather obviously concerns itself with the relationship between texts and events, there has been marginally more work done on its relationship to social and political developments. In a volume published in 1987, both Don E. Wayne and Walter Cohen noted the connections between 1960s radicalism and theory,[14] and Jonathan Gil Harris has published an essay on the relationship between Stephen J. Greenblatt's subversion, containment thesis and the Cold War (an updated, revised version appears in this volume, *Historicizing Theory*).[15] Brook Thomas also scatters interesting observations about the relations between theory and history throughout *The New Historicism and Other Old-Fashioned Topics* (1991).[16] But three essays and occasional comments in a book represent a miniscule fraction of the over four hundred items listed in the Modern Language Association International Bibliography (MLAIB) on the New Historicism,[17] and twelve years separates the publication of Harris's essay from the two in *Shakespeare Reproduced*. Clearly, historicizing the New Historicism is not (yet) a "hot" topic.

Instead, the vast majority of work on the New Historicism follows the same trajectory as that on French theory. For example, in the introduction to his 1989 anthology simply entitled *The New Historicism*, H. Aram Veeser notes that after the seminal texts were published at the start of the 1980s, "In a decade the New Historicism has mustered able cadres across several periods and disciplines and produced a substantial body of publications."[18] But neither Veeser nor any of his extremely able contributors (including Greenblatt, Louis A. Montrose, Catherine Gallagher, Jonathan Arac, Gerald Graff, Lentricchia, Vincent Pecora, Gayatri Chakrauorty Spivak, and Stanley Fish) devote significant attention to unearthing what conditions made the New Historicism attractive to these "cadres" or what social, political, or economic circumstances contributed to the formation and dissemination of this particular approach. In fact, with one exception, the issue is never even raised.[19] Again, my intention is not find fault with Veeser's anthology, but to point out that this book, like Lentricchia's *After the New Criticism*, continues to represent the state of discourse, for the subsequent work on Greenblatt and the New Historicism has been largely uninterested in historical or sociopolitical matters.

The question, therefore, is why has historicizing theory engendered such indifference, if not resistance? Why, at a time when—to give a few admittedly random examples—critics have no problem situating Geoffrey Chaucer's *Miller's Tale* in the context of the Peasant's Rebellion, More's *Utopia* in the context of humanist debates over the morality of Europe's actions in the New World, John Milton's *Paradise Lost* in the context of the English Revolution, and Daniel Defoe's fiction in the context of the South Sea Bubble, when, in other words, the act of historicizing literature (however broadly construed) has become almost axiomatic in both scholarship and the classroom, has there been little sustained interest in historicizing *theory*?[20] And why is the narrative history of theory almost identical to the narrative history of literature that theory helped to supplant with one more sophisticated and historically rooted?

There are several answers to this question. First, the generational issue. It is, perhaps, unreasonable to expect the founders of theoretical discursivity to historicize themselves. That project generally requires some distance from the events themselves. Consequently, Terry Eagleton, born in 1943, can situate the social and political roots of the New Criticism, whose founders, John Crowe Ransom and Cleanth Brooks, were born, respectively, in 1888 and 1906. Yet, significantly, Eagleton, like Lentricchia, stops historicizing once he reaches poststructuralism, at least partly because he belongs to their generation.[21] The task of historicizing theoretical developments after the New Criticism, it seems, has largely fallen to the "Next Generation" of literary critics, a group I define elsewhere as academics who "received the various approaches and epistemologies signified by the shorthand term *Theory*, second-, if not thirdhand."[22] In other words, the academic family dynamic seems to have students historicizing their elders. The contributors to *Historicizing Theory* (with the sole exception of Morris Dickstein) are all members of the "Next Generation," and as this volume demonstrates, their attention is now turning to precisely this issue.

But in addition, the resistance to historicizing theory arises from the connection, noted by Montrose, Wayne, and Cohen but not at the time or subsequently explored in any depth, between theory and the Sixties. The reluctance to digging any further, I suggest, stems from how this connection has so often been used as a means of *discrediting* theoretical approaches. Starting with Allan Bloom's *The Closing of the American Mind* (1987), there has been a steady stream of crediting French theory (and often theoretical approaches in general) with the decline of Western Civilization. Bloom, for example, bemoaned the abandonment at Cornell University in the Sixties of "the old core curriculum" to a professor of comparative literature, whom Bloom explicitly and snidely identifies as "an assiduous importer of the latest Paris fashions," who of course defends this development.[23] Following Bloom, Roger Kimball remarks that:[24]

> It has often been observed that yesterday's student radical is today's tenured professor or academic dean. The point of this observation is not

to suggest that our campuses are littered with political agitators. In comparison to the situation that prevailed in 1968, when colleges and universities across the country were scenes of violent demonstrations, the academy today seems positively sedate. Yet if the undergraduate population has moved quietly to the Right in recent years, the men and women who are paid to introduce students to the great works and ideas of our civilization have by and large remained true to the emancipationist ideology of the Sixties.

Dinesh D'Souza, in *Illiberal Education* (1991), also asserts that "Older, traditionally liberal professors are retiring and making way for a new generation, weaned on the assorted ideologies of the 1960s," and substantiates this charge with a series of quotes taken from interviews and articles in the popular (as opposed to academic) press from such prominent figures as Henry Louis Gates, Jay Parini, and Annette Kolodny attesting to the roots of their scholarship in the protests of the 1960s.[25]

Perhaps the most extraordinary instance of the Sixties being used as a club against theory is the "affair" surrounding Cambridge University awarding Derrida an honorary degree. Cambridge's proposal occasioned a letter to the *Times* (London), signed by twenty philosophers from all over the globe, urging the university to not go through with this plan. The reason for their dismissal of his work is as follows: "M. Derrida's career had its roots in the heady days of the 1960s and his writings continue to reveal their origins in that period. Many of them seem to consist in no small part of elaborate jokes and the puns 'logical phallusies' and the like. . . ."[26]

In the interview concerning this letter, Derrida responds in the two ways we have come to expect. The first is to completely ignore the charge, and for most of the interview, both the questioners (the editors of the *Cambridge Review*) and the subject do not address the topic of what Derrida's work may owe to the Sixties. But toward the end, one question delicately points to the main charge against Derrida:[27]

> It has often been alleged of your work (but not of yours alone) that it is intimately bound up with not only a French, but a distinctively Parisian, intellectual situation, and indeed that it loses its force and some of its intelligibility when removed from this context. There is obviously an implicit charge of parochialism here: how would you respond to this allegation?

Derrida's response is instructive. At first, he seems to admit the historical embeddedness of his work: "It is true that what I'm trying to do, *especially back in the 1960s* and principally in *Of Grammatology* will be better understood if aspects of the French, and more narrowly, Parisian university and cultural scene are taken into account . . ." (my emphasis).[28]

Derrida seems about to situate his work in the uproars roiling the Parisian university scene, and it is important to note that a reader familiar with his work might very well expect such a response, for despite the supposed ahistoricism of deconstruction, Derrida has explicitly invited this type of analysis. In the introduction to a much earlier essay, "The Ends of Man," Derrida pinpoints with great precision its historical parameters. He conceived this essay in

> the month of April, 1968: it will be recalled that these were the weeks of the opening of the Vietnam peace talks and of the assassination of Martin Luther King. A bit later, when I was typing this text, the universities of Paris were invaded by the forces of order—and for the first time at the demand of a rector—and then reoccupied by the students in the upheaval you are familiar with. This historical and political horizon would call for a long analysis.[29]

Furthermore, in "Deconstructions: The Im-Possible," published in the recent anthology, *French Theory in America* (2000),[30] Derrida repeats this invitation (although with typical complexity, he also undercuts this invitation) for a "long analysis" of theory's relationship to historical events of whatever type:

> Let's suppose the historical analysis of a paradigm in the sense of [Thomas] Kuhn or an episteme in the sense of [Michel] Foucault, some "themata," or as they say, an historical analysis of givens, a configuration that explains that at a certain moment an invention was made possible, that it became practicable under certain conditions, technical, economic, social, psychological, scientific, et cetera. According to this analysis that I hold to be necessary and, to be sure, legitimate, and which we must push as far as possible, the invention of this possible will have done nothing but make explicit . . . that which was already there. . . .[31]

Yet, to return to the Cambridge University affair, when Derrida actually has an opportunity to speculate on the "historical and political horizon" of his work, he declines, preferring to conclude the sentence thus: "for example, the hegemony of structuralism, of a certain Althusserian Marxism, of Lacanian psychoanalysis, of [Maurice] Blanchot, Lévi-Strauss, Foucault, Barthes, and so on."[32] When Derrida refers to the "Parisian university and cultural scene" surrounding his work, he pointedly does *not* mean what is going on in the streets (or the hallway outside his office). He does not mean *Sixties* culture. Instead, by "cultural," Derrida means *intellectual* culture, or what is more generally known as "intellectual history." The occupation of the university is forgotten, as are the "certain conditions," be they technical, economic, social, psychological, scientific, or whatever, which surrounded the origins of Derrida's seminal works.

Derrida's response to this question demonstrates a key aspect of the resistance to historicizing theory. First, granting the connection between deconstruction or New Historicism or any other flavor of theory and the Sixties seems to play directly into the hands of one's enemies (e.g., Bloom). As we have seen, between the writing of "The Ends of Man" in 1968 and the Cambridge Affair in 1992, theory in general and Derrida in particular were consistently denounced as "relics" of the Sixties. Therefore, it is better strategically to deny the connection altogether or at most, to grant it the most cursory treatment and to quickly move on.[33] Consequently, most sympathetic discussions of theory, including Derrida's own, prefer minimal contact with this topic. Hence Derrida's simultaneous invitation to, and denigration of, historicizing theory. The tendency to regard history as the enemy of theory was unfortunately strengthened by the revelation of de Man's anti-Jewish wartime newspaper columns, which obviously invited invidious comparisons between his earlier and his later writings.[34]

Therefore, the strategy of shifting attention toward theory's intellectual or philosophical roots, to see theory in the context of the Western metaphysical tradition—C. W. F. Hegel, Heidegger (who obviously has his own problems), and Edmund Husserl, to analyze its relationship to less problematic (in terms of public relations) roots than, say, the invasion of "the universities of Paris [by] the forces of order," constitutes a *defensive* move. Put bluntly, the association of theory with the Sixties does not work to theory's advantage, does not enhance its credibility, and in the face of considerable hostility from nonacademic writers (who have, truth be told, many sympathizers within the university), I suggest that the interpretive community of metatheoretical scholars implicitly decided to not only quarantine this area of investigation, but to direct attention away from history and to move attention toward theory's relationship with philosophy.[35]

Historicizing Theory seeks to break this pattern and to begin a concentrated effort at situating various theories and theoreticians within their manifold social, political and economic contexts. In "The Poetics and Politics of Culture," Montrose argues that part of the burden of New Historicism is to recover "the cultural specificity, the social embedment, of all modes of writing," recognizing that such recovery will inevitably be partial and proceed "from our own historically, socially and institutionally shaped vantage points."[36] Montrose's main object is, of course, early modern writing, but his statement can, I think, be applied with equal effect to theory itself. That, in short, is this anthology's burden.

∞

The organization of this volume is roughly chronological. Evan Carton, in "The Holocaust, French Poststructuralism, the American Literary Academy, and Jewish Identity Poetics" situates poststructuralism within the parameters of the second World War in his discussion of the ambivalent subtextual struggles of a generation of postwar French intellectuals with the fact of the Holocaust. Imported in the 1970s, with little attention to its historicity (its encipherment of Auschwitz and its implication in the longer French cultural struggle with *la question juive*), this body of thought came to comprise the field of "theory" in the American literary academy, and thus to shape the disciplinary inquiries of professors and students of English into matters of language, reason, history, knowledge, and power. A curious feature of this phase of poststructuralism's journey was its embrace and institutionalization by Jewish American critics for whom literary studies' disciplinary legitimation crisis coincided with a more personal crisis of spirit, of cultural community, and of Jewish self-identification. Carton's essay traces out some of the chains of circumstance and meaning that connect the Holocaust to French poststructuralism and to the recent history of the American literary academy, which connect Jewish "identity poetics," whether in France at early or midcentury or in the United States at century's end, to the issue of the intellectual vocation.

Karen Raber's "Michel Foucault and the Specter of War" historicizes Foucault's early work as a response to the French experience of World War II, suggesting that the historical vision that underwrites Foucault's politics and philosophy is mobilized both by the historical events of the war, and by France's attempts at revisionism about its role in cooperating with the Nazi Occupation in the years following Liberation. Raber connects Foucault's understanding of the medicalization of crime, the function of the state in policing public hygiene and purifying the "body" of its people, and the creation of the disciplined "docile" body of the individual, with the institutions and expressions of Nazi thought whether manifested in the rhetoric and actions of the Vichy government or through the direct presence of Nazi rule during Occupation.

James J. Paxson, in "Historicizing Paul de Man's Master Trope, Prosopopeia: The Nazi *Volkskörper*, and Allegories of the Body Politic," bridges continental developments and theory's career in the United States. Although the mandarin theories of language, literature, and tropes developed by de Man continue to see explication in sporadically appearing articles and books, and in the wake of the fact that the historical scandal of de Man's at-times anti-Semitic and potentially collaborationist "wartime writings" of the early 1940s has faded from the current scene in theory, Paxson proposes to historicize de Man's greatest theoretical tool: his "master trope," prosopopeia, by showing how the Nazi rhetoric of *Gleichschaltung* (coordination or organic synthesis) and its subjacent master trope, *Der Volkskorper* (People's Body), find phantom regeneration in de Man's mature theoretical master trope of poetics, prosopopeia, or personification.

Lee Morrissey's "'Nostalgeria' and Jacques Derrida's Structure, Sign, and Play in the Discourse of the Human Sciences'" situates Derrida's highly influential essay, "Structure, Sign, and Play," in terms of the relationship between Paris and Algeria, especially in the context of the Civil War of the late '50s and early '60s. What emerges, as Morrissey writes, "is a Derridean argument much more politically and historically aware than his work is generally thought to be, especially in the earlier essays."

"Jean Baudrillard and May 68: An Acoustic Archaeology" by Andrea Loselle takes as its historical source material the noise of May 68 and contemporary developments in sound technology and portable gadgets. In his early books and in his essays for the journal *Utopie*, Baudrillard examined the role the media played in neutralizing student and worker protests. Loselle's piece links his reading of the media's participation with other more powerfully resonant images underlying the post-'68 feminist movement in France and the then gendered technical divisions between the plugged-in, noisy, domestic gadgets destined for women and the comparatively soothing, self-absorbing, portable gadgets advertised for men. Baudrillard, however, has been known more for his treatment of visual images and objects, not noise, audio gadgets, and gendered technical divisions. His involvement in May 68 and his recollections allude to these latter topics in a way that invites historicizing his emphasis on the visual through them. By placing Baudrillard's work in the cultural context of noise, it is possible to historicize, in turn, the fragmentation of the traditional stage of revolutionary action, the street, and the "multiple self-referential spaces of personalized passage and mininarratives of cultural accumulation" produced by the spread of public gadgets that channel and process the unpredictable subversiveness of noise.

In "Stephen Greenblatt's 'X'-Files: The Rhetoric of Containment and Invasive Disease in 'Invisible Bullets' and 'The Sources of Soviet Conduct,'" Jonathan Gil Harris historicizes Greenblatt's infamous theory of subversion and containment with respect to its language. Even as Greenblatt reacts obliquely against Reaganism, the rhetoric of his essay "Invisible Bullets" uncannily parallels that of an important Cold War-era document written by "X," aka George F. Kennan, the architect of the U.S. foreign policy of Soviet containment. Both Greenblatt and "X" reproduce a rhetorical nexus in which "containment" is figured in relation to invasive disease; as a consequence, both Greenblatt and "X" attribute the origins of social pathology and change to factors external to the social organism. The paradigm of invasive disease that informs their rhetoric has a long history; it is a prominent feature of both Renaissance English political writing and mid-twentieth-century functionalist anthropology. In all of its incarnations, the rhetorical nexus of containment and invasive disease serves a largely conservative role, deflecting responsibility for social ills from what often are contributory internal factors.

Ivo Kamps, in "New Historicizing the New Historicism; or, Did Stephen Greenblatt Watch the Evening News in Early 1968?" gives what some may call a "New Historicist treatment of the New Historicism." Noting that significant work has been done in recent years to trace new historicism's theoretical lineage, Kamps's essay addresses an as yet barely explored dimension of new historicist criticism, namely, that of the historical conditions that went into its own making. There is something odd about a critical method that vigorously professes to historicize the objects it investigates but apparently has little interest in historcizing itself, and Kamps sets out to begin the rectify this situation. Employing something like a new historicist method himself, Kamps turns to one of the most traumatic periods in the Vietnam War, the Tet Offensive of early 1968. In particular, Kamps revisits the television coverage of the Tet Offensive by such reporters as Morley Safer and Walter Cronkite to investigate how both the style and substance of their coverage may have shaped the synchronic, associative tendencies of new historicism, as well as new historicism's fondness of anecdotes.

Loren Glass, in "The End of Culture," argues that the New Historicist work of Walter Benn Michaels—and particularly his theorization of the term "culture"—must be understood in the historical context of the Reagan era. Reagan's domestic and foreign policies—dismantling the welfare state at home and trumpeting American economic and military superiority abroad— formed the cultural milieu of Michaels's major work. Glass aligns Michaels's participation in the "Against Theory" debates with the rise of a neo-conservative and xenophobic orthodoxy in American English departments, and then connects Michaels's theorization of the ubiquity of capitalism in his first book, *The Gold Standard and the Logic of Naturalism*, to America's incipient "victory" in the Cold War and the associated globalization of American free-market ideology. Finally, Glass offers *Our America* as a complex allegory of these very historical developments, which symptomatically elides the very decade that formed Michaels's generation of literary critics. Thus Glass concludes that a consideration of the Sixties is crucial to an understanding of the contemporary debates over "culture."

Marc Redfield's essay, "Literature, Incorporated: Harold Bloom, Theory, and the Canon," explores ways in which Bloom served as a symbolic representative and peculiarly literalized embodiment of "the Canon" during the era of the canon wars in the late 1980s and early 1990s. Redfield suggests that both Bloom's writings and his theatrical self-fashionings display an anxiety about those aspects of literariness that resist aestheticization as an embodied canon. A synonym for such literariness, in the late twentieth century, is "theory," particularly the sort of theory associated with the work of de Man. Redfield suggests that we read Bloom's theatrical engagements with de Man as a phantasmatic recoding of anxiety as personal agon, and proposes that the specter of literariness as theory may in turn be aligned with what Walter Benjamin termed the "shock experience of modernity."

David R. Shumway in "The Sixties, the New Left, and the Emergence of Cultural Studies in the United States" argues against the common assumption that the Cultural Studies movement in the United States originates in the Birmingham Centre for Contemporary Cultural Studies. Shumway, however, proposes an alternative genealogy by arguing that cultural studies in Britain and the United States derive from differing New Left movements and their academic offshoots. In the United States, left-wing political movements of the 1960s produced, besides campus protests, changes in the knowledges taught and studied at universities. There are four of these that help account for the rise and particular character of American cultural studies: (1) the rise of mass culture as an object of academic study; (2) the widespread rejection of the belief that genuine knowledge is politically disinterested; (3) the rise of academic feminism and the development of women's studies; and (4) the growth of African-American studies and the recognition of racism as pervasive cultural evil that universities should address. This essay will argue that these changes in the American academy fostered the emergence of cultural studies here, and that the influence of Birmingham, while certainly significant, came late and provided, in Richard Ohmann's words, "a way of gathering and naming a so-far inchoate movement."

H. Aram Veeser looks to how Edward Said's engagement with the Palestine Liberation Organization (PLO) stands at the fountainhead of postcolonial theory. In 1989, Said engaged in a series of angry exchanges with Yaser Aberdrabbo, the PLO spokesperson in Tunis, and Veeser finds in this public debate paradigmatic postcolonial questions about hybrid identity, geographic determination, and catachretic ruptures of Enlightenment-style reasoning. These three concepts are, not coincidentally, essential to postcolonial theory, and we can see in Said's exchange with the PLO an attempt at convincing them to adopt his own enthusiasm for permanent exile, unlocatability, and a complete break with the past.

Benjamin Bertram, in "The Spectrality of the Sixties," is concerned with the tradition of Sixties utopian thinking in critical theory. Bertram proposes that Jacques Derrida's notion of the "messianic" in *Specters of Marx* (1994) is one of many indications that radical utopian thinking has not died out since the Sixties, and he compares Jameson's notion of utopia and Derrida's "messianic" as a means of thinking about the complex legacy of Sixties' utopianism for contemporary critical theory.

The book concludes with an afterword by Morris Dickstein. After first situating himself within the theoretical developments and the sixties and seventies, wryly noting that if his first book on Keats' verse "was an advance on the New Criticism of the mid-1960s it must have looked hopelessly backward ten years later," after the advent of Derrida, Foucault, Barthes, and de Man, Dickstein both praises and critiques the project of historicizing theory. While, he grants, there is obviously much to be gained by this project, there are drawbacks also, such as a potential lack of rigor, and the possibility of diminishing "writers and movements by reducing them to their local circumstances. Yet, Dickstein concludes, while one can argue over details, the larger justification for historical interpretation is twofold. First, we want to know as much as possible about writers who have so profoundly affected our intellectual lives. But also, "historical interpretation is an indispensable way of comprehending culture and shedding light on the theories and practices through which [theory] has always tried to make sense of itself."

❧

A confession: this volume began its life by taking seriously the common perception that various theoretical discourses originated in the Sixties. I wanted, in other words, to transform an accusation into an opportunity. But as *Historicizing Theory* developed, it became increasingly clear that my sense of chronology needed to be significantly broadened. Clearly, some of theory's origins lie in the Sixties, and a number of essays in this book investigate precisely those connections. Yet as proposals came in and as the essays themselves went through various drafts, I learned that theory's historical roots are both longer and shorter than conventionally understood. That is to say, events preceding the Sixties, for example, World War II, Algeria, and the Holocaust, as well as developments after this decade, such as the Reagan/Thatcher era of the Eighties, including the Canon Wars, also shaped theoretical writing of various kinds. *Historicizing Theory* thus seeks to correct two widely shared misapprehensions: the first is that history is unimportant to theory, and the second is that theory's historical roots are largely restricted to the Sixties. While we disagree with Derrida's assessment that this project "will have done nothing but make explicit . . . that which was already there," *Historicizing Theory* accepts Derrida's invitation for a "long analysis" of theory's "historical and political horizon[s]," and we hope that this volume marks the beginning, not the end, of a concerted, concentrated effort at understanding how history shapes theory, in all its guises.

NOTES

1. Fredric Jameson, *The Political Unconscious: Narrative as a Socially Symbolic Act* (Ithaca: Cornell University Press, 1981), 9.

2. There have been a few, scattered instances of historicizing theory over the years. In addition to Terry Eagleton's *Literary Theory: An Introduction* (1996) (see n.

21), Vincent Leitch makes some gestures in this direction in *American Literary Criticism from the Thirties to the Eighties* (New York: Columbia University Press, 1988), in particular his chapters on Marxist criticism in the 1930s (1–23), the New York Intellectuals (81–114), and "Leftist Criticism from the 1660s to the 1980s") (366–407); Gerald Graff generally historicizes the profession in *Professing Literature: An Institutional History* (Chicago: University of Chicago Press, 1987). See also Aijaz Ahmad in *Theory: Classes, Nations, Literatures* (London: Verso, 1992); Jeffrey Williams, "Packaging Theory," *College English* 56.3 (1994): 280–98; "The New Bellestrism," *Style* 33.3 (1999): 414–42; and "The Posttheory Generation," in *Day Late, Dollar Short: The Next Generation and the New Academy* (Albany: State University of New York Press, 2000), 25–44. These essays, however, are the exceptions that prove the rule.

3. While Frank Lentricchia published *After the New Criticism* (Chicago: University of Chicago Press, 1980) over twenty years ago, in many ways it set the standard for discussions of poststructuralist criticism. Furthermore, *After the New Criticism* is still being read. As of this writing (2004), the book remains in print (both paperback and textbook editions) and it is the subject of an interesting exchange on *amazon.com*.

4. Ibid., xi.

5. Ibid., 3.

6. Ibid., 4–5.

7. Ibid., 157.

8. This list is meant to be illustrative and suggestive rather than delimiting the area of inquiry. The open-endedness of "the Sixties," and the term's lack of historical specificity, is what makes it useful for my purposes. My point is that an infinity of stuff is going on in the world, but the literature on theory has, for the most part, chosen to make use of almost none of it.

9. Lentricchias, *After the New Criticism*, ibid., 159.

10. Ibid., 169. "Structure, Sign, and Play" would appear in America in 1973.

11. French critics, on the other hand, have been much more open to this kind of analysis. See, for example, Luc Ferry and Alain Renault, *La pensée 68: essai sur l'anti-humanisme contemporain (French philosophy of the sixties: An essay on antihumanism)* (1985; reprint, Paris: Gallimard, 1988).

12. Christopher Norris, *Deconstruction: Theory & Practice*, chapter 1, discusses deconstruction's relationship to structuralism and to the New Criticism.

13. For example, *Deconstructions: A User's Guide*, ed. Nicholas Boyle (New York: Palgrave, 2000), Norris, *Deconstruction and the 'Unfinished Project of Modernity'* (New York: Routledge, 2000); and *The Emperor Redressed: Critiquing Critical Theory*, ed. Dwight Eddins (Tuscaloosa: University of Alabama Press, 1995).

14. In "Political Criticism of Shakespeare," Walter Cohen devotes exactly two paragraphs to the social origins of theory (Cohen, "Political Criticism of Shakespeare," in *Shakespeare Reproduced: The Text in History and Ideology*, eds. Jean E. Howard and Marion F. O'Connor [New York: Methuen, 1987], 18–19). Don E. Wayne, in his essay

in the same volume, explores at greater length the issue of how "the political crucible of the 1960s" influenced the shifts in understanding Shakespeare (Wayne, "Power, Politics, and the Shakespearean Text," 47–67).

15. Jonathan Gil Harris, "Historicizing Greenblatt's 'Containment': The Cold War, Functionalism, and the Origins of Social Pathology," in *Critical Self-Fashioning: Stephen Greenblatt and the New Historicism,* ed. Pieters Jurgen (Peter Lang: Frankfurt, 1999), 150–73.

16. Brook Thomas, *The New Historicism and Other Old-Fashioned Topics* (Princeton: Princeton University Press, 1991). See esp. 19–20. Even so, historicizing the New Historicism is not the main burden of Thomas's work.

17. As of this writing (2004), the MLAIB lists 448 items.

18. H. Aram Veeser, Introduction, to *The New Historicism* (New York: London, 1989), xiii.

19. Louis A. Montrose is the sole contributor to ibid. to address this problem:

the reorientation in the field under way since at least the beginning of the 1980s is largely the work of scholars who were students during the turbulent '60s, and who have responded to the radically altered socio-political climate of the current decade—and perhaps, to their own discomfortable comfort within its academic establishment—with intellectual work that is explicitly sociopolitical in its manifest historical content, although not always such in its own historical positioning. (Montrose, "The Poetics and Politics of Culture," 25)

20. The major exception to this rule is feminism, which has been copiously historicized, and I imagine that the reason is that this mode of analysis originates *outside* of academia, and its history is more obviously bound up with political events. Furthermore, the history of feminism (in practice, if not in name) stretches at least as far back as the early modern period (see, e.g., Constance Jordan, *Renaissance Feminism: Literary Texts and Political Models* [Ithaca: Cornell University Press, 1990]).

21. However, in the afterword to the second edition of *Literary Theory* Eagleton gives a very broad history of developments in theory since 1982 that is historical in orientation. I am grateful to Edith Frampton for alerting me to Eagleton's afterword.

22. Peter C. Herman, Introduction: '60s Theory/'90s Practice to *Day Late, Dollar Short: The Next Generation and the New Academy* (Albany: State University of New York Press, 2000), 1.

23. Allan Bloom, *The Closing of the American Mind* (New York: Simon & Shuster, 1987), 320.

24. Roger Kimball, *Tenured Radicals: How Politics Has Corrupted Our Higher Education* (pbk. edition, Chicago: Ivan R. Dee, 1998), 5–6.

25. Dinesh D'Souza, *Illiberal Education: The Politics of Race and Sex on Campus* (New York, Free Press, 1991), 17–18. Annette Kolodny, for example, proclaims, "I see my scholarship as an extention [*sic*] of my political activism" (D'Souza, 18, quoting Alan Sanoff, "60s Protesters, 80s Professors," *U.S. News & World Report,* 16 January 1989, 54).

26. "Letter from Professor Barry Smith [editor of *The Monist*] and Others," in *Jacques Derrida, Points: . . . Interviews, 1974–1994,* ed. Elisabeth Weber, trans. Peggy Kamuf et al. (Stanford: Stanford University Press, 1992), 418.

27. Ibid., 415.

28. Ibid., 416.

29. Jacques Derrida, "The Ends of Man," in *Margins of Philosophy,* trans. Alan Bass (Chicago: University of Chicago Press, 1992), 114.

30. Ironically, the one essay in *French Theory in America* that promises to fulfill this invitation, Sande Cohen's "*Critical Inquiry, October,* and Historicizing French Theory," follows the pattern I have been sketching in this introduction. In place of looking at the various extratextual circumstances that attended or made possible the reception of French theory in America, Cohen emphasizes, as Derrida himself does, intellectual history, in particular the debt these two journals owed to Nietzsche and to the Frankfurt school (*French Theory in America,* eds. Sylvère Lotringer and Cohen [New York: Routledge, 2000], 191–216).

31. Derrida, "Deconstructions: The Im-Possible," in *French Theory in America,* 23.

32. Ibid., 426.

33. Another example: in his interesting and useful primer, *New Historicism and Cultural Materialism* (New York: St. Martin's, 1996), John Brannigan admits the influence of conservative politics on both sides of the Atlantic on the work of Alan Sinfield, among others (10), but does not include contemporary politics in his chapter significantly entitled "Key Contexts and Theorists." Reagan's America and Thatcher's England, in other words, do not constitute a "key" context. On the other hand, Brannigan devotes several pages each to Marxism, Raymond Williams, anthropology, and the like. He returns to the connections between New Historicism and Reagan's ascendancy later in the book, noting (without providing sources) that "To some commentators, then, new historicism in its eager confirmation of, and relentless focus on, Renaissance modes of power, has succeeded more fully in propagating and reinforcing power in the late twentieth century" (78). But he cites this sentiment only to diminish its importance ("To assert that these criticisms are valid about all new historicist critics is to believe that all new historicists are the same . . . [78–79]).

34. See, for example, David Lehman, *Signs of the Times: Deconstruction and the Fall of Paul de Man* (New York: Poseidon Press, 1991). The many contributors to *Responses: On Paul de Man's Wartime Journalism,* eds. Werner Hamacher, Neil Hertz, and Thomas Keenan (Lincoln: University of Nebraska Press, 1989) perforce historicize de Man's writing, but it is clear that the act feels both unnatural and traumatic. Also, most of the contributors are deeply troubled by any connections between de Man's earlier writings and his later theoretical project

35. In "Interpreting the *Variorum,*" Stanley Fish gives this definition:

Interpretive communities are made up of those who share interpretive strategies not for reading (in the conventional sense) but for writing texts, for constituting their properties and assigning their intentions. In other words, these strategies exist prior to the act of reading and therefore determine the shape of what is read rather than, as is usually assumed, the other way around. If it is an article of faith in a particular community that there are a variety of texts, its members will boast a repertoire of strategies for making them. (Fish, *Is There a Text in This Class? The Authority of Interpretive Communities* [Cambridge: Harvard University Press, 1980], 171).

My point is that history's unimportance to theory constitutes exactly such an "article of faith" for the interpretive community of literary theoreticians.

36 Montrose, "Poetics and Politics of Culture," in Veeser, *New Historicism,* 20, 23.

1

The Holocaust, French Poststructuralism, the American Literary Academy, and Jewish Identity Poetics

EVAN CARTON

> Thus the Jew remains the stranger, the intruder, the unassimilated at the very heart of our society.
> —Jean-Paul Sartre, *Reflexions sur la Question Juive*

> "Auschwitz," and "After Auschwitz," that is to say, Western thought and life today.
> —Jean-François Lyotard, *The Differend*

> Theory in the United States institution of the profession of English is often shorthand for the general critique of humanism undertaken in France in the wake of the Second World War and then, in a double take, further radicalized in the mid sixties in the work of the so-called poststructuralists.
> —Gayatri Chakravortyt Spivak, *The Post-Colonial Critic*

At a 1980 colloquium honoring Jacques Derrida entitled "The Ends of Man," Jean-François Lyotard delivered a lecture, "Discussions, or Phrasing 'after Auschwitz,'" in which he spoke the epigraphic phrase that I just cited. During the discussion that followed, Derrida enjoined: "if there is somewhere a *One must*, it must link up with a *one must make links with Auschwitz;* . . . I mean to say that the unlinkable of Auschwitz prescribes that we make links."[1] Over the next decade, French intellectuals—especially leading poststructuralist philosophers, textual critics, and social theorists—voluminously obliged. Spurred by a series of unsettling political and cultural events that spanned the 1980s and continued to resonate in the 1990s (the national reexamination of the history of Vichy and indigenous fascism; the resurgence of anti-Semitic violence in Paris; the Holocaust negationism of Robert Faurisson and others; the screening of Claude Lanzmann's *Shoah;* the Klaus Barbie trial; the politi-cal inroads of Jean-Marie Le Pen and the National Front; and the Martin Heidegger and Paul de Man affairs), these intellectuals explicitly linked their critical projects and situations to Auschwitz.

Works such as Lyotard's *Differend* (1984) and *Heidegger and "the jews,"* (1988), Derrida's *Cinders* (1987), Maurice Blanchot's *Writing of the Disaster* (1980), Jean Lacoue-Labarthe's *Heidegger, Politics, and Art* (1987), and Julia Kristeva's *Powers of Horror* (1980), belatedly confirmed the Holocaust's con-stitutive presence—its long absent presence, or presence as absence—in French poststructuralist thought.[2] The widely disseminated and applied social, philosophical, historical, and linguistic paradigms of postwar French theory, it now appeared, had emerged in large measure from the theorists' ambivalent subtextual struggles to "make links with Auschwitz." From its outset, I will argue, French poststructuralism at once confronted, commemorated, deflected, and veiled the Holocaust. Nor were these complicated relations fully revealed or resolved by the retrospective 1980s and 1990s assertions of the Holocaust's link or presence to contemporary intellectual life— articula-tions that themselves tended to effect a kind of disarticulation, an unlinking or absenting, as well.

Lyotard's and Derrida's quoted remarks begin to suggest why this is so. Taken together, they invoke Auschwitz as modernity's principle of identity and its principle of alterity—linked and unlinkable at once by virtue of its irre-ducible otherness (Derrida) and its ubiquity (Lyotard) to thought and life today. The word "Auschwitz" itself—which indicates both a locus of horrible destruction and a boundless destructiveness and horror—helps enact this con-vergence of identity and alterity, presence and absence. Yet, whether as the most notorious site of the Nazi Final Solution or as the abyss in and of mod-ern consciousness, "Auschwitz" here displaces another phrase—*la question juive*—by which the shapers and inheritors of twentieth-century French social, literary, and intellectual history are powerfully and particularly con-nected to it. To make this observation is to insist that the implicit "before Auschwitz" of Lyotard's hypostatic "'Auschwitz'"/"'after Auschwitz'" be inter-rogated and that both the "One" and the "must" of Derrida's *"One must"* be historically specified. However categorical and cataclysmal, the Holocaust is situated for contemporary French intellectuals within chains of cultural cir-cumstance and meaning that long predate and postdate it.

As, for French cultural theorists, the Holocaust is situated within, and mediated by, historical chains of circumstance and meaning, so is it (differently) situated and mediated for American literary critics. Indeed, the central link between the Holocaust and the contemporary discipline of literary study in America is French poststructuralism itself. Imported in the 1970s, with little initial exploration of its historical conditions or recognition of its inscription or encipherment of the Holocaust, this body of postwar French thought came to comprise the field of "theory" in the U.S. literary academy, as Gayatri Chakravorty Spivak observes in the last of my epigraphs, and to shape the disciplinary inquiries of professors and students of English into matters of language, reason, history, subjectivity, knowledge, and power.[3]

If the poststructuralist theory that would afford fin de siècle American literary academics many of their basic tools and vocabularies of analysis arose in part as a French response to Auschwitz, and to the longer shadow of *la question juive* in French intellectual and cultural history, the U.S. scholars who imported that theory did so in response to different cultural, disciplinary, and sometimes personal circumstances. The post-Vietnam and Reagan-era critique of U.S. imperialism and the rise of subcultural identity politics to contest totalizing constructions of the nation and atomizing constructions of the self provided the broad historical frame for poststructuralism's American appropriation. Framed by these cultural concerns, the academic profession of literature—which, since its modern establishment in the 1940s, had generally conducted itself by formalistic methods, circumscribed and validated itself by aesthetic discriminations, and organized itself by national categories—began to look, in the eyes of many practitioners, less like a site of freedom and fulfillment than like an apparatus of containment. The "theory revolution" supplied some of the concepts and discourses for the multiform disciplinary self-examination of which the canon wars; the rise of cultural studies; the articulation of the knowledge/power nexus; and the debates about validity, authority, and ideology in interpretation are all expressions.[4] And, again, these poststructuralist concepts and discourses, by means of which American literary academics conducted and continue to conduct our disciplinary legitimation crisis, were themselves forged in the (also continuing) legitimation crisis for Western philosophy that at once consumed and stimulated French thought "'after Auschwitz.'"

This essay, then, proposes to illuminate some links in the chain of circumstance and meaning that connects the thinking of French poststructuralists and, at a further remove, the recent course of the American literary academy to the Holocaust. In the first and longer of its two parts, "Nous sommes tous des Juifs allemands," I survey the recent assertions and earlier hints of the Holocaust's centrality to the work of postwar French intellectuals and examine several problematic figures and functions of the Holocaust in

French poststructuralism: as an absolute and irreparable historical and conceptual break; as the end of figuration and functionalism; and, paradoxically,
as a source of what poststructuralist *avant la lettre* Maurice Blanchot has
called "the unavowable community."[5] This first section also situates poststructuralism and its engagement with the Holocaust in relation to earlier
and later circumstances and discourses within French social, literary, and
intellectual history. Section 2, "The Poststructuralist American Academy and
the Profession of Jewish Identity," outlines one vivid dimension of poststructuralism's appropriation in America: its embrace by Jewish American literary
academics for whom the crisis of disciplinarity—precipitated in part by the
breakdown of humanist ideals (or triumphalist illusions) of American identity, liberal individualism, and Western tradition under the pressure of multiculturalism—also entails or coincides with a more personal crisis of spirit,
of cultural community, and of Jewish self-identification. In their disciplinary
deployments of French poststructuralism, these American professors unearth
and recast its informing Jewish question, which, whether in France at early
or mid-century or in the United States at century's end, is bound up with the
question of the vocation and social legitimacy of the intellectual.

The trace of the Holocaust in poststructuralist theory, my argument concludes, leads back and forward to the trope of *la question juive,* a figure for the
curious reciprocity or transformativity between "Jewishness" and intellectual
vocation, the passage between literary intellectual and Jew that accommodates
movement in either direction and operates on two continents. By means of
this trope, a postwar anti-philosophy ostensibly committed to dissipating
identity categories and undoing the metaphysics of the subject is able to forge
an ironic and problematic poetics of intellectual identity: poststructuralism's
figure of the Jew, in other words, preserves the purpose and possibility of the
French intellectual, though the French intellectual—both before the war and
after it—failed to preserve actual Jews. And this poststructuralist identity
poetics, though originating in a project susceptible to the charge of emptying
the category of Jewish identity of distinctive substance, comes to afford American literary academics a (problematic and ironic) disciplinary avenue of Jewish expression or return.

NOUS SOMMES TOUS DES JUIFS ALLEMANDS

In May of 1968, at the height of the student and labor strikes that nearly toppled the government that had presided in France since the end of the Second
World War, tens of thousands of young French men and women marched to
the chant: *Nous sommes tous des Juifs allemands* (We are all German Jews). Most
immediately, this slogan signified solidarity with Daniel Cohn-Bendit, the

leader of the first student uprising at the Nanterre campus of the University of Paris. The son of German Jewish refugees from Hitler, Cohn-Bendit, who grew up in France, had been vilified throughout the spring as a foreign subversive, dubbed the "German Jew" in right-wing publications, and recently barred from the country as an undesirable. But the slogan's response to the attempted purgation of Cohn-Bendit from the French body politic carried older and deeper historical resonances that were made explicit when members of the National Union against Marxist Subversion counterdemonstrated to the cry of "Cohn-Bendit to Dachau."[6]

The slogan *Nous sommes tous des Juifs allemands,* that is, clearly jabbed at the psychic wound of French cooperation with the Final Solution, associating the contemporary scapegoating and exile of Cohn-Bendit with the xenophobia and racism of the collaborationist leaders who helped the Nazis identify and transport first Jewish refugees and recent immigrants, and then Jews of long-standing French nationality. But, beyond this conscious allusion, the phrase uncannily registered the informing literal or symbolic presence of Germans and Jews at every watershed moment of French cultural, political, and intellectual life since the middle of the nineteenth century. From the fall of the Paris commune, through the Dreyfus Affair, the Action Française, the Vichy regime, the postwar purges, and the establishment of a Heideggerian intellectual avant-garde, to the upheaval of 1968, and extending further to the trials, revisionisms, political scandals, and racial violence of the 1970s and 1980s and the national self-examinations these provoked, modern French identity has been thought in relation to Germany and, conjointly, to "the Jewish Question."

Jean-Paul Sartre explicitly interconnects Jews, German history, and the issue of French identity in his first postwar publication, *Reflexions sur la Question Juive.* "We are all bound to the Jew, because anti-Semitism leads straight to National Socialism," he observes in closing, and bids each Frenchman understand "that the fate of the Jews is *his* fate."[7] Sartre's identification of Frenchman and Jew here pointedly opposes a nationalist discourse which, since Edouard Drumont's 1886 best-seller, *La France Juive,* had routinely and pervasively constituted the Jew as "the negative pole" of French identity and characterized as Jewish "what[ever] is not French in France."[8] To be sure, the representation of Jews and French people generally as common victims of National Socialism elides obvious incommensurabilities and tends to obscure the fact that, before Hitler's rise, not Germany but "France was the center of anti-Semitic agitation in Europe."[9] Nonetheless, by titling his book *Reflexions sur la Question Juive,* Sartre provocatively recalls and recasts a notorious locution of French racism and cultural nationalism, one which, as Susan Suleiman observes, "evoked tens and hundreds of anti-Semitic pamphlets and articles and special issues of newspapers published in France from the 1880s through the Second World War."[10] The Jewish Question obsessed the French cultural conservatives whose project to establish the "True France" "saturated all the 'places of memory' in the first half of this century."[11] Even without the adjective, the phrase *La Question* remained powerfully evocative in 1958, when the French government seized and banned a book of that title in which Algerian Communist Party member Henri Alleg describes his torture by French officers, who boasted that their interrogation techniques were derived from those the Gestapo had used to extract information from Resistance fighters.[12]

The same phrase anchors the brooding, reiterative, incantatory meditation on the possibility "of founding the community, within the world, of those who are still called philosophers" with which, in the months that followed Algerian independence, the young French Algerian Jewish Heideggerian Derrida began his first major essay.[13] The absent presence of the Holocaust is almost palpable in this opening section of "Violence and Metaphysics," a complex personal dialogue with the avowedly ethical and Jewish post- or counter-Heideggerian philosophy of former German prisoner of war Emmanuel Levinas, and the longest and arguably most impassioned piece in *Writing and Difference* (1967, 1978)—the collection of Derrida's early writings (including his dramatic American debut performance, "Structure, Sign, and Play in the Discourse of the Human Sciences") that secured and extended deconstruction's influence in the U.S. literary academy.

> A community of the question about the possibility of the question. This is very little—almost nothing—but within it, today, is sheltered and encapsulated an unbreachable dignity and duty of decision. An unbreachable responsibility. Why unbreachable? Because the impossible has *already* occurred. The impossible according to the totality of what is questioned, according to the totality of beings, objects, and determinations, the impossible according to the history of facts, has occurred: there is a history of the question, a pure memory of the pure question which in its possibility perhaps authorizes all inheritance and all pure memory in general and as such. The question has already begun—we know it has—and this strange certainty about an *other* absolute origin, an other absolute decision that has secured the past of the question, liberates an incomparable instruction: the discipline of the question.[14]

"From the start," claims Suleiman, "the 'Jewish Question' was indissociable from [French] reflections on identity and difference."[15] It was similarly indissociable from Derrida's earliest reflections on writing and difference. In its relentless references to totality, purity, and the absolute, and its insistence on remembering the impossible historical facts with which these philosophical terms and ambitions are implicated, Derrida's language here seeks to bear the burden of responsiveness, or responsibility, to the Holocaust and even to suggest the inseparability of the disciplinary question of philosophy's past and future from the question of the other, *la question juive.* Written in 1963, this paragraph exemplifies the way in which a generation of French intellectuals would approach (and, arguably, sublimate) the Holocaust: as the catastrophic end product of modernity's politico-philosophical history, a history that mutually implicated France and Germany as it did abstract thought and realized power, revolution and the state, and, ultimately, humanism and totalitarianism. In this conceptual frame, moreover, Jews, the primary victims of modern history, come to be figured as its limit—at once its unassimilable other and its ineradicable and saving (though unsaved) internal principle of resistance.

Such informing figures and concerns of recent French thought, as I have indicated, were belatedly recognized. In fact, it took Victor Farias's 1987 *Heidegger and Nazism,* which triggered an explosive debate about Heidegger's politics during the early years of the Third Reich and about the meaning of his deconstructive and anti-humanist legacy in France, to prompt general acknowledgment and direct examination of the centrality of the Holocaust and of *la question juive* to the work of postwar French intellectuals.[16] Yet, Derrida—and other prominent French poststructuralists—had been grappling with this unspoken knowledge long before his explicit proposal, in the opening words of his response to Farias, *Of Spirit: Heidegger and the Question,* to "speak of ghost, of flame, and of ashes."[17] The knowledge resonates not only in "Violence and Metaphysics" but in the short chapters, "Exergue," and "The Supplement of (at) the Origin," which frame *Of Grammatology* (1967, 1976). Derrida thus begins his most extended critique of the philosophy of the Logos by announcing "the ethnocentrism which, everywhere and always, had controlled the concept of writing . . . from the pre-Socratics to Heidegger"; and he concludes by casting the deconstructive insight that identities are constituted by difference in terms that evoke the rhetoric of modern anti-Semitic ethnocentrism: "the sickness of the outside (which comes from the outside but also draws outside, thus equally, or inversely, the sickness of the homeland, a homesickness, so to speak) is in the heart of the living word, as its principle of effacement and its relationship to its own death." To think the ontologically unthinkable possibility of "an originary supplement," this passage goes on to suggest, would be to "no longer see disease in substitution [since] the substitute is substituted for a substitute."[18]

Several years before the appearance of *Of Grammatology,* Derrida had already explicitly associated writing (the site and force of resistance to, or originary supplementation of, the philosophy of the logos) with Judaism and modern Jewish history. Two essays on the work of Jewish poet-philosopher and exile Edmund Jabes, collected in *Writing and Difference* but generally unaddressed by American readers, explore this association. The first, "Edmund Jabes and the Question of the Book," considers "a certain Judaism as the birth and passion of writing," perceiving each to constitute a "form of exiled speech" that articulates "the strange relation between law, wandering, and nonidentification with the self." The second essay, written expressly to conclude *Writing and Difference*, and suggestively entitled "Ellipsis" (at once, etymologically, defect or shortfall, and the mark of an absence), introduces— by means of a critical pun—the image of ashes that would become a recurrent motif in Derrida's later writings: Ou est le centre? Sous la cendre (Where is the center? Under ashes), Derrida quotes Jabes here.[19] So central had this image become for Derrida by the 1980s, that it provides the title for a poetic self-colloquy, written in 1982 and expanded and republished in 1987, in which Derrida both collects and annotates the textual sites of *la cendre* throughout his work and notes that, for him, "the best paradigm for [the key deconstructive concept of] the trace . . . [is] the cinder—what remains with- out remaining from the holocaust, from the all-burning, from the incineration the incense."[20]

Aligning Derrida's Jewish lineage and certain details of his early life with such coy textual invitations as he provides, critics such as Geoffrey Benning- ton have ascribed to him "a Jewish thought in some way opposed to the tyranny of the Greek logos."[21] Yet, both Derrida's "Jewish" aversion to logo- centrism and his work's inscription of the Holocaust and of the conceptual figure and historical fate of the European Jew are common to the writings of his non-Jewish poststructuralist compatriots. Lyotard's *Postmodern Condition* (1979, 1984), for instance, nowhere mentions "the Final Solution" in its seemingly dispassionate account of the postmodern as a condition of "incredulity toward metanarratives" or unifying discourses of legitimation. But the report turns—between chapter 9, "Narratives of the Legitimation of Knowledge," and chapter 10, "Delegitimation"—on a paragraph devoted to Heidegger's notorious 1933 Rector's Address, "The Self-Assertion of the German University," in which the Heideggerian theme of Being's struggle toward its self-assertion folds into the Hitlerian theme of National Social- ism's struggle toward Germany's destiny. Lyotard's chapter break immedi- ately follows this last-cited "episode in the history of legitimation," and his succeeding chapter opens, "In contemporary society . . . [where] the grand narrative has lost its credibility."[22]

Within a year of the publication of *The Postmodern Condition*, Lyotard had inserted the name "Auschwitz" into this gap, in the lecture (mentioned earlier) that became the central chapter of *The Differend* (1983, 1988). "Auschwitz," Lyotard contends here, is the place where the first-person plural pronoun, "in effect the linchpin for the discourse of authorization," was per- manently shattered.[23] Modeled by the inconceivable discourse community of Nazi exterminators and exterminated Jews—addressors and addressees of the decree to die—this shattered "we" extends beyond the camps to the "we" for whom, cognitively and affectively, "Auschwitz" is at once indigestible and unpurgeable. The Holocaust, in "Phrasing 'after Auschwitz,'" thus designates the continuing self-rupture and self-revelation of "[our] Western thought and life."[24]

Versions of this view pervade the work of other contemporary French intellectuals. In the year of Lyotard's lecture, for instance, Blanchot, the éminence grise of the younger academic theorists whose work came to define French poststructuralism in the United States, published *The Writing of the Disaster*. Blanchot's "disaster" shares key features of Lyotard's "postmodern," and its degree zero, as well, is the Holocaust: "The unknown name, alien to naming: The holocaust, the *absolute* event of history—which is a date in history—that utter-burn where all history took fire, where the movement of Meaning was swallowed up" (25). In the same year, 1980, Lacoue-Labarthe and Jean-Luc Nancy presented a paper entitled "The Nazi Myth," in which they argued that National Socialist ideology, "with its double trait of the mimetic will-to-identity and the self-fulfillment of form, belongs profoundly to the mood or character of the West in general," and that its analysis must comprise "one element in a general deconstruction of the history in which our own provenance lies."[26] And, three years earlier, inspired in part by Michel Foucault's unfolding vision of modernity as *panopticon,* Andre Glucksmann's *Master Thinkers* had charted this same history of the present as the realization of the project of German metaphysical or idealist philosophers (the "master thinkers")—a project of intellectual mastery, never separable from the dream of political domination, which logically culminates (but does not die) with Hitler.[27]

While Foucault's own major writings do not indicate that the Holocaust and the figure of the Jew hold originary places in his thinking, Foucault did remark, in an interview shortly before his death, that his constant state of fright as a high school student in occupied Poitier, amid refugees, political assassinations, informants, and deportations, formed "the nucleus of [his] theoretical desires."[28] Indeed, it is difficult not to recall Foucault's adolescent experience of Nazi occupiers and cooperating zealots of "True France" when one reads his injunction "not to discover the roots of our identity, but to commit [ourselves] to its dissipation," or when one considers his critical fixation on "the effects of truth that . . . power produces" and his insistence that "we all have a fascism in our heads."[29] If, as Dominick LaCapra has remarked (voicing a familiar reservation), Foucault's depictions of the history of disciplinary society tend to posit "a totalitarian organization . . . that is beyond the dreams of even recent regimes," it may be that Foucault's imagining of that history is shadowed by the prodigiously organized dreams of the Thousand Year Reich.[30] And, in fact, upon the publication of *The Master Thinkers,* Foucault promptly endorsed it in a magazine review in which he agreed that modern European anti-Semitism was "the matrix of all the racisms branding madmen, deviants, aliens" and named the Jew, "because he represents the absence of land, money that circulates, vagabondage, private interest, the immediate bond with God," as disciplinary society's prototypical insubordinate.[31]

"The Jew," as figured here by Foucault, stands as a sort of "originary supplement" to "Auschwitz" (conceived, in Blanchot's words, as "that utter-burn where all history took fire, where the movement of Meaning was swallowed up") in the philosophico-political imaginary of French poststructuralism. I mean to suggest that "Auschwitz" or the Holocaust, in this body of postwar French thought, marks the *end* of Meaning in the double sense of "consumption" and "consummation." National Socialism or the self-assertion of the German state is, as Lyotard implies, the West's ultimate—and ultimately delegitimizing—"grand narrative." The Final Solution is, as Glucksmann argues, the instrumental nightmare of the German (or Franco-German) metaphysical dream of Reason's or Spirit's realization in history.[32] Jews, of course, were the target of the Final Solution, their bodies the principal ones consumed in the Holocaust's "utter-burn." Yet, as the Other, the representative of difference, which originally informs Europe's totalizing projects of Identity, "the Jew" undoes such projects, figures their deconstruction. The Holocaust indeed "negates thought" and "suffocates language," as Richard Stamelman observes; but, for postwar French intellectuals, it is not the "absolute senselessness"[33] of "Auschwitz" so much as its totalitarian *consummation* of Meaning that arrests thought's, language's, and meaning's possibility—a deadly consummation that the figure of "the Jew" resists.

This trope of "the Jew," though it is inescapably linked to "the *absolute* event of history" and though it implicates the French intellectual tradition and its heirs in the long chain of responsibility for that event, also affords French poststructuralists a means of escape from, or resistance to, the Holocaust's absoluteness. For, the recovery of this trope allows postwar French intellectuals to return to—and then, by embracing and transvaluing it, to turn from—a prewar anti-Semitic figuration of the Jew as, in Geoffrey Hartman's vivid summary, "the very principle of the non-solid, of what is essentially groundless, rootless, shape-shifting, cerebral, cunning, abstract, and—like money in distinction to landed property—an agent of perpetual displacement and dissolution."[34] Closely and ambivalently associated since the Dreyfus Affair with the vocation of the intellectual in France, the figure of "the Jew" returns to signify for French poststructuralists both the possibility and the anti-disciplinary form of intellectual vocation after Auschwitz, the ironic faith of what Derrida calls "the community, within the world, of those who are still called philosophers . . . [after] the impossible has *already* occurred."

The transvaluative figuration of "the Jew" by postwar French intellectuals is already evident in *Reflexions sur la Question Juive*, where Sartre identifies the Jew with the salutary "spirit of free criticism . . . originating spontaneously in modern society" yet demonized by those who "fear . . . the human condition" as "the satanic spirit of negation, a virus of destruction."[35] Blanchot elaborates this characterization in an essay entitled "Etre juif" (Being a Jew, or, read in dialogue with the philosophical tradition, Jewish Being), which appears among a group of pieces gathered under the heading "The Limit Experience" in his 1969 collection, *L'entretien infini* (The infinite interview). Jewish being, Blanchot writes, ensures "that the idea of exodus, and the idea of exile as a just movement can exist" and that "the experience of strangeness can affirm itself near us in an irreducible connection"; it avows "a truth of exile, . . . the dispersion which summons to a residing without place [that] ruins all fixed relations of power . . . [and], in the face of the demand of the All, brings forth another demand and finally forbids the temptation of Unity-Identity."[36] Two decades later, Lyotard's *Heidegger and "the jews"* (1988, 1990) further developed this conception of Jewish being, while explicitly differentiating it from the Jewish people as an historical collectivity by placing the term "the jews" between quotation marks and using a lowercase *j*. "The jews," in this work, comprise the fissure in the foundation of foundational thinking, the repressed absence that elicits and undoes the metaphysics of presence, and the name of "every writing worthy of its name."[37]

A sign of "the spirit of free criticism," a "summons to a residing without place [that] ruins all fixed relations of power," a name for "every writing worthy of its name," Jewishness *(etre juif)* indicates the project of French poststructuralism itself. Such acts of "Jewish" self-denomination (re)iterate poststructuralism's link to the Holocaust. Yet, as I've suggested, the doubling of "Auschwitz" by "the Jew" in French poststructuralist discourse marks not only a catastrophic convergence but a resistant—if nothing so confident or oblivious as a saving—difference. The space of this difference may be mapped by superimposing upon Blanchot's figure of The Disaster (the absolute that "disorients the absolute"; "the thought which leads one to keep one's distance from thought"; that which "ruins everything, all the while leaving everything intact") his figure of Jewishness ("a residing without place [that] ruins all fixed relations of power . . . [and], in the face of the demand of the All, brings forth another demand and finally forbids the temptation of Unity-Identity"). It is the space between the ruin of everything and the ruin of the All, between a renunciative distance from thought and a critical residing without place: the space, that is, of intellectual vocation.

Inhabiting this space allowed French poststructuralists, after Auschwitz, to continue to think—in the form of unthinking—the powerful speculative tradition of the German master thinkers (particularly G. W. F. Hegel,

Friedrich Nietzsche, and Heidegger) and the intimately interconnected political and intellectual histories of Germany and France. And, it allowed them to
continue to possess—in the form of cultural burden—the troubled legacy of
their French pre- and postwar forebears (protofascist 1930s aesthetes; self-
serving or self-exculpating prosecutors of the late 1940s purge of politically
impure intellectuals; and radical 1950s apologists for the policies of Stalin)
who, in the name of difference, liberation, and resistance, had complied with
the barbarous sacrifice of the Other. Out of the treasure and trauma of these
inheritances, French poststructuralists fashioned their paradoxical project: the
deconstructive reconstruction of intellectual vocation around a simultaneous
insistence upon, and struggle against, the complicity of regimes of knowledge
with regimes of power.

One key component of this project would expose the chain of events,
ideas, and influences (outlined in n. 32) that interlinks French revolutionary
ideology, German metaphysics, the Holocaust, and poststructuralist thought
itself. If, as Heidegger imperially remarked of modern French philosophers
in a 1966 interview in *Der Spiegel,* "when they begin to think they speak German," postwar French intellectuals reciprocally viewed the National Socialism that in some measure came to speak Heidegger himself as the disastrous
German articulation of originally rational and liberatory French concepts.[38]
Of course, as was becoming painfully clear during the decades of poststructuralism's emergence, fascism and even the Holocaust had also been spoken
in French.

Like long-gagged political prisoners, or repressed memories, newly
released, the facts of French anti-Semitism and French responsibility for the
arrest and deportation of nearly seventy-six thousand Jews, few of whom
returned, began in the 1960s to announce themselves everywhere. The year
1968, historian Henry Rousso states in *The Vichy Syndrome* (1991), was the
"turning point in France's thinking about the Occupation,"[39] inaugurating a
passionate and painful reevaluation of the reciprocal myths of an externally
compelled, promptly repudiated, and ideologically aberrational Vichy regime
and a massive popular Resistance. Fueled in the 1970s not only by prolific historical examinations of the war years but by Marcel Ophuls's film *The Sorrow
and the Pity* (1971), by juridical and journalistic attention to the unpunished
war crimes of French fascists Paul Touvier and Louis Darquier de Pellepoix,
and by an apparent increase in anti-Semitic expression and activities, this project of reevaluation also coincided with an intense and public Jewish renewal
movement that centered on the preservation of Jewish memory of the catastrophe and on the reclamation of Jewish identity in France under the banner
of *le droit de la différence* (the right of difference).[40]

This moment of traumatic national recollection of French fascism, as the
Left-sympathizing poststructuralists well understood, was by no means a

moment of vindication for the intellectual Left. On the contrary, the moment is marked—both in public historical discourse and in the discourse of post-structuralist theory—by the delegitimation of traditional narratives of complicity and resistance and the destabilization of this opposition itself. In keeping with the developing poststructuralist reading (elaborated in n. 38) of the self-co-optation of ontotheological philosophy's most radical challengers, Zeev Sternell and other historians of the interwar years in France were charting "the process whereby certain mentalities and intellectual trends generally associated with the left slid toward fascism."[41] Moreover, these mentalities and trends were genealogically and rhetorically linked to those of poststructuralism itself, and, indeed, had arisen in response to an earlier "date in history . . . where the movement of Meaning was [thought to have been] swallowed up"—not the Holocaust, but World War I.

In the wake of the First World War's physical and psychological devastation of Enlightenment dreams of "the rational and just society," avant-garde writers and artists such as the young Blanchot cultivated what Alan Stoekl has identified as the characteristic, and agonistic, "sacrificial gesture" of twentieth-century French intellectuals.[42] These intellectuals cast themselves and their work as guardians and communicants of a vitality—an emanation of the sacred—that refuses political or aesthetic recuperation, a force of resistance to rationalized society that paradoxically sustains itself in resistance through rituals of self-sacrifice. Blanchot elaborates this logic of sacrifice in his 1937 essay "From Dread to Language," where he suggests that the word *writer* designates not an occupation but "a human condition" characterized by dread. To obey and write this dread, Blanchot continues, in terms disturbingly akin to those he would apply to the Holocaust forty years later in *The Writing of the Disaster*, is to accept "the nothingness that dread makes appear to [the writer] as his own object" and thus "to lose himself, without that loss being compensated by any positive value." Yet this self-sacrifice generates a creative energy, in the form of an uncivil work of art whose "usefulness is to express that useless part without which civilization is not possible."[43]

Recognizing the paradox of the essential utility of writing's absolute uselessness, Blanchot observes that "the depth of [the writer's] dread is tied to the fact that this dread cannot do without methodic realization," cannot avoid "seeking a complete solution to a situation that would be ruined and transformed into its opposite by a complete solution."[44] In other words, the sacrificial energy of self-abandonment and aesthetic resistance to instrumental use remains fundamentally susceptible to social recuperation and totalization. And indeed, amid the deepening economic despair and civil disintegration of the late 1930s, the thinking of iconoclastic literary intellectuals such as Blanchot himself and Georges Bataille, another crucial forerunner of French poststructuralism, proved susceptible to the barbarous recuperative project of fascism.[45]

The chain of *trahisons des clercs* that comprised one of the French post-structuralists' cultural inheritances did not end with fascism's fellow travelers in the 1930s or with the Vichy collaborators but extended into the postwar period.[46] The fervid purge *(epuration)* of collaborationist intellectuals in the mid-1940s, for example, so discredited itself by its "combination of verbal violence, selectivity, and bad faith," in historian Tony Judt's characterization, that Albert Camus, an early proponent, soon judged it to have increased the moral cynicism it was intended to combat.[47] Ultimately more damaging, though, for the French intellectual Left of the immediate postwar years was the rigid adherence of its most esteemed representatives (Sartre, Maurice Merleau-Ponty, and numerous others) to the sacrificial logic by which they theorized and justified the purges, show trials, and domestic and imperialist violence of Stalin's Soviet regime. Common to each of these episodes in modern French intellectual and political history is the writer's or thinker's sacrifice of *le droit de la différence* to the violent claims and attractions of collectivity and power. (Common to several of them, as well, is the persecution of Jews.)

A 1937 remark of Bataille's succinctly elucidates the intellectual's persistent temptation to such sacrifice—a crucial poststructuralist theme that the foregoing pages have sought to contextualize. Depressed by the claim of France's most esteemed Hegelian philosopher, Alexandre Kojeve, that the consummation of history and philosophy— emblematized for Hegel in the figure of a man on horseback—had arrived with Stalin, Bataille described the intellectual at such a moment as "the man of 'unemployed negativity.'"[48] It is possible, if reductive, to plot French intellectual history of the first sixty years of the twentieth century as a series of capitulations to the positivity of that consummate figure, whether in the form of fascism, the Vichy government, the corrupt *epuration* of postwar French culture, or Stalinism. French poststructuralism, in turn, may be viewed as a philosophy, a psycho-sociology, and a hermeneutics of resistance—under the sign of "the Jew"—to the deadly temptation of positivity, of ontotheology, of cognitive or cultural essentialism, of final solutions. Yet, the echoes and convergences between figures of Auschwitz, Jewishness, writing, and intellectual vocation in the discourses of such thinkers as Blanchot and Lyotard raise a question about the character and objective of the poststructuralist enterprise: Is French poststructuralism a means of assuming an "unbreachable responsibility," in Derrida's phrase, to the fact of the Holocaust and to the task of radically interrogating all regimes of putative Truth or is it a means of restoring Bataille's anxious 1930s intellectual, the man of unemployed negativity, to disciplinary employment?

The Poststructuralist American Academy
and the Profession of Jewish Identity

Finding postwar disciplinary employment in U.S. universities, and eventually rising to an appointment at Yale, Paul de Man played a key role in the establishment of poststructuralism as, for a time at least, the lingua franca of the American literary academy. Ironically, given de Man's posthumously exposed wartime contributions to a collaborationist Belgian newspaper and the consequent reading (by some) of his deconstructive hermeneutics as an intellectual apparatus for obscuring the meaning of those writings and disidentifying with their author, the poststructuralist discourse that de Man helped transport to America was first taken up by Jewish intellectuals for whom it came to underwrite a new poetics of Jewish identity. More ironic still are the constructions by some of his more forgiving commentators, most notably Hartman, of de Man's own transgression as an instance of the bidirectional passage between intellectual and (figurative) Jew.

In "Judging Paul de Man," Hartman speculates that de Man's most damaging collaborationist article, "Les juifs dans la litterature actuelle," expressed a "self-protective" impulse. Wishing to deflect prevalent charges of rootlessness and negativity against modern literature and its devotees, Hartman suggests, de Man "decoys reader or censor by projecting on the Jew the intellectual's own [qualities]."[49] (In neither's finest moment, Shoshana Felman and Derrida also allegorize the postwar and the posthumous de Man, respectively, as Holocaust witness and Holocaust victim.)[50] Whatever the merit, though, of Hartman's argument that the early de Man protects himself and buttresses modernist literature by projecting his own intellectual commitments as the work of the Jew, it is only slightly hyperbolic to claim of Hartman's own early scholarship and that of his Yale colleague Harold Bloom that the inverse is the case: that these critics decoy disciplinary readers and censors, credentialize themselves, and challenge modernist criticism by projecting their Jewish commitments as the work of the literary intellectual.

In *The Academic Postmodern and the Rule of Literature,* David Simpson defines "the academic postmodern" as the contemporary intellectual milieu or knowledge regime that has resulted from "the exporting of literary-critical categories into disciplines that had previously resisted them" and that typically "[risks] mistaking the internal migration of terms and priorities among the disciplines inside the academy for a radical redescription of the world outside the academy."[51] My essay—particularly in the link between its two sections, between the title's first pair of terms ("the Holocaust and French Poststructuralism") and its second ("the American Literary Academy and Jewish Identity Poetics")—locates the development of some of the "terms and priorities" of the academic postmodern in a series of complex migrations, importations, and redescriptions: not only transdisciplinary but transnational passages, and passages between the academy and the world outside. Such passages include the radical redescription or intellectual historicization of the Holocaust and the transvaluative migration of the anti-Semitic figure of "the Jew" by means of which postwar French philosophers and social theorists at once implicated their disciplines in "that utter-burn . . . where the movement of Meaning was swallowed up" and sustained them beyond it. And they include a radical redescription of literary critical categories in American universities that is made possible, in part, by the importation of Holocaust-haunted, figuratively "Jewish" French theories of displacement, negation, and textuality—an importation which, in turn, makes possible for Jewish American literary academics a reconnection to (or redescription of) Jewish identity and community that at once resists and inhabits the terms and priorities of the academy.

Hartman and Bloom stand historically, disciplinarily, and Jewishly between the first generation of Jewish American critics, who entered the literary academy—or resolutely remained on its fringes—in the late 1930s and 1940s, and the generation (mine) of baby boomer Jewish academics whose current poststructuralist identity poetics I will examine in the closing pages of this essay. The young men of the first generation (Lionel Trilling, Daniel Aaron, Meyer Abrams, Harry Levin, and Leslie Fiedler, etc.) were generally the children of immigrants, who grew up in physically and metaphysically concentrated Jewish environments—whether the form of metaphysical concentration was orthodoxy, spoken Yiddish, Freudianism, or Marxist theory and labor activism. At some point, however, such concentration had failed to yield them intellectual or communal sustenance. As Alfred Kazin put it, reflecting on the passage of many of his peers from New York Jew to American literary intellectual: "you were lonely as a Jew and lonely in a strange land, lonely, always lonely, even in the midst of people."[52] Not a matter of lack of company, such loneliness bespoke, for Kazin and his colleagues, their inability to experience Judaism, or even any of the modern projects of displaced Jewishness, as a vital, participatory, purposeful community of belief. "The Republic of Letters," as Fiedler referred to his youthful vision of the house of literary study, seemed to offer such a community, and in order to become a "full-fledged, up-to-date citizen" of it, Fiedler recalls, he willingly overlooked evidence of anti-Semitism in the writings of the modernists he loved.[53] This generation of critics, then, deflected some and perhaps sublimated others of their Jewish acquisitions and sensibilities as they found in the literary academy a way out of Jewish difference and, perhaps, Jewish identity.

Entering university life after the establishment of these predecessors, after the Holocaust, after the troubled military creation and political ratification of the State of Israel, and at a moment of high-profile Jewish literary productivity in the United States, academics of Bloom's and Hartman's generation were in one sense freer, and in another bound, to bring a more active Jewish self-consciousness to their critical vocation. Biographical particulars as well (Bloom's Talmudic training, and Hartman's refugee childhood) doubtless underpinned such self-consciousness in the early careers of these two critics, as did the conservatism of the Yale English department in the 1950s. With characteristic agon, Bloom recalled its intellectual environment as "an Anglo-Catholic nightmare . . . [in which], no matter what you read or how you taught it or how you wrote, you were supposed to gravely incline the head and genuflect to the spirit of Mr. Thomas Stearns Eliot, God's vicar upon earth, the true custodian of Western tradition."[54] Hartman more temperately described the "gentlemanly sort of Christianity" that was expressed, in part, by the elevation of Eliot, John Donne, and seventeenth- and eighteenth-century studies over "the adolescent and faintly disreputable Romantics."[55]

Against prevailing critical orthodoxy, and—one might say—against gentlemanly Christianity itself, the first books of both twenty-something Jewish critics champion romantic poets. Both Hartman's *Unmediated Vision* (1954) and Bloom's *Shelley's Mythmaking* (1959) refer to Jewish interpretive traditions on their first pages, but neither claims a vision of the Romantics or a disciplinary practice that is mediated by Jewish experience and knowledge. On the contrary, Jewish references such as Bloom's opening citation of Martin Buber are more or less strictly analogical and illustrative, and the religious establishment that the Romantics are said to succeed and exceed is undifferentiated: William Wordsworth initiates modern poetry's "almost total break from Judeo-Christian traditions," writes Hartman; Percy Shelley works "in parallel opposition to the mythmakings of formalized religions," writes Bloom.[56] Only with their intellectual assimilation of French theory at a moment, the late 1960s, when the U.S. social and academic landscape shifted (a moment that featured the deconstruction of the figure of American commonality, the Left's positive revaluation and embrace of difference, and the decisive replacement of Jews by other minorities as bearers of difference in the polis and the literary academy), would Bloom and Hartman begin insistently to distinguish Jewish from Christian forms and traditions, to link mediation and textuality with Judaism, and to identify their own disciplinary positions and perspectives as Jewish ones.

Both critics early emphasize the "Hebraic" quality of Derridean deconstruction, a response that probably contributed to Derrida's more direct engagements, in later writings, with his own Jewish heritage and with the Holocaust. Echoing and glossing Derrida's famous exposition of the "two interpretations of interpretation," Hartman names these competing orientations "Patristic, chiefly typological, and Rabbinic, which stands in 'negative' relation toward the Messianic event as a fulfillment of time and of the Word" and offers literary studies a "welcome . . . semiotic [counterperspective]" to the

long-dominant "logocentric or incarnationist thesis."[57] Accordingly, five years
after Derrida began his series of American visits and a year after de Man's
appointment to the Yale faculty, Hartman writes a new preface, "Retrospect
1971," for the reissue of his 1964 study of Wordsworth in which he laments
the disciplinary conventionalism or timidity that allowed him "to evade [his]
own insights."[58] Foregrounding these insights now, Hartman depicts a
Wordsworth who does not "break from Judeo-Christian traditions" or "seek
the hellenic innocence of the senses," as he'd written previously, but who
"relives on the very ground of his senses the religious struggle between Hellenic (fixed and definite) and Hebraic (indefinite, anti-anthropomorphic) representations of the divine" and who thus exemplifies an agonistic poetics of
error that resembles the way avant-garde European films converge on a center that is an absence and illuminate a darkness that has no heart.[59]

It was poststructuralism's theorization of the romantic conflation of
sacred and secular texts and of the play of sacralizing and secularizing energies in all writing and reading that most engaged and enabled Bloom. Thus,
the revisionary ratios of *The Anxiety of Influence* (1973), which Bloom began
to draft before the Yale critics had taken significant stock of French theory,
are themselves revised in *A Map of Misreading* (1975) and *Kabbalah and
Criticism* (1975) by Bloom's desublimation of his talmudic training and Jewish Gnostic theology and his increasingly open and anxious confrontation
with the influence of his Jewishness. Following upon the dramatic success of
the trilogy's first volume, the latter two books announce a strong *Jewish*
reader who, as Bloom puts it at the beginning of *A Map of Misreading*, has
"[opened] received texts to his own sufferings, or what he wants to call the
sufferings of history."[60] For Bloom, these sufferings include his own post-
Holocaust Jewish turn toward what he describes as the originally anti-Jewish Gnostic vision of "an alien God set against an evil universe," and, the
trilogy suggests, they include "the kabbalistic pathos" of his personal
attempt "to exalt aspects of Exile" and to live his Judaism by means of the
breaking of its vessels.[61]

Textuality is the sacred vessel of both Hartman's and Bloom's Jewish
identity, but both also understand it to be a broken one. While Hartman
defends as ethical insight, rather than fatal blindness, what incarnationist
thought deems the "wilderness error" of Jewish textualism, he would understand Bloom's remark that "the obsession with 'language' is . . . a defensive
trope" to describe the predicament not only of "modern literary discourse" but
of the Jewish literary intellectual as well.[62] Vigilantly alert to "the pathological
potential in collective types of thought [including Jewish ones] that claim to
unify or heal a community," Hartman is nonetheless troubled by the privatiz-
ing consequences of such wariness.[63] Bloom's judgment on the disciplinary
and religious limits of textualism is compatible. After summarizing the three

stages of creation in Lurianic Cabala—*Zimzum*, "the Creator's withdrawal"; *Shevirath ha-kelim*, "the breaking-apart-of-the-vessels"; and *Tikkun*, "restitution or restoration"—Bloom observes:

> The first two stages can be approximated in many of the theorists of deconstruction, from Nietzsche and Freud to all our contemporary interpreters who make of the reading subject . . . what I myself would call a new mythic being. . . . Such a reader, at once blind and transparent with light, self-deconstructed yet fully knowing the pain of his separation both from text and from nature, doubtless will be more than equal to the revisionary labors of contraction and destruction, but hardly to the antithetical restoration that increasingly becomes part of the burden and function of whatever valid poetry we have left or may yet receive.[64]

This three-stage kabbalistic story of creation—with its third and restorative stage remaining incomplete, figured only in desire—suggestively approximates both the disciplinary history of postwar literary study and one (if not the) narrative of Jewish subjectivity in the American literary academy. For critics such as Fiedler and Trilling, literary disciplinarity offered a haven from, or sublimation of, Jewish identity; for their generational successors, Hartman and Bloom, Jewish interpretive traditions and commitments—underwritten by, and partly rewritten as, emergent poststructuralist discourses of textuality, rupture, and exile—offered both a tool for disciplinary revision and desacralization and a means of dialogizing professional labor and Jewish subjectivity. And, for a third generation of Jewish academics—born after the war, when the simultaneous compulsion and disqualification to "make links with Auschwitz" at once comprised and helped attenuate Jewish identity in America[65]—the poststructuralist academy has itself sometimes provided a site for the convergence of disciplinary and Jewish profession and a law (or Logos) of Jewish return.

To effect, or at least explore, such a convergence was the recent project of *People of the Book: Thirty Scholars Reflect on Their Jewish Identity* (1996), a volume of essays commissioned and edited by Jeffrey Rubin-Dorsky and Shelley Fisher Fishkin. Both the title of the collection itself, in its tropic doubling of its contributors' religious heritage and professional commitment, and that of the editors' introduction, "Reconfiguring Jewish Identity in the Academy," nominate the academy as a vital site of contemporary Jewish experience and render reciprocal the practices of "literary academic" and "Jew." This reciprocity, for the contributors who are most attracted by it, tends to be imagined and articulated here in terms of the institutionalized discourse of French poststructuralism, which, more often than Jewish vocabularies and traditions themselves, has made current and articulable to my generation of academics the notion of Jewishness as a principle, locus, or legacy of *differance*.[66] Accordingly, Raphael Sassower writes: "In some uncanny way, I found (not just rediscovered) my Jewishness in postmodernism, and especially in the writings of Jean-François Lyotard, . . . [which] gave me some answers about my own jewish (read: marginal-because-critical) identity."[67]

Signaled in part by the Lyotard-inspired slippage from upper- to lowercase Jewishness, the problems that readily present themselves in this narrative of Jewish self-discovery have to do with the experiential specificity of Jewishness as difference and resistance, and (as Bloom and Hartman worried) with whether such an identity may be occupied, let alone transmitted, except in and as intellectual atomism and abstraction—or in and as the practice of academic criticism. In the collection's most probing essay, and certainly its wittiest one, Maria Damon also worries about such questions, ironizing "this tale of heroic survival thru exegesis" and wryly reflecting: "no matter how many essays I write in which I 'problematize' 'identity' by taking 'the Jew' as the archetypal identity-problematizer (Reb Coyote-shmoyote), everyone knows I'm not real."[68] While, at moments, Damon writes, she justifies a Jewish identity experienced "as *a priori* fragmentary: an essence characterized by evanescence, an entity defined by its indeterminacy," at others she mourns a Jewishness "which I have . . . tried to reassemble as if it were some thing that had been shattered."[69]

Itself a broken vessel, an effect if not of God's withdrawal during the Holocaust then of the legitimation crisis of the European ontotheological philosophical tradition in its wake, poststructuralism became a tool that American literary academics of the past thirty years have used to break the vessels of false or forsaken disciplinary and cultural gods. Bloom's "[custodial] spirit of Mr. Thomas Stearns Eliot"; New Criticism's poetic icon or well-wrought urn; the self-evident literary masterwork and the monumental canon of Western literature to which it distinctively belonged; the integral disciplinarity of literary study itself; American identity; the freestanding individual subject or liberal self: these are among the idols that French postwar theory has helped American professors to topple or deconstruct. The critical assault on such hegemonic categories of identity or value has been accompanied by, and often pursued in the interest of, a valorization of otherness, difference, marginality, hybridity, and multiplicity. If this decentralizing trend in the American literary academy and in American cultural life at large on the one hand "forbids the temptation of Unity-Identity," in Blanchot's phrase, on the other it intensifies such temptation, whose object it relocates in sub- or multicultural rather than dominant and national identities and politics. The personal narrative that feminist critic and queer theorist Bonnie Zimmerman outlines in *People of the Book* bears the mark of both of these impulses: among feminist critics in the seventies, Zimmerman recalls, "nobody was talking much about being Jewish"; by the late eighties, she continues, "I had been evading my Jewish identity for over a decade," until, in a book published in 1990, "I . . . added Jewish to the identity litany."[70]

By the time Bloom and Hartman began to produce their distinctive disciplinary midrashim on poststructuralism, Jews had ceased to betoken difference within U.S. institutional cultures. In the larger society, too, Jews had been more or less thoroughly supplanted by other Others, as intimated by the dedication—"Sixty Million and more"—of the most influential and academically celebrated American novel of the last quarter century, Toni Morrison's *Beloved* (1987). Hence, among progressive younger Jewish academics of the 1970s, whose childhoods and intellectual formations generally had not occurred in distinctively Jewish environments, "nobody was talking much about being Jewish." Hence, too, the belated effort to recover an identity freighted with the possibility both of restored legacy and community (Damon's "thing that had been shattered") and of reclaimed cultural difference (now an *avowable* object of desire and basis of—rather than disqualification for—social and academic authority in multicultural America).

The editors of *People of the Book* report "the delicious sense of community we felt when several of us would share and debate our ideas [about] the question of our Jewishness in the academy."[71] As one of the volume's final contributors observes, however, taking as his essay's epigraph a fragment of a remark by Claude Lanzmann ("I had no concept; I had obsessions, which is different . . ."), it is "hard . . . for communities to perpetuate a sense of their collective identities without rituals of some kind, without a dogma that goes without saying."[72] Lacking "a dogma that goes without saying," this collection of Jewish professors can only be—like Derrida's "community, within the world, of those who are still called philosophers"—a community of the question, whose location is the university and whose identity is underwritten by poststructuralist theories and discourses of difference: an intellectual identity poetics, an academic *question juive*.

NOTES

1. Quoted by Jean-François Lyotard in "Discussions, or Phrasing 'after Auschwitz,'" in *Auschwitz and After: Race, Culture, and 'the Jewish Question' in France*, ed. Lawrence D. Kritzman (New York: Routledge, 1995), 174.

2. As Lawrence D. Kritzman writes in his introduction to ibid.: "The memory of Auschwitz and the question of Jewish identity have been key critical *topoi* in French political, cultural, and intellectual life since the end of World War II" (1). Indeed, long before the memory of French governmental and popular complicity in the Nazi effort to identify, deport, and exterminate Europe's Jews was allowed explicitly to pierce the

"self-protective silence . . . [that] prevailed for close to fifty years after the occupation" (Geoffrey Hartman, "The Voice of Vichy," in ibid., 16), advanced French thought had embraced or been invaded by "'a new shape of knowing' . . . the motif of some lasting violation" (Michael Andre Bernstein, "Lasting Injury: Competing Interpretations of the Nazi Genocide and the Passionate Insistence on Its Uniqueness," *Times Literary Supplement*, 7 March 1997, 3). Often signaled by the prefix "post-," the new shapes of, or resistances to, knowing that French intellectuals have largely pioneered—"the crisis of representation in poststructuralist approaches to history and language" and the "proliferation of images, identities without substance, and textuality-centered culture" that "we roughly call postmodernism"—are most aptly historicized, as David Suchoff argues in his translator's preface to cultural historian Alain Finkielkraut, *Le juif imaginaire* (1980) (*The imaginary Jew* [Lincoln: University of Nebraska Press, 1994]), as expressions of "the post-Holocaust era," xiii, xvii.. Key French texts, in addition to Finkielkraut's, which confirm this historicization include Andre Glucksmann, *The Master Thinkers* (1977), trans. Brian Pearce (New York: Harper, 1980); Maurice Blanchot, *The Writing of the Disaster* (1980), trans. Ann Smock (Lincoln: University of Nebraska Press, 1986); Julia Kristeva, *Powers of Horror: An Essay in Abjection* (1980), trans. Leon S. Roudiez (New York: Columbia University Press, 1982); Lyotard, *The Differend: Phrases in Dispute* (1984), trans. Georges Van Den Abbeele (Minneapolis: University of Minnesota Press, 1988); Jacques Derrida, *Cinders* (1987), trans. Ned Lukacher (Lincoln: University of Nebraska Press, 1991); Jean Lacoue-Labarthe, *Heidegger, Politics, and Art* (1987), trans. Chris Turner (Oxford: B. Blackwell, 1990); Derrida, *Of Spirit: Heidegger and the Question* (1988), trans. Geoff Bennington (Chicago: University of Chicago Press, 1989); Lyotard, *Heidegger and "the jews"* (1988), trans. Andreas Michel (Minneapolis: University of Minnesota Press, 1990); and Julia Kristeva, *Stranger to Ourselves* (1988), trans. Leon S. Roudiez (New York: Columbia University Press, 1991).

3. Insofar as such interrogations of the workings and relations of language, reason, history, subjectivity, knowledge, and power continue to occupy the attention—if not define the scholarship—of American literary academics, the widespread reports of theory's demise in the past decade seem premature. The fact that the signature critical idioms of the early "theory revolution" have become less fashionable attests not to poststructuralism's abandonment but to its disciplinary incorporation and domestication. Has the Holocaust, too, therefore, been quietly and unreflectively incorporated in the terms of our contemporary disciplinary practice? If, in other words, the Holocaust is belatedly recognized as a central presence (even in its absence) to the critical discourses that have centrally influenced American academic thinking about language, reason, history, subjectivity, knowledge, and power, how should our understanding and use of these discourses now reflect this recognition? How, if at all, does it alter our estimation of the powers and limits, or the conditions of applicability, of our interpretive paradigms? In historicizing French poststructuralism, its American appropriation, and the intellectual and cultural "identity poetics" that it underwrites, in France and in the United States, my essay proposes to open such questions for exploration, though satisfactory answers to them are beyond its scope.

4. For a succinct narrative of the relation between the rise of literary studies as an institutionalized academic profession and the mid-twentieth-century triumph of

critical formalism see "Groping for a Principle of Order: 1930–1950," in Gerald Graff, *Professing Literature: An Institutional History* (Chicago: University of Chicago Press, 1987), 145–61. For a book-length history of the modern literary academy in the last half century and of the role of the "theory revolution" in that history, see Evan Carton and Graff, "Criticism since 1940," in *The Cambridge History of American Literature*, vol. 8, ed. Sacvan Bercovitch (New York: Cambridge University Press, 1996). Of course, the political orientation, consequence, and utility of the "theory revolution" have been widely debated. Assailed by conservatives as subversive and by leftists as counterrevolutionary (and, in response to biographical revelations about Martin Heidegger and Paul de Man, by both as crypto-fascist), poststructuralist theory typically refuses easy or categorical ideological classification. A number of factors contribute to this classificatory difficulty or ideological instability: indeterminate relations between discursive and material instruments and measures of power; the nonequivalence between different forms or arenas (cultural, disciplinary, class, and international) of politics; and poststructuralism's double-edged destabilization of fixed identity categories—a destabilization that implicitly challenges naturalized hierarchies but that also implicitly resists or defers reconstituted political self-definitions in favor of the kind of infinite transformative potential that is (arguably) all too serviceable to intellectual disciplines and careers that depend on renewable interpretive work rather than on decisive social action. Again, my narrative of poststructuralism's emergence in France and appropriation in the United States does not resolve the problematic of the politics of theory so much as it deepens that problematic and offers one view of its historical grounds.

5. Maurice Blanchot, *The Unavowable Community* (1983), trans. Pierre Joris (Tarrytown, NY: Station Hill Press, 1988). Like the "community of the question about the possibility of the question" that Derrida poses in a key passage from the essay "Violence and Metaphysics" that I will discuss shortly, Blanchot's "unavowable community" is powerfully and pervasively informed (and deconstructed) by the Holocaust. Of this pointedly "negative community," a community that inscribes absence and is predicated on "someone else's death," Blanchot writes:

> What, then, calls me into question most radically? Not my relation to myself as finite or as the consciousness of being before death or for death, but my presence for another who absents himself by dying. To remain present in the proximity of another who by dying removes himself definitively, to take upon myself another's death as the only death that concerns me, this is what puts me beside myself, this is the only separation that can open me, in its very impossibility, to the Openness of a community. (9)

6. Les Evans, ed., *Revolt in France, May-June, 1968; A Contemporary Record* (New York: Les Evans, 1968), 90.

7. Jean-Paul Sartre, *Anti-Semite and Jew*, trans. George L. Becker (New York: Schocken, 1948), 151, 153.

8. Elaine Marks, *Marrano as Metaphor: The Jewish Presence in French Writing* (New York: Columbia University Press, 1996), 70, 72.

9. Zeev Sternhell, *Neither Right nor Left: Fascist Ideology in France* (Berkeley: University of California Press, 1986), 30.

10. Susan Suleiman, "The Jew in Sartre's *Reflexions sur la question juive,*" in *The Jew in the Text: Modernity and the Construction of Identity,* ed. Linda Nochlin (London: Thames & Hudson, 1995), 204.

11. Herman Lebovics, *True France: The Wars over Cultural Identity, 1900–1945* (Ithaca: Cornell University Press, 1992), xiii.

12. Henri Alleg, *La question* (Paris: Editions de Minuit, 1958).

13. Derrida, *Writing and Difference,* trans. Alan Bass (Chicago: University of Chicago Press, 1978), 79. Derrida wrote "Violence and Metaphysics" shortly after his parents emigrated from Algeria in 1962 during the final days of a general Jewish exodus. Ironically, the vast majority of the nearly 140,000 Jews who left Algeria during and just after its war of independence, between 1954 and 1962, resettled in the country which, under Vichy, had stripped them of French citizenship (and expelled twelve-year-old Derrida from public school). For Derrida, questions of Algerian identity and colonial violence were intimately entangled with *la question juive,* with memories of fascism, and with the transport and destruction of communities later signified by the word "Auschwitz." In an essay revised and expanded for this collection from its original publication in the electronic journal *Postmodern Culture,* Lee Morrissey challenges "the commonly accepted notion that Derrida's work avoids, overlooks, or prevents a relationship with history and/or politics" by reading his best-known essay "in terms of the 'liberation' of Algeria" (Morrissey, "Derrida, Algeria, and 'Structure, Sign, and Play,'" *Postmodern Culture* 9.2, [1999]: 1). My essay joins this challenge but locates the central (absent) historical and political presence—the constitutive "rupture"—for Derrida's work, and for poststructuralism generally, in the Holocaust.

14. Derrida, *Writing and Difference,* 80.

15. Suleiman, "The Jew in Sartre's *Reflexions sur la question juive,*" 202.

16. Victor Farias, *Heidegger and Nazism* (1987), trans. Paul Burrell (Philadelphia: Temple University Press, 1989). *Heidegger and Nazism* derived its particular impact in France not from its "outing" of Heidegger's early (and possibly late) Nazi sympathies, which had been charged and debated before in European intellectual circles. Appearing at the height of a belated national examination of the extent of French complicity with Nazism and of the country's continuing susceptibility to anti-Semitic prejudice and violence, Farias's book instead suggested to some that postwar French philosophy, which was heavily indebted to Heidegger, comprised a form and a continuation of such complicity or, at the least, complacency. Philosophers such as Derrida, Lyotard, and Lacoue-Labarthe responded with books that at once contested or complicated Farias's account of Heidegger's politics, engaged the Holocaust and the Jewish Question much more directly than their earlier work had done, and contended that these issues had, however cryptically, been present—even central—to their thinking all along.

17. Derrida, *Of Spirit,* 1.

18. Derrida, *Of Grammatology*, trans. Gayatri Chakravorty Spivak (Baltimore: Johns Hopkins University Press, 1976), 3, 313–14. For generations, French and German anti-Semitic writers and polemicists had typically associated Jews with "the sickness of the outside" that came to infect and parasitically feed on a natural and national host. Derrida here complicates this trope when he writes of a self-destructive "sickness of the homeland . . . in the heart of the [Christian?] living word." Derrida's figure of the "originary supplement" also approximates, and shares the ontological critique of, the "othered" self of French poststructuralist psychoanalytic theory—an otherness that is likewise cast in sociopolitical terms. Compare, for example, the "supplemental logic" of Kristeva's argument in *Stranger to Ourselves* that "Freud brings us the courage to call ourselves disintegrated in order not to integrate foreigners and even less to hunt them down, but rather to welcome them to that uncanny strangeness, which is as much theirs as it is ours. . . . The foreigner is with me, hence we are all foreigners. If I am a foreigner, there are no foreigners" (191–92).

19. Derrida, *Writing and Difference*, 67, 69, 297.

20. Derrida, *Cinders*, 43.

21. Geoffrey Bennington and Derrida, *Jacques Derrida*, trans. Bennington (Chicago: University of Chicago Press, 1993), 293. Derrida himself entertains this view most suggestively in "Circumfession," his pendant to Bennington's interpretive biographical essay, "Derridabase," in which he announces himself "a sort of *marrane* [i.e., a secret Jew] in French Catholic culture" and closes by promising "the ultimate periphrasis," to "speak of the Final Solution" (170, 310).

22. Lyotard, *The Postmodern Condition: A Report on Knowledge*, trans. Bennington (Minneapolis: University of Minesota Press, 1984), 37.

23. Lyotard, *Differend*, 98.

24. Ibid., 88.

25. Blanchot, *Writing of the Disaster*, 47.

26. Phillipe Lacoue-Labarthe and Jean-Luc Nancy, "The Nazi Myth," *Critical Inquiry* 16 (winter 1990): 312.

27. Glucksmann, *Master Thinkers*. In the course of his narrative, Glucksmann explicitly amends Foucault's account of the inception of modern society in Enlightenment Reason's categorical self-differentiation from madness. "The Reason of the classical age never locked up the 'madman' only," he observes. Citing a passage from G. W. F. Hegel's *German Constitution* (1893) that equates the madman and the Jew, twin affronts to Reason and to the self-fulfillment of the German state, Glucksmann argues that the figure of the Jew occupies an originary place "alongside the madman in the exclusion-area of Hegelian reason" (95–96).

28. Didier Eribon, *Michel Foucault*, trans. Betsy Wing (Cambridge: Harvard University Press, 1991), 10.

29. Michel Foucault, *Language, Counter-Memory, Practice*, trans. Donald F. Bouchard (Ithaca: Cornell University Press, 1977), 162; Foucault, *Power/Knowledge*, trans. Colin Gordon (New York: Pantheon, 1980), 93, 99.

30. Dominick LaCapra, *Soundings in Critical Theory* (Ithaca: Cornell University Press, 1989), 20.

31. Quoted in Jeffrey Mehlman, *Legacies of Anti-Semitism in France* (Minneapolis: University of Minesota Press, 1983), 20–21.

32. This understanding of twentieth-century fascism as the twisted or inhumanly perfected product of eighteenth-century philosophical ideals broadly corresponds to the postwar analyses of the exiled Frankfurt school philosophers, most notably that of Theodor Adorno and Max Horkheimer in *Dialectic of Enlightenment* (1944). "Enlightenment is totalitarian" by virtue of an "'irrationalism' [that] is deduced from the nature of the dominant *ratio* itself," Adorno and Horkheimer argue. "Not merely the ideal but the practical tendency to self-destruction has always been characteristic of rationalism," in which "the submission of everything natural to the autocratic subject finally culminates in the mastery of the blindly objective and natural" (Adorno and Horkheimer, *Dialectic of Englightenment,* trans. John Cumming [New York: Continuum Publishing Company, 1991], 6, xvii, xvi).

For postwar French intellectuals such as Glucksmann and Derrida, history and the future of philosophical thought demanded that they come to terms with the role of the French intellectual tradition in this dialectic. Evident enough was the fact that German speculative philosophy—in particular, the work of Hegel, Friedrich Nietzsche, and Heidegger—had powerfully engaged French intellectuals throughout the twentieth century, especially since the 1930s, when Alexandre Kojeve's legendary seminars on Hegel at the Ecole des Hautes Etudes had shaped an entire generation. But this tradition of German thought itself could be viewed as a philosophical speaking of French revolutionary ideals of freedom and the reign of Reason. The French Revolution variously inspired the thought of J. G. Fichte, Hegel, and Karl Marx. Central to Hegel's project, in fact, as explicated by Kojeve in Paris, was the figure of Napoleon, who embodied the fullness of action—Man's self-perfection "through his total integration with History"—that it is the task of the *Phenomenology* (1807) to bring into the fullness of thought. This synthesis of action and knowledge, Kojeve had written, is the revelation of Absolute Spirit and its realization "by the universal and homogeneous State" (Denis Hollier, ed., *The College of Sociology,* trans. Betsy Wing [Minneapolis: University of Minnesota Press, 1988], 88).

French poststructuralist theorists encountered the Holocaust in the context of this philosophico-political tradition in which the mutual implication of France and Germany was the implication of abstract thought and realized power, of revolution and the state, and, ultimately, of humanism and totalitarianism. Thus, Lyotard links the French revolutionary narrative of universal liberation and the German idealist narrative of absolute knowledge—both prominent among the modern discourses of legitimation that he writes, "have given us as much terror as we can take" and that postmodernity must strive to unlearn (Lyotard, *Postmodern Condition,* 81). And Foucault finds the greatest contribution of Glucksmann's *Master Thinkers* to lie in its recognition of the "turn [by which] German Philosophy [was] able to make of Revolution the promise of a true and good State, and of the State the serene and accomplished form of the Revolution" (Mehlman, *Legacies of Anti-Semitism in*

France, 18). This turn—in which, Foucault writes, "all of our submissions find their principle"—is at once a trope of accomplishment and betrayal, of accomplishment *as* betrayal.

33. Richard Stamelman, "The Writing of Catastrophe: Jewish Memory and the Poetics of the Book in Edmond Jabes," *Auschwitz and After,* 267.

34. Geoffrey Hartman, "The Voice of Vichy," in ibid., 21.

35. Sartre, *Anti-Semite and Jew,* 118, 54.

36. Blanchot, *L'entretien infini* (Paris: Gallimard, 1969), 183, 184 (my translation).

37. Lyotard, *Heidegger and "the jews,"* 34. Recent critics have noted, often with discomfort or dismay, the reiterative, objectifying, and derealizing tendencies or potentialities of such ostensibly transvaluative figurations of the anti-Semitic trope of "the Jew" as Sartre, Blanchot, and Lyotard perform. Thus, Mehlman describes "France's anti-Marxian philosemitism" as predicated on a "chiasmic reversal in the paradigm through which anti-Semite and Jew retain their relation" (Mehlman, *Legacies of Anti-Semitism in France,* 21), and Alan Stoekl observes of Blanchot's *etre juif,* as others have pointed out about Sartre's "Reflexions sur la question juive," that "in [the] essay one collectivity—the Jews—tends to disappear in their specificity before our very eyes, while another, the anti-Semites, is very precisely identified, its threat noted as very real" (Stoekl, "Blanchot, Violence, and the Disaster," in *Auschwitz and After,* 139). Tobin Siebers holds Lyotard's lowercase appropriation of "the jews" to "writing" to be a "repulsive tactic" of Holocaust evasion that is consistent with the broader tendency of a Cold War intellectual skepticism "to eschew the political plane of existence in order to win a charismatic and worldless subjectivity for the critic" (Siebers, *Cold War Criticism and the Politics of Skepticism* [New York: Oxford University Press, 1993], 101, 12). If non-Jewish French theorists have alienated Jewish identity from lived religious and cultural experience, community, and commitment, their figure of "Jewish being" has nonetheless been advanced and lived by Jewish intellectuals both in Europe and in the United States. As Irving Howe reports, for example, many of the New York Intellectuals in the 1950s tended to experience and value their Jewishness as a trope or avenue of alienated modernity, a "Jewishness of question and risk" rather than of religious observance or association (Howe, *A Margin of Hope: An Intellectual Autobiography* [New York: Harcourt, 1982], 260). While I recognize and share many of the concerns articulated by the critics cited in this note, my principal interest in this essay, as summarized in its introductory section, is not simply to repudiate on moral, political, or religious grounds the curious reciprocity or transformativity between "Jewishness" and intellectual vocation but to sketch its history and to explore its cultural and disciplinary functions and implications.

38. Gunther Neske and Emil Kettering, eds., *Martin Heidegger and National Socialism: Questions and Answers,* trans. Lisa Harries (New York: Paragon House, 1990), 63. The responses of Derrida, Lyotard, Blanchot, and Lacoue-Labarthe to the question of Heidegger and Nazism, accordingly, all hinge on the poststructuralist (and Heideggerean) insight of achievement's or fulfillment's self-betrayal, of consumma-

tion's destructive self-consumption. Heidegger's philosophy remains profound and compelling, these thinkers argue, not *despite* his abiding commitment (or temporary susceptibility) to National Socialism, but *because* of it. Heidegger's Nazism, in this reading, shockingly validates Heidegger's point about Western philosophy's pervasive and devastating tendency to betray authentic Being by yielding to the metaphysical temptation to objectify it—a temptation to which even radical deconstructors of the metaphysical tradition such as Nietzsche (for Heidegger) and Heidegger (for the French poststructuralists) have succumbed. With Heidegger, revolutionary philosophical thought completes and betrays itself in fascism.

39. Henry Rousso, *The Vichy Syndrome: History and Memory in France since 1944*, trans. Arthur Goldhammer (Cambridge: Harvard University Press, 1991), 99.

40. Rousso provides an account of the reassertion of Jewish memory and identity in France during these years in ibid., chapter 9, "Obsession (After 1974): Jewish Memory."

41. Sternhell, *Neither Right nor Left*, 19.

42. Alan Stoekl, *Agonies of the Intellectual: Commitment, Subjectivity, and the Performative in the Twentieth-Century French Tradition* (Lincoln: University of Nebraska Press, 1992), 5, 11. At once cultural dissident and representative, Stoekl's twentieth-century French intellectual is a devotee of an illimitable originary energy and a lawgiver. This figure is early exemplified by Emile Durkheim's secular priest or rational shaman. On the basis of his anthropological investigations, Durkheim argued that the seemingly irrational and often violent rites observed in "primitive" religions were in fact totem acts that at once constituted, legitimated, and vitalized social collectives. Upon such acts, moreover, the life of any society—including modern "rational" ones—depended. The modern Durkheimian intellectual, in Stoekl's account, recuperates the primal energy of the sacred, reinterpreted as "moral enthusiasm," and places it "at the disposal of the rational and just society" (5). At work here is a double logic of sacrifice in which, in the first place, community originates in sacrificial ritual and, in the second, the ecstatic originary force—in other words, the play of the signifier—must be sacrificed to the establishment of the communal order of the signified.

43. Blanchot, *The Gaze of Orpheus, and Other Literary Essays*, trans. Lydia Davis (Tarrytown, NY: Station Hill Press, 1981), 5, 7, 9, 8.

44. Ibid., 11, 12.

45. Georges Bataille would come to see the energies of transgression and heterogeneous excess that he cultivated in the mythico-political collectives he organized in 1935 and 1936 appallingly harvested, three years later, in a season of total war. And his short-lived "sacred sociology," which called (in the closing words of the October 1938, declaration of principles that he coauthored) for the reconstruction of "a collective mode of existence that takes no geographical or social limitation into account and that allows one to behave oneself when death threatens" (Hollier, *The College of Sociology*, 46), was answered within the year by Hitler. Indeed, as Carolyn Dean observes in *The Self and Its Pleasures: Bataille, Lacan, and the History of the Decentered Subject* (Ithaca: Cornell University Press, 1992), the avant-garde artists and thinkers who "redefined

male identity in masochistic terms" and theorized convergences "between art and violence—between art and death" were responding to the same "cultural crisis in interwar France" that underlay fascism's growing political appeal: their "belief in the transgressive, anti-utilitarian, and hence revolutionary quality of self-loss . . . was not always easy to distinguish from a fascist celebration of self-sacrifice, from the paradoxical self-fulfillment through self-annihilation to which fascist sympathizers such as Pierre Drieu la Rochelle and Henri de Montherlant so often alluded" (202, 212, 3, 228).

46. Julien Benda coins this phrase ("the treason of the intellectuals") in his 1923 book of that title, *La trahison des clercs,* in which he states prophetically that the distinguishing feature of the twentieth century will be "the intellectual organization of political hatreds" (Benda, *The Betrayal of the Intellectuals,* trans. Richard Aldington [Boston: Beacon, 1955], 21.

47. Tony Judt, *Past Imperfect: French Intellectuals, 1944–1952* (Berkeley: University of California Press, 1992), 69–70.

48. Hollier, *College of Sociology,* 92.

49. Hartman, *Minor Prophecies: The Literary Essay in the Culture Wars* (Cambridge: Harvard University Press, 1991), 136.

50. In "After the Apocalypse: Paul de Man and the Fall to Silence," in *Testimony: Crises of Witnessing in Literature, Psychoanalysis, and History* (New York: Routledge, 1992) that she coauthored with psychoanalyst Dori Laub, Shoshana Felman reads an "altogether different personal and historical significance" (121) into de Man's lifelong silence about his youthful collaborationist writings and anti-Semitic utterances. After the trauma of the Holocaust and its implication of an entire generation of European intellectuals, Felman suggests, "the act of bearing witness could no longer be repeated as a simple narrative act but had to turn upon its own possibility of error to indicate—and warn us against—its own susceptibility to blindness" (138). Hence, de Man's silence about his past and his criticism's deconstruction of simple narrative and intentional acts and meanings is in fact a masterpiece of testimony. By breaking with country, family, politics, and history, de Man (who had admired and translated *Moby Dick*)

> dies as Ahab and survives as Ishmael in his inside knowledge of the compellingly seductive and radically delusional quality of the event, and in his later vision of the entanglement and the complicity, of the bankruptcy of all conventional historical divisions and the blurring of all boundaries. . . . Indeed, in his afterlife as Ishmael, in his later writings and in his teaching, de Man, I would suggest, does nothing other than testify to the complexity and ambiguity of history as Holocaust. (136–37)

The tastelessness of Derrida's sanctification of a martyred de Man in his essay "Of Sound and Silence," originally published in *Critical Inquiry* and reprinted in *Responses: On Paul de Man's Wartime Journalism,* eds. Werner Hamacher, Neil Hertz, and Thomas Keenan (Lincoln: University of Nebraska Press, 1989), is mitigated, if at all, only by the bond of friendship and act of personal loyalty that the essay performs. "He *was* the war," Derrida pronounces (124), a man who bore, "through the ruptures, exile, the radical reconversion, what I begin to see clearly is . . . an enormous suffering, an agony, that we cannot yet know the extent of" (147). "He must have thought that well-tuned ears knew how to hear him, and that he did not even need to confide to anyone about the war in this regard. In fact, that is all he talked about" (156). Indeed, even now, Derrida muses, "is it not de Man who speaks to us 'beyond the grave' and from the flames of cremation?" (153).

51. David Simpson, *The Academic Postmodern and the Rule of Literature: A Report on Half-Knowledge* (Chicago: University of Chicago Press, 1995), 2.

52. Alexander Bloom, *Prodigal Sons: The New York Intellectuals and Their World* (New York: Oxford University Press, 1986), 25.

53. Leslie Fiedler, *Fiedler on the Roof: Essays on Literature and Jewish Identity* (Boston: D. R. Godine, 1991), 9.

54. Imre Salusinszky, ed., *Criticism in Society* (London: Routledge, 1987), 61.

55. Hartman, *The Longest Shadow: In the Aftermath of the Holocaust* (Bloomington, University of Indiana Press, 1996), 19.

56. Hartman, *The Unmediated Vision: An Interpretation of Wordsworth, Hopkins, Rilke, and Valery* (New Haven: Yale University Press, 1954), xi; Bloom, *Shelley's Mythmaking* (New Haven: Yale University Press, 1959), 101.

57. Derrida, *Writing and Difference*, 292; Hartman, *Minor Prophecies*, 152; Hartman, "The Poetics of Prophecy," in *High Romantic Argument: Essays for M. H. Abrams*, ed. Lawrence Lipking (Ithaca: Cornell University Press, 1981), 35.

58. Hartman, *Wordsworth's Poetry* (New Haven: Yale University Press, 1971), xvii.

59. Ibid., xviii-xix.

60. Harold Bloom, *A Map of Misreading* (New York: Oxford University Press, 1975), 3.

61. Bloom, *Kabbalah and Criticism* (New York: Seabury Press, 1975), 3, 46.

62. Ibid., 105.

63. Hartman, *The Longest Shadow*, 50.

64. Bloom, *A Map of Misreading*, 5.

65. For a representative account and critique of this reorientation—and disorientation—of Jewish American identity around the "absent presence" of the Holocaust, see Robert Alter's "Deformations of the Holocaust," *Commentary* 71.2 (1981): 48–54. Alter writes:

> the institutional centering of a victimization so unprecedented as to resist meaning may be more than anything else an appeal to Jewish masochism, an attempt to base collective identity on a sense of dread or—if we are utterly honest about these matters—on the special *frisson* of vicariously experiencing the unspeakable, in all the material comfort and security of our American lives. (53)

66. The contributors to *People of the Book: Thirty Scholars Reflect on Their Jewish Identity*, eds. Jeffrey Rubin-Dorsky and Shelley Fisher Fishkin (Madison: University

of Wisconsin Press, 1996) who are most attracted by the idea that professional and Jewish identity are linked tend to be the younger ones. Significantly, the older scholars represented here respond more guardedly, even resistantly, to the volume's project. With varying degrees of pointedness, Herbert Lindenberger, Paul Lauter, and Joel Porte all use their essays to decline the invitation to fuse or even dialogize literary critical disciplinarity and Jewishness.

67. Raphael Sassower, "The 'Jew' as 'Postmodern': A Personal Report," in ibid., 301–2.

68. Maria Damon, "Word-landslayt: Gertrude Stein, Allen Ginsberg, Lenny Bruce," in ibid., 380, 385.

69. Ibid., 380.

70. Bonnie Zimmerman, "The Challenge of Conflicting Communities: To Be Lesbian and Jewish and a Literary Critic," in ibid., 206, 207.

71. Rubin-Dorsky and Fishkin, "Reconfiguring Jewish Identity in the Academy," in ibid., 8.

72. Michael S. Roth, "Shoah as Shivah," in ibid., 403.

2

Michel Foucault and the Specter of War

KAREN RABER

> I remember very well that I experienced one of my first great
> frights when Chancellor Dollfus was assassinated by the Nazis in,
> I think, 1934. . . . The menace of war was our background, our
> framework of existence. Then the war arrived. Much more than
> the activities of family life, it was these events concerning the
> world which are the substance of our memory. . . . Our private life
> was really threatened. Maybe that is the reason why I am fasci-
> nated by history and the relationship between personal experience
> and those events of which we are a part. I think that is the nucleus
> of my theoretical desires.
> —Michel Foucault, *Politics, Philosophy, Culture*

The last two decades of critical reflection on the legacy of Michel Foucault
have given us a substantive and dynamic portrait of the theorist as Parisian
intellectual, sexual revolutionary, and political dissident—all roles Foucault
consciously adopted and polished, while leaving the factual skeleton of his life
deliberately unfleshed. Indeed, critical views of Foucault have often reproduced his own reluctance to connect his thought to a life: David Macey,
Didier Eribon, even to a great extent James Miller and the many critics who
offer brief biographies as part of their critical studies of Foucault's works all
seem to discover that the attempt to tell a relatively traditional form of biography is complicated enormously both by Foucault's position on his own
legacy, and by his reluctance to make information about his life part of the
written record. Macey begins his book with an exhaustive list of the various

philosophical traditions that have claimed Foucault, or that might have influenced his work, concluding that to tell the life story is to tell the intellectual history Foucault did willingly leave behind: "To say that the history of his books is to a large extent the biography of Michel Foucault is, at one level, almost a truism," Macey observes, and clarifies, "His biography is, that is, the story of a thought, a work in progress."[1] David Cousins Hoy remarks that "there may not be a single 'Foucault,'" and so attempts to find consistency in his works are unlikely to succeed.[2] Miller, whose discussion of *The Passion of Michel Foucault* (1993) inspired heated and venomous arguments among Foucault scholars for deliberately foregrounding Foucault's sexuality, may nonetheless be most tellingly criticized for telling a wholly conventional psychologized biography: Lynn Hunt observes that Miller's treatment of the man who wished "to efface himself and decenter all of mankind," represents the resurrection of all Foucault assaulted and should, if you believe his positions have merit, have successfully dismantled.[3] At the moment the critic believes she has found the ultimate "life story" of "Foucault" it turns out the author is simply not where we expected him to be.

We have inherited from Foucault, these examples suggest, a skeleton, a ghost, a mind, some thoughts, but perhaps not precisely a system of thought, and certainly not an individuated, coherent corpus—physical or intellectual, disciplined or otherwise. Yet, even in the absence of a system, consistency or a body, there is still history—discontinuous, problematic in its reconstruction, subject to Foucault's own skeptical methods, but a kind of history. A history like that, derived exclusively from texts, history that is the story of thoughts or what the academy has classified as "intellectual history," however, is also a tradition thoroughly assaulted in Foucault's early works. But if we are looking to historicize Foucault, should we not be looking for a social history, a local history, which suggests the environment, the historical context that produced 'Foucault'—the "nucleus of [his]theoretical desires?" Such a history, proceeding from a skeptical posture, is in fact precisely the project Foucault's work invites from us.

Some, mainly Foucault's critics and intellectual heirs, have tried to do just that. Most critical accounts of the relationships between Foucault's life and work break his development into periods—Hoy, for instance, is typical in dividing the work into three decades, each with a particular set of interests, implications, and outcomes. And most generally agree about locating the connections between his theoretical positions, his political work, and in turn his sudden and tremendous influence on European and American theory and politics, in the turbulent events, the maimed bodies, the political crises of the 1960s and 1970s: Vietnam, Algeria, the Tunisian and Parisian student uprisings of 1967 and 1968, and Attica and European prison riots. Yet I think these gestures toward historicizing Foucault are incomplete, hindered by some important oversights and omissions. The Tunisian students whose violence Foucault approved as "an utterly remarkable act of existence" were nearly fifteen years Foucault's junior, adherents of a brand of Marxism he had repudiated.[4] The same is true about the students of Paris in '68. Whatever social paradigms shaped these students' lives, they were not the same as those that had already shaped Foucault's. In his responses to these movements, and to the work of the *Gauche Proletarienne,* we detect Foucault's sense of *exteriority* to their motivations and a clear resistance to the idea that their history is the most significant shaping force in his own life: "For *those young people* [the Tunisian students], Marxism did not merely represent a mode of analyzing reality; it was at the same time a kind of moral energy."[5] In an interview with Ducio Trombadori at the end of 1978 a characteristic battle takes place between the interviewer, who insists on locating Foucault's formation in the events of the 1960s, and Foucault himself, who tries to suggest other perspectives. Asked what May '68 meant to him, Foucault responds: "During the month of May 1968, as in the period of the Algerian War, I wasn't in France; again, I was a little out of phase, an outsider."[6] Undaunted, the interviewer remarks that Foucault tends to dismiss the events of May, and suggests that they were more formative to European politics and intellectual life than Foucault would allow; indeed, several questions later, we find Trombadori still inviting discussion on the centrality of May '68. The author, however, offers quite a different historical context for his work: "The experience of the war (World War II) had shown us the urgent need of a society radically different from the one in which we were living, this society that had permitted Nazism, that had lain down in front of it, and that had gone over en masse to de Gaulle."[7] Yet this insight is quickly passed over and categorized by Trombadori not so much as a reference to Foucault's work, but as a comment on the marginality of Jean-Paul Sartre's thought for Foucault.

I want to take the hint from Foucault, and disinter the specter of war buried in his work and his life—not the war in Algeria, not the Vietnam War, not the war inside prisons or on the streets of Paris, but The War, the defining event of France's modern history and of Foucault's early life. Among all the other things the Paris student riots were, they were also importantly the death-knell for France's vision of itself under Charles de Gaulle, the final dismantling of de Gaulle's imperial rule, and with it France's lingering identity as a victim-survivor of the Second World War. By conjuring a potent and persistent set of ghosts—the phantoms of Vichy, of collaboration, of fascism, of the discipline of the body in concentration camps, of the covalent discipline of Nazism, of totalitarian discourse represented as Nazi propaganda—that haunted Foucault's childhood and early adulthood, as they haunted French intellectuals and the proletariat alike, I hope to offer an historical explanation for both Foucault's triumphant displacement of the "imperious agent of causality," and for his insistence that all aspects of everyday life are "organized and controlled down to [their] oddest and smallest details,"—the source of many critics' complaint that Foucault's thought seems to enforce the modern subject's "entrapment in a totalitarian narrative."[8] But I also want to suggest that with all the historical work Foucault himself did, the history he told over and over was not the history of the ancient Greeks, or the history of the "classical age" of the ancien regime, or in fact any of the histories that do appear in his works. Rather, I want to argue that lurking unwritten in all the fascination these histories hold for Foucault is a history he did not tell, the history of France during World War II.

To put it another way: I intend to take seriously—literally and historically—the implications of Foucault's own comments in "Two Lectures," that politics is war by other means.[9] Although Foucault offers this inversion of Clausewitz's assertion—"war is politics by other means"—in order to question the presumed relationship between power and violence, I would argue that we have here another hint about how to read the French experience of war, its violence, and its violation of European illusions about consensus, representation, and political cohesiveness in Foucault's work. In an early summary of one of his university seminars Foucault poses a series of questions that ground the course's examination into "how relations of subjectivation can manufacture subjects," among them, "Should war be considered as a primary and fundamental state of things in relations to which all the phenomena of social domination, differentiation, and hierarchization are considered as secondary?"[10] States, Foucault concludes, are born out of war, and rather than imposing peace, rely on war's continuation in organizing the social body. "It is not enough," Foucault warns, "to find this war again as an explanatory principle; we must reactivate it, make it leave the mute larval forms in which it goes about its business . . . and lead it to a decisive battle that we must prepare for if we intend to be victorious."[11] Rather than a "shaping fantasy" for French intellectuals of the '60s and '70s, World War II might best be characterized as a shaping nightmare, a "mute" larva awaiting reanimation, an incubus demanding exorcism in a wholly new concept of power and political process. "We wanted a world and a society that were not only different, but that would be an alternative version of ourselves: we wanted to be completely other in a completely different world."[12]

EXHUMATION

James Bernauer's essay on Foucault and Auschwitz may be one of the few critical pieces to reconsider which history we should connect Foucault with when explicating his politics and ethics. Bernauer seizes on a photograph in the tribute volume, *Michel Foucault: Une histoire de la verité,* to argue that Foucault's philosophy, especially his later work on sexuality, represents a critique of "recent world wars and our current atomic situation . . . as the outcome of a power-knowledge regime that is committed to the administration of life itself."[13] The photograph captures a moment in Foucault's visit to Auschwitz in 1982, accompanied by Simone Signoret and Bernard Kouchner:

> A visit to another prison? Only after consulting the information at the back of the book did I realize it was Auschwitz. Of course, It was only to be expected that he would have wanted to see Auschwitz with his own eyes, the eyes which stare sternly out at the photographer. If Claude Lansmann's *Shoah* has permitted us to hear the voices of that distant hell, I believe Foucault has enabled us to see its nearness, to feel its intimacy, and to challenge its logic.[14]

Those who write Foucault's biographies, however, largely ignore this connection. Miller, like Trombadori, refers to World War II only as the origin of Sartre's philosophy in order to qualify Foucault's relationship to his elder colleague. Although Miller comments that "Foucault . . . came of age in a world where the threat of death was ubiquitous yet largely invisible, more a nightmarish rumor than a tangible reality," he assumes that the too-young Foucault "experienced the war at one remove."[15] Miller's one brief insight remains undeveloped and buried in the—to him—more interesting passages of Foucault's adult life. Macey also glances at one possible ideological impact of the French experience of war: "During Foucault's teens, homosexuality was viewed with horror by the ideologues of Vichy, obsessed as they were with the defense of the values of the patriarchal family."[16] But Macey also hurries along to focus far more intently on the young Paul-Michel's experience at school in 1945 and after.

Granted, each of these biographers has a particular agenda not necessarily satisfied by examining more carefully the aftermath of German occupation or the various monstrosities of the Vichy regime; yet I find fascinating about their diminution of war's influence and importance in Foucault's life the fact that it replays a larger historical repression, a communal forgetting that characterizes postwar France's treatment of its own recent history. Henry Rousso calls France's selective amnesia "the Vichy Syndrome," arguing that only in the 1970s was the "carefully constructed myth" about France's behavior during the war shattered through a "return of the repressed."[17] Prior to the 1970s, France underwent a purgation of memory, the transformation of the war through de Gaulle's revisionist reading of his country's experiences—France was, in de Gaulle's words, "humiliated . . . martyrized . . . [but] Liberated by itself, by its own people with the help of the armies of France . . . of the true France."[18] The desire to forget France's collaboration with the Nazis was so strong, the

mythologies that arose out of it survived nearly intact until—not coincidentally—1968. Marcel Ophuls's film *The Sorrow and the Pity*, exposing Vichy's
willing collaboration with the Nazis, and French anti-Semitism and the persecution of Jews under Vichy rule, was filmed in 1967 and 1968, and shown
in 1971, but not televised until more than a decade later due to extreme opposition to its views of the past. Other events continued the "shattering" process
described by Rousso: the pardon by Georges Pompidou in 1971 of Paul Touvier, who had aided the Nazis in destroying Resistance units during the war.
Touvier was a "real" (i.e., not fictional or filmic) collaborator who "appeared
almost like a ghost—a collaborator with real crimes and authentic victims to
his credit."[19] These early breaks began a cascade, ushering in an era of self-cas-
tigation and self-examination analogous to that experienced by the Germans
following the exposure of the concentration camps and the revelations of the
Nuremberg Trials, with the sole exception that for the French enlightenment
was delayed, belated.

What emerges in the resulting orgy of self-disgust versus self-justification
is a picture of France's wartime embrace of the worst aspects of Nazism. But
we should not forget that this picture is a reconstructed, partial one—a gory
corpse too-soon buried, requiring a messy exhumation. Bernauer's treatment
of Foucault and Auschwitz fails, despite the splendid insights of his conclusions, to fully appreciate this. The Foucault who visits Auschwitz is a foreigner, an outsider to that experience as he was to so many others—he is a
tourist, if a somber one, in search of a past that is not precisely his own, trying to listen to ghosts he may have once thought had little to do with his own
past. Bernard Kouchner's essay accompanying the photo notes that the three
were visiting a place they had *only* seen in films and in their imaginations, and
that they found the experience inadequate.[20] Bernauer connects Foucault's
ethic with repugnance for Nazism and the recognition that the Nazi regime
functioned according to its own sense of the moral, the right and the good,
making it continuous with, not radically different from, the "virtuous" non-
German national regimes that fought it. But Foucault is French, not German;
his connection to the concentration camps, to the extermination of the Jews,
and to Nazi thought is mediated by that difference. While such a reminder
might seem intended to diminish the impact of Nazi actions in the formation
of Foucault's philosophy, it isn't. Rather, the experience of the belated discovery of the past (that we see practically registered in the very late date of the
epigraph to this essay in which Foucault finally acknowledges the importance
of his childhood memory of war), especially when that discovery *aligns* French
propaganda and behavior with Nazi extremes, intensifies the shock of discovery, and the shock of recognition of the commonality of Nazi and non-Nazi
potentialities. Bernauer suggests that arguments that place Nazism on the far
side of an abyss from "moral" systems of politics and culture allow us to avoid

"any anxiety that we ourselves might share a moral kinship in the Nazi king-dom of death."[21] But France was forced in the 1970s and after to accept that kinship. To wake up from the dream that France was an innocent victim of an outside force, and realize that it had cooperated in global and local ways with its "oppressor" is to become suddenly awake also to the need for a new kind of historical analysis that will defeat such effects of deliberate denial and oblivion, the analysis that Foucault's historiographical methods make possible.

WAR AND/VERSUS POLITICS

Poitiers, Foucault's childhood home, was occupied during the war by the Germans, and suffered most of the kinds of treatment any occupied town did—Jews were collected and deported, wounded were brought to town, troops first retreated through the town, then with the advance of the Allies, came through on their way to liberate Paris: "Operation Bulbasket" sent a team of British Special Air Servicemen into the area in 1944 to disrupt rail traffic; a number were caught, and shot in July of that year. There were air raids, food was scarce; people lived with the constant fear of arrest and punishment; some collaborated, some resisted. Some repudiated the Vichy government and its leader, Pétain, but all at least officially accepted its propaganda.

The Vichy government embraced a rhetoric of purification and discrimination entirely compatible with Nazi self-described "humanistic" values. In the interests of "strengthening" France's culture and society, whose weaknesses had led to the nation's quick defeat by the Germans, an intense effort was applied to "dividing 'good' French from 'bad,'" and indigenous from 'foreign" influences.[22] A propaganda poster signed by Pétain announces the goals of the National Revolution the Vichy regime supported, including the following:

6. Any citizen who pursues his own interests outside of the common interest goes against reason and even against his own interests.

7. Citizens owe their labor, their resources, and even their lives to the fatherland. No political conviction, no doctrinal preference relieves them of these obligations.

10. The state must be independent and strong. No group can be tolerated that brings citizens into conflict with one another or that discredits the authority of the state. All cliques imperil the unity of the nation. The state must smash them.[23]

This poster, displayed in all French schools, implicitly justifies French cooperation and even independent enforcement of deportations and round-ups, especially of Jews, using language worthy of any Nazi document—repeated

evocation of the "fatherland" that must be purified, the use of "reason" to dele-
gitimize resistance and explain repression, and so on. Jews, according to the
propaganda, owed no allegiance to any nation: Rudolph Van Wehrt's film
Frankreich auf der Flucht ("France in Flight," 1941) tells the story of several
Germans who meet a fleeing Jew in Occupied France who, believing his new
travel companions are refugee Jews like himself, announces that he defends no
borders because he is not French, nor German, nor English. Propaganda like
Hermann Esser's *Die jüdische Weltpest* ("The Jewish Plague," 1939) or *Der
ewige Jude* ("The Eternal Jew," 1940), produced by Joseph Goebbels's ministry
of propaganda) which depicted scenes of swarming rats and flies to illustrate
the notion that Jews were a filthy infestation, were intended to sway occupied
populations to embrace German Aryanism. Vichy France embraced this kind
of anti-Semitic image of the Jew.

The French did not carry out mass deportations with the efficiency one
might expect from these facts. There was sufficient local resistance to a number
of increasingly punitive policies against French Jews to mitigate the ferocity of
either the anti-Semitic Vichyites or the Nazi occupiers. Some 70,000–80,000
Jews in all were deported from France to the east by both German and French
police—but this number is far less than the total Jewish population of the country before the war, and far less as well than the number of French workers
deported to labor in German factories.[26] Yet the historical exhumation of
France's role in sending its Jews east during the war involved countless wrenching stories that overwhelmed de Gaulle's calculated mythologizing of France's
past as triumphant survivor of its "martyrdom." The whole notion of France as
the nation of Resistance—as a military organization, but also as a posture of
heroism—is emptied of its apparent truth-value by such stories.

While only male Jews and other undesirables were being deported, the
French public could persuade itself that these men were destined for no worse
fate than native French who were being supplied for labor. But when the
deportations shifted to include women, and then mainly children below the
age of fifteen, no mistake was possible. A witness recalls, "We saw little children who did not even know their last names deported without parents and
without name tags"—this, she notes, was impossible to explain away. Poitiers
too lost its share of Jews.[27] On 27 January 1944, the regional prefect was
ordered to arrest local Jews. "After demanding and receiving authorization

from his French superiors, he obeyed with a vengeance. . . . French police caught 484—an astounding 76 percent."[28]

To many witnesses of roundups in France, Germany or other countries, the most striking thing about the targets of deportations and other forms of repression was their passivity, their docility: while there are stories of escapes during the French police actions, and numerous accounts of Jews being sheltered by clerics or ordinary citizens, most French Jews went without violent resistance, and certainly without an organized, armed response. Susan Zuccotti notes that the apparent reason why the Poitiers Jews were caught in such great numbers as late as 1944 was that they simply could not assimilate the idea that they were in danger from French as well as from German authorities (191). Many Jews threatened with deportation petitioned the Vichy leadership on the basis of individual claims to citizenship in France, and especially to military service to the nation; some asked exemption on the basis of illness, age, or other debility. But as the punitive and comprehensive nature of the deportations became clear in the later years of the occupation, there was still no extralegal, organized, militarized opposition. These were simply far too well-disciplined citizens to take that option. In other words, the inclusion of France's Jews as members of the nation under the Third Republic, and their enfranchisement as citizens may have actually contributed to their greater compliance with a state to which they felt they owed allegiance. Incorporated into the regime of rule, educated to accept its power, disciplined in their adherence to law and order, France's Jews may well not have recognized themselves in Pétain's poster as those whose participation in a "clique" must be "smashed," or those whose doctrinal "preference" made them an "irrational" threat to the healthy body of the state. And so they marched compliantly to their deaths.

Compliance with power, the inscription of the individual with the regimes of power, and the production of docile, disciplined bodies find their most thorough expression in Foucault's *Discipline and Punish* (1979), a text that I believe owes more than we have recognized as Foucault's experience of the war. To illustrate that claim, let me begin with my own moment of dawning understanding, á la Bernauer's account of Foucault at Auschwitz. To introduce a chapter on "Docile Bodies," Foucault offers the reader the historical accout of the seventeenth- versus the eighteenth-century soldier's increasing subjection to discipline or "dressage":

> Let us take the ideal figure of the soldier as it was still seen in the early seventeenth century. To begin with, the soldier was someone who could be recognized from afar; he bore certain signs . . . movements like marching and attitudes like the bearing of the head belonged for the most part to a bodily rhetoric of honour. . . . By the late eighteenth century, the soldier has

become something that can be made; out of a formless clay, an inapt body, the machine required can be constructed; posture is gradually corrected; a calculated constraint runs slowly through each part of the body, mastering it, making it pliable, read at all times, turning silently into the automatism of habit. . . .[29]

Now this is a compelling example, but as a scholar of early modern culture I have always thought that the history it pretends to tell is simply inaccurate—the eighteenth century did not invent the automatism of habit, nor did soldiers from prior historical periods owe their training only to a system based on honor. Roman soldiers were subject to an equally "machinelike" form of the dressage, drilling constantly and learning a marching gait called the "military step." They too were "made" as if out of formless clay, and their success in battle often derived from their impressive disciplined uniformity far more than from individual skill with arms. The early Persians likewise are paragons of discipline and mechanical precision; even the supposed rabble of medieval infantry has recently been shown to be a fiction manufactured after the fact. In all these cases, the body is treated in what Foucault calls "'retail,' individually" in order to produce a mass effect; in all cases what is at stake is the "economy, the efficiency of movements, their internal organization" (137).

I'm not arguing that Foucault was a bad military historian (although that may well be true also), or that the example of the soldier doesn't speak eloquently about a different social process, one that is genuinely the focus of *Discipline and Punish*. Rather I detect in the example of the soldier a prior and different fascination, which I see borne out in another remark Foucault makes later, in a 1976 interview, that he has always wanted to engage in a full-length study of the army "as a matrix of organisation and knowledge," suggesting that his use of the soldier in *Discipline and Punish* is not an isolated element of his thought.[30] No one has, to my knowledge, found this statement curious, given Foucault's declared interest in those groups and members of society usually deemed marginal. What is marginal about the army? How would a study of the military cooperate with a career built on analyzing prisoners, the insane, the medical profession, and sexuality?

Foucault's fascination with the soldier should, I would rather suggest, be read as the lingering aftermath of his early exposure to the one modern military force that could truly be distinguished for its application, if not the invention, of discipline, namely, the soldiers of Nazi Germany. Recognizable from a distance? Automatons? In *Discipline and Punish*, Foucault cites Frederick II, "the meticulous king of small machines, well-trained regiments and long exercises," to support his view of the "puppet" soldier (136). Is it an accident that the best example of such a formula for modern militarism is Austrian, or that his talents and emphases so neatly match those of his latter-day incarnation,

Hitler? While Foucault may not have consciously offered an historical method for interpreting the "work" of the German military, and its continuousness with the submission of entire populations to deportation and death, it is nevertheless true that the history he tells in *Discipline and Punish* accomplishes precisely that.

In *Discipline and Punish*, Foucault observes that "The judges of normality are everywhere. We are in the society of the teacher-judge, the doctor-judge, the educator-judge" (304). The dispersal of judgment, the power of the norm to define and delimit behavior, the internalization of the judges' standards, all contribute to the self-disciplining subject. The ability, the desire, the *imperative* to recognize and report this systematic inscription of the individual within the disciplinary state, I would argue should be linked to both to France's general revisitation in the '70s of the rhetoric of Vichy and the abuses of power in which it engaged; and to Foucault's specific experiences of the police state during the war. Although *Discipline and Punish* locates the historical transition to a "disciplined" order in the eighteenth century, I believe that the necessary trigger *to perceive* that historical shift does not arrive until the 1940s in Europe. In the 1940s France and Foucault witnessed the machinery of the German army, but also the effects of the regimentation and militaristic nature of its own society. Again, the compliance of the Jews, of the French police, and of ordinary French citizens in the deportation process signals continuity with, not distinction from, the army's machinery of violence. The soldier and the citizen are not polar opposites, but mirrors of each other and reflections of the power of discipline and the disciplines of power to generate the subject. The Vichy government's admiration for Nazi organization and purification, its belief that the state will be saved when "good" French are separated from "bad" French and the latter purged, exemplify the notion that the violence of war is not divisible from the violence of the discursive construction of the modern subject of a rationalized and systematized social order in peacetime. Politics is war by other means.

The Camp and the Clinic

The Jews rounded up in the waves of French deportations from 1942 through 1944 were headed for concentration camps, and by 1944 their destination was primarily Auschwitz. Whether the French realized this or not is still debatable. Public fictions about internment camps, slave labor, and a separate "Jewish reservation" in the East wore thin and finally broke when the trains left stations filled with children. In 1942, because orders had not yet arrived from Germany about how to handle children under the age of fourteen, French police at the Vel h'Hiv' holding camp and other temporary internment camps separated children from parents so that the trains east might be filled per established quotas. This meant later trains had to be filled with children alone. Clearly these were not suitable laborers, nor could children without parents or guardians be expected to survive either a prison camp or a "reservation," meaning French witnesses either refused to make the logical leap that these deportations were to extermination sites, or understood but did nothing—at least officially—about their suspicions.

It is tempting to try to map the concentration camp onto the carceral systems Foucault describes in *Discipline and Punish,* but the camps had nothing to do with prisons in that respect. While some camps did provide labor to the Nazis, most were not prisons, but extermination sites clearly dedicated to killing mass numbers of "undesirables," especially Jews following 1942 and the Wannsee Conference. The camps collected bodies en masse, identified only groups and not individuals, and while surveillance was ubiquitous, it bore little resemblance to the comprehensive internalized form encouraged by the Panopticon. A far more legitimate and convincing connection is found in Foucault's assertions about the overlap—practical and ideological—of the prison and medical discourse in "Body/Power":

> On the contrary, it's the body of society which becomes the new principle in the nineteenth century. It is this social body which needs to be protected, in a quasi-medical sense. In place of the rituals that served to restore the corporal integrity of the monarch, remedies and therapeutic devices are employed such as the segregation of the sick, the monitoring of contagions, the exclusion of delinquents. The elimination of hostile elements by the *supplice* (public torture and execution) is thus replaced by the method of asepsis—criminology, eugenics and the quarantining of "degenerates." . . .[31]

In a later lecture, Foucault describes the creation of the "dangerous individual" in nineteenth-century legal and medical thought, and reflects that recent attempts to incorporate a regime of punishment based on who one is, rather than what one does, generates "a foreboding of the dreadful dangers inherent in authorizing the law to intervene against individuals because of what they are; a horrifying society could emerge from that."[32]

Needless to say, that danger was already historically manifest in the cooperation of the medical and penal systems in Nazi-controlled Europe. In the camps, medicine, purification, and the "remedying" of degeneration through the scientific application of death merged. The camps were thus what Bernauer describes as representative occasions of the exercise of "biopower" as described in *The History of Sexuality:*

> One of these poles—the first to be formed, it seems—centered on the body and a machine: its disciplining, the optimization of its capabilities, the extor-

tion of its forces, the parallel increase of its usefulness and its docility . . . *an anatamo-politics of the human body.* The second, formed somewhat later, focused on the species body, the body imbued with the mechanics of life and serving as the basis of the biological processes: propagation, births and mortality, the level of health, life expectancy . . . *a biopolitics of the population.*[33]

According to Bernauer, "The ethic of National Socialism is regarded as a form of applied biology . . . the practice of killing as a moral imperative to enhance biological life" (203).

Today's prisons have their attached clinics, their version of a medicalized approach to crime and punishment. Foucault's sensitivity to the collaboration of medicine and repression, to the connection between the clinic and the barracks (the disciplined body precedes, as this quote indicates, the exercise of biopower in the broadest domain) seems again based in his prior awakening to the significances of the Nazi regime and France's participation in its agenda. Although *The History of Sexuality* locates its historical interest in an earlier era, it, like *Discipline and Punish,* is enabled and compelled to speak of that era only by virtue of Foucault's intimate understanding of how the modernity he describes culminated in the war in 1940s Europe. A number of German concentration camps (variously called by the German relocation camps, "prison camps" and "labor camps") also contained clinics, but in them unimaginable experiments were conducted on prisoners in the name of a new Nazi science. Camp doctors found their highest purpose in promoting the more efficient annihilation of camp inmates, characterizing death on a massive scale as the "medicine" the new, perfected Aryan state required to survive and thrive. Thus, death-dealing was not antithetical to the Nazi medical establishment's view of life, but part of its exercise of biopower, and so entirely compatible with its valuable medical achievements on behalf of non-Jewish citizens. As Foucault notes, biopower involves the connection between protecting life and eradicating the right to life: "One might say that the ancient right to take life or let [one] live was replaced by a power to foster life or disallow it to the point of death."[34] Robert Lifton's study of the Nazi medical establishment's "biomedical vision" offers important insights to this relationship: the profession was reorganized at all its levels, a process of *Gleichschaltung* or "coordination," which made it more fully systematic and comprehensive.[35] The Nazi doctors "exhibited a certain élan in extending various forms of medical care to the entire German population . . . spectacular operative results and humane employment arrangements for people who had lost hands or limbs" (40). The medical professions embraced the discourse of healing that included the aggressive treatment of "illness" or corruption in the racial character of the nation: "The unifying principle of the biomedical ideology was that of a deadly racial disease, the sickness of the Aryan race; the cure, the killing of all Jews" (16). As James J. Paxson points out in his essay for this volume, *Historicizing Theory*, the Nazi concept of the German *Volk* was a powerful instance of prosopopeia, reinventing the body politic in the image of a single, organic individual. The imperative to purge and heal, then, must "logically" extend to whole populations, while the language of illness and healing, of purification and the elimination of "dirt" and "vermin," legitimizes any degree of violence, indeed invites the systematic application of violence whether to the individual body or to the "body politic."

The Nazi cure began with sterilization, and continued through the organization of mass "euthanasia" and finally to camp exterminations in the gas chambers. Lifton recounts the progress: carbon monoxide was suggested as the means for efficient "medicalized killing" by Dr. Ernst von Grawitz on the basis of its successful use to "euthanize" large groups in "killing centers," usually converted mental institutions or nursing homes. Dr. Irmfried Eberl became the commandant of Treblinka; Dr. Hermann Pfannmüller devised a policy to starve children to death in order to save the cost of drugs; Dr. Werner Heyde planned the structure and methods for the mass "euthanasias." Dr. Sigmund Rascher studied the effects of altitude on inmates at Dachau. And then of course there was Dr. Mengele, who *"exemplified the Nazi biological revolutionary . . .* part of a vanguard that saw its mission as noble and viewed courage and cruelty (or 'hardness' as the Nazis were fond of saying) . . . as personal virtues" (377). Those who wished to participate in the killing sometimes adopted the posture of physicians even when they had no right to the title—witness Joseph Klehr, a "semiliterate laborer and medical orderly" who would don his white coat in order to inject prisoners with lethal doses of phenol (265).

Lifton describes two links between the structure of the German medical profession and the concentration camps: the first is "the *ideological bridge* from the killing of those considered physiologically unworthy of life to the elimination, under the direction of doctors, of virtually anyone the regime considered undesirable or useless; that is, from direct medical to medicalized killing" (138). The other connection is material, in the institutions the doctors created for carrying out the grand design of healing, which provided the legal, medical, and organizational practices that ultimately governed the camps. As this description should confirm, and as this list of doctors suggests, the Final Solution could not have been achieved, or perhaps even imagined, without the contribution of the Nazi medical professions.

The Nazi doctors also supervised their own version of "the birth of the clinic" in the experimental units of the camps, most notoriously Block 10 at Auschwitz. Block 10 was organized carefully as a scientific facility, divided between laboratories, each with its own set of "investigators," and its own patients. In a certain sense, Block 10 was the direct product of the trajectory of modern medicine: "Nineteenth century medicine . . . was regulated more in accordance with normality than with health. . . . When one spoke of the life of groups and societies, of the life of the race, one did not think first of the internal structure of *the organized being,* but of the medical bipolarity of *the normal and the pathological.*"[36] Auschwitz and the other concentration camps were the means for separating Nazi-defined pathological humans from the "normal." Block 10 investigated, among other things, the possibility of "normalizing" pathological subjects—one experiment devised by Mengele was intended to see whether non-Aryan features could be biologically converted into Aryan characteristics, or brown eyes to blue. Other experiments involved breeding, inherited traits, "scientific" criteria for distinguishing undesirables from normal humans, and so on. The health of the "organized being" was sacrificed to address the polarity of normal versus pathological. In a bizarrely logical completion or extreme of the history of modern medicine, instead of forcing death to render its dark secrets up as enlightenment, instead of, as one chapter in the *Birth of the Clinic* (1973) has it, "Open[ing] up a few corpses," Block 10 merely confirmed that once pathology was generalized to a people that could then be excised from the healthy body of the race, the separated and categorized individuals were merely walking corpses. Their deaths did not need to precede their autopsies.

Lifton recounts the testimony of "Marie L." a prisoner-physician detailed to assist in Block 10 (272) whose French origins remind us that a significant percentage of Auschwitz's inmates had arrived on French deportation trains. At the same time, the story of the prisoner-physicians has a chilling dimension to it: while around them the Nazi doctors created insane experiments, prisoners with medical experience assigned to Block 10 attempted to devise more "legitimate" experiments themselves. One such inmate was a Polish neurologist who pursued electroshock experiments, apparently in the hope that the "scientifically interesting" results would protect the role of the prisoner-physicians (299–300). And some prisoner-physicians maintained records of the effects of deprivation, which functioned as a kind of testimony after the camps were liberated. Yet in either case, prisoners with medical training became complicit with the regime that justified mass murder and torture in the name of science—thus, even its victims, those with the ability to recognize the madness that had become "normal" in the camps, could not escape the totalizing effects of the Nazi system.

Again, in the case of Auschwitz and the Nazi medicalization of killing it is not so important for our purposes of understanding Foucault to determine that he, or his fellow French knew at the time about where their deported Jews were headed, even though the greatest percentage of France's Jewish population did indeed end up at Auschwitz. The French did not see themselves on trial, at least initially, in the Nuremburg "medical trials" where the first confirmation of what happened in Block 10 and why it happened emerged. In the 1970s, however, when the cultural representation of France's experience of the war shifted to emphasize collaboration and complicity, the collective impact on the French intellectual community as well as on the public at large forced a crisis in the connection between history and knowledge. From this, the need to replay the horrors of Auschwitz in order to bridge the apparent distance between France and Germany, between Paris and the camps, propels Foucault to physically visit Auschwitz's ruins seeking that other history in the camp's silences. But he has already, as I see it, been visiting the camps all along, in the work he has produced that connects the clinic with the prison, or the army barracks with the gas chamber—the "anatamo-politics of the human body," with the "biopolitics of population."

Lentricchia remarks that New Historicism has absorbed from Foucault "the feeling, usually just evoked, almost never argued through, that all social life is organized and controlled down to its oddest and smallest details" (234). Bernauer suggests that we must find the reason for this totalizing vision in the totalizing nature of the Nazi regime, a proposal with which I emphatically agree. In fact, I suspect that much of what makes critics uneasy about Foucault's thought can be traced to those early experiences, both of war, and of the discovery of the false position France occupied in regard to its own past following the war. His resistance to totalitarian systems of thought, to master-narratives of history, to a teleological and continuous version of history, a focus on marginalized groups, the desire to write "archaeolog[ies] of silence,"[37] all have a part of their origins in the history of French collaboration, the ghosts of Auschwitz, and the consequences of historical revisionism. The events and discourses that shaped Foucault's early life and France's collective memory of war shaped the historical vision that made both possible

In conclusion, I'd like to change direction and look ahead, as well as behind for a moment. It seems to me especially important to understand Foucault's relationship to the specter of the Second World War at this particular moment in our own history. Because we, the American academic establishment, have been to our own reckoning more clearly shaped by the distinct experiences of the Vietnam War (as Ivo Kamps demonstrates elsewhere in this volume), and by a differently complicated relationship to the generation that fought and won the Second World War, our grasp of the nuances of defeat, occupation, and failed resistance to Nazi philosophies in Europe before, during, and after the war, is more tenuous. A disturbing tendency has arisen lately to lionize our elders, those "best and bravest," "The Greatest Generation," who fought during World War II, and to do so without any vestiges of the skepticism we supposedly learned from Vietnam. The successful labors of the two Toms—Brokaw and Hanks—and others, engaged to celebrate the morality, integrity, and individual accomplishments of the "war generation" should remind us that unlike France we have not been directly confronted with our own historical complicity in Nazism, which may explain how and why our "'60s generation" has managed—despite lingering but attenuated effects on the politics of theory within the academy—to put Vietnam behind them, and returned to the fold of their fathers. The disgust we register in Foucault's comment about "this society that had permitted Nazism, that had lain down in front of it, and that had gone over *en masse* to de Gaulle" is missing from our cultural conversations about World War II and seems to be leaching out of our discussions even of Vietnam. The attack on the United States in September of 2001 only accelerated this already-locomotive trend, leading to a new tone in the production of both high and low culture.

The high priest of this movement, author Stephen Ambrose, remarks in an interview about the miniseries based on his popular book, *Band of Brothers,* that he believes the country is newly interested in its history, which is

> something that young people, especially, didn't want to hear about in the '60s and '70s, because of everything else going on—the civil rights movement, women's rights movement, Vietnam. Now that 25 years later those issues aren't at the forefront anymore, young people are aware that we're living in the freest and richest nation that ever was, and we owe that to somebody. Where did this wealth and these liberties come from? That's the 180–degree turn in attitude about history in this country. And World War II is the greatest event of the century that we just passed through, and the answer to some of those questions.[38]

This image of the "young people" of an earlier generation ignoring history, rather than rejecting its messages, denatures the protest and anti-war movements of our own immediate past, and devalues the lessons they, and we, should learn from their interrogation of historical method, among other things. A new kind of forgetting is happening, a new erasure; and the next generation of "young people" may find themselves in turn having to exhume an ugly past made possible by their own faith in the lies their fathers and mothers tell them. Instead of watching the myths of war and peace fall apart in Vietnam on the nightly news, or watching the young Dan Rather telling a horrified nation about the realities of war no one wanted him to convey, we may find ourselves, like Foucault standing at Auschwitz decades after its ghosts were created, seeking a disturbing past that can't be recovered, trying long after the damage is done to analyze what is missing from the "history" we wish to believe now. Perhaps as we fashion our own fantasies about who we are and what our history makes us, we require and should welcome further haunting by the ghost(s) of Foucault.

NOTES

Michel Foucault, *Politics, Philosophy, Culture: Interviews and Other Writings, 1977–1984,* ed. Lawrence D. Kritzman (New York: Routledge, 1988), 6–72.

1. David Macey, *The Lives of Michel Foucault: A Biography* (New York: Pantheon, 1993), xii. See also Didier Eribon's *Michel Foucault,* trans. Betsy Wing (Cambridge: Harvard University Press, 1991) for an alternative but equally representative biography.

2. David Cousins Hoy, ed. *Foucault: A Critical Reader* (Oxford: Basil Blackwell, 1986), 2.

3. Lynn Hunt, "The Revenge of the Subject/The Return of Experience," in *The New Salmagundi Reader,* eds. Robert Boyers and Peggy Boyers (New York: Syracuse University Press, 1996) 504–12, quote is from 504. Many of the essays in this volume comment on James Miller, *The Passion of Michel Foucault* (New York: Simon & Schuster, 1993).

4. Miller, "Foucault's Politics in Biographical Perspective," in the *New Salmagundi Reader,* 490–503, esp. 495.

5. Macey, *Lives of Michel Foucault,* 504 (my translation).

6. Foucault, *Power: Essential Works of Foucault, 1954–1984,* vol. 3, ed. James D. Faubion (New York: New Press, 1994, 280–81.

7. Ibid., *Power,* 248.

8. Frank Lentricchia, "Foucault's Legacy: A New Historicism?" in *The New Historicism,* ed. H. Aram Veeser (New York: Routledge, 1989), 231–42, quotes from 231, 234–35.

9. Foucault, *Power/Knowledge: Selected Interviews and Other Writings, 1972–1977,* ed. Colin Gordon (New York: Pantheon, 1977), 90–91.

10. Foucault, "Society Must Be Defended," in *Power: Essential Works of Foucault: 1954–1984, vol. 1: Ethics: Subjectivity and Truth,* ed. Paul Rabinow (New York: New Press, 1994), 59–65, quotes from 59, 60.

11. Ibid., 61.

12. Foucault, *Power,* 251–52. Foucault suggests that his professional calling was determined by his sense of impending doom in the interview quoted in the epigraph: "We did not know when I was ten or eleven years old, whether we would die or not in the bombing and so on" (Foucault, *Politics, Philosophy, Culture,* 7). His assocation of the lack of a certain future with the turn to scholarship and particularly philosophy inspires the desire for "knowledge as a means of surviving by understanding."

13. Karlis Racevskis, ed. *Critical Essays on Michel Foucault* (New York: G. K. Hall, 1999), 191.

14. James Bernauer, "Beyond Life and Death: On Foucault's Post-Auschwitz Ethic," in *Critical Perspectives,* 190–207, esp. 190.

15. Miller, *Passion of Michel Foucault,* 38, 39.

16. Macey, *Lives of Michel Foucault,* 15.

17. Henry Rousso, *The Vichy Syndrome: History and Memory in France since 1944,* trans. Arthur Goldhammer (Cambridge: Harvard University Press, 1991), 10.

18. Ibid., 16.

19. Ibid., 117.

20. Bernard Kouchner, "Un vrai samurai," in *Michel Foucault: Une histoire de la vérité* (Paris: Syros, 1985), 85–91, esp. 88.

21. Bernauer, "Beyond Life and Death," 202.

22. John F. Sweet, *Choices in Vichy France: The French under Nazi Occupation* (New York: Oxford University Press, 1986), 99.

23. Ibid., 33.

24. Ibid., 118.

25. Michael R. Marrus and Robert O. Paxton, *Vichy France and the Jews* (New York: Basic, 1981), 241.

26. Sweet, *Choices in Vichy France,* 127; Marrus and Paxton, *Vichy France,* 219. It is possible, however, to argue that the early halt to deportations in France due to the Liberation accounts for this limited number. At least one historian suggests that had the end of the war come later, France would indeed have eliminated its entire Jewish population (Marrus, *Vichy France,* 44).

27. Susan Zuccotti, *The Holocaust, The French, and the Jews* (New York: Basic, 1993), 137.

28. Ibid., 190–91.

29. Foucault, *Discipline and Punish: The Birth of the Prison,* trans. Alan Sheridan (New York: Vintage Books, 1979), 135.

30. Foucault, *Power/Knowledge,* 77.

31. Ibid., 55.

32. Foucault, *Politics,* 151.

33. Foucault, History of Sex, 139.

34. Foucault, *History of Sexuality,* 138.

35. Robert Lifton, *The Nazi Doctors: Medical Killing and the Psychology of Genocide* (New York: Basic, 1986), 33–41.

36. Michel Foucault, *The Birth of the Clinic: An Archaeology of Medical Perception,* trans. A. M. Sheridan Smith (New York: Pantheon, 1973), 35.

37. Ibid., xix.

38. Interview with Stephen Ambrose, "Historian Stephen Ambrose Author of "Band of Brothers": The Story of Easy Company" at *Http://usmilitary.about.com/library/milinfo/bandofbrothers/blbbambrose.htm.*

3

Historicizing Paul de Man's Master Trope Prosopopeia

Belgium's Trauma of 1940, the Nazi Volkskörper, *and Versions of the Allegorical Body Politic*

JAMES J. PAXSON

The recovery of Paul de Man's wartime writings spurred a flurry of research that seemed to end quickly. While some theorists still concentrate on decoding the arcane vocabulary in de Man's mature work, the task of understanding the presence of his earlier in his later work remains. As an exemplar of de Manian "arcanism" we might take Tom Cohen; as the exemplar of historicizing the mature de Man as an often ghostly refraction of the young de Man, we take Lindsay Waters.[1] A potential collaborator with National Socialist thought after the fall of Belgium in spring 1940, de Man himself has been tainted in the modern academy, while deconstruction has waned and been waked in a climate of historically driven (and dominant) cultural studies. History and historicism dominate theory in the contemporary scene of theory; while the endorsements of historicism, certainly of conventional literary history, have always militated against the sort of rigorous rhetorical reading cultivated by de Man and his followers.[2] Reading de Man's works rhetorically therefore seems at odds with an attempt to "historicize" those works and his personal and professional life. And it might furthermore seem that my project in this essay is at odds with trying to historicize the rhetoricality of de Man—

de Man understood both as the Man whose early career tainted his later one; and de Man as the Voice of revolutionary theories of reading. Peggy Kamuf has declared that in this "waning twilight" of deconstruction precipitated by the discovery in the late 1980s of de Man's wartime collaboration, "one can nevertheless still frequently discern the sentiment that 'deconstruction' (more or less *personified*) ought to be banned from critically, historically responsible debate about the future of our literary institutions."[3] De Man himself has become that very "personification," perhaps moreso than Jacques Derrida, of deconstruction. And I thus contend that the best insights in historical, psychoanalytic, and deconstructive analysis can still help to amend many of the discrepancies and differences between rhetorical and historical thought, helping to lift that ban. "Deconstruction" understood exactly as Kamuf understands it—as an institutional or cultural "reserve" that guarantees, like an endless credit system, the cognitive and rhetorical futures for impossible readings, impenetrable languages we call "literature," irreconcilable *pasts,* secrets, scandals, and collaborations,[4]—actually supports my interests in working out how and why de Man's theoretical productions arrived *when* they did.

And so the burden of this essay is to investigate the historical relations between the life and work of the early de Man, writer of collaborationist journalism known for offensive anti-Semitic pronouncements, and the work of the later de Man, dean of American deconstruction whose career rose in the 1960s and climaxed at the moment of his untimely death in 1983. On one hand, the discovery of de Man's wartime writings nearly ruined the methodological and institutional cachet of deconstruction as a philosophical and critical practice; sanctimonious sermons, coming from the likes of David Lehman, equated deconstruction, de Man, and fascism in a simple-minded way.[5] On the other hand, the entire historical affair of the late 1980s when his wartime writings were discovered could be exploited to carry out a more in-depth "historicization" of de Man, of what seemed the best in his grand intellectual project—the articulation of an exhaustively rhetorical or tropological theory of texts, knowledge, and human language replete with an unsurpassed conceptual panoply. Even de Man's loyal adherents, such as Rodophe Gasché, have not yet taken this needed course,[6] though Waters alone, as I've already noted, has gone that route.

First and foremost among de Man's conceptual panoply, his "thinking enterprise of the later writings" (as Gasché terms it), stands *prosopopeia,* the almost preternaturally idolatrized "master trope of poetic discourse."[7] Traditionally, prosopopeia or personification means the figurative giving of human identity to that which is not human, although for de Man prosopopeia records its own semiotic unmaking as well as the making of *prosopon,* a "face." And even though theory most commonly associates de Man with allegory, prosopopeia takes a detour through allegory—the figure of othering, loss, and temporal passage—in ways that might enable the sort of historicization that this essay sees as needed and inevitable. For a few of de Man's adherents, allegory did lead to prosopopeia anyway, but not in historical terms.[8] So in an effort to help historicize postmodern theory in general, I shall try to historicize de Man's master trope prosopopeia by revisiting the subject that engrossed American theory studies a decade or so ago: the wartime writings scandal in terms of the figural constructions that I believe to have constituted "historical" life for the young de Man, a Belgian who endured the worst times of his native land.

More specifically, I shall consider the early writings of de Man in terms of the contextual ideology and constituent rhetoric of Nazism, in particular the nebulously understood, so-called "People's Body" or *Volkskörper* central to German thought in the 1930s and 1940s that was exported as part of the greater German *Gleichschaltung* or "coordination" of cultures and political systems in a newly emergent organic whole—via military and violent as well as cultural or ideological means—experienced by young de Man and everyone else in the expanding fascist or totalitarian empire of the Third Reich. This should help us to better understand how a single and singular rhetorical trope, prosopopeia, or personification, could come to be superelevated to a divine or deific status in de Man's deconstructive machine—the "machine" of language serving as de Man's favorite catachresis.[9] I will try to connect some of the images and sentiments that one finds sprinkled among de Man's intellectual or authorial juvenilia in *Le Soir* and *Het Vlaamsche Land* with the climactic, mature productions in deconstructive poetics during his years at Yale University in the 1970s and early 1980s. Such would be a connection between early trauma and later triumph, a psychoanalytic configuration of great import though also a fracture running, in this special case, between psychoanalysis and deconstruction themselves.[10] In so doing—in so invoking some of the language of a psychoanalytical model treating de Man's early formation under the semiotic aegis of the *Volkskörper* and his mature idolatrization of prosopopeia—I mean to demonstrate far more than the crude boosterism of anti-deconstruction seen in the fulminations of Lehman or the psychoanalysis of de Man's personal guilt expressed by others.[11] De Man no doubt suffered certain personal tragedies having to do mostly with close family members; but his trauma as a Belgian national living in 1940 may speak more fully regarding the semiotic terms I seek to articulate in this essay since deconstruction's figural mechanisms of language operate not just at localized textual levels but at collective, public, and political levels as well. It might be said that I seek to forge a cognitive, tropological, and historical linkage between the ideology of a self-ascribed master race and de Man's master trope. I shall, perhaps reminiscent of the phenomenological critics who sought to descry large cognitive patterns in the "life" of a writer and with whom the de Man of the 1950s and

1960s shared intellectual community,[12] read the first inscriptions of de Man's magisterial prosopopeia in his early though ominous journalism—a body of work where it has *never* been located by other theorists writing about the young de Man. I shall in turn reflect upon American culture and ideology that circumscribed the sage de Man of the early 1980s, an era dominated by a hitherto unrealized neo-conservative, Right-center government personified in the guise of Ronald Reagan and his own political machine. This may help answer the question of why de Man's universal prosopopeia gained intellectual ascendancy in the late 1970s and early 1980s. But as well, the connections among de Man's supertrope prosopopeia, Nazi master tropes of social or biological collectivity, and the Belgian experience of 1940 invite historicization of other "versions of the allegorical Body Politic" prior to the Reagan years, as this essay's title promises: here, consequently, lies the parallel importance of the life and writings of German émigré Ernst Kantorowicz, near-victim of the Holocaust and paramount theorist of allegorical Bodies Politic. If other essays in this volume, *Historicizing Theory,* by Karen Raber and Evan Carton treat the "ghost" or the "veiling" of the Holocaust in French poststructural thought, this essay's tandem narrative of de Man and his shadow Kantorowicz reveal how allegorical tropes in medieval or modern theory studies so strongly depend upon one another and on the trauma of Nazi violence and social engineering during the Second World War.

❧

After twenty-three centuries of classical rhetoric's tabulations of tropes, figures, and schemes for use by orators and poets, de Man trumped others in the postmodernist game of redefining and co-opting the classical figures for newer purposes. The narratologist Gérard Genette often strained the conventional senses of the master tropes of discourse in order to write a rhetoric of narrativity in the modern, Proustian novel.[13] To be sure, even the term "trope" has taken over completely for just about all critics and theorists nowadays, standing in metonymically for the other categories of eloquence well-exercised by Aristotle, Demetrius, Cicero, Quintilian, Donatus, or Bede.[14]

But it was de Man who not only rechristened allegory by following postromanticist developments in the theory of tropes;[15] he expanded prosopopeia or personification, the trope whereby one gives animate and sentient human consciousness to inanimate or nonhuman things or ideas, to an expansive para-cognitive category—a sort of potential or competence for language and consciousness themselves. Prosopopeia traditionally meant making a "local" or discursive rhetorical ornament in which a thing in nature momentarily takes on some human attribute: "today, the sun smiles." Or, it meant the full-scale creation of a character in a sustained narrative who stood as an embodied abstraction lent personality and voice: here we must beware of Prudentius' Vices in the late-classical *Psychomachia* or Spenser's myriad warlike personifications in *The Faerie Queene*. But de Man complicated this old picture. Even if prosopopeia or narrative personification persisted for de Man in a particular poetic text or utterance to look like a "medieval" literary effect, it offered not the epistemological closure or cognitive capsulization long attributed to such a trope; it systematically and symptomatically *defaced* its own epistemological and semiotic foundations. The trope whereby one en-faces the nonhuman—*prosopon poiein* means "to make a mask or face" in the Hellenic Greek of late classical rhetorical theory[16]—often erases, undermines, or deconstructs the semiotic logic of the ontological and grammatical transformation itself.[17] De Man's master trope, when deployed as a local rhetorical ornament in a line of lyrical verse, thematized its own semantic constitution and semiotic structures (the notion of a facade over a substrate, an outside encasing a hidden inside) while obliterating the linguistic and cognitive possibility of that rhetorical moment as an event of cognitive closure or completion. Nowhere was this process better theorized than in de Man's "Autobiography as Defacement," one of his signal essays on Wordsworth's figural poetics;[18] yet it was in select essays that appeared in his final book, *The Resistance to Theory*, that the theorization of prosopopeia as the ultimate mechanism for culling the epistemological values in poetic conceptions of time, place, memory, and desire reached its most concentrated form. All of the major scholars using de Man's theory of allegory—from Carol Jacobs to J. Hillis Miller—agreed that each distinctive-looking formulation of the mode involved the phenomenology of *temporality*. Likewise, prosopopeia was the ultimate temporal procedure in semiosis. Prosopopeia became the ghost that haunted every non-self-coincidence of human reading or understanding according to deconstructive theory.

Postmodernists often sever de Man's revisionist theory of prosopopeia and allegory from roots in premodern rhetorical theory, while traditionalists (usually classicists or medievalists in literary studies) ignore the achievements made in deconstruction.[19] Diplomats like myself have tried to rethink classical and medieval literary forms aggressively within de Man's framework. De Man confined his discussions of allegory and prosopopeia almost exclusively to romantic texts and to localized lyrical lines or passages, with primacy of attention given to Wordsworth, Shelley, Nietzsche, Hugo, Proust, and so forth; but his approach can shed invaluable light on the narratologically more complex dispositions of prosopopeia in full-scale, allegorical character invention.[20] Rhetorical traditionalists—usually medievalists in the literary academy by trade—might condemn arguments that articulate the epistemological and linguistic aporias of narrative personification in allegory;[21] here, to repeat, one finds an institutional and territorial corollary to postmodernists' insistence

that premodern allegory bears little or no value for the study of modern cultural forms and linguistic effects. But de Man's theories of personification or
prosopopeia and allegory have remained far-reaching and powerful enough,
by my estimation, to help solve problems involving even the gender structure
of early literary allegory, to wit, the narrative casting of female allegorical
abstractions exclusively as women—in light of the charge that de Man's project never could account for matters involving gender or the feminine.[22]
Although it seemed to break from earlier, traditional definitions of allegory
and personification, de Man's theory remains unmatched in power and utility,
even though it in turn falls short in mediating between rhetoric and history.[23]
If, in my opinion, the constructedness of gender could be accounted for using
de Man's theory, so history might hold similar promise. Now we are ready to
force his theory to confront its own historical past.

❧

One of the most dominant rhetorical props in Nazi thought during the
1930s and 1940s was the collective *Volk*. In short, the *Volkskörper* or "People's Body" was the Nazis' revised conception of early Christian notions of
sacred collectivity or community and of the pagan Body Politic, a very old
idea that traced its fabular origins to Roman folk history and that perhaps
culminated, as Kantorowicz had authoritatively shown, in the Elizabethan
juridical theory of early modern England.[24] When Shakespeare has Mene-
nius Agrippa tell the allegory of the state body in *Coriolanus,* he of course
cribs Plutarch.[25] A favorite Roman idea to be sure, the Body Politic also surfaced decisively in nineteenth-century German *volkism*—the theory of a
racially distinct *Volk,* a "people" or "tribe," tied to a particularly archetypal
and paternal landscape, "homeland," or *Heimat* in the fertile plains and fast
mountains of central and eastern Europe, perhaps even of far western Asia.[26]
The idea took off under the Nazis, exciting contemporary philosophers such
as Martin Heidegger. Robert Jay Lifton affirms its sense as a revision of the
early Christian, Pauline *corpus mysticum* and of the Roman *patria* governed
by its special ethos of *pietas.* Drawing upon historian George L. Mosse,
Lifton summarizes:

> One must address this ultimate dimension . . . if one is to begin to grasp the
> force of the Nazi projection of the "Thousand Year Reich." The same is true
> of the Nazi concept of the *Volk*—a term not only denoting "people" but con-
> veying for many German thinkers "the union of a group of people with a
> transcendental 'essence' . . . [that] might be called 'nature' or 'cosmos' or
> 'mythos,' but in each instance . . . was fused to man's innermost nature, and
> represented the source of his creativity, his depth of feeling, his individuality,
> and his unity with other members of the *Volk*."[27]

Regarding one particular SS surgeon, Lifton condenses further the corpus idea in medicalist terminology: "Thus, Johann S. spoke to me with pride about the principle of being 'doctor to the *Volkskörper*' . . . and of 'our duty . . . to the collectivity.'"[28] The *Volkskörper*, like all ideologically focal Body Politic figurations, meant the personified state or collective presence of the "healthy" nation. It was the ultimate historical prosopopeia.

And yet, the Nazi version of this old juridical, even theological, concept was a bit of sham scenery in the theater of totalitarian or fascist consolidation. As commentators on totalitarian polity in Nazi Germany have shown, prior rhetorics of collective society as well as theologically sanctioned concepts achieved a "phantomlike" status.[29] All such political figurations compete as authentic, while they only record, as de Man himself would eventually recognize, their own figural invention and effacement.[30] But the Nazi Body Politic was an especially phantomlike "emanation of pure evil" since the actual social process of society, most fully embodied in the destruction of the Jews and other enemies of (or infections in) the state, was the merely totalitarian drive toward societal self-immolation, of finding a perpetual stream of victims that must never reach exhaustion, as Hannah Arendt and thinkers following her have argued.[31] Certainly the logic of such ends still astonishes one, as Lifton's most striking example of an SS surgeon's rationalization makes clear:

> But there is another perspective on medicalized killing that I believe to be insufficiently recognized: *killing as a therapeutic imperative.* That kind of motivation was revealed in the words of a Nazi doctor quoted by the distinguished survivor physician Dr. Ella Lingens-Reiner. Pointing to the chimneys in the distance, she asked a Nazi doctor, Fritz Klein, "How can you reconcile *that* with your [Hippocratic] oath as a doctor." His answer was, "Of course I am a doctor and I want to preserve life. And out of respect for human life, I would remove a gangrenous appendix from a diseased body. The Jew is the gangrenous appendix in the body of mankind."[32]

The acknowledgment of a pervasive though phantom *Volkskörper* susceptible to disease or surgery may be a good but frightening starting point in a project to historicize de Man's own master trope, prosopopeia. I can offer only a sketch here in this essay toward working out the rhetorical, cognitive, structural, psychological, and material connections between the vast, superordinate personified "People's Body" imagined to constitute the state of the Third Reich (or even the body of all "mankind") and the manifestation of that body in the conceptual frameworks plied by certain speakers, writers, or artists who ruminated upon their own concomitantly aesthetic, symbolic, technical, or political agency.

Such a technical agent was Fritz Klein. But can we imagine such an aesthetic agent in the person of the young de Man? A nobody, an opportunist eking out a living on a collaborationist publication, he later reached the apex of institutional power in the American university and ended up receiving thorough excoriation for hiding his anti-Semitic writings completed in that germinal early period. Tobin Siebers has already made the strongest case for linking the aesthetics of beauty at the heart of National Socialist thinking and the trajectory that de Man's thinking takes from his earliest writings through his ascent in, and break with, New Critical formalism by the 1960s. De Man's final ruminations on the romantic symbol, as a counterpart to temporal allegory, marks the peak of that ascent and the break. "The Nazis described every relation, every possible link, within society in terms of organic or natural unity," writes Siebers, and he continues, "For de Man, then, the natural culmination of the aesthetics of beauty is National Socialism. He knows because he saw it happen. He loved beauty too much, and it happened to him."[33] Siebers's conclusions generalize well, I think, the historical significance (which cannot be underestimated) of the Nazist cult of organic wholeness and unity—the primary personification or anthropomorphism of which was the *Volkskörper*—at many conscious or unconscious levels.

The specific quality of the national tragedy suffered by the Belgian people in 1940, however, uncannily feeds into the imaginary experience of the National Socialist personified body. Military invasions and conquests compare to one body's defeat, mutilation, or absorption by another; so much had always been evident in the political rhetoric of warring nations in the late Middle Ages and Renaissance, as Shakespearean discourse well attests.[34] A narrative thus emerges of peculiarly coincidental energy and moment: de Man began to come of age precisely when the German invasion of his native Belgium destroyed his nation's sovereignty. The disastrous events of late spring 1940 spelled a signal, indeed symbolic, end for Belgium's own symbolic body: the German blitzkrieg penetrated the coastal plane, invading Belgium in a stroke by "decapitating," as contemporary Pentagonese jargon would have it, the small nation's own carefully prepared military corps. The Belgian defenses had, of course, been built to withstand the sort of protracted suffering experienced in 1914 when Kaiser Wilhelm's German troops put to siege strategic forts, such as Liége, using their gigantic, 40 cm howitzers (the well-known "Big Berthas"), and then, after a lengthy and enervating forced march, conducted a large civilian slaughter against partisans in Belgian towns and cities. As Jeffrey Mehlman has pointed out, de Man himself was well aware of the distinction between the gradually unfolding miseries of 1914 experienced by Belgian soldiers and citizenry and the mental shock of instantaneous collapse that was a "whirlwind" escaping signification itself in May 1940.[35]

The defeat of spring 1940 did come as an absolute shock, a sudden death that cannot be exaggerated. Like the French to the west and south, the Belgian military put its trust in the impenetrability of the Ardennes Forest and in static fortifications. Actually, this meant one single and singular fortress in the special case of Belgium—the underground Fort Eben Emael that was, by world standards, an absolutely "impregnable" bulwark of tunnels, barracks, and 75 mm gun emplacements protected by ten-inch-thick forged steel *cloches* or "cupolas." If we imagine a geographic body for Belgium, its mailed fist—or perhaps its martial heart or head—had to be the imposing and indestructible Fort Eben Emael that guarded the eastern frontier and controlled access to the Albert Canal and the Meuse River.[36]

As the French themselves would shortly learn, new technology and tactics had antiquated such singular and, let us say, symbolically overdetermined kinds of war tools—sunken, reinforced concrete forts bristling with guns—by the year 1940. Using the elite paratroops of the *Luftwaffe,* the Germans seized the impregnable Fort Eben Emael lodged in the banks of the strategically important Albert Canal on 10–11 May. German engineers crossed the canal by boat, planting bombs in the fort's viewports and turrets; meanwhile, the first-ever "vertical insertion" (another Pentagon metaphor, if I may) landed *Luftwaffe* paratroops on the fortress's earthen roof where the troopers planted 110-pound shaped charges on entry ports, steel-wrapped gun emplacements, and machine gun casemates. After a siege that lasted less than a day, the world's most ingeniously designed and unconquerable fort lay in German hands. It was a military event—workable through the tactics of blitzkrieg, the military expression of what Waters calls the pervasive "cult of action" of the day—that would be repeated in the following month's siege of the French Maginot Line; and indeed, we might think productively of Eben Emael, the geographical head of the Belgian military and geographical "body," also as a (northernmost) synecdoche, a microversion, of the entire static defense system the Western democracies had prepared against German expansionism from the east. Ironically, "neutral" Belgium had capitulated—the paranomastic value of this word taking on a greater fullness in light of the geographical parable I have just summarized—in an intensively fast moment of shock and trauma in the eyes of its people, its government, and its press.[37] The Body Geographic was decapitated in Eben Emael's swift capture.

The Body Politic of Belgium lost its head too; and it may serve us to pursue further some of the then-commonplace thinking on Belgian nationalism and the people's belief in kingship as these beliefs were constituted in terms of the "geographic" role and destiny of the royal head of the national Body Politic. Consequent to the lightning invasion and occupation, Belgium's King Leopold III ordered his army to lay down its arms without the consultation of the French or English governments and with little backing from the (theoretically) more primary Belgian Parliament, as some accounts have it.[38] This was an act taken by Belgians and by all the European democracies as an abjuration of kingly power. Leopold became a hollowed-out effigy of a king, certainly a pale and failed shadow of his more vigorous and charmed father, Leopold II, who, "when the Germans invaded Belgium in August 1914 . . . assumed personal command of the army in keeping with the tradition and acquired tremendous popularity as the 'Soldier-King' *(Le Roi Chevalier)* who stayed and fought with his troops until final victory."[39]

This appraisal, written by historian of Belgium's occupation Werner Warmbrunn, goes on to invoke the theologized language of kingship that would characterize Kantorowicz's charismatic-typological imagery of the "medieval" king: "[Leopold II] retained this *nimbus* of glory and veneration throughout his life until his tragic end in 1934" in a travel accident,[40] the moment when Leopold III thus ascended the throne. But before this great change in 1934, Warmbrunn adds, then-prince Leopold was himself shaped by seminal historiographical thought that expressed early-twentieth-century Belgium's own self-ascription as an organic Body Politic personified in an exceptional king:

> At the University of Ghent [Leopold III had] also attended lectures of the dean of Belgian historians, Henri Pirenne. Pirenne is famous as the articu-lator of the *idée belge,* the notion that Belgium, on the basis of her history, culture and her *geographical situation,* had an ancient historical tradition and an *historical mission* at the crossroads of Europe. Pirenne thus viewed the Belgian state of 1831, far from being an artificial creation of Great Power politics, as the *embodiment of an historic and organic community.*[41]

Could a Belgian intellectual as sensitive as de Man have avoided, or resisted, this allegorically laden portrait of the Belgian king as the "embodiment" of "organic" and "geographic" signification?

In the allegory of conflicting bodies politic, the loss of national indepen-dence and governmental efficacy through instant surrender to Nazi Germany might have seemed semiotically overdetermined. *Gleichschaltung* implied the erasure or absorption of competing or adjacent personified bodies/states. Per-haps like the combatants in a medieval *psychomachia,* warring personified states can often exist only by corollary elimination or absorption.

Above all, what I emphasize as an imaginary allegorical narrative had real and painful sources and effects: the Belgian nation—all Belgians, as compli-cated as their own fractious history between Flemings and Walloons had been—suffered a sudden trauma from which recovery must have seemed far out-of-sight. The king, embodiment of the people and land in the unique *idée belge,* and Eben Emael, architectural and technological reification of the nation's unusual geographic status as a "crossroads," were cut off, erased, as a new allegorical body supplanted what had been. In a once celebrated memoir written by Belgian Anne Somerhausen about the invasion and occupation, *Written in Darkness* (1946), the language of medieval allegorism arrives right on the book's very first page as the brave woman begins to record her family's plight—her husband and three sons are named, aptly, Mark, John, Matthew, and Luke[42]—while the typological, parabolic, pastoral, and ecclesiastical vocabulary of old allegory quickly comes into service to convey her sense of the Belgian people's plight in regards to their "lost" king and to a correspondingly lost church leader of theirs, as a July 1940 entry reads:

> *Sheep without a shepherd.* We are now a bewildered nation—just a flock of sheep, running about without guidance. Not a word has come from the King since that of May 10, exhorting us to resist; he capitulated, quarreled with the government, and seems now to consider himself a defeated army commander and a prisoner of war. Not a word has come from the Cardinal to a nation of which surely ninety percent are Catholics and wait for a guiding word.[43]

And later: "Why, then, did [the Germans] let us celebrate our national holiday three days ago, whereas now they make us feel that we are no longer a nation, but only a defeated flock without a King?"[44]

It was in this historical moment that the young de Man first fled for the imagined security of the borders of Spain, only to return in a few short months to eventually secure his slot on the writing staff of *Le Soir.* Whatever a Belgian's personal sentiments in those awful times, his or her experience of the national disaster should call for special attention and understanding on our parts, with especial care concerning the sort of supercharged typological or allegorical vocabulary that we see in eyewitness Somerhausen's characteristically levelheaded account. But speaking solely of the ideological adjustments made under National Socialist domination in occupied Belgium, Siebers summarizes that the *aesthetic* principles many thinkers have linked to the formative experiences of young de Man "must have wheedled their way into [his] ears."[45] The localized personification of ideas "wheedling" themselves inward, like cunning if patient little tricksters, sells too short the giant trauma of the actual historical state of affairs. If I were to "excuse" de Man's collision (and collusion) with his first Ghost of Prosopopeia, it would be through this national tragedy and trauma, experienced by all Belgians of 1940 who had seen their national Body Politic demolished or beheaded in the two senses I've described: the geo-military seizing of the talismanic Eben Emael and the abjuration of Leopold III (who was also seen as the vanished shepherd of a Christologically cemented "flock"). The semiotic components of Nazi rhetoric arrive not as wheedlers-into-the-ears but as traumatizing decapitators. The "singularity" in later deManian thought that Gasché writes of materializes already as a specter of traumatic defeat, of the decapitation and trampling of de Man's national Body Politic followed by the spectral replacement of that social (or mystical) body by another, more rarefied but gigantic and universal version. As personal experience or allegorical fiction, the Occupation becomes almost impossible even to exist in memory.[46] Thus, the historical sketch I have provided really puts flesh on the skeletal argument (I echo Karen Raber's rhetoric regarding the early Foucault's need for enfleshment in his eventual 1960s-1970s embodiment) proffered by Mehlman concerning de Man's infamous reading of a Hugo poem that allegorized the Spanish invasion of Flemish territory in the seventeenth century—a reading that Mehlman in turn allegorizes as a repression of de Man's guilt over his own collaboration during the twentieth-century German occupation of his homeland.[47]

During the Occupation and during the war, then, the way was open for de Man to take part in the inexcusable rhetoric of National Socialist political thought: the condemnation of inferior or dangerous members in the new Body Politic. His work on *Le Soir* made public that suffusive rhetoric in the rediscovered writings haunting us in the late 1980s and beyond. And those writings, dare I say, speak for themselves. The dual tomes brought out by the University of Nebraska testify to the import of this experience. Yet we must continue to read even these scurrilous writings tropologically, rhetorically. The *Wartime Journalism* (1988) volume and its companion text *Responses* (1989) treat, in the reprinting of de Man's key statements like the now infamous 4 March 1941 column on the Jewish Question ("Les deux faces du judaisme") and its several commentaries by our own contemporary scholars, the significance of de Man's will to cultivate a sophisticated sort of anti-Semitism in the mould of de Man's uncle, Hendrik,[48] even though such statements had ignited the whole late 1980s firestorm about a blatantly anti-Semitic de Man.

But there are moments when the rarefaction of de Man's rhetoric seems to parallel, or emanate from, the allegorical substance of collective bodies, souls, and states. I shall follow suit by dwelling for a moment on the most often cited among the incriminating pro-Nazist passages of early de Man: the formulation from the 28 October 1941 book review, "*Voir La Figure*, de Jacques Chardonne." Some months after the article on "The Two Faces of Judaism," de Man considers a new art in the making as Europe is transformed aesthetically and politically:

> La guerre n'aura fait qu'unir plus étroitement ces deux choses si voisines qu'etaient des l'origine l'àme hitlérienne et l'àme allemande, jusqu'à en faire une seule et unique puissance. C'est un phenoméne important, car il signifie qu'on ne peut juger le fait hitlérien sans juger en même temps le fait allemand et que l'avenir de l'Europe ne peut etre prévu que dans le cadre des possibilités et des besoins du génie allemand.
>
> [The war will only bring about a tighter union of these two things that were so close from the start—the Hitlerian soul and the German soul—to the point that they will become a single and unique power. This is an important

phenomenon, because it means that one cannot judge the fact of Hitler without at the same time judging the fact of Germany and that the future of Europe can be envisioned only in the framework of the possibilities and the needs of the German spirit.][49]

Rodolphe Gasché employs litotes, or understatement, when he judges that claims such as these "give in . . . to some Nazi stereotypes which they are naive enough to believe that they can circumvent and undo by textual maneuvers."[50] I would go farther: clearly such postings in *Le Soir* adopt the vocabulary of Nazist *Gleichschaltung*. They subscribe to the tropological vitality of a superordinate cultural, political, and cosmic "soul" coeval, I should think, with the desired and still-forming Nazi *Volkskörper* imagined by the social engineers of the Third Reich. The *Volkskörper* would be that fantasized, futurological (and eschatological) combination of *l'ame hitlérienne, le génie allemande,* and *l'ame allemande* into a new and *unique puissance* just in the birthing during the early 1940s. Prosopopeia, both *vis* and *figura*, has already become the master trope of the master race.

The tendency in much of the scholarship of the second of these volumes, *Responses*, is to separate the occupationist writings (of 1941–42) from earlier and much later productions; and so is the case with Gasché's musings coming at the close of *The Wild Card of Reading* (1998), a document I take to be the most thoughtful and meaningful book-length response to the whole historical affair. But it is uncanny that even the very earliest writings of de Man that we have—indeed the very first entry dug up by Werner Hamacher, Neil Hertz, and Thomas Keenan and placed at the head of their *Wartime Journalism* volume—is an aptly dull piece of hackwork, "L'examen médical des étudiants." It is an editorial (published in the liberal college weekly newsletter *Jeudi*, 23 March 1939) that discusses the medical status of Belgian university students and culminates by decrying "l'absence d'un *organisme central,* capable de diriger et d'organiser les services medicaux" in the Belgian and French university systems.[51] Admittedly, the bit of editorializing is a minor reflection on institutional organization. But its rhetorical system, in an uncanny or aleatory flow, fully presages organic or corporeal *Gleichschaltung* precisely in the medical language of the *Volkskörper* figuration. And it is the medical or medicalist cant of the *Volkskörper* figure that bears most significantly in all of our current returns to the evils and horrors of Nazism—the humiliation and murder of the Jews in the Holocaust preeminently.[52]

Medical or physiological discourse predominates such flows and figural crossings-over. The *Volkskörper*, one could say, was the intellectual implosion on a whole cultural scale of the field of professional medicine in the Third Reich, as Lifton, in his book *The Nazi Doctors* (1986), has so well illuminated. Robert Proctor's *Racial Hygiene* (1988) fills out further that picture of a social order and its medical dimension that was fully *gleichgeschaltet,* "coordinated."[53] In order to "heal" the corporate Body Politic of the German people, SS surgeons themselves literally, and at the micro- or cellular or compartmental level of a social body (governed by *un organisme central,* one could say in French) administered to its diseased tissues, limbs, organs: they murdered Jews, Gypsies, and homosexuals, by administering or presiding over the administration of poisonous compounds to those unfortunates chosen for extermination at the death camps. I find it plausible that de Man's meagerly early ruminations in his politicized hack writings, his journalistic juvenilia, somehow form not just a synecdoche of the People's Body but a prolepsis of the phantom trope that would come to dominate his mature theoretical production. "Hilterian souls," "German souls," and "central organisms" presage, in the rhetorical function a proleptical synecdoche (if I might transumptively so combine these two tropes), the soul of the great linguistic "machine" identified by Miller as "prosopopeia," itself a kind of catachresis (and another over-productive trope).[54]

∞

I can insure the validity of my effort to "historicize" de Man's master trope, prosopopeia, and the Nazist rhetoric of *Volkskörper* and *Gleichschaltung* in light of the historical tragedies of spring 1940 by calling up another biographical narrative of a correspondingly monumental twentieth-century allegory theorist. In taking up the medicalized *Volkskörper* as it has been treated by Lifton, I have of course drawn on the great German historian of law and medieval literature, Kantorowicz. His opus magnum, *The King's Two Bodies* (1957) still stands as required reading for students of medieval and Renaissance politics, theories of kingship, and historical writing; indeed, we cannot dissociate Kantorowicz's seminal chapter on Shakespeare's *Richard II* from any considerations of politics or power in Elizabethan culture.[55] The *Volkskörper,* as I've already intimated, served as a rarefied, cheapened, "phantomlike" version of the Body Politic trope, the trope fully crystallized by Elizabethan jurists in England's sixteenth century though partially realized as an important device of thought as early as Carolingian or Ottonian polity on the European continent. The king possesses "two bodies": a Body Natural and personal, which, like all of our individual bodies, perishes after seven or eight decades if we're lucky; and a Body Politic, a collective body that is, in short, the personification of the nation's collective society of all persons as well as an embodiment of the geographic land itself. The king serves as the "head" of the Body Politic; and thus the literal *beheading* of Charles I by the radical Puritan Parliament of 1649 was the most fitting of symbolic executions in English history.[56]

If residual effects of this enduring trope can be traced even into twentieth-century political systems, it is not a leap to follow Henri Pirenne and think of Belgium's Leopold III, the withdrawn monarch of his nation (in contrast not just to his numinous and charismatic father Leopold II but to, say, contemporaneous King Christian of Denmark who willfully and arrogantly paraded daily in the streets of Copenhagen to defy the German occupation of his nation), as the severed head of the social and geographic body of swiftly beaten Belgium. The king may be the "head" of the personified body of state/landscape; though he must of course be identified with the whole itself: thus, in celebration of *Volkskörper* rhetoric, Rudolf Hess jubilantly would proclaim at Nazi rallies (and as we've all seen many times in old newsreels), "Hitler ist Deutschland." The führer of the Third Reich indeed was the head of the personified nation, just as French rulers could be personifications of their states: no more need be said of Charles de Gaulle's greatest cliché paraphrasing the words of the Sun King, *L'état c'est moi.*

For historical or poetical research on the medieval or early modern Body Politic, Kantorowicz's magisterial study still serves as the main textbook, although it has supplements in sequel studies done by more theoretically progressive scholars. (Indeed, Louis Marin's *Portrait of the King* stands as the greatest successor to *The King's Two Bodies*.)[57] Just as I have followed a hunch that something productive could be made of de Man's life during the Belgian Occupation and its relation to the eventual hypertrophy of prosopopeia, so the life of Kantorowicz—a Jew who had to leave the German university prior to his coming to America—might urge a similar linking of later theorization and earlier trauma caused by National Socialism. I take a lead from Alain Boureau's book, *Kantorowicz* (1991), which purports to understand how Kantorowicz, an historian who was moreso a theorist of medieval law, developed his model of the "king's two bodies" following his experiences of soldiering in World War 1, efforts at taking part in commercial life in Weimar Germany, inevitable persecution as a Jewish academic in the 1930s German university, eventual emigration to New York in 1939, tenure at Berkeley in the 1940s that culminated in resignation after his refusing to take what was a startlingly familiar Oath of Allegiance in 1949, and final settling in at Princeton's Advanced Institute for Research in the 1950s, where Kantorowicz finally won the luxurious independence only few academics could ever enjoy and that allowed him to finish his opus magnum, *The King's Two Bodies*.[58] In a sincerely speculative series of narratives (the author of Kantorowicz's "biography" admits to the challenging fact that Kantorowicz left behind no personal papers, correspondence, or journals), Boureau reconstructs a picture in which the brilliant German-Jewish thinker seemed always co-opted by the tensions and forces of service to authoritarian bodies—the kaiser's Imperial army, a lucrative and demanding family business that dealt in wine wholesaling, the university of early Nazi Germany (Boureau does give attention to the restructurings of 1933, an event that led to the ending of the careers of Jewish scholars in Germany en masse), but even moreso the conservative American university of the 1950s.

In Boureau's picture, two poles establish themselves not unlike the historical structure I am positing as an armature for de Man's life: the polar historical context for the ultimate production of *The King's Two Bodies* demarcates an arc that went from grim military service in World War 1 to the institutional persecutions of the McCarthy era.[59] We are taken from a scene of trauma to a time of troubles. And, although Boureau reminds the reader of the fallout of 1933, the year in which careers of eminent German thinkers from Husserl to Kantorowicz fell apart, he strangely leaves out of his speculative picture any mention of the German *Volk*. I emphasize what should not need emphasizing: how could a Jewish intellectual in Germany, however much he might have been disturbed by the trench warfare he'd experienced in 1914–18, not be *increasingly* more affected, traumatically so, by the caustic rhetoric of *Gleichschaltung* and bodily purity from 1933 through 1940? How could he not suffer personally from the instituting of the Nuremburg Laws or the eventual thuggery of *Kristallnacht*—historical events underway well before the obscenity of the death camps?

It is not that Boureau elides or downplays this general state of affairs; but I find astonishing the fact that Boureau does not posit any version of this figural phantasm—German *Gleichschaltung* or the *Volk*—which was already vital in early National Socialist rhetoric and that might have served as the trigger in Kantorowicz's anxious desire to write a history of the medieval Body Politic. Any Jew in Germany living through the 1930s must have felt the pressures of an imaginary rhetorical institution in a very real sense. After dozens of stunning pages that trace the Body Politic in German culture to the theological concepts organizing medieval polities ranging from the court of Frederick II to the slogans of the pro-Emperor Italian Ghibellines, from the language of biblical typology imbued in medieval kingship to premodern and self-ascribed images of Parousia, Boureau locates the actual inception of *The King's Two Bodies* in one of Kantorowicz's few autobiographical sketches concerning his own apprehension not of the "secret Germany" he so well understood but of *postwar American corporate culture*. Boureau writes (in a story worth citing at length):

> On his arrival at Berkeley in 1939, Ernst met Max Radin, a specialist in legal theory possessed of enormous intellectual curiosity. In 1957, Ernst Kantorowicz dedicated *The King's Two Bodies* to the memory of Max Radin. In the preface, he explains how the idea for the project arose out of a lively argument between him and Radin that took place in 1945. Still imperfectly acculturated to the United States, Kantorowicz had shown Radin a document published by the Order of Saint Benedict, Inc. Kantorowicz was bemused that a religious order should incorporate itself. Radin explained to

his younger colleague that in America all religious institutions were organized as limited liability corporations. "It is the same for the dioceses of the Roman Catholic Church, and, for that matter, even the archbishop of San Francisco can be considered, in legal terms, 'a unitary corporation'." From that point, the conversation turned to another "single member corporation," the English crown in the sixteenth century, the legal substance of the king and of the theory of the two bodies that Kantorowicz would analyze for the next fifteen years.[60]

That the presumed "source" or trigger for Kantorowicz's investigative drive in the first place was a document involving ecclesiastical organization fits, to be sure, with the theological and religious dimensions of figural language constituting Kantorowicz's master trope. Yet it is an American cultural peculiarity—the parallelism between religious organizations in modern America and the well-known Americanist commercial corporation—that presumably served Kantorowicz as the ground zero of his grand historical project!

The memory is odd, to say the least, since the conversational trajectory that Kantorowicz provides in summary and that Boureau selectively recapitulates—Roman Catholic Church . . . Archbishop of San Francisco . . . the English Crown . . . the King's Two Bodies—elides what must have been, to two German émigrés speaking to each other at the end of World War II, the most apparently modern figural successor to Frederick II: the Nazi führer, Adolph Hitler, and his transcoded *Volkskörper* of the Third Reich. One detail that Boureau excludes, in fact, might be cause for a further, ironic chill. Regarding what Boureau takes as Kantorowicz's "imperfect acculturation," Kantorowicz had in fact written in his preface:

> To a scholar coming from the European Continent and not trained in the refinements of Anglo-American legal thinking, nothing could have been more baffling than to find the abbreviation *Inc.*, customary with business and other corporations, attached to the venerable community founded by St. Benedict on the rock of Montecassino in the very year in which Justinian abolished the Platonic Academy in Athens.[61]

The bit of autobiographical confession itself happens to allegorize nothing less than the genealogy of (premodern) allegory: (1) Platonism and its early scholastic heritage; (2) revitalized hegemony of Roman law (under the sixth-century Emperor Justinian, sponsor of the *Corpus Juris*); (3) the typological founding of one of the great Italian communities of learning (literally *super petram*, as the Gospel of Matthew had it regarding the very origins of the Catholic Church); and (4) final and triumphal Americanist incarnation of European ecclesiasticism. Like Somerhausen's shepherdless flock or her nuclear family of Gospel antitypes (Mark, John, Matthew, and

Luke), Kantorowicz's founding rock *(petrus),* along with what it leads out of and into, invokes the vocabulary of allegorism.

Yet, could the two discussants have missed the modern historical significance of the great Benedictine Abbey of Montecassino precisely in *1945?* In the year before the conversation between Kantorowicz and Radin on Benedictine incorporation had taken place, the Allies demolished the great Abbey of Montecassino (built, incidentally, in the form of a perfect square like the New Jerusalem of Revelations or the Virtues' military *campus* in Prudentius's *Psychomachia*) from the air. This was to the horror of many observers even among the Allies, and even though Waffen SS troops (who'd "helped" the Benedictine monks and abbots save the treasury of medieval documents housed in the structure) had probably occupied the Abbey (using it as an artillery spotting post) during the Allied forced march up the Italian peninsula that was halted in its attempts to cross the Rapido River near Montecassino and to break through the formidable Gustav Line. Thus, through an innocuous opening anecdote in Kantorowicz's grand *opus,* the corporative destinies or histories of Church and Third Reich—and corporate America— coincide: a de Manian "allegory" of the figural aporias of memory and narrative underwrites the vocabulary of medieval typological allegory (*aedificabo meum ecclesiam super petram*—"I will build my church on this rock"—as Christ put it to Simon Peter in the Synoptic gospels); and Nazi soldiers passed themselves off as the protectors of a Church Abbey while the American devastators flew overhead in their bombers.[62]

In psychoanalytic terms, the anecdote by Kantorowicz (as well as by that anecdote's reinforcer, Boureau) transposes the collective and corporative actions of the continuous German Reich—second and third versions—with those of America, perhaps as a screen memory or ascesis (a willed act of forgetting).[63] But the transposition, perhaps a chiasmus, records and effaces a figural superposition of modern America, Third Reich, and "allegorical" (in the old, pre-de Manian sense of the term) or imagined "medieval" past. The figural rhetoric of the *Volkskörper* hides itself under Kantorowicz's narrative of investigatory origins, while it programs an emergent narrative of a pancorporatist America—an America in which even ecclesiastical bodies, the heirs of early Christian *ecclesia* as well as Roman *patria,* could be configured with the dominant political, social, and economic engines or machines—the great corporations—of a nation as it would look for all subsequent decades and into the next century. De Man managed to survive and function in the social world of Occupied Belgium, a world devastated, as a Body Politic, by a singular defeat and removal of its own holy Crown, its Head. The trauma of this lived encounter with the residuum of medieval typological allegory, it is quite possible, resonates with a similar symbolic narrative that describes the intellectual "life" of Kantorowicz. Can it be that both survivors of, and émigrés from, the Third Reich had revisited the traumas or anxieties concomitant upon life in that totalitarian regime precisely in their creation of reconstituted (and deconstructive) "theories" about what we are variably calling "allegory"? Rather, if Kantorowicz's superprosopopeia, the corporative king's Body Politic, could be seen as a phantomlike version of the Nazi *Volkskörper* he fortunately escaped as a Jewish intellectual (for he, like all Jewish émigrés, would one day have been surgically excised from that *Körper* had he remained in the Reich), could de Man's superprosopopeia, the prosopopeia of allegory's non-convergence with itself in the human act of *reading*, be taken as history's corollarily produced conceptual "phantom"? We can say that Kantorowicz and de Man have been produced by history—such is the historicizing of theory promised by this very volume—but as allegorical agents who have symptomatically opted to produce further theories of allegory, history's hidden and generative script. De Man and Kantorowicz, preeminent theorists of allegory and prosopopeia, become ghosts of each other, ghosts produced by a violent historical era that culminated in the great Nazi Terror and its aftermath of American (imperial) intervention.

If Kantorowicz sought to uncover the theological and typological fabrics of medieval and early modern political thought, the modern historian Conor Cruise O'Brien centralizes the historiography of typological language in the formation of, in particular, the modern Western democracies—France, Britain, Germany, and especially the United States. The corporate America (and new *imperium*) that inhabits Kantorowicz's portentous Preface as a merely fugitive flicker takes center stage in the rhetorical model of O'Brien. Irish cultural activist, political scientist, and former British Parliamentarian, O'Brien proffers an eloquent, tripartite historiographical scheme that shows the derivation of the modern United States to be typological and religious in origin.[64] (To say the least for the moment, the conceptual scheme well explains the "special relationship" enjoyed by modern Israel and the United States—the latter being a typological refiguration of the former and the trigger, so understood, of the world's current, early twenty-first-century political maelstrom involving the final assault of fundamentalist Islamic states and movements against the "Great Satan" of Israel and the United States.) Hermetic images and language embellish this historiographical arc:

> The story of the [American] Great Seal also has some bearing on that scale . . . of "chosen people," "holy nationalism," and "deified nation." . . . Americans were, in some sense, a chosen people. But a chosen people might well have to be punished, like the Jews, for breaches of the Covenant. Yet the design [of the Great Seal] actually approved by the Continental Congress in June 1782 tended to move America from the conditional and therefore relatively chastened status of "chosen people" into the complacencies of "holy nation" and in the direction of "deified nation."[65]

O'Brien sets up a typologically laden and durable historiographical model. Most important is his idea that certain democracies reached the condition of "deified state" in a late historical phase; and in this phase, constitutional powers could be curbed while juridical or legalistic processes might appear to be supermagnified. Without hesitation, O'Brien names this moment in German society as the emergence of the Nazi Third Reich in the early 1930s (with its crystallization of nationalist self-expression in the exclusionary Nuremburg Laws); in the United States, it comes at the beginnings of the Reagan years, around 1980.[66] O'Brien's deified state turns out to be the apotheosis of the Body Politic, one at first seen as a "chosen" or "holy" body favored and then imbued by a transcendent deity. As it was allegory and prosopopeia's fate within deconstruction of the 1970s and 1980s to become phantomlike apotheoses of their former, typological, medieval versions, perhaps it has been America's fate toward the end of the twentieth century to become a self-deifying projection of itself commanding powers which, when iconized, seem cosmic and supernatural.[67] Opponents of de Man's prosopopeia—opponents or detractors of the magical, divine, even deific "abracadabra" that climaxed de Man's career and thought, as Mehlman has put it—might readily see it as part and parcel to an historical moment when the culture that produced it and deconstruction became an apotheosized emanation from earlier, typological, and theological semiotic substances or processes.

Throughout this essay, I have argued that de Man's production of a universal prosopopeia, the rarefied or apotheosized emanation of language's "machine," records the trauma or the anxiety of survival that occurred after his native, national homeland had fallen to the Nazis, creators of their own "phantomlike emanation" of an allegorical Body Politic or Deity Politic during the historical moment when their "deified nation" came to life. I have then implied that O'Brien's model of early 1980s America as a deified nation, a Deity Politic, may have something to do with prosopopeia's conceptual apotheosis in late deManian deconstruction.

And although de Man's theory reaches its conceptual climax and the zenith of its institutional power and influence by the early 1980s, just at the time of de Man's own death, the beginnings of this upper trajectory of prosopopeia, its final apotheosis in deconstruction, should still be emphatically traced *back to the 1960s*—an historicistic move somewhat in keeping with the historical drift of the articles in this volume, *Historicizing Theory*. The signal text marking the radical break in theorizing "allegory" and its traditionally related tropes, such as prosopopeia, in contradistinction to the intellectual traditions of premodern literary scholars (medievalists in the main), was of course "The Rhetoric of Temporality," first written in the mid-1960s and recognized by de Man himself as the standout piece that he later collected in *Blindness and Insight*. The essay, de Man admitted for the theory of allegory, "augurs what seemed . . . to be a change, not only in terminology and in tone but in substance."[68] The ghost or phantom of the medieval Body Politic, realized first as the Nazi *Volkskörper* and later as that phantom's second-order emanation, de Man's Universal Prosopopeia, begins to take rhetorical or discursive shape in that signal essay on allegory and irony, "The Rhetoric of Temporality," a shape of new "terminology," "tone," and "substance," to be sure. But it would not be until de Man's death in 1983 that the Prosopopeia Ghost would be at home in a changing America, taking shape as a powerful monarch, maybe a tyrant, to haunt and command us by the end of that portentous decade. If we imagine critical theory as a Body Politic—a Body Theoretic, shall we say—then de Man's master trope has risen as the restored king, the head, in that imaginary body during the singularly reformative years of the 1980s. The rhetorical engine of the Body Politic topos is of course synecdoche, the figural taking of the part for the whole or the whole for the part. Jon Whitman, in some recent and very incisive commentary on the institutional value and use of "The Rhetoric of Temporality," implies that the historical *failure* of de Man's theory of allegory and prosopopeia may rest in this synecdochal process—the very process that I have implied all along controls in part the macroprosopopeia of the Nazi *Volkskörper*. Whitman writes:

> In retrospect, the appeal to "allegory" in de Man's work and in much post-structuralist writing frequently tends to privilege part of that broad subject as if it were nearly the whole—radically stressing temporal dissolution over strategies of negotiation, textual dissonance over dimensions of resonance, tensions in structure over transactions of sense. Such a view of "allegory" and history needs itself to be historically situated. . . . [I]t is critical to scrutinize more intensely the historical forces that enter into the composition of texts—including deconstructionist texts about "allegory" . . . [f]or theories of "allegory" are not only themselves historical acts. With their changing definitions and drives, they repeatedly display provocative efforts to construct and reconstruct the process of history itself.[69]

In what I think is one of the best current histories of allegory theory, ancient through poststructuralist, Whitman's overview captures the current drive to keep "decoding the arcane vocabulary" in de Man's work (as I noted in the opening lines of this essay) while it anticipates, more importantly, this essay's attempt to historicize de Man's master trope, prosopopeia.

NOTES

1. See Tom Cohen, *Ideology and Inscription: "Cultural Studies" After Benjamin, De Man, and Bakhtin* (Cambridge: Cambridge University Press, 1998); and Rodolphe

Gasché, *The Wild Card of Reading: On Paul de Man* (Cambridge: Harvard University Press, 1998); see as well Lindsay Waters's unsurpassed historical sketch of Paul de Man's tripartite intellectual life—historist, phenomenological, or "interiorist," and the turn to the rhetorical—in his "Introduction, Paul de Man: Life and Works," de Man, *Critical Writings, 1953–1978* (Minneapolis: University of Minnesota Press, 1989), ix–lxxiv. My essay's focus on the violence of Nazist allegorical rhetoric builds squarely on Waters's articulation of the contemporaneous Nazist "cult of action" (xviii) and social "charismatic force" (xxv) which Waters's introduction shows so completely shaped young de Man's aesthetic and historical consciousness.

2. In *The Rhetoric of Romanticism* (New York: Columbia University Press, 1984), we have one of de Man's most celebrated phrases: "the terminology of traditional literary history, as a succession of periods or literary movements, remains useful only if the terms are seen for what they are: rather crude metaphors for figural patterns rather than historical events or acts" (254).

3. Peggy Kamuf, *The Division of Literature, or The University in Deconstruction* (Chicago and London: University of Chicago Press, 1997), 4 (my emphasis).

4. Ibid., 5–6.

5. See David Lehman, *Signs of the Times: Deconstruction and the Fall of Paul de Man* (New York: Poseidon Press, 1991).

6. Even Gasché concludes, "I shall abstain from categorizing the link that may exist between the early journalistic work and the thinking enterprise of the later writings. To call this link either a continuation or a covering up of the undeniably unpardonable aspects of some of the earlier texts is to miss the leap and the rupture that de Man's critical and philosophical writings have undertaken." See Gasché, *Wild Card of Reading*, 268.

7. De Man's phrase, "master trope of poetic discourse," appears in de Man, *The Resistance to Theory* (Minneapolis: University of Minnesota Press, 1986), 48.

8. See J. Hillis Miller, "Reading Part of a Paragraph in *Allegories of Reading*," eds. Lindsay Waters and Wlad Godzich (Minneapolis: University of Minnesota Press, 1989), esp. 166–69.

9. Humanists and psychoanalysts have attacked the nonhuman sense of de Man's language machine, referring to the oft-cited statement coming near the end of *Allegories of Reading* (New Haven: Yale University Press, 1979): "The deconstruction of the figural dimension is a process that takes place independently of desire; as such it is not unconscious but mechanical, systematic in its performance but arbitrary in its principle, like a grammar" (298). A few pages earlier, de Man had written: "The machine-like quality of the lie is more remarkable still . . ." (294); and "The machine not only generates, but also suppresses, and not always in an innocent or balanced way" (294). I want to emphasize that "machine" may be one of de Man's greatest catachreses—catachresis being the trope favored by de Man among his panoply of tropes whereby we use words from our lexicon for things that really have no name in the lexicon. So far, Andrzej Warminski has provided the most thoroughgoing exculpation of de Manian catachrestic rhetoric in my opinion; see especially his "Introduction: Allegories of Ref-

erence," in de Man, *Aesthetic Ideology*, ed. Warminski (Minneapolis: University of Minnesota Press, 1996), 8.

10. In paying respect to the achievements of psychoanalysis in the special case of this essay, I refer to the important work on trauma and memory by Cathy Caruth. See her own curiously prosopopoetic language in describing how trauma and its witnessing, which involves a grasp of "the impossible," further can mean being "chosen by" that impossibility; Caruth, "Trauma and Experience: Introduction," in *Trauma: Explorations in Memory*, ed. Caruth (Baltimore and London: Johns Hopkins University Press, 1995), 10. For the best discussion of deconstruction's links and debts to psychoanalysis, see Stephen Melville, *Philosophy beside Itself: On Deconstruction and Modernism* (Minnesota: University of Minnesota Press, 1986), 84–114.

11. See Peter L. Rudnytsky, "Rousseau's *Confessions*, de Man's Excuses," in *Autobiography, Historiography, Rhetoric: A Festschrift in Honor of Frank Paul Bowman*, eds. Mary Donaldson-Evans, Lucienne Frappier-Mazur, and Gerald Prince (Amsterdam: Ralopi, 1994), 215–43.

12. Phenomenological criticism, as such, was characterized not by the intensive or close reading of an individual text nor by the drive to understand the workings of the Language Machine. Rather, it sought to build up a kind of biographically based model about the unique workings of one writer's mind and life; as such, it valorized each individual act of reading while eschewing any "theory" that could circumscribe critical work from text to text. Since, as Miller reminds us regarding the history of de Man's methods and work during the 1950s and 1960s, phenomenology (of "the important categories . . . consciousness, intentionality, and temporality") helps understand the arc of such a unique career; and since I in part try to embody such apprehension in this project, I want to conjure with the now neglected or depleted approach. See Miller, "An Open Letter to Professor Jon Wiener," in *Responses: On Paul de Man's Wartime Journalism*, eds. Werner Hamacher, Neil Hertz, and Thomas Keenan (Lincoln and London: University of Nebraska Press, 1989), 337.

13. Most trenchant is Gérard Genette's modification of Quintilian's term "metalepsis": for Quintilian, it is a "transition from one trope to another"; that is, a middle or linking image left out of a mixed, complex metaphor (see Quintilian, *Institutio oratoria*, vol. 3, trans. H. E. Butler [Cambridge: Harvard University Press, Loeb Classical Library, 1920], 8.9.38–39). For Genette, it is the passage of a fictional character from one level or layer of diegesis outward or inward to another (see Genette, *Narrative Discourse: An Essay in Method*, trans. Jane E. Lewin [Ithaca: Cornell University Press, 1980], 234). Quintilian's definition of prosopopeia can be found in the *Institutes* at 6.1.25, 9.2.31, 11.1.41.

14. In cultural studies work in particular, "trope" has come to denote the older concepts of "theme" or "topic." If many historians of rhetoric bristle at the lack of distinction between "figure" and "trope" (for which de Man or I am guilty), further generalized usages are often seen by conservative scholars as part of a downward spiral in literary and linguistic study. For an important discussion of the relation between de Man's vocabulary of rhetorical terms and that vocabulary's medieval rhetorical antecedents, see John Guillory, *Cultural Capital: The Problem of Literary Canon Forma-*

tion (Chicago and London: University of Chicago Press, 1993), 207–11. Guillory's chapter on de Man, "Literature After Theory: The Lesson of Paul de Man" (176–265), triangulates among a sociological theory of de Man's institutional charisma (in a manner following the work of Pierre Bourdien), the psychoanalytical theory of displacement (following Freud and Lacun), and a formalist description of de Man's conversion of linguistic and grammatical concepts into rhetorical ones.

15. The story of Romanticism's disparagement of allegory in favor of symbol is now commonplace in the history of de Manian deconstruction; see his version of the split and distinction in "The Rhetoric of Temporality," in *Blindness and Insight: Essays in the Rhetoric of Contemporary Criticism,* 2d. ed. (Minneapolis: University of Minnesota Press, 1983), esp. 187–208.

16. See the concise history of the term's philological provenance in Jon Whitman, *Allegory: The Dynamics of an Ancient and Medieval Technique* (Cambridge: Harvard University Press, 1987), 269.

17. My approach to reading both postmodern and ancient treatments of the trope prosopopeia has been to follow de Man in his articulation of systematic "defacement": see James J. Paxson, *The Poetics of Personification* (Cambridge: Cambridge University Press, 1994), esp. 67–70.

18. De Man, *Rhetoric of Romanticism,* 67–81.

19. Taking as a literary test case William Langland's strange fourteenth-century poem, *Piers Plowman,* see Howard H. Schless, "The Backgrounds of Allegory: Langland and Dante," *Yearbook of Langland Studies* 5 (1991): 129–42, as an example of the latter kind of quarantining. A more recent essay collection that tries to cover the gamut of historical theories of allegory and prosopopeia while offering some pieces that attempt synthesis or reconciliation is *Interpretation and Allegory: Antiquity to the Modern Period,* ed. with introductory essays by Jon Whitman (Leiden, Netherlands: Brill, 2000).

20. I work through the distinctions, implicit in traditional rhetoric, between localized personification and personification as a form of character invention, in Paxson, *Poetics of Personification,* esp. chapter 2.

21. Above all, personification is still viewed as a means not for opening epistemological holes but for providing closure and certainty. Critics often thus see it as absolutely distinct from the effects of allegory. See Schless, "Backgrounds of Allegory," 131; John M. Steadman, *The Lamb and the Elephant: Ideal Imitation and the Context of Renaissance Allegory* (San Marino, CA: Huntington Library, 1974), 75; and Thomas E. Maresca, "Personification vs. Allegory," in *Enlightening Allegory: Theory, Practice, and Contexts of Allegory in the Late Seventeenth and Eighteenth Centuries,* ed. Kevin L. Cope (New York: AMS Press, 1993), 21–39.

22. Although de Manian allegory/prosopopeia theory has come under attack for its exclusion of problems in gender (though one important general critique of, and remedy for, this situation that arrived by the 1980s was Barbara Johnson, *A World of Difference* [Baltimore and London: Johns Hopkins University Press, 1987], 184–89), see Paxson, "Personification's Gender," *Rhetorica* 16 (1998): 149–79, for a de Manian

analysis of female personification characters in late classical or early medieval cosmic allegories—from Prudentius's *Psychomachia* to Bernardus Silvestris's *Cosmographia*.

23. Responding to de Man's aphoristic claim about history's own figurality (see n. 2), Kevin Newmark provides an excellent discussion of the practical problems that have ensued from de Man's remark; see Newmark, "Paul de Man's History," in ed. Lindsay Waters and Wlad Godzich, *Reading de Man Reading* (Minneapolis: University of Minnesota Press, 1989), 121–35.

24. Ernst Kantorowicz, *The King's Two Bodies: A Study in Medieval Political Theology* (Princeton: Princeton University Press, 1957).

25. Plutarch, *The Lives of the Noble Grecians and Romans,* trans. John Dryden, revised by Arthur Hugh Clough (New York: Modern Library, n.d.), 266:

> Menenius Agrippa . . . after much entreaty to the people, and much plain-speaking on behalf of the senate, concluded at length with the celebrated fable. "It once happened," he said, "that all the other members of a man mutinied against the stomach, which they accused as the only idle, uncontributing part in the whole body, while the rest were put to hardships and the expense of much labour to supply and minister to its appetites. The stomach, however, merely ridiculed the silliness of the members, who appeared not to be aware that the stomach certainly does receive the general nourishment, but only to return it again, and redistribute it amongst the rest. Such is the case," he said, "ye citizens, between you and the senate. The counsels and plans that are there duly digested, convey and secure to all of you your proper benefit and support."

Later allegorical schemes would, of course, translate the stomach into the heart or head of the Body Politic; fantastic, para-allegorical versions of the fable would tender the literal separations and mutinies of body parts, as in Gogol's well-known short story, "The Nose." More recent and pulpy-popular in contemporary American horror fiction is Clive Barker's short story, "The Body Politic," in which everyone's hands (and then feet) detach and kill their former owners; see Barker, *The Inhuman Condition* (New York: Pocket Books, 1987), 67–117.

26. The theory of the *Volk* perhaps began in linguistic or philological thinking of the early nineteenth century: the search for a primal homeland was a philological search for the beginnings of Aryan or Indo-European community and speech. See the fascinating summary chapter, "The Indo-European Homeland," in J. P. Mallory, *In Search of the Indo-Europeans* (London: Thames and Hudson, 1989), 143–85.

27. Robert Jay Lifton, *The Nazi Doctors: Medical Killing and the Psychology of Genocide* (New York: Basic, 1986), 14. The citation from George L. Mosse is taken from his *Crisis of German Ideology: Intellectual Origins of the Third Reich* (New York: Grosset, 1964), 4.

28. Lifton, *Nazi Doctors,* 30.

29. I take the terms "phantomlike" and "emanation," which I use throughout this essay synonymously with "deific," from Orwell critic Isaac Deutscher's formulation

about the totalitarian party of Oceania in *1984:* "The party is not a *social body* actuated by any interest or purpose. It is a *phantomlike emanation* of all that is foul in human nature"; from Deutscher, "*1984:* The Mysticism of Cruelty," in *Twentieth Century Interpretations of* 1984, ed. Samuel Hynes (Englewood Cliffs, NJ: Prentice-Hall, 1971), 39 (my emphases). I owe cognizance of this formulation to a citation of Deutscher in Melvyn New, *Telling New Lies: Seven Essays in Fiction, Past and Present* (Gainesville: University Press of Florida, 1992), 126. (New's chapter first appeared as "Orwell and Anti-Semitism: Toward *1984,*" *Modern Fiction Studies* 21 [1975]: 81–105.) I am grateful to Heather Lawson for recommending to me New's essay on Orwell and anti-Semitism.

30. As speculative wisdom seems to have indicated, de Man's projects in the 1980s, had he survived, would have treated the texts of Marx.

31. See New, *Telling New Lies,* 121–24.

32. Lifton, *Nazi Doctors,* 15–16 (emphasis in original).

33. Tobin Siebers, "Allegory and the Aesthetic Ideology," in *Interpretation and Allegory,* 475 and 478.

34. The metonymic references to, say, the king of France simply as "France" or of the king of England as "England" in Shakespeare's plays are too numerous to catalog; but the decisively violent imagery of personified confrontation, capitulation, and then mutilation and decapitation (or defacement?) appears in a singularly arresting conceit from *1 Henry 6* when Joan of Arc cries: "Now the time is come, / That France must vail her lofty-plumed crest, / And let her head fall into England's lap (5.3.24–26).

35. See Jeffrey Mehlman, "Perspectives: on De Man and *Le Soir,*" in *Responses,* 324: "Hitler's jolt to European sensibilities—too devastatingly rapid, as de Man repeatedly suggests in *Le Soir,* to have registered in psychological terms—and Derrida's, that is . . . are nodes of a complex continuum one name of which may be the 'life of Paul de Man.'" In de Man's own words, as expressed in his 23 December 1941 *Chronique littéraire* from *Le Soir,* titled "Recits de Guerre," we hear how "Avant le 10 mai, elle traina une vie morne, d'ou toute trace d'héroisme était exclue. Ensuite, les choses se précipitèrent à une telle allure que tous, soldats et civils, eurent l'impression d'ètre entrainés dans un tourbillon dont ils ne comprenaient pas la signification"; from de Man, *Wartime Journalism, 1939–1943,* eds. Werner Hamacher, Neil Hertz, and Thomas Keenan (Lincoln and London: University of Nebraska Press, 1988), 174.

36. The technically informative summary account of the German assault on Fort Eben Emael is from Col. James E. Mrazek (Ret.), *The Fall of Eben Emael: Prelude to Dunkirk* (Washington, DC: Luce, 1970).

37. See ibid., 15–18, regarding Belgian realization that their geographic situation and heritage had always been "impossible" and at the same time extraordinary.

38. Werner Warmbrunn, *The German Occupation of Belgium, 1940–1944* (New York: Peter Lang, 1993), 14.

39. Ibid.

40. Ibid. (my emphasis).

41. Ibid., 15–16 (my emphases).

42. Anne Somerhausen, *Written in Darkness: A Belgian Woman's Record of the Occupation, 1940–1945* (New York: Knopf, 1946), preface.

43. Ibid., 17–18 (emphasis in original).

44. Ibid., 20.

45. Siebers, "Allegory and the Aesthetic Ideology," 477.

46. In my attempt to work up a rhetoric that draws on deconstruction and psychoanalysis, I admit the need to proceed cautiously in drawing a generalized picture about Belgium's history. The reshaping of memories of war, invasion, conquest, and Occupation finds a more in-depth thematic treatment in recent French historical writing, which might serve as a more expansive model. See, for instance, Henry Rousso, *The Vichy Syndrome: History and Memory in France since 1944,* trans. Arthur Goldhammer (Cambridge and London: Harvard University Press, 1991). Rousso promises to theorize and help create a "new history of memory" (3) in order to study the greatest trauma of modern French history. His summary paragraph about the trauma and its resultant, long-term, collective suffering—dubbed by him *le syndrome Vichy*—parallels my historical summary about the tragedies suffered in the young de Man's homeland: "Why have memories of the Occupation (1940–44) proved so enduring and controversial? The first reason is of course that the tragedy that France suffered in those years was one of unprecedented gravity. The country, already shaken by the events of the 1930s, was subjected within a few short years to a series of terrible blows. The war of 1939–40 was brief but disastrous: some 90,000 French soldiers died, and nearly two million French troops were taken prisoner. Crushing and unexpected military defeat led to a humiliating and ferocious Occupation by foreign troops. France was divided into separate zones, and the Empire disintegrated as Vichy and de Gaulle vied for control of its component countries. Within France, civil war attained its peak in 1944 but continued after the Liberation in the form of the so-called *épuration,* or "purge" of those alleged to have collaborated with the Nazis. Finally, France rejoined the Allied war effort in 1944–45 as it also began to face the problems of economic, political, and moral reconstruction. Such well-known facts scarcely bear repeating except to emphasize that these wrenching events were squeezed into a period roughly equal to the term of a single legislature in peacetime; the French had no time to grasp, come to terms with, and mourn what had befallen them in one catastrophe before they found themselves caught up in yet another. It was under Vichy, and with Vichy, that people first began to take the measure of the defeat, and it was through the purge that the majority of Frenchmen became aware of what the Pétain regime had been" (5). I am grateful to historian Fred Corney for introducing me to Rousso's provocative book and for suggesting its program as a model for reconstructing the Belgian national experience in 1940–45.

47. Mehlman, *Genealogies of the Text: Literature, Psychoanalysis, and Politics in Modern France* (Cambridge: Cambridge University Press, 1995), 131–38, contains his important response to de Man's celebrity as monarch of prosopopeia and allegory theory, entitled "Prosopopeia Revisited." Mehlman writes: "But to the extent that Hugo's Time and Mind are . . . figures of Spanish occupant and Flemish victim, de Man has

implicitly rewritten the poem as a scenario of Flemish collaboration with a foreign occupant, a rehearsal, as it were, forty years after the fact, of one of those Germano-Flemish cultural events celebrated by de Man in the pages of *Le Soir*" (138). Mehlman here responds to de Man's reading of Hugo's "Carillon," in "Hypogram and Inscription," in *Resistance to Theory*, 45–47.

48. See Michael Sprinker, "Determinations: Paul de Man's Wartime Journalism," in *Responses*, 370–74.

49. De Man, *Wartime Journalism*, 158; translation taken from Lehman, *Signs of the Times*, 163.

50. Gasché, *Wild Card of Reading*, 245.

51. De Man, *Wartime Journalism*, 3 (my emphasis).

52. It should also be remembered that war in any form had become, in the rhetoric of American isolationism at the time, construed as a "contagion," as President Roosevelt had decried in more than one public address.

53. See Lifton, *Nazi Doctors*, esp. 14–18; see also Robert Proctor, *Racial Hygiene: Medicine under the Nazis* (Cambridge: Harvard University Press, 1988), esp. 70–74.

54. Miller, "Reading Part of a Paragraph," 169.

55. See Kantorowicz, *King's Two Bodies*, 24–41.

56. Ibid., 21–23.

57. Louis Marin, *Portrait of the King*, trans. Martha M. Houle, foreword Tom Conley (Minneapolis: University of Minnesota Press, 1988).

58. Alain Boureau, *Kantorowicz: Stories of a Historian*, trans. Stephen G. Nichols and Gabrielle Spiegel, foreword Martin Jay (Baltimore and London: Johns Hopkins University Press, 2001).

59. See ibid., esp. 29–39, 80–83.

60. Ibid., 47.

61. Kantorowicz, *King's Two Bodies*, vii.

62. For the details of this important aspect of the Allies' campaign in Italy, see Fred Majdalany, *The Battle of Cassino* (Boston: Houghton, 1957).

63. See n. 11 regarding Rudnytsky's psychoanalysis of de Man's excuses, repressions, and lies.

64. Connor Cruise O'Brien adheres to a strong program meant to revise modern historiographical models according to the prototype afforded in medieval models of historical repetition: I refer to the "figuralist" system, based on the findings of Erich Auerbach, which has been espoused by Hayden White. See especially selected essays in White's *Figural Realism: Studies in the Mimesis Effect* (Baltimore and London: Johns Hopkins University Press, 1999).

65. O'Brien, *God Land: Reflections on Religion and Nationalism* (Cambridge: Harvard University Press, 1988), 62.

66. Ibid., 65.

67. See ibid., 68–70, for an anecdote about his visit to the Smithsonian Air and Space Museum during a special celebratory showing, closed to the public, during night hours one evening in April 1987. O'Brien saw the technological and cosmic self-celebration of the museum as peculiarly representative of a self-deifying quality never before discernible in American history. As he summarizes, "The level of hubris in the American atmosphere had become disturbingly high by 1986" (70). O'Brien's remarks about the uncanniness of the Air and Space Museum (repository of divine technology with its special aesthetic power) tellingly echo Tobin Siebers's closing point (484–85) about the incredible increase in the number of museums being built in the late-twentieth-century West.

68. De Man, *Blindness and Insight*, xii. On the connection between de Man's emergent thought in the 1960s and the repression of the national trauma of the Vietnam War, see David Simpson, "Going on about the War without Mentioning the War: The Other Histories of the Paul de Man Affair," *Critical Quarterly* 31 (1989): 58–68; I am grateful to Peter C. Herman for this reference.

69. Jon Whitman, "Present Perspectives: The Late Middle Ages to the Modern Period," in *Interpretation and Allegory*, 302–3.

4

"Nostalgeria" and "Structure, Sign, and Play in the Discourse of the Human Sciences"

LEE MORRISSEY

More than thirty years after Jacques Derrida first read his essay "Structure, Sign, and Play in the Discourse of the Human Sciences" (1966) at the Johns Hopkins Conference on "The Language of Criticism and the Sciences of Man," it may seem redundant to return to the "originary" moment of Derrida's spectacularly successful—and simultaneously remarkably simplified—American reception. However, now that, reportedly, "deconstruction . . . is dead in literature departments today"—as Jeffrey T. Nealon writes in *Double Reading* (1993) it may be possible to reconsider its "birth," particularly the commonly accepted notion that Derrida's work avoids, overlooks, or prevents a relationship with history and/or politics.[1] While the historicizing approach of this essay is made possible in part by the increasingly explicit treatment of historical and political questions in Derrida's recent works, such as *Specters of Marx* (1994) and *Jacques Derrida* (1991), it is also made possible by "Structure, Sign, and Play"'s second "interpretation of interpretation," that which "affirms play."[2] If, as "Structure, Sign, and Play" contends, "Being must be conceived as presence or absence on the basis of the possibility of play and not the other way around," I am revisiting this early essay to play with the possibility that the recent focus on politics (presence), neglected though it was (absence), had been there from the "beginning" (play). Specifically, I consider Derrida's essay, in terms of the relationship between Paris and Algeria or Francophone North

Africa, what the recent *History of Structuralism* (1997) calls "the continental divide of structuralism."[3] By "playing" with Derrida's "Structure, Sign, and Play" essay in terms of the "liberation" of Algeria (ca. 1962), what emerges is a Derridean argument much more politically and historically aware than his work is generally thought to be, especially in the earlier essays.

During the initial discussion after his reading of "Structure, Sign, and Play," Derrida stated, "I don't destroy the subject; I situate it. . . . It is a question of knowing where it comes from."[4] As he has discussed more frequently in his recent works, Derrida happens to come from Algeria, where he lived until he was nineteen years old. He has recently described, in part, his experience of Algeria in terms of "Vichy, official anti-semitism, the Allied landing at the end of 1942, the terrible colonial repression of Algerian resistance in 1945 at the time of the first serious outbursts heralding the Algerian war."[5] The war in Algeria, which lasted eight years, "toppled six French prime ministers and the Fourth Republic itself," with casualties of "an estimated one million Muslim Algerians and the expulsion from their homes of approximately the same number of European settlers."[6] Derrida returned to, and lived in, Algeria for two years during the war. Where "Structure, Sign, and Play" tentatively claims that "perhaps something has occurred in the history of the concept of structure that could be called an 'event,'" and answers the obvious question—"what would this event be then?"—with the cryptic claim that "its exterior form would be that of a *rupture*" (278), this essay, on the one hand, treats the Algerian liberation as that rupture, while on the other, considering the cryptic, tentative tone of Derrida's essay as symptomatic.

The fact that this context has not informed the typical response to "Structure, Sign, and Play" over the past thirty years probably has more to do with American unfamiliarity with the Francophone North African situation than with the famous opacity of Derrida's writing. When, for example, the editors of the influential anthology, *Yale Critics* (1983), set out "to stimulate serious, careful assessment of [deconstruction] in relation to recent American criticism and to the critical tradition," they argue that in order "to achieve this initial location, [they] had to refrain from pursuing other important current concerns, such as feminism, semiotics, and ethnic and regional studies."[7] It is not clear what one is left with when one excludes so many fields that cover so many issues. This rather comprehensive list of exclusions turns out to have included issues that the recent work of Derrida, the key figure in the approach the editors of *Yale Critics* were trying to survey, indicates has been of central importance. Overlooking what they call "regional studies" means that they might have missed precisely the trans-Mediterranean context that Derrida's recent work so directly discusses.

Jean Hyppolite, the first person to ask a question regarding "Structure, Sign, and Play" when it was first read, asked what remains the "central" question; recognizing that the "technical point of departure of the presentation" is Derrida's discussion of the center, Hyppolite asked "what a center might mean." Hyppolite wondered, "is the center the knowledge of the general rules which, after a fashion, allow us to understand the interplay of the elements? Or is the center certain elements which enjoy a particular privilege with the ensemble?"[8] Derrida's answer, "I don't mean to say that I thought of approaching an idea of the center would be an affirmation,"[9] echoes his essay's claim that *"this affirmation then determines the noncenter otherwise than as loss of the center"* (292). However, if we were to do to the word "center" what Derrida says the center does—making a "substitution of center for center" so that "the center receives different forms or names"—his essay can describe the complexity of Algeria's decolonization (292).

Derrida's definitions of "the center" constitute abstracted definitions of a political center: "The center, which is by definition unique, constituted that very thing within a structure which while governing that structure escapes structurality" (279). The center "governs" and is "constituted"; the political implications of Derrida's terms here are very important. We are all familiar with how centers manage to escape structurality: consider, for example, South Africa's National Party's 1997 contention before the Truth and Reconciliation Committee that its leaders had no knowledge of what members of the army (in "Structure, Sign, and Play"'s terms, "the structure") were doing to black South Africans. When pressed, the center says that power was always elsewhere. In this sense, then, "the center is not the center" (279). Or, as Derrida also says, "the center is, paradoxically, *within* the structure and *outside* it" (279). Like a governmental center, the "center of a structure permits the freeplay of its elements inside the total form" (278–79), even as it also "closes off the freeplay it opens up and makes possible" (279). Some possibilities cannot be considered even by the freest of centers.

According to "Structure, Sign, and Play," this comparative narrowness of possibilities is the result of centering: "The structurality of structure . . . has always been neutralized or reduced, and this by a process of giving it a center or referring it to a point of presence, a fixed origin" (278). The center thus controls, in the sense of "containing," the structurality of the structure, reducing it; the extremes are neutralized by the center. For many people (although Derrida's essay might say, for "the structure"), this containment is a good thing: "the concept of centered structure is in fact the concept of play based on a fundamental ground, a play constituted on the basis of a fundamental immobility and a reassuring certitude" (279). Limiting freeplay is reassuring, "and on the basis of this certitude anxiety can be mastered" (279). The center, which governs, allows certain freedoms, and even if allowing these closes off others, it is considered preferable to the absence of centering because with it a reassuring certitude, through which anxiety can be reduced, is implied.

"Structure, Sign, and Play" emphasizes that the center is "not a fixed locus but a function" (280). In one sense, then, the governmental function need not be put in one place; the function can be distributed throughout the structure. This is another way of understanding that the center is not the center; the center of power need not be at the central place. Even decentralized power functions as power. Moreover, if the center is a function, not a place, then it is highly variable; not only can the function be fulfilled from different places, but different centers can fulfill the same function. "If this is so," according to this essay, "the entire history of the concept of structure, before the rupture of which we are speaking, must be thought of as a series of substitutions of center for center" (278). In governmental terms, whatever fulfills the function of the center is itself just a substitute for a (previous) center; the function remains the same even if the center has moved, that is, is not a fixed locus.

"Structural" conditions in Algeria made these issues all the more complicated and important. The Crémieux Decrees of 1870 automatically made Algerian Jews French citizens, and left Algerian Muslims French "subjects," with the option to apply for citizenship. However, legislation that permitted Algerian Muslims to be subjected to Islamic, rather than French, law "became in effect a prison, because Muslims wishing to adopt French citizenship had to renounce these [Islamic] rights, thereby virtually committing an act of apostasy," according to Alistair Horne.[10] Moreover, French was simultaneously made the official language of the land, Arabic being considered foreign, and with Koranic schools shut down, anyone who wanted an education would need to attend a French school, where they would learn about "their" French culture. As a consequence, "by 1946," write David and Marina Ottaway, "about forty-six thousand Algerians out of a total population of seven and a half million had full French citizenship."[11] This, it seems to me, is an instance of the structurality of the structure.

According to *Jacques Derrida* (1991), in 1942, when Derrida was twelve years old, the French government in Algeria, which had not been occupied by Germany, revoked the Crémieux Decrees; consequently, as it is put in one of the *three* accounts of it in *Jacques Derrida*, "they expelled from the Lycée de Ben Aknoun in 1942 a little black and very Arab Jew who understood nothing about it."[12] In addition to being expelled from school, Derrida also lost his French citizenship. Overnight he was a Jew and no longer French. Being both was seemingly no longer possible. A teacher said that day that "French culture is not made for little Jews."[13] In terms of "Structure, Sign, and Play," Algeria had undergone a substitution of center for center, and in 1942, this new center neutralized a possibility for freeplay, mastering a certain anxiety; but the center, the structure, had repositioned Derrida: "thus expelled, I became the outside" (289). From the point of view of Algeria (perhaps especially the point of view of a schoolboy expelled for being Jewish), it could be said that Paris governs while escaping what is applied to the rest of the structure, the governed.

From 1870 on, whether one were "Muslim" or "Jewish" had a significant impact on one's relationship with the center; but whereas "Muslim" could include a variety of origins—Kabyle, Chaoui, M'zabite, Mauretanian, Turkish, and Arab, for example—to simply refer to all these peoples as "Muslim" was itself a distortion that says something about the structural possibilities for freeplay at the center. The marker of difference was Islam, to which all other differences were relegated. Even the phrase *pieds noirs* could refer to French, Spanish, Italian, and Maltese immigrants. As for how these questions worked in practice, consider the following transaction from the Algerian Assembly in 1947, seven years before the war:

> M. Boukaboum—"Don't forget that I'm an Algerian, first and foremost!"
>
> M. Louvel—"That's an admission!"
>
> *From several benches, in the center—"You are French, first and foremost!"*
>
> M. Boukaboum—"I am a Muslim Algerian, first and foremost!"
>
> M. Musmeaux—"If you consider the Muslim Algerians as French, give them all the rights of the French!"
>
> M. Louvel—"Then let them declare they're French."[14]

From this example, we can see that it was understood that the structure demands/asks people to "be" one thing, and then treats them in different ways if/once they "are."

This argument can be read in relation to a famous passage from "Structure, Sign, and Play," according to which "the history of metaphysics, like the history of the West, is the history of these metaphors and metonymies" (282). Although that essay is usually read in terms of "the history of metaphysics," this analogy between metaphysics and the history of the West works both ways, relating to the history of the West as much as it does to the history of metaphysics. After all, as Derrida's essay points out, "we have no language—no syntax and no lexicon—which is foreign to this history" of metaphysics (280). In claims such as "I am an Algerian," and "I am a Muslim," metaphors and metonymies posit existence, or, in terms of "Structure, Sign, and Play" would seem to be the "determination of Being as *presence* in all the senses of this word" (279). Although metaphors claim to state that this is that, or while metonymy, as its root indicates, makes possible changes of names, in fact, they are nothing but descriptions with reference to some center. Their power is rhetorical, and, granted, that is substantial and real. But words do not necessarily establish what the object is; they instead participate in "a history of meanings" (279). Moreover, because saying that you are somebody, or something, takes the form of both a metaphor (x = y) and a metonymy (a name change, "I" am "something else"), what you are may still be different than either the metaphor or the metonymy can suggest. "We live in and of difference," according to Derrida.[15] We are not who we say (we are). In fact, we cannot be, because when we say who we are we are only using metaphors and metonymies.

Insofar as there is a difference between Being and a metaphor, we live in difference. Those metaphors and metonymies only have meaning in relation to some center that contains the freeplay of the structure so as to master a certain anxiety, probably the anxiety of difference, which is also the anxiety of similarity. The "rupture," with which "Structure, Sign, and Play" begins, "comes about when the structurality of the structure had to begin to be thought" (278). Once people begin to recognize that the structure is a structure, and nothing else, a rupture can occur; prior to that, when people believe that the structure is something other than a structure (e.g., "the way things are"), they have instead fallen for metaphors. Once people become conscious of how the structure structures them, then there can be an event, which, when considered externally, could be called a "rupture." To some extent, by the mid-1960s this thinking of the structurality of the structure happened in Algeria, temporarily suspending the usual substitution of center for center, resulting in what is called a "rupture." The word "rupture" is used by others to describe the results of the Algerian civil war: Jacques Soustelle, for example, refers to the "rupture between the Sahara and France,"[16] and the entry "Algerie: les intellectuels avant la decolonization," in *Dictionaire des intellectuels français* (1996) refers several times to *les ruptures*.[17] While both examples suggest an "Algerian," and 1960s, usage of the word "rupture," "Structure, Sign, and Play" claims that it is only "before the rupture of which we are speaking" that the entire history of the concept of structure must be thought of as a series of substitutions of center for center (278). The rupture, which might "be called an 'event,' if this loaded word did not entail a meaning which it is precisely the function of structural—or structuralist—thought to reduce or to suspect" (278), has changed that pattern of substitution.

According to "Structure, Sign, and Play," *"this affirmation then determines the noncenter otherwise than as loss of the center"* (292). On the one hand, the noncenter (either the "margins," or "the rupture") is not necessarily a loss; the decolonizing rupture is not a loss. But of course, on the other hand, the extraordinarily qualified, tentative tone of this affirmation clearly mitigates against celebrating the rupture that this essay suggests has occurred. There are several reasons for such reserved appreciation of the rupture. First, it is not clear that there is such a thing as a "rupture," a total break. As Edward Said explains, "imperialism did not end, did not suddenly become 'past,' once decolonization had set in motion the dismantling of the classical empires."[18] Describing change as a rupture, as a break, suggests that all that came before has stopped, that there has been an ending, or a new beginning, a claim that must, of course, overlook continuities, or traces. Jean-François Lyotard's claim—made as early as 1958—that "there is already no longer an *Algerie française*, in that 'France' is no longer present in any form in Algeria,"[19] for example, replays the dichotomizing logic of the center, by overlooking what persists (including, most obviously, the French language, although that too has become an issue recently). Or as Derrida's essay puts it, "one can describe what is peculiar to the structural organization only by not taking into account . . . the problem of the transition from one structure to another, by putting history between brackets" (291).

With reference to his own experience in Algeria, Derrida has recently spoken about what persists despite (or through) change, about what survives the brackets. Although Derrida "always (at least since 1947) condemned the colonial policy of France in Algeria," during the emigration of Jews from Algeria "he even put pressure on his parents not to leave Algeria in 1962. Soon afterward he recognized his illusions on this matter."[20] Although he describes these "illusions" as "his 'nostalgeria,'"[21] to see how nostalgeric Derrida was, and/or how controversial it is to claim that the rupture was not a rupture, it is important to note that of an estimated 140,000 Jews in Algeria before the outbreak of the war in 1954, only 10,000 remained by 1962, and by 1970, that number had dropped to 1,000 with only one Talmud Torah in the entire country. And this drop, in most cases, was precipitous as Independence approached: "whereas in 1961 as many as 22,000 Jews lived in Oran, during the summer of 1962 only 1,000–5,000 remained."[22] Moreover, the social circumstances in "the Algerian Jewish scene [were] totally different from that in either Morocco or Tunisia," according to Michael M. Laskier's study of *North African Jewry in the Twentieth Century* (1994).[23] Algerians Jews were more Francophilic; only 10,000 emigrated to Israel between 1954 and 1962; most of the rest went to France. Of course, in his ambivalence over how to respond to decolonization, Derrida is not unusual: Francine Camus, for example, admitted, "I feel divided . . . half-French and half-Algerian, and, in truth, dispossessed in both countries which I no longer recognize, since I never imagined them separated."[24]

If it is possible to understand Derrida's "Structure, Sign, and Play" in terms of this historical "event," it is nonetheless still a question as to "why, despite the revolutionary rhetoric of his *circa* 1968 writings, and despite the widespread, taken-for-granted assumption that he is 'of the Left,' Derrida so consistently, deliberately, and dexterously avoided the subject of politics. Why, for example, has he danced so nimbly around the tenacious efforts of interviewers to pin him down on where he stands vis-à-vis Marxism?"[25] Precisely because this hesitant relationship with communism is thought to represent Derrida's hesitancy with the Left in general, it is important to remember how the Algerian and French Communist parties responded to the Algerian War. In Algeria, the Communist Party, "which tended to support *petits blancs* rather than the Muslims," "strongly condemned the Sétif Uprising [May 8, 1945], and was actually reported to have taken part in the reprisals."[26] The French Communist Party, "by granting the Guy Mollet-Lacoste government full power for its North African policy, the vote of the French Communist Party not only resulted in the escalation of the colonial war, but also caused a schism in the traditional Left."[27] By "knowing where it comes from," mistrust of the Communist Party in Algeria might be seen as politically progressive.[28]

Regardless, Thomas McCarthy is not alone in believing that "Derrida's discourse, it seems to me, lives from the enormous elasticity, not to say vagueness and ambiguity, of his key terms."[29] But that elasticity moves his writing beyond the categorical imperative that might be placed on it by a "metaphysics of presence" ("Structure, Sign, and Play," 281). Derrida has recently said, "I'd like to escape my own stereotypes," meaning, in a sense, he'd like to substitute an absence for a presence.[30] With its "elasticity," his essay can be as hybrid, as multiple, as his work suggests identity is. "I absolutely refuse," writes Derrida, "a discourse that would assign me a single code, a single language game, a single context, a single situation; and I claim this right not simply out of caprice or because it is to my taste, but for ethical and political reasons."[31] Readers have long wondered how it could be "ethical," not to mention "political," to refuse a single code. Ernesto Laclau recently pointed out that "this does not sound much like an ethical injunction but ethical nihilism."[32]

However, the point is not that no position will be taken, but rather that the code that marks positions will be refused, precisely because of how it has been centered, a point that may make more sense when considered in the postcolonial situation represented by Algeria. For example, in his influential article and subsequent book, Samuel P. Huntington contends that "culture and cultural identities . . . are shaping the patterns of cohesion, disintegration, and conflict in the post-Cold War world."[33] Huntington's claim, that "world civilizations" predating Cold War alignments are reshaping the world, is the type of assumption that "Structure, Sign, and Play" challenges, for ethical reasons. Huntington, and others, would, on one level, reduce the complexity of identity to a single code, a single language game, and so forth, and, on another level, would perform the same centering operation on the structure that Derrida's essay describes. They would be, as even Huntington admits, "groping for groupings."[34] Derrida's essay asks us to examine how those "groupings" are claims to identity, rather than identity itself.[35] (With that essay it can be seen that recent arguments over the so-called "third way" also run the risk of simply recentering within a new structure.)

"As an adolescent," Derrida has recently said, "I no doubt had the feeling that I was living in conditions where it was both difficult and therefore necessary, urgent, to say things that are not allowed."[36] In its "elasticity," or in its "refusal of a single code," "Structure, Sign, and Play" entails both of those perceptions: the difficult conditions, and the interdiction against speaking. The essay could be understood as part of what Hal Foster describes as "a shift in conception" "from reality as an effect of representation to the real as a thing of trauma," as a traumatic response to an event.[37] In *Unclaimed Experience* (1996), Cathy Caruth describes trauma "in terms of its indirect relation to reference," according to which both the violent event and the violence of that event cannot be fully known.[38] This traumatic indirect relation to reference may account for the oft-noted elasticity, obscurity, generalization, and ahistoricism of Derrida's work; it could be the result of a traumatic incomprehension or of the incomprehensibility of the traumatic event. For the problem of reference that haunts the reception of Derrida's work is in fact the problem of reference that is indicative of a response to trauma, that is, having the feeling of living in conditions where it was both difficult and therefore necessary, urgent, to say things that are not allowed. Derrida's recent discussion of wanting "to render both *accessible and inaccessible*" could thus be read as the traumatized wish to speak, but not speak too much or too directly, about the trauma.[39]

Recently, Derrida has stated that "what interests me . . . is not strictly called either literature or philosophy," but something for which "'autobiography' is perhaps the least inadequate name."[40] And there is a way in which, by trying "to read philosophers in a certain way" (as "Structure, Sign, and Play" describes it), that essay could be considered an autobiography (288). But "autobiography" is the least inadequate name because there is more to the essay than what it says about Derrida's biography. When read with "play," "Structure, Sign, and Play" is like Derrida's recent definition of literature: "in principle [it] allows one to say everything."[41] As that rhetorical strategy whereby one says more than one has said, literature (and, perhaps more specifically, metaphors) allow one to say one thing and to mean many other things. Like literature, that essay need not, and does not, say everything in order to convey more than it actually does say—about metaphysics, about the history of the West, or, perhaps, about nostalgeria.

With *La mésentente* (1995), Jacques Rancière claims that this is a paradox: "a determinate type of speaking situation: where one of the speakers at the same time intends and does not intend." Neither a "misreading" nor a "misunderstanding"—for "the concept of misunderstanding assumes that one or the other of the speakers, or both of them . . . may not know what one or other says"—in *la mésentente* conversants know what is being said, even if it strikes them as a contradiction. For Rancière, knowing the contradiction makes *la mésentente* the image of politics, which he also describes as "the art of the local and singular construction of the universal case."[42] Although "Structure, Sign, and Play" could describe a decolonizing experience in Algeria, that word, "Algeria," is but a metonymy for a confluence of factors, larger than, and also visible elsewhere besides, Algeria. Like literature or *la mésentente,* more is said here than just references to metaphysics or the history of the West. What Derrida says in *Specters of Marx* (1994) concerning apartheid could also apply to his own experience in Algeria: "one can decipher through its singularity so many other kinds of violence going on in the world."[43] Algeria, like apartheid, is an example of what is going on in many places; it is a local and singular example of the universal case.

Although Derrida has claimed that if "one has an interest in this, it is very easy to know where my choices and my allegiances are, without the least ambiguity"[44] ("Almost Nothing," 84), the ambiguity, the traumatic elasticity of terms give it its political charge. As a "mésentente," "Structure, Sign, and Play" is intrinsically political, although not in the narrow sense of liberal or conservative, but rather in the much more significant sense of what Slavoj Zizek calls "the struggle for one's voice to be heard and recognized."[45] The fact that in this literary-political struggle for recognition every injustice could potentially represent a universal wrong means that "Structure, Sign, and Play" is applicable without reference to the context of its origin. This "playful" universality is taken to mean that Derrida's work is not political, or, in Eagleton's memorable phrase, "is an injurious as blank ammunition."[46]

At the same time, however, with a universalizing reading, or with what Zizek describes as "the possibility of the metaphoric elevation of her specific wrong," the uniqueness and singularity may be overlooked.[47] It may simply be recentered within a new structure, rather than being recognized in itself. If, as Zizek contends, "politics proper designates the moment at which a particular demand is not simply part of the negotiation of interests but aims at something more,"[48] then the elasticity of the terms of "Structure, Sign, and Play" aims at something more. The consequent play, by facilitating "the movement of signification," "excludes totalization" (289). As "Structure, Sign, and Play" points out, "there is always more" (289). This "something more" represents the uniqueness of the situation that would be lost in restructuring it as universal. Instead of such a polarized, universal—and then "recentered" structure—that essay can be seen as part of Derrida's ongoing argument that "in order to recast, if not rigorously refound a discourse on the 'subject' . . . one has to go through the experience of deconstruction."[49]

NOTES

1. Jeffrey T. Nealon, *Double Reading: Postmodernism after Deconstruction* (Ithaca: Cornell University Press, 1993), 22.

2. Jacques Derrida, "Structure, Sign, and Play in the Discourse of the Human Sciences," in *Writing and Difference,* trans. Alan Bass (Chicago: University of Chicago Press, 1978), 278–93, esp. 292.

3. François Dosse, *History of Structuralism, Vol. 1: The Rising Sign, 1945–1966* (Minneapolis: University of Minnesota Press, 1997), 264.

4. "Discussion," in *The Structuralist Controversy: The Languages of Criticism and the Sciences of Man,* eds. Richard Macksey and Eugenio Donato (Baltimore: Johns Hopkins University Press, 1972), 265–72, esp. 271.

5. Derrida, "'This Strange Institution Called Literature': An Interview with Jacques Derrida," trans. Geoffrey Bennington and Rachel Bowlby, in *Acts of Literature,* ed. Derek Attridge (New York: Routledge, 1992), 33–75, esp. 38–39.

6. Alistair Horne, *A Savage War of Peace: Algeria, 1954–1962* (New York: Viking, 1977), 14.

7. Wallace Martin, Introduction, to *The Yale Critics: Deconstruction in America,* eds. Jonathan Arac, Wlad Godzich, and Wallace Martin (Minneapolis: University of Minnesota Press, 1983), ix.

8. Macksey and Donato, *Structuralist Controversy,* 265.

9. Ibid., 267.

10. Horne, *Savage War of Peace,* 35.

11. David Ottaway and Marina Ottaway, *Algeria: The Politics of a Socialist Revolution* (Berkeley: University of California Press, 1970), 30.

12. Derrida and Bennington, *Jacques Derrida,* trans. Bennington (Chicago: University of Chicago Press, 1991), 58.

13. Ibid., 326.

14. Horne, *A Savage War of Peace: Algeria, 1954–1962* (New York: Viking Press, 1977), 49, 70.

15. Derrida, "Violence and Metaphysics: An Essay on the Thought of Emmanuel Levinas," in *Writing and Difference,* trans. Alan Bass (Chicago: University of Chicago Press, 1978), 153.

16. Quoted in Kristin Ross, *Fast Cars, Clean Bodies: Decolonization and the Reordering of French Culture* (Cambridge: Massachusetts Institute of Technology Press, 1995), 126.

17. Tassadit Yacine, "Algerie: les intellectuels avant la decolonization," in *Dictionaire des intellectuels français: les personnes, les lieux, les moments,* eds. Jacques Julliard and Michel Winock (Paris: Editions du Seuil, 1996), 51–52.

18. Said, *Culture and Imperialism* (New York: Vintage, 1994), 282.

19. Jean-François Lyotard, "Algerian Contradictions Exposed 1958," in *Political Writings,* trans. Kevin Paul (Minneapolis: University of Minnesota Press, 1993), 197–213, esp. 202.

20. Derrida and Bennington, *Jacques Derrida,* 330.

21. Ibid.

22. Michael M. Laskier, *North African Jewry in the Twentieth Century: The Jews of Morocco, Tunisia, and Algeria* (New York: New York University Press, 1994), 334, 338, 344.

23. Ibid., 40.

24. Quoted in Horne, *Savage War of Peace*, 542.

25. Nancy Fraser, "The French Derrideans: Politicizing Deconstruction or Deconstructing the Political?" *New German Critique* 33 (1984): 127–154, esp. 127.

26. Horne, *Savage War of Peace*, 136.

27. Danielle Marx-Scouras, *The Cultural Politics of Tel Quel: Literature and the Left in the Wake of Engagement* (University Park: Pennsylvania State University Press, 1996), 34.

28. Macksey and Donato, *Structuralist Controversy*, 271.

29. Thomas McCarthy, *Ideals and Illusions: On Reconstruction and Deconstruction in Contemporary Critical Theory* (Cambridge: Massachusetts Institute of Technology Press, 1991), 118.

30. Derrida, "This Strange Institution Called Literature," 30.

31. Derrida, "Remarks on Deconstruction and Pragmatism," in *Deconstruction and Pragmatism: Simon Critchley, Jacques Derrida, Ernesto Laclau and Richard Rorty*, ed. Chantal Mouffe (New York: Routledge, 1996), 77–88, esp. 81.

32. Ernesto Laclau, *Emancipations* (New York: Verso, 1996), 78.

33. Samuel P. Huntington, *The Clash of Civilizations and the Remaking of World Order* (New York: Simon & Schuster, 1996), 20.

34. Ibid., 125.

35. Homi K. Bhabha makes a similar point in *The Location of Culture:* "The taking up of any one position, within a specific discursive form, in a particular historical conjuncture, is thus always problematic—the site of both fixity and fantasy. It provides a colonial 'identity' that is played out—like all fantasies of originality and origination—in the face and space of the disruption and threat from the heterogeneity of other positions" (Bhabha, *The Location of Culture* [New York: Routledge, 1994], 77).

36. Derrida, "This Strange Institution Called Literature," 38.

37. Hal Foster, *Return of the Real: The Avant-Garde at the End of the Century* (Cambridge: Massachusetts Institute of Technology Press, 1996), 146.

38. Cathy Caruth, *Unclaimed Experience: Trauma, Narrative, and History* (Baltimore: Johns Hopkins University Press, 1996), 7.

39. Derrida, "This Strange Institution Called Literature," 35.

40. Ibid., 34.

41. Ibid., 36.

42. Jacques Rancière, *La mésentente: politique et philosophy* (Paris: Galilée, 1995), 12, 14, 188 (my translation).

43. Derrida, *Specters of Marx: The State of the Debt, the Work of Mourning, & the New International,* trans. Peggy Kamuf (New York: Routledge, 1994), xv.

44. Derrida, "The Almost Nothing of the Unpresentable," in *Points . . . Interviews, 1974–1994,* ed. Elizabeth Weber, trans. Peggy Kamuf et al. (Stanford: Stanford University Press, 1995), 78–88, esp. 84.

45. Slavoj Zizek. "A Leftist Plea for 'Eurocentrism,'" *Critical Inquiry* 24 (summer 1998): 988–1009, esp. 999.

46. Terry Eagleton, *Literary Theory: A Critical Introduction* (Minneapolis: University of Minnesota Press, 1983), 145.

47. Zizek, "Leftist Plea for 'Eurocentrism,'" 1002.

48. Ibid., 1006.

49. Derrida, "This Strange Institution Called Literature" 34.

5

Jean Baudrillard and May '68

An Acoustic Archaeology

ANDREA LOSELLE

Georges Perec's *Les choses* (1965) has become a canonical reference for the discussion of the displacement of history and the existential subject in postwar France. In this novel, identity and historical consciousness pass into the vacuous world of signs: British-made shoes for Jérôme, a handmade cashmere twin-set for Sylvie, a chesterfield couch, some "para-scientific trifles" for the home, and so on.[1] Sylvie and Jérôme are young market researchers whose aspirations begin and end as passive representatives of French consumer culture. The absence of any nuanced reflection on the relationship between self and history in *Les choses* even turns their brief activism in an anti-Fascist movement into mere playacting. Perec's source material, we learn, was the women's magazine, *Mme Express*. According to the author, reading too many issues of this popular magazine required an occasional dose of Roland Barthes's rigorously distanced structuralist readings of the very products that this kind of magazine might advertise.[2] The magazine, the novel, and the theoretical work all appear, however, whether critical or uncritical, to suggest that the market's construction of the self through inert things (not through a lived relation with the world) is almost inescapable.

Despite the evident solace Perec found in structuralism's critical stance toward popular culture, this influential intellectual movement of the '50s and '60s has not escaped the criticism that, like *Mme Express,* it, too, was just another symptom of "the system." Structuralism merely elucidated the structure of everyday life; it did not change or undermine it. Moreover, the movement denied the importance of history. In *Fast Cars, Clean Bodies* (1995), Kristin Ross has written that "the very breadth of structuralism's reach [across disciplines] ended up in a kind of paranoiac cul-de-sac: in its denial of history as the realm of the unexpected and the uncertain, its denial of the extradiscursive, its denial, finally, of the outside itself."[3] Attempts such as this one to place the era of the 1950s and '60s on trial through its once fashionable theory are bound up with the question of the very belatedness of the post-'60s studies, trials, and scandals surrounding, in particular, the Second World War. Retrospectively, it seems as though structuralists as well as novelists such as Perec were complicitous with the suppression of history. Although this view informs my reading of the Jean Baudrillard of the high '60s and early '70s and his own work on objects, I would like to take a cue from Ross's reference to history as the realm of the unexpected to examine more closely another series of events that most historians and critics, including Baudrillard, agree was unexpected: May '68. Indeed, some credit the events of this month as having been a major catalyst that brought about both structuralism's demise and France's long-delayed reckoning with its former Collaborationist politics.[4] The May movement also marks the period when Baudrillard's work was just beginning to hit the French theory scene with his first book, *Le système des objets* (1968).

The question of history has always been near the center of Baudrillard's work. Beginning with *Le système des objets*, he refers frequently to its disappearance from contemporary interiors. Not surprisingly, *Les choses* helps to illustrate this concern: "despite this interior's kind of thick, cushy nostalgia, it is clear that nothing here has symbolic value anymore. One has only to compare [Perec's] description to a that of an interior by Balzac to see that no human relation is inscribed in things; everything is a sign, a pure sign. Nothing has a presence or a history. . . ."[5] History belongs to the symbolic, that realm of desire and self untouched by the signs of use and exchange value. Baudrillard's reflections on history have continued to evolve in his work as he passes on to other more pervasively popular media than the novel. Twenty years later, in response to Victor Farias's book on Martin Heidegger's Nazi Party involvement, Baudrillard suggested that what we call "history" now is, finally, too little, too late: "We tend to forget too easily that our reality comes down to us through the media, the tragic events of the past included. . . . History had to be understood while there still was history. Heidegger should have been denounced (or defended) while there was still time . . . our amnesia is the amnesia of images"[6] The structuralist reproduction of history's disappearance from the world of things as suggested by Perec's novel no longer tells us anything new. We have to look to the pervasive language of the media to trace this disappearance that fuels the untimely and repeated return to the images of the Second World War.

One of the problems, however, in placing this theorist's comments on history in an historical context is that the Baudrillard we know is almost always his most recent experiment in theory. Except when prodded in interviews, he tends not to return to the past. He enjoys a reputation for being a theoretical "terrorist," who, by his own admission, gambles with his prose to push theory to its own extremes of simulation.[7] This testing of theory's limits diverts us from looking at Baudrillard's work in relation to the cultural history of the technical objects and the media that shaped the '50s and '60s and were participants in May '68's unfolding and demise. We do not overlook these objects because he has outwritten them as a "postmodernist"; rather we remain overly focused on a history of ideas in which Baudrillard *as theorist* is seen by his critics to move beyond the reductive constraints of structuralism. At the same time, Baudrillard would appear to be pushing us to regard history, particularly that of the Collaboration, as a hopeless amnesia of belated images. These factors leave the relationship between Baudrillard's work and the unpredictability of the May movement an open question, if only because it is also a moment in recent French history that is often idealized, even by Baudrillard.

I will be arguing that if May '68 can be idealized, it is due to another related amnesia of images: a nostalgia for an unpredictable innocence suddenly captured and just as suddenly lost. If it has allowed us to read this failed revolution as the historical *rupture* necessary to begin the work of putting the guilty history of the Collaboration to images and words, its innocence is not often enough examined in relation to other historically continuous phenomena. How the Collaboration's belated representation in the media would become for Baudrillard an amnesia of images has, for example, overshadowed his earlier accounts of how the media also actively participated in mitigating the May movement's very unpredictability in real time. The blow-by-blow journalistic processing of the events of May '68 had less to do with retrospectively organizing images than with neutralizing the potentials of public noise and disruption. References to this role played by the media appear in Baudrillard's early work but have yet to be closely examined if only because historicizing things of such unpredictable consequences as public noise itself (not just its aestheticized forms) is working with evidence that seems far more ephemeral than leftover visual images and written words. And yet, there is a wealth of concrete evidence that points to a period involved in developing media and gadgets for the recording and transmission of sound that would segregate, silence, and recycle a range of noises and voices into tamer, less disruptive images of war and revolution. Indeed, as we will see, many of Baudrillard's own *visual* images associated with the '60s recall the historical repression of other more powerfully *resonant* images involving not only the

Collaboration but also the sexual revolution and the French feminist move-ment. By looking back on the media of the '60s, I hope then to provide some-thing of a Baudrillardian acoustic account of a revolution known back then as much for its amplified, recorded, and transmitted noise as its images.

Of course, the media to which Baudrillard refers the most, cinema and television, have the greatest power of simulation, a concept central to his work from the '70s on. Unlike live radio or theater, they are constitutive media reliant on montage, which alters and interprets raw footage as it passes through the editing room. In sound reproduction, montage (the splicing together of taped segments) is generally, though not exclusively, limited to musical performance and experimental works. But here emphasis is not always or necessarily on imposing an interpretive order as in film; montage in music, for example, is frequently driven by a desire for a performative per-fection not otherwise attainable.[8] Musical reproduction does not qualify, for Baudrillard, as simulation and therefore is left untreated in his work. Still, in the '50s and '60s, in addition to standard musical reproduction enhanced by the hi-fi and the long-playing record, the relatively new medium of tape intensified reflection on the nature of noise itself and experimentation with it. John Cage's work on the noise implicit in silence, the tape cutups of William Burroughs, Brion Gysin, and other Beat artists, and the *musique con-crète* of Pierre Henry, Michel Chinon, Pierre Schaeffer, and others are some examples. This channeling of noise into experimental aesthetic forms coin-cided with the channeling of primarily the voice into gadgets for other pur-poses: dictaphone, walkie-talkie, portable tape recorder, cordless phone, and transistor radio. These technical objects, although they appear from time to time as examples in Baudrillard's early work, tend to fall to the margins. They open up a space, however, in which a cultural history of May '68 involving random and organized street noise as a category of subversive unpredicata-bility and the public use of gadgets may become more audible in Baudrillard's persistent visualization of events.

Noise's unpredictability connects, for example, to one late distinction Baudrillard makes between an innocent event and guilty history, that is, between that which was unpredictable (May '68) and that which keeps us coming back for more organized narrative (the Collaboration). The latter is a form of constitutive aesthetic satisfaction that drives this repeated need for closure where there is no expiation; the documentary is, for Baudrillard, exem-plary of this form. The May movement does not, of course, elude a similar fate, having generated its fair share of documentaries and histories. Why Bau-drillard deems it an innocent event has naturally much to do with the fact that it was both an unpredictable and a failed revolution involving neither geno-cide nor routine acts of torture. Unfulfilled expectation better characterizes May '68's passage into history. It also represented, for the theorist, a moment that stood on the cusp of traditional and modern revolutionary modes. It failed, that is, for lack of a better understanding of modern forms of social repression and for not coming up with ways to sustain effective modes of subversive activity. Instead, protestors learned to play to the networks.

Yet, May '68 can still easily be remembered as a brief passage of time punctuated by exuberant and violent talking, chanting, singing, and shouting.[9] Retrospective history insists though on the visual remnants: the deserted barricades, overturned, burned-out cars gone cold, the mounds of litter, the famous paving stones that became decorative momentos in many a former protestor's home, and especially, the graffitied slogans that historians have quoted again and again in the hope that they might deliver up their secret meanings. "[I]t is in the graffiti all over the walls where one must try to grasp the secret point of '68. . . . Do they give away the secret meaning of this unprecedented movement?"[10] As the closest thing to May '68's noise, graffiti are idealized as speech so that even the walls are personified: "'The walls have the floor *[Les murs ont la parole].*'"[11] These end up functioning as the *paroles gelées* of the sudden upsurge of talk across classes and professions[12] and the collective protests demanding not narrative closure in the visual, but an answer back.

❧

As a student of sociology at Nanterre in 1966, Baudrillard was familiar with the work of the campus's leading anti-structuralist figures: Henri Lefebvre, Emmanuel Lévinas, and Paul Ricoeur. He was also drawn to Barthes's semiological approach to the everyday and worked with sociologist Pierre Bourdieu, who was also at Nanterre.[13] He borrowed from structuralism more than he espoused it.[14] It also happened to intersect with his interest in design theory. Combined with his work on technical objects and media of the '60s, Baudrillard's interest in design foreshadows his theory of simulation.[15] It informs one central theme in his first book: ambience. The term applies to a wide range of examples such as the morality of colors, the articulation of rooms by color schemes or by furniture functions, and the "new ergonomics" (a term that came into usage around 1965) of home and office furniture. His third book, *Pour une critique de l'économie politique du signe* (1972), contains an entire chapter on the legacy of the Bauhaus movement in 1960s architectural and interior design. If linguists and literary critics drew upon Ferdinand de Saussure, sociologists interested in the role of objects in postindustrial society could easily look back to Bauhaus's or Adolf Loos's dictum that "ornament is crime," where emphasis is on functionality (denotation) at the expense of decoration (connotation): "the moment of formal theorization (what Bauhaus is for the political economy of the sign) always marks a departure point in the historical process itself;" "it is therefore with [Bauhaus] that one can date, *logically,* the 'Revolution of the Object'."[16]

The '50s and '60s inherit from Bauhaus the social repression of the domestic interior as functional ambiance. Baudrillard couples "ornament is crime" with the popular slogan of Canadian media theorist, Marshall McLuhan, "the Medium is the Message."[17] The suppression of parasitic accumulation (family photos, collectibles, eclecticism, and kitsch) in favor of the ambient interconnectedness of functional design (the medium) serves to create new conceptions of lifestyle and work such as "'[c]ybernetic furniture, adjustable desks of varying configurations. . . .'"[18] As a consequence of postwar modernization, setting one's house in order meant acquiring the technical signs of being modern in such a way that, according to Baudrillard, an ambient form of repression has worked its way into French society as cultural simulation. It neutralizes impetus for social change without by domesticating it first from within. That a noisy revolution nevertheless did erupt outside in the streets, campus buildings, and factories all but demands that it be set in relation to Baudrillard's early formulations of simulation's suppression of the symbolic in private domestic interiors.

The events leading up to May '68 began on Baudrillard's campus, Nanterre, with the March 22 movement, initially a protest against administrative segregation of dorms by sex. Discontent over the educational system as a whole spread to other campuses and escalated in face-offs with university officials and brutal encounters with police. These, in turn, triggered the massive sympathetic workers' strikes that began on 14 May. Until the end of the month, virtually all industry, transportation, and other services in France were brought to a standstill. Baudrillard described the momentum leading up to, and into, the first weeks of May as a revolution of transpolitical dimensions. In addition to reinvigorating Jean-Paul Sartre's existentialism, students and workers embraced new divergent approaches to political involvement that departed radically from traditional Marxist theories of proletarian class struggle.[19] Baudrillard was not only at Nanterre at this time; he also belonged to a group that founded the journal, *Utopie,* described by him as a radical, situationist type of publication "that drew on the energy of revolt that was taking place in one fraction of society."[20]

If it is today commonplace to refer to the mass student demonstrations and workers' strikes as a failed revolution, Baudrillard is no exception when he shows in later interviews that he was not immune to the disappointment that followed in their wake.[21] The straightforward prose of the early essays for *Utopie,* though critically incisive, sounds more affirmative notes than does the writerly euphoric "terrorism" of his later work.[22] Possible solutions are offered in these early essays such as the proposal that a technical culture could be freed of its commercialized, futurist conceptualization by radically restructuring the educational system.[23] He confidently predicts that "we are going to be faced more and more with these unforeseeable transgressions, these convulsions in the system of values."[24] One of the last positive statements about May '68 is also the very last sentence of what is now considered a classic, *La société de consommation* (1970), his second book: "We will await the brutal irruptions and sudden disintegrations that in a manner as unpredictable, yet certain, as in May '68, will come to break up this white mass [consumer society]." Hope appears to recede gradually in these statements; prediction becomes waiting, which will give way, finally, to memory.

Late in life, however, Baudrillard still clings to this moment. In an interview with Sylvère Lotringer, he tells us that "May '68 was an illogical event, irreducible to simulation, one which had no status other than that of coming from someplace else—a kind of pure object or event. Its strangeness derives from a logic of our own system, but not from history."[25] It differs from history in that its "secret" is not what he calls a saturation of an event with explanations. Instead, its secret is "indecipherable," and therefore "innocent." Guilty histories are the aftermath narratives about fascism—itself a narrative of racial superiority that took on frightening momentum of its own. The innocent, "pure" event of the May movement "absorbed its own continuity."[26] What remains for this theorist, then, is the irruptive discontinuity of a few remembered '60s era images, images whose cultural history, I contend, sees them bound up in a dialectic of guilt and innocence. These images recalled by Baudrillard (e.g., the miniskirt and graffiti) intersect with other iconic images of the period: long hair, nudity, free love, beads, folk and rock music, and so on. Their desired innocence excludes their contemporaneously recorded, filmed, and printed means of transmission at the same time that they also operate to mitigate (and not, as is traditionally presumed, to release) other less innocent images of, in particular, the Collaboration.

If visual images ultimately become, for Baudrillard, dominant artifacts or ideographs of reproduction or the simulacrum, some account, then, needs to be taken of how sound devices and noise also played a part in both fueling and absorbing May '68's continuity.[27] These were ubiquitous though today they have been filtered out by greater attention to, for example, graffiti's visual messages. My goal is, first, to read a range of visual images for their implicit connections to noise, and, in the last section of this essay, to look more closely at the technical inventions of the '50s and '60s in relation to the events of May '68 and to their actual reproduction. My approach is inspired by the work of the technician, Richard G. Woodbridge III, who in 1969 theorized that cultural objects such as pots and paintings can innocently capture sounds in their grooves and strokes.[28] In other words, the combination of a potter at a wheel tracing grooves on a clay pot with a stick is a crude recording device capable of picking up ambient sound. The theory was as much about how such objects

could absorb sounds as it was about the scientific possibility of, as on a phonograph, releasing or playing them. Experimentation in this area, dubbed
"acoustic archaeology," has the virtue, as with a lot of '60s happenings and
ideas, of being *groovy,* but it is not so far-out that it cannot be appreciated as
a part of this era's interest and advancements in sound technology. This example serves here as a figurative hieroglyph—an attempt ultimately to decipher
the ideograph and the phonograph in tandem—for the vestiges of the unpredictability of noise not so innocently solidified in the leftover cultural objects
of the '60s. As we will see, one additional outcome of this approach is that the
determination of the guilt or innocence of these objects falls along gendered
lines that reinterpret and re-present innocence and guilt in the technical and
other objects assigned to women and to men. To tame noise it would be necessary to get at women through the domestic interior by turning them into
gadgets and to get at men through the street as distracted manipulators of
portable gadgets.

∽

The collaboration of the Situationist International avant-garde group with the
May '68 student action committees brought to the revolution a fresh slogan
critical of capitalism in its leader Guy Debord's book: *La société du spectacle*
(1967). Later accounts make it a commonplace that the revolution turned the
society of the spectacle into a festival. It is, for example, referenced in Mark
Poster's *Existential Marxism in Postwar France* (1975).[29] But for Baudrillard
just one year after May '68, contemporary mechanisms of social repression
transformed what started out as a potential festival into mere *ludic* spectacle
instead. These were responsible for the very momentum of the May movement dissipating in "the fascination with symbolic street confrontation where
[the police] became repression incarnate . . . *the no. 1 object of consumption* for
the imagination in revolt."[30] For Baudrillard, the ludic is the primary selling
property of the technical object, not a feature of true subversive action. It feeds
off the consumer's fascination with the spectacle of herself in action whether
that be in the self-absorbed manipulation of a gadget or in confrontational
play before the media: "Overt, traditional repression is done in the name of a
puritan morality. Modern repression is done in the name of the game."[31] The
media did not, then, facilitate the diffusion of the revolutionary message as
much as it turned the subversive act into a "gesture," "a function of its repro-
ducibility."[32] Protests are now more often staged events run by organizers and
operatives. A pedagogy exists to teach novices how and what to perform
before the camera, such as how to make their bodies deadweight so that the
camera may be made to record police officers clumsily dragging innocent-
looking protestors off to jail. Accounts such as Poster's praising the brief

recrudescence of Sartre's already dated existential Marxism and the end of structuralism notwithstanding, France's official commemorative festival for the twentieth anniversary of the May movement sold more T-shirts than it did ideas. It is, however, not only the "pure" event of the movement or its commemorations that we should be looking at but also a broader cultural history starting as far back as the '50s that explains what did and did not happen as a result of the revolution and what compels Baudrillard to preserve the innocence of that moment.

Thus certain period phenomena for Baudrillard, because they tap into the symbolic, appear more positively memorable than others. Years later, he recalls the miniskirt: "The miniskirt was perhaps the last episode in the history of fashion that was more than an effect of fashion: it was a sort of event in the history of morals *(moeurs)* to the extent that the rape of appearance came to replace taboo (the anterior fashion). There was in effect a true erotic effect, an irruption of the erotic in the real."[33] Ruptures such as this mid-'60s fashion—hotly contested by the French as the invention of the haute couture designer Courrèges but, in fact, popularized by British designer Mary Quant[34]—are privileged, fleeting moments. Fashion soon steps in to embellish it as one model for the appearance of the erotic—on its way to the anorexic/love-starved look of an Ally McBeal—but not as the irruption of desire itself. Furthermore this "rape," if it symbolized liberation from the restrictive girdle or from the puritanical morality of more voluminous clothing, it only managed to restrict and alter movement and bodily appearance along the lines of an erotic ludism. A more streamlined appearance is bound up with a scripted, playful movement that defines the '60s female body in miniskirt and in other presumably liberated costumes: the "new look" of the bikini, the modern housewife's elegant, little frock, the striptease artist's nostalgic props. It is useful to recall that in keeping with that appearance, pantyhose were invented by the French company Dim in 1968.[35] Called *collants* in French, "skin tights" are the synthetic appearance of the bare, not nudity itself.

More revealing clothes were accompanied by the sense, then, that there was not just less but nothing to see. To draw on Baudrillard's own 1980s example of striptease, like the protestor's play before the camera, "[f]emale striptease puts an act in publicity. . . . This is another ritual of transparency."[36] In the 1950s Barthes had already criticized the striptease as a form of bourgeois "propriété ménagère" (domestic propriety and suitability). Perfectly scripted undressing would be on a par with keeping the appearance of a well-run home.[37] "Gone," as McLuhan also declared in another vein, "are the thrills of striptease"; only total nudity speaks to visual, literate man divorced from "the audile-tactile values of less abstract societies." "[T]he ritualistic exposure of the body indoors and out-of-doors" shares something in common, he adds, with the secret enjoyment of seeing the taboo naughtiness of verbal obscenities outed in print.

Bodily exposure becomes even "heady music"; the epidermis is, moreover, a kind of aural receptor: "[p]sychologists have long taught us that much of our hearing takes place through the skin itself."[38] This aural liberalism of the flesh, although consonant with the free love and expression themes of the '60s revolution ("to shout naked words"[39]), runs up against the enduring myth of the liberation of women through the household gadget: dirty words and a clean house are not the same but in underlying ways they intersect with the aesthetics of the miniskirt. The more it reveals, the more it miniaturizes, the less it is obscene.

In May 1969 when the discussion of women's rights had taken '68's lead, Baudrillard in "La pratique sociale de la technique" illustrates his discussion of the gadget's futurist ideology with a reproduction of an advertisement from *Elle: La Femme-Gadget* or Gadget-Woman ("at last the liberated woman").[40] She is a diminutive figure in minidress and tights with one hand firmly attached to a vacuum cleaner. Over her tower the latest home appliances and gadgets stacked in open cubes. The smaller the clothes, the more innocently doll-like the woman, the more questionable her usefulness as she becomes paradoxically the personification of the gadget. We are reminded that girlish tininess (not thinness), was also *the* cause of Twiggy's failure at first to break into modeling and her eventual success in becoming "'the face of '66.'"[41] Twiggy recalls another well known nickname of the era, Gidget.[42] This nickname cannot escape being placed alongside the word for the littlest, most ludic of gadgets, the widget, a small device of doubtful utility such as Baudrillard's own extreme example of the "Venusik" (ca. 1970), a polished metal cylinder that might in a pinch serve as a paperweight: "'Amateurs of formal beauty and potential uselessness, the fabulous "Venusik" has arrived!'"[43]

What the first miniskirt achieved without was a certain kind of aestheticized revolutionary rupture (heady music, as McLuhan put it) already brought into line by the liberating potential of Gadget-Woman's overpowering vacuum cleaner within the home (listening to noise). For the "audile-tactile" dimension of baring one's skin is assaulted by the very noises of these gadgets that force the skin to listen to the plugged-in extensions that are the aural, not spoken, signs of a well-run household. In thinking about the importance of May '68 in raising consciousness about women's rights in France, we might contrast Gadget-Woman with a first "General Assembly" on women's rights conducted at Vincennes in 1969. Closed to men, the assembly was disrupted by them in the form of shouted insults and obscenities.[44] If there is something intuitive, yet unexplored in McLuhan's linkage of obscenity, nudity, and sound (the skin as ear), measure needs to be taken of the uses of obscenity. The disciplining by and of speech along gender lines raises the question of who speaks, who listens, and through what new means. For it is implied that a woman's voice is her body; if she speaks out, there is something transgressively obscene in the act that invites silencing her with obscenities that reduce her to her physicality. At the same time, it is implied that her voice cannot be properly heard without the body, that is, her voice is her body. The male voice, however, is associated with a resonant power that can withstand being separated from the body in recordings. These assumptions are rooted, in part, in the historical development of sound technology. Theodor Adorno wrote, for example, in 1927 that "the female voice requires the physical appearance of the body that carries it. But it is just this body that the gramophone eliminates, thereby giving every female voice a sound that is needy and incomplete [a fact, he adds, that has nothing to do with technical recording capabilities]. Only there where the body itself resonates, where the self to which the gramophone refers is identical with its sound, only there does the gramophone have its legitimate validity: thus Caruso's uncontested dominance."[45] The '60s is perhaps the last decade in which this form of gender discrimination is still audible while, as we will see later, it is the decade that inaugurates miniaturization of the voice in portable gadgets such as the dictaphone, a device whose primary target is the male voice.

Thus it is important to recognize that the one subversive medium Baudrillard singles out for praise in his early work, graffiti, is also the most anonymous, silent, and disembodied phenomenon of the events of May '68. The slogans of the '60s were furthermore constant countercultural references to the symbolic realm of desire divorced from the frankly obscene and erotic: Power to the Imagination *(Imagination au pouvoir)*; I Take My Desires for Realities Because I Believe in the Reality of My Desires *(Je prends mes désirs pour des réalités, car je crois à la réalité de mes désirs)*; It Is Forbidden to Forbid *(Il est strictement interdit d'interdire)*; Action Must Not Be Reaction but Creation *(L'action ne doit pas être une réaction mais une création)*; Pleasure without Fetters *(Jouissez sans entraves)*; the situationist incitement Under the Cobblestones, the Beach . . . *(Sous les pavés, la plage . . .)*; and the recycling of surrealist mottos, Life Instead *(Plutôt la vie,* taken from a poem of the same title by André Breton).[46] If historical accounts of the May movement ritually repeat these slogans in the vain attempt to disclose their secret, desire makes no secret of its retrospectively innocent self.

Insofar as the slogan is *the* genre of the advertisement, the graffitied countercultural messages function as transgressive publicity that attempts to usurp the code of one-way media control: "the promotional diversion of graffiti after May '68 . . . does not give itself to be deciphered *[ne se donne pas à déchiffrer]* as a text in competition with promotional discourse" says Baudrillard; "it shows itself *[il se donne à voir]* as transgression."[47] But it is not the message that interests Baudrillard as much as it is the medium of the street, a primary site of verbal exchange:

everything . . . is *immediate* inscription, spoken and answered, fluid, at the same time and in the same place, reciprocal and antagonistic. In this sense the street is the alternative, subversive form of all mass media in that it is not, as is mass media, an objectivized medium of messages with no response, a transit network at a distance; the street is the opened up space of the symbolic exchange of ephemeral, mortal speech, speech that is not reflected on the platonic screen of the media. Institutionalized by reproduction, spectacularized by the media, it dies.[48]

In retrospect, the graffiti of this revolution complement more than they transgress the media's "messages without response" insofar as no historian has been able to ask who wrote them, has never been able to respond to them, but offers them up to be consumed far from their immediate context, the street, in streamlined typeface. When the walls are said to speak, graffiti become silent figurative ideographs recollected and recycled for their seeming naive innocence.

The extent to which gadgets and the media repress symbolic rupture in reality relates to the underlying metaphorics of innocence in the miniskirt and graffiti. If both are visual, they recall other transgressive vocalizations of the symbolic insofar as they are implicated in technical and in other forms of silencing. Women's scantier clothes, for McLuhan, are analogous to not the secret pleasure of *saying* obscene words but to that of outing them *in print*. At the same time domestic gadgets miniaturize and drown women out in the name of household cleanliness and propriety. They are drowned out elsewhere by vocal obscenities, an act suggesting that their talk is physically obscene. Graffiti is more clearly the less transgressive extension of the more ephemeral utterance. Obviously, one runs a greater risk of shouting obscenities and slogans in public than in writing them because these acts are more immediately threatening. Graffiti, like the miniskirt, become signifiers of vocal censorship or ideographs that cease to signify where irruptions of the aural symbolic are concerned. For the later Baudrillard, obscenity is no longer "the hidden, the repressed, the obscure, but . . . the visible, the all-too-visible, the more-visible-than-visible; it is the obscenity of that which *no longer contains a secret* and is entirely soluble in information and communication" (emphasis added).[49]

The 1960s is also the era that saw a relaxing of French censorship laws concerning previously banned books along with new interest in historical and contemporary popular slang. The numerous reeditions of out-of-print works and the publication of new studies and dictionaries during this period channeled this language into the proper codes of scholarly inscription.[50] Some of the volitility of offensive language had diminished. This was not (and is still not) the case in some areas of the United States: Country Joe McDonald was fined five hundred dollars by a Massachusetts court and sentenced to have his head shaved for saying "fuck" in public.[51] French demonstrators did not, of course, have their heads shaved for using offensive language in the streets. In

France censorship would focus, in one important case, on what could be seen, not said: the so-called horizontal collaboration by women whose heads were publicly shaved for sleeping with the Nazi enemy. The only woman interviewed in 1969 for the *Sorrow and the Pity*, Mme Solange, is coaxed by Marcel Ophuls into recollecting female prisoners (she herself also having been a prisoner in 1945) returning from a French Liberation tribunal with shaved heads; spliced in American documentary footage accompanied by a Georges Brassens song ("La tondue" or, roughly translated, "The Sheared Woman") gleefully participates in the graphic, public "desexualization" of French women by men. The '60's celebration of the "innocent" sexuality of hair (and nudity), and lots of it ("grow it; show it," according to the 1968 musical *Hair*), would have been recalled in the deliberate irony of the interviewee's profession: Mme Solange is making her living in 1969 as a hairdresser, someone who, judging by the tight perfection of her own seemingly revisionist coiffure (guilty by association), disciplines unruly locks against the countercultural message to let it "all hang out."

This segment of the documentary received some of its sharpest criticism for virtually fabricating the hairdresser's guilt by using montage to splice in lingering, clichéd shots of her hands worrying the edge of her blouse.[52] The visual manipulation of her testimony trumped everything she had to say in her defense, including her memory of being tortured naked in a bathtub. But head-on collision between the innocent sexuality of '60s hair and the desexualization of guilty women in 1945 never occurred. Had it not been for the intervention of the French government, this documentary would have aired on national television. It was a first, major attempt to raise the specter of the Collaboration at the national level. And yet showing it in 1969 would have also upset the fragile politics of resexualizing the present as a form of innocence (concomitant with its ideographic transformation in books and gadgets) away from the unspoken and unspeakable obscenities of the past.

Ready for distribution in 1969, *The Sorrow and the Pity* was finally allowed to be shown in 1971 in a small theater in Paris's Latin Quarter and, eventually, in a larger theater on the Champs-Elysées.[53] To use Baudrillard's terms, the documentary was not permitted to become the event it was meant to be; instead it took on an aesthetic patina by being shown belatedly in the movie theater.[54] Thus, in addition to the representation of women and graffiti, other 1960s loci of the obscene, such as hair, were on the visual fault line of innocence and guilt. But guilt and innocence here are constitutive and, in this case, gendered.[55] If the first innocent transgressions (the miniskirt, graffiti, and long hair) can never be recaptured, historicizing them recontextualizes them in a dialectic of guilt and innocence. The word that Baudrillard used much later to describe this form of history and that also links the miniskirt and graffiti together as '60s artifacts is "anorexia."[56] It contrasts with his earlier far more enthusiastic statements about the subversive, implicitly vocal role of graffiti; for "anorexia" refers to his McLuhanesque observation of ruins from recent events covered over with a "cold history" of graffiti.

Similar to Jean-Luc Godard's 1972 film, *Comment ça va?* which begins with the technical modes (the typewriter and the telex) mediating a communist newspaper reporter's oral dictation of an article on a demonstration in Spain, graffitied walls begin before they even start as the backdrop of news footage and end up in documentaries or as postcards: the voice disappears into mechanical and electronic modes of visual inscription. The movie is revealingly about the production of a documentary on the everyday work involved in producing a communist newspaper. Thus both the projected documentary and other media are being questioned metacritically for their ability to represent the ideals of communist thought and action. It becomes apparent that even an explanatory legend fails at correctly representing a photograph of a Spanish demonstrator when it is juxtaposed with that of a French May '68 demonstrator. They are fraught with ambiguity: the more one looks at the photographs the less decidable they are as visual evidence of an event; the more the figures appear to be playacting. The reporter is even asked to contemplate whether the Spanish demonstrator seen in typical ludic confrontation is smiling or grimacing in pain. Is he even innocent? Eyewitness reportage and transgression are deferred and effaced by production. One senses some of this undecidability of the frozen pose as a similar short-circuiting of symbolic exchange in Baudrillard's own photographs, a medium he picked up in the late '80s. In these photos, a preference is shown for walls, textures, and patterns. Numerous walls are graffitied, such as one taken in New York City (1994) where in spray-painted block letters one reads: CERTITUDE DOES NOT EXIST. Above and below are other inscriptions: responses ("Are you sure?"), antagonistic, territorial tags, and the word, "DESIRE . . . ," rendered wistful by its suspension marks. The photograph indexes and rephenomenalizes them as the object's "maladjusted silence *[silence caractériel]*."[57]

Reflecting on Baudrillard's late involvement with photography, one senses that the profoundly visual nature of his theories has something to do with a loss of speech as a category of the unpredictable. That loss can be traced in the technologization of the voice in sound reproduction and communications. But as we have seen in the Godard and Ophuls examples, the innocent event of May '68 and its ludic dissipation drew attention to the documentary as a powerfully seductive form of historical representation, not to the unpredictability of noise. Events, for Baudrillard, are no longer taking place in the real where history is properly understood as a lived, not televised, happening: "What no one wants to understand is that *Holocaust* [the 1979 documentary series] is *first of all* (and exclusively) an event, or rather a *televised* object

(McLuhan's fundamental rule, which we must not forget). . . ."[58] But the differences between the innocent event and guilty, seemingly simulated event obviate the innocence of the May movement as a demand for, as Baudrillard himself points out, dialogue. It became statically visual. That repression, as Baudrillard argued, took place first from within the home and the workplace. But it is possible to trace another form of ambience directed more specifically at taming the street. Baudrillard would perhaps contest that the street was already archaically symbolic in the 1960s. Still, one condition for the possibility of May '68 was the threatening, albeit traditional, residue of a viable form of urban revolt, enough so that during the May events one could simultaneously hear the deafening symbolic power of the street and its miniaturized waning over the transistor radio.

Consideration of this cultural history of certain gadgets having to do with communication and voice reproduction needs to be seen in relation to the increasing portability of gadgets. For not only did they inevitably become miniaturized, but they were also being liberated from the electrical socket with more battery-operated gadgets and new cordless devices such as the telephone and the electric shaver. Baudrillard is interested in the ludic side of these objects in which their sometimes questionable utility is, unlike the feminized widget, directed toward manufacturing signs of masculine prestige (his examples: variable speed windshield wipers, automated window openers; the car is, of course, a masculinized spectacle).[59] Users play the hierarchical range of variants from the traditional razor to the electric razor to its "liberated" cordless cousin. Here there is an emphasis on the object's little buttons, intimate buzzes, and responsive beeps, which function as mechanical seduction, not as overpowering noise as in the case of the plugged in vacuum cleaner.

One might ask, then, why Baudrillard did not read more into two examples of publicity that he used in his discussion of the ludic dimension of the technical object in *La société de consommation:* the dictaphone and cordless phone. "'You take it up with just one hand, a flick of the thumb, and to it you whisper your decisions, dictate your instructions, proclaim your victories. Everything you say is consigned to its memory. . . . Whether you are in Rome, Tokyo, New York, your secretary will not lose a single syllable . . .'"; and "'[a] telephone finally become an integral part of man, and which allows him to call New York or answer Honolulu from the poolside or the far end of a park'."[60] The fantasy power trip of the dictaphone and portable telephone promised to its targeted user, the businessman, projects the portability of the devices to global dimensions. Here there is, moreover, a privileging of his words offered in devices into which he may pour his important thoughts, as opposed to the noise of the domestic gadget and the widgeting of the miniskirted woman in the frivolous "Venusik," which, as a potential paperweight, stays in its place. If men are seemingly being set free to explore the world through the portable

gadget, they are also visibly being put to work in public. Thus where the documentary and the news photo efface work, new signs of work emerge through
uses of the voice resonantly miniaturized.

The first phonographs and records of the turn of the century were a revolution in reproduction almost on a par with the invention of photography in
1839 (Adorno called records "acoustic photographs"[61]); they profoundly
affected interiors by bringing the sounds of an entire orchestra into one's living room, and spawned, as is the case with the library and photo album, the
record collection or *discothèque*. The phonograph and the television become
furniture that rally around themselves the signs of accumulated cultural prestige, that is, ideal reflections of one's self. (If *Les choses* had been written in the
'80s, Sylvie and Jérôme would have had in addition to their dream *bibliothèque*
and *discothèque*, a *vidéothèque*.) But the invention of tape (resulting in the cas-
sette tape) and new cordless technology liberate the gadget from the home
and send it into the streets, parks, and other public places to domesticate them
in turn. Sylvie and Jérôme prove that they are on the cutting edge with the
portable tape recorder they use to survey the French at the thresholds of their
homes and in public spaces: "Most of the time they would have to go to public gardens, school exits, or the public housing projects in the suburbs to ask
mothers if they had noticed some recent advertisement. . . . They left for the
provinces, a tape recorder under one arm. . . ."[62]

The ludic dimension of tape-based gadgets is even greater than that of
the phonograph because running the tape is at a greater remove with its fast-
forward and rewind buttons and the counter; one can also record one's self and
others with the simple push of a button. The tape recorder comes much closer
to the camera. Like the camera, its ludic possibilities extend to clothing as an
obvious category of the portable. Portable gadgets become adjuncts to one's
clothing (pocket clip, belt attachment, and shoulder strap), or exteriorized
objects of public display and manipulation that differ from the personification
of the miniskirted woman as gadget. But unlike the camera, the conventional
uses of voice gadgets intersect with the outside in different ways as work and
distraction, not as, say, the ritual preservation of memory. As Bourdieu
pointed out in 1965, the personal use of the camera is the mediated preservation of conventional social, leisure practices: vacations, travel, social events,
and rituals such as birthdays.[63] Sylvie and Jérôme's job is to reduce individual
expressions of choice and opinion, tonality and emotion, to predictable consumer signs. Their work is therefore largely defined by the repressive functional ambience of the interior. But other sound gadgets are either public
devices of the business world or a means to smooth the transition from home
to workplace and vice versa, an ambient ergonomics of public passage that
personalizes one's everyday interaction with public space. As Rey Chow has
suggested, the ultimate withdrawal from public engagement is the Walkman

of the '80s. In addition to this device, one can cite the earlier proliferation of other "portable oppressions and portable oppressed objects."[64] These devices had begun to make their presence felt in the '60s.

McLuhan observed that "people can tolerate their images in mirror or photo, but they are made uncomfortable by the recorded sound of their own voices. The photo and visual worlds are secure areas of anesthesia."[65] Here it is possible to read "anesthesia" as a synonym for Baudrillard's "amnesia of images." The '60s stands as an era that actively secures new uses of the voice and, consequently, triggers new conceptions of self-representation. Tapes enable one to hear oneself directly rather than hear one's cultural self in the record collection. Another diverted relation to the self comes into being: the self-referential machine (vs. the female listening machine). Early signs of this relation can be found in Samuel Beckett's *Krapp's Last Tape*.[66] Here Krapp lives his life in a *mise-en-abime;* the taped journal in replay mode turns into repeated, negative commentary on his younger voices. Sensing that this is his last tape, we are aware that his life has been spent listening to himself never accomplish his life; instead his life span is fed through a loop of mutually repellant, discontinuous selves.[67] But Krapp's evident oral pleasure in sounding out the word "spoool" for his reels of tapes points to the diversion that is the medium, an infantile, repetitive diversion that we are reminded was not the original inspiration behind the first "talking machines": recording great moments, such as historic speeches and original musical performances, and its potential uses in the office."[68] If, indeed, it is Krapp's very last tape, the audience is also taken in by the hoax of the medium; for, another use proposed for the first gramophones was to record "the last words of the dying."[69] But Krapp's temporal illusion is not the actual end, but a future past. This extraordinary compact play points to the medium's influence in *telling* time. Krapp uses the tape recorder to preserve himself in a monumental or momentous present, a projective now that never happens. It was this same underlying relation to time that Baudrillard found responsible for the failure of May '68.

Long after the image domesticates society, after one ceases to feel self-conscious of one's own photographic image, after the medium is theorized as reproduction in relation to art (Walter Benjamin), and theorized as a medium worthy of sociological study in the mid-sixties (Bourdieu), recording and communication devices enter the field in multiple new forms. At the same time the collective voice still occupies the space of the street and the square, the municipal park and the marginalized, architectural wasteland of the Nanterre campus hastily built amid grim factories and outcast HLMs (*habitation à loyer modéré* or subsidized housing). Chants and songs filled these public spaces in '68. French authorities have known since before the short-lived Commune the revolutionary potential of songs. Songs heard emerging from bars—common meeting grounds for political dissidents and anarchist cells—

were cause for alarm. The potential threat of the chants about love and creativity and the pacific folk songs were no different . "[E]very noise," writes
Jacques Attali, "evokes an image of subversion. . . ."[70] Such images have a way
of gaining momentum; noise can produce more noise and incite panic, anger,
and ecstasy. But what happens when those images are reproduced?

In addition to playing to the networks, May '68 activism took advantage
of other technical devices. "At a CSF factory in Brest the workers resumed
production, making what they deemed important: walkie-talkies to help the
strike."[71] In "Le ludique et le policier," Baudrillard recalls students during the
memorable night of the barricades (11–12 May) holding transistor radios to
their ears: "Fighting on the barricades, students were at the same time carried
away by their resonant image on transistor radios. Everywhere this society is
looking at itself. . . ."[72] The ease with which he passes from listening to looking might recall the old photographs of proud Communards posing on barricades and toppled monuments that were, on the one hand, personal memen-
tos of triumph and, on the other, documents that would later serve authorities
as convenient mug shots for tracking insurgents. In May '68, "raincoated men"
took pictures of students while students defiantly took pictures of them.[73] The
analogy with photographs works because the transistor radio functioned during the events as a recording device but the photograph requires a certain time
delay for processing this looking at and looking back. The transistor radio,
which was ubiquitous during the riots, was involved in a narrowing of that lag
to divert the present: "It's ten o'clock on the transistors," one eyewitness
account tells us.[74] Students on the barricades listening to themselves participated in the neutralization of subversive action by self-referentially tuning
into the media's feedback loop. And sympathizers from the safety of their
homes acoustically bore witness to it by placing their transistor radios on win-
dowsills.[75] The visual and resonant image amount to more or less the same
reductive, self-referential difference except in the way that time was experienced. Telling time on the transistor radio, if it is an example of hearing one's
self in the act through a radio announcer's narrative, is also a form of paraly-
sis in a sought-for monumental time, a momentous noise holding the protestor in suspense by hearing herself in the process of making history.

What conclusions about the Baudrillard of the '60s and the present can
be drawn? His writings on, and recollections of, May '68 betray for a time
some hope and later a certain nostalgia that escapes the kind of critique he
directs against other images treated by him as technical simulations of history,
culture, and identity. Providing an acoustic account of Baudrillard in the cultural context of the '60s reveals a hole in the technology by which the later
theory of the visual simulacrum is guided and advances but never seems to
look back. What has not been remembered in writing, what has been sublimated as a pure event, is not only noise itself and its potentials but also the

noise heard through the technology of the day (its specific graininess on the LP, over the radio, and the '60s era amp). The revolution's "resonance," as Edgar Morin called it, eventually succumbs to memory's own form of sound decay at the same time that it is gradually supplanted by "hi-fidelity" histories of the movement. Baudrillard heard May '68 happen; graffiti recollected for him verbal exchanges; and he witnessed others hearing reproductions of their own noise and voices. Yet, following Friedrich Kittler, such reproductions are "unwritable" noise material, the physiology of the voice or phonological signifers as opposed to imagistic signifieds and written transcriptions of words.[76] In 1972 Baudrillard confused writing and speech by reading graffiti as a figure for fluid verbal exchange instead of as quotable leftovers or transcriptions, a confusion that he does not make in his photographs. Graffiti can only be the absence of symbolic verbal exchange. The failed, heroic possibilities of recording sound come down to the emptying out of collective noise and exchange. To divert the present from its presence other noise takes the place of vocal momentum, which is perhaps why Baudrillard's late turn to photography is a desire for silence, for its ability to remove the object from its noisy continuum, not for its ability to isolate a moment in time, to record history, or to commemorate an event. "Whatever the noise or violence surrounding it, the photo delivers the object over to immobility and silence"; the photograph "is the only way of traversing cities in silence, of traversing the world in silence."[77] This desire suggests that public noise has lost much of its meaning and presence. In the wake of May '68, a multiplicity of gadgets gradually makes noise a phenomenon of personalized passage or so many mininarratives of cultural accumulation; such gadgets are filled by their hearers as suggested by the quotidian banalities overheard in one-sided cellphone conversations and in the tiny percussive sounds emanating from headphones.

NOTES

1. Georges Perec, *Les choses: une histoire des années soixante* (Paris: René Juillard, 1965), 27. Unless otherwise indicated, all translations are my own.

2. Kristin Ross, *Fast Cars, Clean Bodies: Decolonization and the Reordering of French Culture* (Cambridge: Massachusetts Institute of Technology Press, 1995), 143. For all the emptiness of its characters, Sylvie and Jérôme, the novel was based on the author's personal experience: "he spent two years studying sociology; after a short period as a market researcher he married; he and his wife spent the academic year 1960–1 as teachers in Sfax, Tunisia." The narrative addresses in a more complicated way therefore the question of the subject through the implicit suppression of autobiography. See Arthur Marwick, *The Sixties* (Oxford: Oxford University Press, 1998), 508–9.

3. Ross, *Fast Cars, Clean Bodies*, 195.

4. See, for example, Mark Poster, *Existential Marxism in Postwar France* (Princeton: Princeton University Press, 1975); and Henry Rousso, *The Vichy Syndrome: History and Memory in France since 1944*, trans. Arthur Goldhammer (Cambridge: Harvard University Press, 1991).

5. Jean Baudrillard, *Le système des objets* (Paris: Gallimard, 1968), 279.

6. Baudrillard, "Hunting Nazis and Losing Reality," in *New Statesmen*, trans. Material Word, 19 February 1988, 17.

7. Mike Gane, ed., *Baudrillard Live: Selected Interviews* (New York: Routledge, 1993), 126, 155, 168.

8. Thomas Y. Levin, "For the Record: Adorno on Music," *October* (winter 1990): 46.

9. Angelo Quattrocchi's eyewitness account is filled with references to screaming, crying, chanting, and singing. Much shouting is poured into microphones: "Reporters scream the horror into the transistors. Colder men in manipulating rooms insist that they calm down or switch their voices off. They break with music." Quattrocchi and Tom Nairn, *The Beginning of the End: France, May 1968* (London: Verso, 1998), 31. See also Edgar Morin's account of May '68's "resonance" in Morin, Claude Lefort, and Jean-Marc Coudray, *Mai '68: la brèche, premières réflexions sur les événements* (Paris: Fayard, 1968), 71–74.

10. Michel Winock, "Années '60: la poussée des jeunes," in *Etudes sur la France de 1939 à nos jours* (Paris: Seuil, 1985), 316.

11. Ibid.

12. Poster, *Existential Marxism in Postwar France*, 385.

13. François Dosse, *Histoire du structuralisme, vol. 2: Le chant du cygne, 1967 à nos jours* (Paris: Editions de la découverte, 1992), 144–45.

14. For a detailed discussion of the influence of structuralism and Marxism on Baudrillard in his early work, see Gane, *Baudrillard's Bestiary: Baudrillard and Culture* (New York: Routledge, 1991).

15. "The Bauhaus project of total design is certainly one of the most important episodes in the evolution of simulation, which marks the passage of the sign from the dialectic of the real to the order of the sign itself." Gane, *Baudrillard Live*, 143. See also, Gary Genosko, *McLuhan and Baudrillard: The Masters of Implosion* (London: Routledge, 1999), 71.

16. Baudrillard, *Pour une critique de l'économie politique du signe* (Paris: Gallimard, 1972), 229, 239.

17. In 1967 Baudrillard wrote a skeptical review of Marshall McLuhan's *Understanding Media: The Extensions of Man*, 2d ed. (New York: Signet, 1964). He faulted the book for its idealism, but, as can be seen in the frequency with which he refers to him in his work, McLuhan has had a lasting influence on Baudrillard. The review

appeared in *L'Homme et la société*, no. 5 (July-September 1967): 227–30. For a thorough discussion of the French reception of McLuhan see Genosko, *McLuhan and Baudrillard*.

18. Baudrillard, *La société de consommation* (Paris: Gallimard, 1970), 171. Baudrillard is quoting the "technician of the art of living," André Faye.

19. Gane, *Baudrillard Live*, 74.

20. Ibid., 72.

21. "I sometimes find myself longing for the lightness of spirit we had in the sixties, when people had more zest for collective interventions and group action, even when they did it anonymously and secretly." Ibid., 189–90.

22. One might, for example, juxtapose his reflections on the "realized utopia" of 1986 in *America* to those in the *Utopie* pieces.

23. Baudrillard, "La pratique sociale de la technique," *Utopie*, nos. 2–3 (May 1969): 155.

24. Baudrillard, "Le ludique et le policier," in ibid., 15.

25. Gane, *Baudrillard Live*, 118.

26. Ibid., 115.

27. "I plunge into the negative ecstasy of radio." "Hot, sexual obscenity is followed by cool communicational obscenity." Baudrillard, *The Ecstasy of Communication*, trans. Bernard Schutze and Caroline Schutze (New York: Semiotext[e], 1988), 24, 25.

28. Richard G. Woodbridge III. "Acoustic Recordings from Antiquity," *Proceedings of the IEEE* 57.8 (August 1969): 1465–66.

29. Mark Poster, *Existential Marxism in Postwar France*, 385.

30. Baudrillard, "Le ludique et le policier," 3.

31. Ibid., 12.

32. Baudrillard, *Pour une critique de l'économie politique du signe*, 215.

33. Gane, *Baudrillard Live*, 42.

34. Marwick, *Sixties*, 466.

35. Bernard Chapuis and Ermine Herscher, *Qualités: objets d'en France* (Paris: Editions du May, 1987), 34. The year 1962 saw the first seamless hose.

36. Baudrillard, *Ecstasy of Communication*, 34.

37. Roland Barthes, *Mythologies*, 2d ed. (Paris: Seuil, 1970), 150.

38. McLuhan, *Understanding Media*, 116.

39. Quattrocchi and Nairn, *Beginning of the End*, 11.

40. Baudrillard, "Pratique social de la technique," 154.

41. Marwick, *Sixties*, 420.

42. In the television series Gidget's given name is Frances, a name her father uses only when Gidget is bad. My thanks to Toni Sol for recalling this tidbit.

43.Baudrillard, *Société de consommation*, 169.

44. Ibid., 694–95.

45. Theodor Adorno, "The Curves of the Needle," *October*, trans. Thomas Y. Levin (winter 1990): 54.

46. See Poster, *Existential Marxism in Postwar France*, 382–83; Winock, "Années 60," 316; and Marie-Claire Lavabre and Henri Rey, *Les mouvements de 1968* (Florence: Casterman-Giunti, 1998), 36.

47. Baudrillard, *Pour une critique de l'économie politique du signe*, 228.

48. Ibid., 218.

49. Baudrillard, *Ecstasy of Communication*, 22.

50. Jacques Cellard and Alain Rey, "Avant-propos," in *Dictionnaire du français nonconventionnel* (Paris: Hachette, 1980), 10.

51. Jacques Attali, *Noise: The Political Economy of Music*, trans. Brian Massumi (Minneapolis: University of Minnesota Press, 1985), 105.

52. For a detailed discussion of the filming of this interview and its critiques, see Marcel Ophuls, "Nous n'y étions pas," in *Le chagrin et la pitié* (Paris: Editions Alain Moreau, 1980), 253–59.

53. Rousso, *Vichy Syndrome*, 110.

54. That added aesthetic meaning is nowhere more apparent than in Woody Allen's *Annie Hall* (1977) in which an opening scene involves the pompous recycling of McLuhan's theories by a media studies professor, who is overheard by Alvie as he stands on line with Annie to see the *The Sorrow and the Pity*. A cameo appearance by McLuhan himself, who will tell the professor that he has failed to understand his work, asks in other ways what the documentary then becomes. For the professor, it is clearly not functioning as a representation of history; the medium itself transforms the film into an aestheticization of history.

55. The hairdresser's fabricated guilt would appear to underlie one scene in *Annie Hall* where Alvie asks Annie if she could withstand real torture. Annie replies that the documentary makes her feel guilty. Alvie slyly suggests that Annie is guilty of collaboration with consumer society; torture for her would mean the taking away of her Bloomingdale's card, he says. The hairdresser and Annie are then connected by their weaknesses or lack of heroism.

56. Baudrillard, "The Anorexic Ruins," in *Looking Back on the End of the World*, trans. David Antal (New York: Semiotext[e], 1989), 35, 38.

57. Baudrillard, *Car l'illusion ne s'oppose pas à la réalité: photographies* (Paris: Descartes et Cie, 1998), n.p.

58. Baudrillard, "*Holocauste* (suite)," *Cahiers du cinéma*, no. 302 (July-August 1979): 72. "It is too late now; we have been moved on to other things, as we have seen with *Holocaust* and even with *Shoah* on television. These phenomena were not understood at the time when we still had the means to understand them." Baudrillard, "Hunting Nazis and Losing Reality," 17.

59. Baudrillard, *Société de consommation,* 170.

60. Ibid., 169–71.

61. Adorno, "Curves of the Needle," 50.

62. Perec, *Choses,* 31.

63. Pierre Bourdieu, *Un art moyen: essai sur les usages sociaux de la photographie* (Paris: Editions de Minuit, 1965), 113–34.

64. Rey Chow, "Listening Otherwise, Music Miniaturized: A Different Type of Question about Revolution," in *The Cultural Studies Reader,* ed. Simon During (New York: Routledge, 1993), 384.

65. McLuhan, *Understanding Media,* 181.

66. The play was first written and staged in English in 1958; the French version premiered in 1960.

67. Of course, one may also read the title of this play to mean the last tape heard or made that particular evening. The title does not exclude the possibility that Krapp, though quite old, will live to see the next day. Still, whether or not his life ends that night, his recorded predicament remains the same.

68. Samuel Beckett, Krapp's Last Tape *and Other Dramatic Pieces* (New York: Grove, 1960), 12–13.

69. Friedrich Kittler, "Grammophone, Film, Typewriter," in *Literature, Media, Information Systems,* trans. Dorothea Von Mücke with Philippe L. Similon, ed. John Johnston (Amsterdam: Overseas Publishers Association/G+B Arts International, 1997), 40.

70. Attali, *Noise,* 122.

71. Poster, *Existential Marxism in Postwar France,* 377. See also, Quattrocchi and Nairn, *Beginning of the End,* 59.

72. Baudrillard, "Le ludique et le policier," 11.

73. Quattrocchi and Nairn, *Beginning of the End,* 4.

74. Ibid., 28. Quattrocchi's account contains references to radio on almost every other page. Its presence is like a Greek chorus at times echoing the cause of the revolution, at others denouncing it.

75. Ibid., 28.

76. Kittler, "Grammophone, Film, Typewriter," 44, 46.

77. Baudrillard, *Car l'illusion ne s'oppose pas à la réalité,* n.p.

6

Stephen Greenblatt's "X"-Files

*The Rhetoric of Containment and
Invasive Disease in "Invisible Bullets"
and "The Sources of Soviet Conduct"*

JONATHAN GIL HARRIS

Stephen Greenblatt's essay "Invisible Bullets"—subtitled "Renaissance Authority and its Subversion"—first appeared in print in 1981, a year after the election of Ronald Reagan. In this essay, Greenblatt offered his now famous double reading of the Elizabethan philosopher, scientist, and New World colonist Thomas Harriot's seemingly subversive encounters with Algonquian culture and Prince Hal's seemingly subversive encounters with London's underworld culture. Both instances, Greenblatt argued, demonstrate that power is not threatened by what might seem to undermine it; rather, subversion is "the very condition of power."[1] To describe this process of co-optation, which bears the unmistakable imprint of Michel Foucault's account of power, Greenblatt employed a term that was to become as influential in Renaissance literary and cultural criticism as it has been dogged by debate and controversy: "containment."

Greenblatt's theory of containment has prompted criticism from several quarters. Some of these critiques concern the utility of Greenblatt's version of Foucault: if early modern authority was so utterly resourceful in turning all subversion to account, Greenblatt's detractors have asked, how could the English Civil War—indeed, how could change of *any* kind—have ever taken place? Another related critique, powerfully voiced by cultural materialists in particular, is that Greenblatt's essay unwittingly says much more about the "entrapment" and ineffectiveness of leftist American cultural and literary critics during the Reagan years than it does about the operations of power in early modern culture.[2] This specific critique is a local instance of a more general misgiving repeatedly expressed about the new historicism. As many have noted, if new historicists insistently point to the historical specificity of early modern ideologies and practices, they have tended to avoid reflection on the historical situatedness of their own critical discourses and preoccupations. This neglect has prompted Alan Liu's counterproposal that "'acknowledgment' of the present's intervention in the past should blossom into disciplined study. We *should* see our own prejudices and concerns in such constructs as the 'Renaissance,' in other words."[3]

To argue that Greenblatt's conception of Renaissance containment is inflected by his own pessimistic response to Reaganism might seem to take up Liu's challenge. For all its attractiveness, however, such an argument seems to me to perform only a partial historicization at best, understanding the "present's intervention in the past" mostly at the level of authorial affect. In its author-centered approach, the critique is not that far removed from the idealist tendency to historicize theoretical movements simply in terms of what their leading practitioners may have read and studied. Greenblatt's allegedly despairing response to Reagan, or his demonstrably deep debt to Foucault, is thereby transformed into the "historical" ground on which his critical methodology stands. I would like instead to attempt a critique that attends less to what Greenblatt may have been feeling or reading when he wrote "Invisible Bullets," than to the historicity of his essay's rhetoric. In particular, I shall argue, its critical lexicon reproduces a rhetorical nexus prevalent during the Cold War, a nexus that links "containment" to a potent vocabulary of invasive disease.

Inasmuch as I focus on certain key documents that articulate this nexus— a U.S. State Department policy paper and the writings of functionalist sociologists and anthropologists—my critique of Greenblatt might at first glance seem to replicate the very "history of ideas" approach that I and the other contributors to this volume, *Historicizing Theory*, seek to avoid. But my point is that the nexus of containment and disease does not simply belong to the world of "ideas." By regarding rhetoric as material in both its forms and its effects, I seek a history in and through Greenblatt's essay that cannot be confined to the idealist sphere of authorial intention and influence. Jacques Derrida's dictum, that "the writer writes *in* a language and *in* a logic whose proper system, laws, and life his discourse cannot dominate absolutely," is particularly apposite here.[4] Greenblatt may or may not have read any of the documents that I examine in this essay. Nevertheless, the rhetorical configuration of which these documents are local expressions has also provided one of the discursive horizons of possibility for his critical practice and, more importantly, for policies and actions within the realm of international relations. This configuration is not politically neutral. No matter how much the argument of Greenblatt's essay may be seen as a reaction against Reaganism, its rhetoric inhabits the familiar Reaganite Cold War binaries of health and pathology, stasis and revolution, and containment and subversion.

I would also argue that to understand the history of this configuration is now of considerable and even pressing importance. As I write this, in the year after the events of September 11, 2001, the rhetorical nexus of containment and disease seems to be acquiring a new power in American political discourse. The Bush administration has vowed to "fight" and "contain" an invading "virus": terrorism. Inasmuch as the administration's promise has sought to lend legitimacy to new military adventures in the Middle East and elsewhere, the history of its rhetoric needs urgent unpacking. By attending to this history, which in my narration dates back from the Cold War to the European Renaissance, we might not only begin to see what the present can tell us about the past, as Liu has suggested. We might equally use the past to critique the present.

I

Greenblatt's use of the word "containment" certainly warrants contextualization and historicization. "Containment's" history as a term disclosing the operations of authority does not, of course, begin with the publication of his essay. In its modern political sense of "keeping a hostile nation or ideology within limits" (OED definition 11d), the term extends back to the escalation of superpower tension at the beginning of the Cold War. Its currency can be dated to 1947, when *Foreign Affairs* published an article, penned by the pseudonymous "X," called "The Sources of Soviet Conduct."[5] "X" was George F. Kennan, a high-ranking official in the State Department. His article popularized what was to become not only a linchpin of American foreign policy, but also a hegemonic rhetoric: calling for a "patient but firm and vigilant containment of Russian expansive tendencies" (87), "X" contributed to America's growing rejection of its prewar isolationism. Since then, mainstream U.S. political rhetoric has often defined the nation not only in opposition to its putative enemies (whether Soviet, Marxist, or Islamic), but also in terms of its capacity to fight, control, and eliminate them.

But to understand the history of "containment" in its political application, we must also recognize the other discursive fields in which the term participated when "X" first employed it. The powerful symbolic freight that has attached to "containment" since the Cold War can blind us to how the term has been a staple of medical vocabulary since the nineteenth century. To contain a disease is to prevent its entry into the body, or to diminish its effects once it has invaded. Here, the "limits" within which political containment attempts to consign undesirable foreign matter (at least according to the OED) possess a distinctly corporeal dimension. We can see at a glance how this dimension directly informs the Cold War rhetoric of containment. For "X," the Russians—and more generally communists—are foreign bodies of a pathogenic order, whom he characterizes as a contaminating "fluid stream." The United States, "X" argues, must contain this pathogenic matter through aggressive intervention overseas. But the task of containment also demands self-enclosure: the "good health" of Americans can be insured only by "pulling themselves together as a nation" (90). The U.S. body politic's limits, and particularly its vulnerable points of access, must be vigorously policed to minimize the risks of pathological incursion.

Indeed, the common ground between political and pathological discourses of containment was repeatedly assumed in the Cold War era, and not just in relation to communist enemies. A U.S. educational film from the 1950s, to give just one example, depicted the germs that cause tuberculosis as bayonet-wielding Japanese invaders.[6] But for all its rigid binaries distinguishing "us" from "them," Americans from foreigners, healthy victims from pathological predators, the rhetoric of pathological invasion was frequently predicated on a fear that such distinctions may not be quite so clear-cut, and were in need of reassertion. Andrew Ross has shown how Cold War fears of invasion were accompanied by a

> chorus of similar hysterical discourses that contributed to the Cold War culture of germophobia, and the many fantasmatic health concerns directly linked to the Cold War—Is Fluoridation a Communist Plot? Is your washroom breeding Bolsheviks? Cold War culture is rich with the demonology of the "alien," especially in the genre of the science fiction film, where a pansocial fear of the Other—communism, feminism, and other egalitarianisms foreign to the American social body—is reproduced through images drawn from the popular fringe of biological or genetic engineering gone wrong.[7]

As Ross makes clear, the rhetoric of germ invasion worked not only to contain the invading "alien"; it also united the nation against those pathological organisms "foreign to the American social body" that were nonetheless native to it—communism and feminism. Containment of an external threat thus shaded into, even as it concealed, containment of elements *within* the body politic.

For all its suasive force in our own moment, the notion of disease as an invasive foreign body is a comparatively recent one. So naturalized has this notion of disease become that it is easy to forget there once was a time when people's pathological fears were not figured in terms of viruses, bacteria, germs, or any other foreign body. According to the dominant pathological model of medieval and early modern medicine, disease was not an invasive organism with a determinate identity, but an internal state of imbalance. This imbalance was situated primarily in the humors, the four fluids that were believed to circulate in each body; the physician's task was to restore these to a state of equilibrium or homeostasis. Although external elements—noxious vapors, bad food, poor climate, and celestial bodies—were believed to trigger humoral disarray, disease was understood to be an endogenous or internally generated condition.

Partly as a result of recurrent epidemics of plague and the devastating emergence throughout Europe of syphilis in the sixteenth century, however, notions of disease and contagion inexplicable in terms of internal humoral balance had come to have increasing currency.[8] Speculation about the origins of epidemic disease was rife on both sides of the Atlantic in an age where contact between Native Americans and Europeans had exposed both to unfamiliar viruses (influenza, measles, and smallpox in the case of the former, possibly syphilis in the case of the latter) against which their immune systems had no defense. In "Invisible Bullets," Greenblatt examines how Harriot recorded the "ignorance" of Algonquian physicians who, unable to arrest a mysterious epidemic that swept through those native communities visited by English colonists, concluded that the disease had an unusual cause: the English "did make the people [. . .] die . . . by shooting invisible bullets into them."[9] Greenblatt, noting that this conception of disease "uncannily resembles our own," nonetheless offers what would appear to be a self-evident caveat: "but a conception of the biological basis of epidemic disease lies far, far in the future" (35).

Greenblatt is right, of course: it was only in the nineteenth century that the fledgling science of microbiology elaborated its theories of bacterial and viral infection. But Greenblatt's assessment is somewhat misleading nonetheless, inasmuch as it implicitly assumes that sixteenth-century Europeans lacked the conceptual apparatus that would have enabled them to regard the Algonquian explanation for the epidemic as anything other than "ignorant." Prior to Harriot's New World encounters, however, two continental physicians had already proposed theories of contagion remarkably close to the "invisible bullets" hypothesis. In his treatise *De Contagione et Contagiosis Morbis et Eorum Curatione* (1546/1930), Veronese physician Girolamo Fracastoro offered a detailed and novel hypothesis regarding the transmission of plague. Although he still insisted upon the humors' privileged role in maintaining or jeopardizing the health of the individual organism, he deviated from humoral orthodoxy in asserting that epidemic diseases could be spread over distances by miniscule agents of infection, which he called the *seminaria prima*, or "primary seeds," of contagion. These seeds were absorbed through the mouth, where they would seek out and adhere to the humor for which they felt a natural affinity; the humor then conveyed the *seminaria* to the heart, at which point the effects of the illness would become palpable.[10]

A similar conception of disease as an invasive entity rather than as a disruptive state was proposed at much the same time by iconoclastic Swiss physician Paracelsus. Breaking altogether with the old system of the humors, he created a new science of pathology based on cosmic chemical principles. This led him to assert that although disease manifests itself as a disturbance of any of the body's proper functions, it is not simply an internal state; it is an entity in its own right, whose origins lie outside the body in a foreign invader that he variously termed a "homunculus" or a "seed." This seed of disease was in most cases a mineral (from the earth) or gaseous element (from the stars) of the minutest corporeality. Motivated by its "inner schedule," or *archeus*, the seed would direct itself through the body's orifices or pores toward the organ to which it was related by a predestined sympathy. From the conjunction of seed and organ was engendered the disease, a parasitic complex with a life of its own.[11]

Fracastoro's and Paracelsus's notions of disease as a determinate invader may not have had a particularly significant long-term impact on scientific pathology; indeed, versions of the humoral paradigm of disease continued to hold sway in the medical establishment until the mid-seventeenth century. But Fracastoro's and Paracelsus's ideas did resonate in the popular imagination, and nowhere more so than in political writing. As I have argued elsewhere, sixteenth-century political treatises bear witness to a significant shift in understandings of the nature and cause of the body politic's diseases.[12] Whereas writers endebted to the earlier humoral paradigm were quick to attribute the causes of social illness to internal problems within the body politic (e.g., unequal distributions of wealth, and imbalances of power), late Tudor political writers, making use of Paracelsus's notion of disease in particular, increasingly attributed the origins of the body politic's diseases to foreign "pathogens" such as Catholics, Jews, witches, and even commodities imported from overseas.

The popularity of the new invasive paradigm, at least in political writing, had less to do with its scientific accuracy than with its political expediency. The humoral paradigm of disease was fraught with perils for those who wished to serve as apologists for Tudor authority, inasmuch as a pathological model that insisted on the internal origins of disease opened up the possibility that the causes of social discord and conflict were powerful institutions within the body politic, such as the monarchy, the judiciary, or the ruling classes. The attribution of social disease to foreign bodies was thus often part of a concerted attempt to displace popular perception of the causes of social illness from these powerful internal agents to exotic, easily vilified bogeymen.

At the beginning of the twenty-first century, we have inherited this rhetorical strategy of displacement, even if we are seldom aware of it. Not only have we refined and consolidated the invasive paradigm of disease in our modern theories and practices of pathology; we also use it—often unwittingly—to organize our thoughts about a variety of nonmedical phenomena, including politics, economics, and colonialism. The attribution of disease to foreign bodies inaugurated in early modern Europe has become a reflex gesture for most Westerners. "X"'s rhetoric of Soviet containment may have lost much of its signifying force in recent years, and become an old-fangled relic of the Cold War era; but hasn't its underlying invasive model of disease persisted in economists' and stockbrokers' fears in the late 1990s about the so-called "Asian contagion," or in the characterization of the terrorist attacks on the World Trade Center and the Pentagon as "lethal viruses" that "rode the flow of the world's aerial circulatory system"?[13]

These mainstream discourses of social pathology have been paralleled, and perhaps even fueled, by academic writing in the Cold War era. The attribution of a social organism's ills to foreign bodies was axiomatic in the influential functionalist movement of the social sciences, particularly in its analyses of so-called "primitive" cultures and their encounters with the "contagion" of "civilized" nations. That functionalist method enjoyed its heyday in the North American academy during the decade after the Second World War is, I believe, no coincidence. The rhetoric of functionalism and of the Cold War have much in common: a predilection for organic models of social formation; a studied blindness to conflict and contradiction produced within the social organism; and a shared conviction that the integration of the organism's component members is paramount, in a fashion that allows the interests of the powerful to be readily mystified as the interests of the "whole." This common ground testifies to the deeply conservative political agenda that functionalism often served.[14]

Just as importantly, though, this is common ground in which any historicist critique of Greenblatt's "Invisible Bullets" might take a profitable interest, to the extent that functionalist social science is demonstrably as much a part of the prehistory of the essay's critical lexicon as is the Cold War rhetoric of containment. What I want to pay special attention to here are the ways in which functionalist conceptions of deviance and social transformation were informed by a corporeal model of society derived from medical discourse and, in particular, by a presumption of the exogenous origins of disease. In a manner that problematically parallels (but cannot be simply aligned with) one of the characteristic strategies of Cold War rhetoric, this presumption led functionalists to attribute the origins of social pathology and change almost exclusively to external factors. I shall dwell on the functionalist movement in some detail, in order to explain how it not only consolidated and refined Renaissance notions of disease as a foreign invader, but also anticipated Greenblatt's rhetorical gambits in his analysis of literature and culture in "Invisible Bullets." "X," academic functionalists, and Greenblatt alike are thus all heirs to a Renaissance discourse of social pathology which, at its inception, was employed to mystify or erase the internal origins of social conflict and contradiction. In deploying this discourse, we need to be aware of the mystifications and erasures it has performed. Such awareness might encourage us to embrace other models of social, if not natural, pathology—including, perhaps, those archaic models of endogenous disease that political writers in the Renaissance discarded.

II

From Auguste Comte and Herbert Spencer in the nineteenth century to Bronislaw Malinowski and Talcott Parsons in the mid-twentieth, social scientists repeatedly resorted to biological models of society, in large part to legitimize their work as "scientific," but also to explain the ways in which the various components of a social "organism" function to maintain its integrity. "The physiologist studies the functions of the average organism," Emile Durkheim observed; "the same is true of the sociologist."[15] Refinements in social science long kept step with paradigm shifts in medicine and biology: more than a century after Comte asserted "a true correspondence between Statistical analysis of the Social Organism in Sociology, and that of the individual Organism in Biology,"[16] Parsons drew on contemporary developments in genetic science to compare the function of genes to that of "units of cultural inheritance," align the relationship between cell nucleus and cytoplasm with that between cultural institutions and their subsystems, and characterize the family both as the body politic's "germ plasm" and the "primary organism for the transmission of the fundamentals of the pattern of culture."[17]

Possibly the most comprehensive and self-conscious theorization of the organic analogy was undertaken by English anthropologist A. R. Radcliffe-Brown. In his essay, "On the Concept of Function in Social Science," Radcliffe-Brown explains how "the concept of function applied to human societies [which for him invariably meant primitive societies] is based on an analogy between social life and organic life." He asserts that "the life of an organism is conceived as the *functioning* of its structure. It is through and by the continuity of the functioning that the continuity of structure is preserved." His definition of "function" almost ineluctably commits him to a highly static conception of the social organism: "the function of any recurrent activity," he says, "such as the punishment of a crime, or a funeral ceremony, is the part it plays in the social life as a whole and therefore the contribution it makes to the maintenance of the structural continuity." As this assertion demonstrates, Radcliffe-Brown assumes that any social institution or activity can be understood only in terms of its "maintenance" of order; he finds it virtually impossible to conceive of any "recurrent activity" that may be disruptive or dysfunctional.[18]

Not surprisingly, the fetishization of social integration and cohesion that is the hallmark of functionalist organicism has prompted widespread criticism from many quarters of the social sciences. Pierre Bourdieu, for example, questions the tendency of functionalist anthropology "to credit historical systems with more coherence than they have or need to have in order to function. In reality, these systems remain . . . 'things of shreds and patches.'"[19] Clifford Geertz supplements Bourdieu's quibble over the functionalist emphasis on social integration with an even more telling criticism: "where the functional approach has been least impressive," he argues, "is in dealing with social change . . . the emphasis on systems in balance, on social homeostasis, and on timeless structural pictures, leads to a bias in favor of 'well-integrated' societies in a stable equilibrium."[20] Victor Turner makes a similar criticism: "the functionalists of my period in Africa tended to think of change as 'cyclical' and 'repetitive' and of time as structural time, not free time." He adds that he did not find it helpful "to think about change as *immanent* in the structure of Ndembu society, when there was clearly a 'wind of change,' economic, political, social, religious, legal, and so on, sweeping through the whole of central Africa and originating *outside* all village societies."[21]

Turner rightly registers here the inability of functionalist methodology to explain anything other than cyclic change. Nevertheless, his critique is itself problematic. At the same time as he displaces questions of social transformation from the synchronic to the diachronic, from consideration of cyclic change to the economic and political origins of more radical cultural upheaval, he is nonetheless inclined to view social transformation as originating in factors external to the social organism rather than as a consequence of developments, conflicts, or contradictions within its systems of organization. In fairness, he is speaking about the colonial process, where the drastic transformation of "primitive" societies has for the most part been prompted by agencies extrinsic to them. But it is precisely cultural anthropology's imbricatedness within one of the master-narratives of European colonialism—that is, the fantasy of a perfectly integrated, timeless, prelapsarian society transformed (and transformable) only by the contaminating apparition of the powerful white colonist—that has contributed to its functionalist practitioners' characteristic difficulty in conceiving of change arising from factors within a society.

For example, although Radcliffe-Brown does attempt to theorize social dysfunction—"to return to the analogy of social life and organic life, we recognize that an organism may function more or less efficiently and so we set up a special science of pathology to deal with all phenomena of disfunction"—it is significant that he conceives of social disease, and change, as emerging from external rather than internal factors:

while an organism that is attacked by virulent disease will react thereto, and, if its reaction fails, will die, a society that is thrown into a condition of functional disunity or inconsistency (for this we now provisionally identify with dysnomia) will not die, except in such comparatively rare instances as an Australian tribe overwhelmed by the white man's destructive force, but will continue to struggle toward some sort of eunomia, some kind of social health, and may, in the course of this, change its structural type. This process, it seems, the "functionalist" has ample opportunities of observing at the present day, in native peoples subjected to the domination of the civilized nations.[22]

As with Turner's account of change in Ndembu culture, in other words, Radcliffe-Brown's social pathology emerges from a problematic positing of the devastating encounter between "civilized" and "primitive" societies as paradigmatic of cultural transformation in general.

It would be inaccurate, however, to claim that functionalists have been entirely neglectful of the possibility of disease emerging from factors *within* the social organism. Nonetheless, as Jean-François Lyotard observes in *The Postmodern Condition* (1984), functionalist sociologists from the postwar period have tended to regard even the most obviously endogenous social "ills" (e.g., unemployment or political upheaval) as mere "internal readjustments" of the organic whole that serve simply to augment the system's "viability."[23] Such recuperations of social disease owe a considerable methodological debt to Durkheim's study of deviance. More than any other subsequent functionalist, Durkheim attempted to lay the basis for a scientific social pathology in his *Rules of Sociological Method* (1895). His chapter on "Rules for the Distinction of the Normal from the Pathological" starts with a conventional analogy between social well-being and bodily health familiar to readers of Plato's *Republic:* "for societies, as for individuals, health is good and desirable; sickness, on the other hand, is bad and must be avoided."[24] In what amounts to an ingenious reversal, however, Durkheim asserts that "pathological" behavior need not be injurious. On the contrary: social illness, he argues,

cannot fail to entail a special consequence esteemed to be harmful to society, and on these grounds it will be declared pathological. But, granted that it does bring about this consequence, it can happen that its deleterious effects are compensated, even over-compensated, by advantages that are not perceived. Moreover, only one reason will justify our deeming it to be socially injurious: it must disturb the normal operation of the social functions. (90)

In other words, Durkheim's project is to demonstrate a paradoxical proposition: how seemingly pathological behavior can contribute to rather than disrupt "the normal operation of the social functions."

This ultrafunctionalist organicist perspective—that even anti-social elements can be recuperated for the good of the "social organism"—shapes

Durkheim's account of the role played within the body politic by criminal behavior. Crime, he concedes, is "a fact whose pathological nature seems indisputable" (97). Nonetheless, in an about-turn that he admits "is apparently somewhat paradoxical," he boldly asserts that crime "is a factor in public health, an integrative element in any healthy society." Most importantly, Durkheim claims, crime helps clarify and ratify the boundaries and "collective values" of the social organism. He also insists—a little contentiously—that crime is a universal, and hence "normal," social activity:

> there is no phenomenon which represents more incontrovertibly all the symptoms of normality, since it appears to be closely bound up with the conditions of all collective life. To make crime a social illness would be to concede that sickness is not something accidental, but on the contrary derives in certain cases from the fundamental constitution of the living creature. (98)

With this assessment, Durkheim hints at, if only to repudiate, a radical social pathology. Many early modern political writers endebted to the humoral paradigm of disease willingly make the concession that Durkheim refuses here, and assert that the body politic's illnesses are indeed potentially produced by contradictions or imbalances in its "fundamental constitution."

However, Durkheim rejects this explanation of the origins of social illness for two primary reasons. First, he subscribes to the functionalist premise that every "fundamental" component or product of the body is "normal," and therefore must contribute in some way to its health. Second, he endorses the exogenous explanation of illness formulated by Paracelsus and Fracastoro, consolidated by nineteenth-century "germ" theory microbiologists such as Louis Pasteur, and replicated by anthropologists like Radcliffe-Brown—namely, that disease originates not in the "fundamental constitution" of the body, but in an external, invading pathogen to which the body has been "accidentally" exposed.[25] Both of these positions implicitly inform Durkheim's conclusion that "contrary to current ideas, the criminal no longer appears as an utterly unsociable creature, a sort of parasitic element, a foreign, unassimilable body introduced into the bosom of society" (102). Durkheim figures the criminal as an invading, "foreign" pathogen, but he does so precisely so that he can disqualify the suggestion; because the criminal is not foreign to the body but is produced by and in it, his or her presence cannot be regarded as invasive and hence pathological.

III

What is remarkable is just how closely Durkheim's account of deviance, and the invasive paradigm of disease that informs it, anticipates Greenblatt's theory of containment in "Invisible Bullets." Greenblatt offers a compelling exposé of power in early modern England and what he characterizes as its delusive subversive effects. Evaluating the alleged atheism of Harriot, Greenblatt is reluctant to assign atheism in general any positivist identity within the Tudor body politic; "atheism," he maintains, "was almost always thinkable only as the thought of another" (22). Instead, he focuses on the functional utility of atheism accusations in consolidating authority. "The pervasiveness and frequency of these charges," Greenblatt argues, "does not signal the existence of a secret society of free thinkers, a School of the Night, but rather registers the operation of a religious authority, whether Catholic or Protestant, that confirms its power by disclosing the threat of atheism." And he concludes this portion of his argument with the now infamous line, redolent not only of Voltaire but also of McCarthyist Cold War rhetoric: "If the atheist did not exist, he would have to be invented" (23).

The specific case of the atheist is but one instance of what Greenblatt regards as a larger pattern of Tudor authority's self-legitimation through the production of subversion—a pattern evident not only in Hal's flirtation with *Henry IV*'s underworld of thieves and masterless men, but also in Harriot's encounters with Algonquian Indians in the Virginia colony. Discussing Harriot's "subversive inquiries" about Algonquian beliefs in his *Briefe and True Report of the New Found Land of Virginia* (1587/1972), Greenblatt offers a thoroughly functionalist explanation of Tudor power and its "subversion":

> But why, we must ask ourselves, should power record other voices, permit subversive inquiries, register at its very center the transgressions that will ultimately violate it? The answer may be in part that power, even in a colonial situation, is not monolithic and hence may encounter and record in one of its functions materials that can threaten another of its functions; in part that power thrives on vigilance, and human beings are vigilant if they sense a threat; in part that power defines itself in relation to such threats or simply to that which is not identical with it. Harriot's text suggests an intensification of these observations: English power in the first Virginia colony *depends* upon the registering and even the production of potentially unsettling perspectives. (37)

Greenblatt's analysis of the effects and functions of "subversive inquiry" involves a revealing movement from an antagonistic model of society, in which subversion is disruptive of a nonmonolithic authority, to a functionalist model, in which "transgressions," "threats," and "unsettling perspectives" are somehow integral to the maintenance of a homeostatic social organism—or its Foucauldian near-synonym, "power."[26]

For Greenblatt, the most complex instance in Harriot's treatise of how the "apparent production of subversion is . . . the very condition of power" (65) is its author's recourse to what Greenblatt terms "Machiavellian anthropology." The Machiavellian hypothesis that religion originated "in an imposition of socially coercive doctrines by an educated and sophisticated lawgiver on a simple people" (27) was, at least for Elizabethan political and religious authority, radically subversive. But, Greenblatt maintains, Harriot succeeded in testing and confirming the hypothesis by performing precisely this sort of imposition on the Algonquian Indians. The latter, impressed but bewildered by the European colonists' array of technological gadgets and accomplishments, thought—or so Harriot supposed—that these "were rather the works of gods then of men, or at the leastwise they had been given and taught us of the gods."[27] Consequently, according to Harriot, the native priests experienced a crisis of belief, and began to suspect that the Europeans were the custodians of genuine religion with privileged access to the "true" (or more accurately, most powerful) God. Harriot thus placed himself in a position, Greenblatt claims, to "disclose the power of human achievements—reading, writing, perspective glasses, gunpowder, and the like—to appear to the ignorant as divine and hence to promote belief and compel obedience" (30). Greenblatt's conclusion is as mischievous as it is brilliant: the very same subversive "Machiavellian anthropology" that could provoke accusations of atheism (and, subsequently, lead to torture, imprisonment, and execution) was deployed by Harriot as a means of consolidating rather than questioning Elizabethan religious and political authority.

Nonetheless, the "Machiavellian anthropology" that Greenblatt claims to recognize in Harriot allows him to cloak his own indebtedness to modern *functionalist* anthropology. After all, his claim that "the *Discourses* treats religion as if its primary function were not salvation but the achievement of civic discipline, as if its primary justification were not truth but expediency" (24) is just as much a gloss on Durkheim's *Elements of Religious Life* as it is a synopsis of Niccolò Machiavelli. As Greenblatt revealingly lets slip in his explanation of the subversive "Machiavellian" hypothesis, "a strictly functionalist explanation even of false religions was rejected by Christian theologians of the period" (34). With such claims, we can begin to glimpse the complex relay of ventriloquism that Greenblatt's essay performs. Harriot's "patriotic" voice, Greenblatt invites us to realize, daringly discloses itself to be Machiavelli's; but Greenblatt conceals from the reader how, on occasion, the very "voice" he attributes to Machiavelli also originates elsewhere—not in the political discourses of sixteenth-century Italy, however, but in a twentieth-century functionalist lexicon. As Greenblatt himself remarks: "the *social function* of popular belief is underscored in Harriot's note to an illustration showing the priest carefully tending the embalmed bodies of the former chiefs. . . . We have then, as in Machiavelli, a sense of religion as a set of beliefs manipulated by the subtlety of priests to help instill obedience and respect for authority" (26, my emphasis). Here, Greenblatt in effect invokes Durkheim's *Elements of Religious Life,* in which it is claimed that religion's "social function" is to instill order, in such a way as to validate Durkheim's *Rules of Sociological Method* (1982), in which anti-social transgressions are understood to consolidate rather than disrupt the functions of the social organism.[28]

Greenblatt's decidedly Durkheimian conception of Tudor subversion's origins and effects can be deciphered in the very title of his essay. At one level, "Invisible Bullets" suggests a danger erased, a pathology depathologized, and a transgression contained. It is not so much that Harriot's apparently subversive, "Machiavellian" inquiries are ideological "bullets" that turn out to be blanks, or at least too small (or "invisible") to have any genuinely disruptive effect. More specifically, the "bullets" are themselves products of power, and the means by which power maintains itself.

Nonetheless, Greenblatt also asserts that Elizabethan culture was characterized by a "relation between orthodoxy and subversion [that] seems, in the same interpretive moment, to be both perfectly stable *and dangerously volatile*" (35). This alternative "volatile" relation can also be witnessed in a second meaning of Greenblatt's title. As I have noted, Greenblatt takes the phrase "invisible bullets" from a passage in which Harriot records, and implicitly discredits, the Algonquian theory of the origins of the epidemic disease that swept through the Indian villages visited by the Europeans. The irony, of course, is that these "invisible bullets" *do* have the power to harm or transform an organism, at least from the vantage point of modern microbiology. We all know the lethal effects of the viruses brought over to the Americas by the New World explorers and colonists, and Greenblatt's essay trades on that knowledge. In other words, the seemingly recuperated transgression initially suggested by Greenblatt's title presumes a genuinely disruptive, pathological potential.

It is precisely because of this potential that "Invisible Bullets" concerns itself with not only Tudor power and its maintenance, but also the nature and origin of cultural disruption and transformation. The changes that Greenblatt examines, however, are confined exclusively to Algonquian culture in the aftermath of its encounter with the English colonists. In addition to the catastrophic social tumult produced by the outbreak of epidemic diseases, Harriot's testing of the "Machiavellian" hypothesis about religion also produces substantial transformations among the Algonquian priests: the "testing . . . could only happen once, for it entails not detached observation but radical change, the change Harriot begins to observe in the priests." Harriot and his fellow colonists, Greenblatt implies, were equipped with ideological as well as microbiological "invisible bullets," both capable of effecting "radical change."

In Greenblatt's analysis of early modern power and cultural transformation, we may recognize two of the characteristic features of functionalist organicism. First and more obviously, as I have already noted, Harriot's deviance is contained—as it is in the sociology of Durkheim and Parsons—by being shown to contribute to the health of the "social organism," or in this case, the maintenance of "power." More subtly, but just as importantly, Greenblatt borrows from the Algonquians via Harriot an exogenous explanation of disease ("invisible bullets") as a figure for the origin of "radical change." By employing this figure, he not only echoes the organicism of social scientists from Comte to Parsons; he also follows functionalist anthropologists in positing the encounter between "civilized" and "primitive" cultures as paradigmatic of social upheaval and transformation. For Greenblatt as for Radcliffe-Brown—and indeed, as for "X"—European culture infects, literally and metaphorically, that of the New World: social change is a contagion contracted from an external, invading foreign body.

Nevertheless, the extent to which social "illness," subversion, and transformation may afflict either culture—Old or New—as a consequence of factors or agents *within* its structural organization remains undisclosed. One might ask, for example, In what ways did shifts within the institutions of education, religion, and the state in the years following Henry VIII's abolition of the monastic orders help make possible the subversive "Machiavellian anthropology" of Harriot? What domestic social fractures, conflicts, and upheavals may have lent impetus to the Elizabethan vogue for recording the beliefs and practices of foreign peoples, in opposition to which a normative, homeostatic "English" culture might be produced? How was the colonial experiment in Virginia implicated within rapidly changing modes of production and consumption in an England distinguished by a growing mercantile class, newly and increasingly hungry for imported luxury commodities? (Harriot's account of Virginia returns repeatedly to native goods, including luxury foods and medicines, for which there was high consumer demand in London.[29]) Or, for that matter, how may the "radical changes" that Harriot witnessed in the Algonquian priests have been prompted just as much by social tensions and factional conflicts within their communities as by their encounters with the English colonists?

Such questions remain unposed by Greenblatt, for whom the contagion of social illness and change originates in a foreign body. We should be careful when making any critique of Greenblatt's use of the "invisible bullets" paradigm not to finesse or erase the enormity of the disruptions—cultural, ecological, and microbiological—unleashed by the European conquerors and colonists in the New World, which he records in sensitive detail. But we should think also of the costs of using the "invisible bullets" paradigm to explain all social change. Does it not work to deprive the Algonquians of any agency in the transformation of their society? And in the process, might not the attribution of social change to foreign contagions itself be a potential mode of containment, working to conceal internally generated conflicts, disfunctions, and transformations?

IV

Consider the following remark that concludes "X"'s article:

> The thoughtful observer of Russian-American relations will find no cause for complaint in the Kremlin's challenge to American society. He will rather experience a certain gratitude to a Providence which, by providing the American people with this implacable challenge, has made their entire security as a nation dependent on their pulling themselves together and accepting the responsibilities of moral and political leadership that history plainly intended them to bear. (90)

If one were to substitute "Spanish" for Russian, "English" for American, and "Armada" for Kremlin in the extract I have just quoted, one would be left with a passage that, in many respects, could have been written in the late 1580s. "X"'s conclusion serves to situate Cold War-era containment within an illuminating rhetorical configuration that might sound very familiar to a critic of early modern literature or culture—the confident appeal to providence, the quasi-functionalist veneration if not of the enemy themselves, then of the "challenge" they present, and, perhaps most interestingly, the domestic agenda implicit in that challenge, recuperated as that which will "pull the nation together." This last phrase suggests a second, implicit gesture of containment that is just as important as the first. This second containment serves to enclose within the encircling unity of vigilant nationhood a country which, riven by internal differences, needs to be "pulled together." Fingering a foreign contagion is for "X" a convenient way of diverting attention from, and "treating," local pathologies.

"X"'s discourse of social pathology mirrors a dual process repeatedly enacted also in Tudor and Stuart political writing. Demands for the containment of an allegedly disease-bearing foreign body often entailed a second-order, yet largely disacknowledged, containment of the body politic's domestic pathologies. I do not have the space here to illustrate in any sustained detail this dual process of early modern containment. However, one example will allow me to offer a preliminary sketch. I have chosen it because it is an integral component of Shakespeare's second Henriad, the sequence that also provides Greenblatt with his literary exemplum of containment.[30] For Greenblatt, Hal's dalliances with prostitutes, drunkards, and thieves, together with his effortless acquisition of underworld slang, are comparable to Harriot's "Machiavellian" recording and testing of Algonquian culture; both men's seemingly subversive encounters with otherness serve to consolidate rather than disrupt the apparatus of English power. However, there is another, larger pattern of subversion and containment shadowed within the Hal plays, one that in certain crucial respects more closely matches both Greenblatt's account of the interplay between English and New World culture, as well as the exogenous model of disease recorded in Harriot's *Brief and True Report of the New Found Land of Virginia.*

The second part of *Henry IV* repeatedly invokes metaphors of disease to present an initial image of a body politic afflicted by the selfish actions of the ruling members: Bolingbroke's usurpation of Richard II, the factional clashes of the aristocracy, and Hal's dissolute lifestyle are all singled out as causes of England's illnesses, upsetting the nation's delicate internal balance.[31] The discourses of social pathology employed in this play are loosely modeled, then, on the humoral paradigm of disease. But the play's resolution offers a blatant disclosure of the mechanisms of displacement that allow threats to the body politic's health to be perceived as emerging from external rather than internal causes. After he has triumphed over his aristocratic adversaries, the dying Bolingbroke tells Hal that a foreign enemy must be found to erase the memory if not the existence of domestic problems: "Be it thy course to busy giddy minds / With foreign quarrels, that action hence borne out / May waste the memory of the former days" (4.5.213–15). This politic counsel, of course, provides Hal in *Henry V* with the unspoken pretext for going to war against France at the head of an army shot through with conflict and dissension between not only its different ethnic groups and social classes, but the members of its ruling fraction as well. The fight against a common enemy achieves not simply the ideological effect of national unity, however; with Hal's accusation against the French at Harfleur that "you yourselves are cause" of the "filthy and contagious clouds / Of heady murder, spoil and villainy" (3.3.19, 31–32), he displaces the origins of disease from inside to outside the English body politic.[32]

In early modern English as in Cold War-era U.S. writing, therefore, containment does not necessarily entail a confident, monolithic power turning all subversion to account, as Greenblatt's model has often been criticized as implying. More often than not, the production and containment of an external, pathogenic threat involves an anxious negotiation—and repudiation—of genuinely disruptive problems within the body politic, as a result of which the locus of social conflict and change is symbolically (if not actually) displaced from inside the body to its boundaries and vulnerable apertures. Shakespeare's, Greenblatt's, and "X"'s narratives of containment disclose, albeit in very different ways, the extent to which encounters with foreign disease can work to efface the internally generated pathologies of a social formation.

This is not to suggest that strategies of containment in early modern England and the modern United States are identical. But it is to acknowledge that we are in a position to recover certain aspects of early modern culture from the vantage point of our own in a fashion that can illuminate both. It is to acknowledge also that Greenblatt's theory of containment might have much more in common with the paradigms and lexicons of early modern pathology—both medical and social—than just the phrase "invisible bullets." Most of all, it is to subject to historical scrutiny the long-standing rhetorical configuration that works to attribute the origins of social pathology and change to exclusively external factors. The title of my essay, "Greenblatt's 'X'-Files,'" is intended to hint at the logic of this rhetoric. Both Greenblatt's and "X"'s explanations of the causes of social pathology anticipate the slogan of the popular television program, *The X-Files: The Truth Is Out There*. As we attempt to understand strategies of containment in the past and in the present, however, we may find that the Truth Isn't Always *Out There*. Sometimes it's far closer to home.

NOTES

I have learned much more about some of the subject material in this essay than I will ever be able to communicate from my little sister, Naomi Harris Narev, who sadly did not live to see this in print. Her strength, courage, and imagination put mine to shame. It is with great love and pride that I dedicate this essay to her.

Parts of this essay have been previously published elsewhere, though in rather different forms, in *Foreign Bodies and the Body Politic: Discourses of Social Pathology in Early Modern England* (Cambridge: Cambridge University Press, 1998), chapters 1 and 2; and "Historicizing Greenblatt's Containment: The Cold War, Functionalism, and the Origins of Social Pathology," in *Critical Self-Fashioning: Stephen Greenblatt and the New Historicism*, ed. Jürgen Pieters (New York and Frankfurt: Peter Lang, 1999), 150–73. I thank auditors at the University of Kansas for helping me think through my argument in this version.

1. Greenblatt, *Shakespearean Negotiations: The Circulation of Social Energy* (Oxford: Clarendon Press, 1989), 65. There are four versions of Greenblatt's essay: "Invisible Bullets: Renaissance Authority and its Subversion," in *Glyph 8: Johns Hopkins Textual Studies* (Baltimore: Johns Hopkins University Press, 1981), 40–61; "Invisible Bullets: Renaissance Authority and its Subversion, *Henry IV* and *Henry V*," in *Political Shakespeare: New Essays in Cultural Materialism*, eds. Jonathan Dollimore and Alan Sinfield (Manchester: Manchester University Press, 1985), 18–47; "Invisible Bullets: Renaissance Authority and its Subversion," in *Shakespeare's 'Rough Magic': Renaissance Essays in Honor of C. L. Barber*, eds. Peter Erickson and Coppélia Kahn (Newark: University of Delaware Press, 1985), 276–302; and *Shakespearean Negotiations*, chapter 1.

2. See Alan Sinfield, *Faultlines: The Politics of Dissident Reading* (Berkeley: University of California Press, 1992), 289. See also, Frank Lentricchia, "Foucault's Legacy: A New Historicism?" in *The New Historicism*, ed. H. Aram Veeser (New York: Routledge, 1989), 231–42; and, most recently, John Brannigan, *New Historicism and Cultural Materialism* (New York: St. Martin's, 1998), 78.

3. Alan Liu, "The Power of Formalism: The New Historicism," *ELH* 56 (1989): 721–72, esp. 753.

4. Jacques Derrida, *Of Grammatology,* trans. Gayatri Chakravorty Spivak (Baltimore: Johns Hopkins University Press, 1976), 158.

5. "X" [George F. Kennan], "The Sources of Soviet Conduct," in *Containment: Documents on American Policy and Strategy, 1945–1950,* eds. Thomas H. Etzhold and John Lewis Gaddis (New York: Columbia University Press, 1978), 77–90.

6. Lisa Cartwright, *Screening the Body: Tracing Medicine's Visual Culture* (Minneapolis: University of Minnesota Press, 1995), 152–53.

7. Andrew Ross, *No Respect: Intellectuals and Popular Culture* (New York: Routledge, 1989), 45. For a reading of Cold War-era germophobia that includes analysis of "X"'s article, see Jonathan Paul Eburne, "Trafficking in the Void: Burroughs, Kerouac, and the Consumption of Otherness," *Modern Fiction Studies* 43 (1997): 53–92, esp. 60–63.

8. For a more extensive discussion of the contest between humoral and new paradigms of disease, see Jonathan Gil Harris, *Foreign Bodies and the Body Politic: Discourses of Social Pathology in Early Modern England* (Cambridge: Cambridge University Press, 1998), chapter 2.

9. Thomas Harriot, A *Briefe and True Report of the New Found Land of Virginia* (1587; reprint, New York: Dover Publications, 1972), 29.

10. See Girolamo Fracastoro, *De Contagione at Contagiosis Morbis et Eorum Curatione,* transl. Wilmer Care Wright (1546; reprint, New York: Putnam, 1930), 34–35. For an illuminating overview of Fracastoro's theory of disease within the history of pathological medicine, see Vivian Nutton, "The Seeds of Disease: An Explanation of Contagion and Infection from the Greeks to the Renaissance," *Medical History* 27 (1983): 1–34.

11. For Paracelsus's account of the *seminaria* of disease, see "Von Blatern, Lähmi, Beulen, Löchern und Zitrachen der Franzosen und irs Gleichen," in Paracelsus, *Sämtliche Werke,* ed. Karl Sudhoff (München, Germany, R. Oldenbourg: 1922), 14 vols, vol. 6, esp. liber II, cap. 10. The most thorough analysis of Paracelsus's theory of pathology is Walter Pagel's *Paracelsus: An Introduction to Philosophical Medicine in the Era of the Renaissance* (Basel, Switzerland: S. Karger, 1958), esp. 134–40.

12. See Harris, *Foreign Bodies and the Body Politic,* chapters 2 and 3.

13. Hendrik Hertzberg, "Comment: Tuesday, and After," *New Yorker,* 24 September 2001, 27. I discuss the rhetoric of invasive disease underwriting the "Asian Contagion" crisis in "'The Canker of England's Commonwealth': Gerard de Malynes and the Origins of Economic Pathology," *Textual Practice* 13.2 (1999): 311–28.

14. For a critique of functionalism's political conservatism, see Jonathan H. Turner and Alexandra Maryanski, *Functionalism* (San Francisco: Benjamin/Cummings, 1979), 113–17; for a specific critique of functionalism's conservatism in the context of postwar politics, see also, Ralf Dahrendorf, *Class and Class Conflict in Industrial Society* (Stanford, CA: Stanford University Press, 1959), esp. 241–48.

15. Emile Durkheim, *Rules of Sociological Method,* trans. W. D. Halls (New York, Macmillan, 1982 [1895]), 92. Durkheim speaks repeatedly of the "social organism"

throughout his study; see esp. chapter 3. For an important critique of Durkheim's functionalist organicism, see Jürgen Habermas, *The Theory of Communicative Action, vol. 2: Lifeworld and System: A Critique of Functionalist Reason,* trans. Thomas McCarthy (Boston: Beacon, 1987), esp 112–15.

16. Auguste Comte, *System of Positive Polity,* vol. 2 (New York: Burt Franklin, 1875), 239–40. For a useful discussion of how Comte's organicism influenced subsequent functionalist paradigms, see Turner and Maryanski, *Functionalism,* chapter 1.

17. Talcott Parsons, "A Note on Some Biological Analogies," in *Family, Socialization and Interaction Process,* eds. Parsons et al. (Glencoe, IL: Free Press, 1955), 396–99.

18. A. R. Radcliffe-Brown, "On the Concept of Function in Social Science," in *Functionalist Sociology,* ed. Paul Colomy (Aldershot, England: Edward Elgar, 1990), 30, 31, 32.

19. Pierre Bourdieu, *Outline of a Theory of Practice,* trans. Richard Nice (Cambridge: Cambridge University Press, 1977), 218 n. 7.

20. Clifford Geertz, *The Interpretation of Cultures* (London: Hutchinson, 1975), 407–8.

21. Victor Turner, *Drama, Fields, and Metaphors: Symbolic Action in Human Society* (Ithaca: Cornell University Press, 1974), 31–32.

22. Radcliffe-Brown, "On the Concept of Function in Social Science," 33, 34.

23. Jean-François Lyotard, *The Postmodern Condition: A Report on Knowledge,* trans. Geoff Bennington and Brian Massumi (Minneapolis: University of Minnesota Press, 1984), 11–12. See also, for example, Robert K. Merton, *Social Theory and Structure* (New York: Free Press, 1949), in which the author devotes attention to dysfunction while typically concentrating on the positive, integrative functions of social and cultural formations. For other critiques of such functionalist recuperations of dysfunction and deviance, see Gareth Stedman Jones, *Languages of Class: Studies in English Working Class History, 1832–1982* (Cambridge: Cambridge University Press, 1983), chapter 2; and Steven Lukes, *Power: A Radical View* (London: Macmillan, 1974), 27–28.

24. Durkheim, *Rules of Sociological Method,* 86. Plato resorts to a pathological vocabulary to represent the causes of social "illness" in *The Republic,* Book 9, section 6, 556e (see Plato, *The Republic,* trans. Desmond Lee [Harmondsworth, Middlesex: Penguin, 1987], 375).

25. For a discussion of theories of the origins of disease in nineteenth-century pathology, see Georges Canguilhem, *The Normal and the Pathological,* trans. Carolyn R. Fawcett and Robert S. Cohen (New York: Zone Books, 1991), chapter 1. Significantly, though, Durkheim did not always view pathological states as being produced by external factors; in *The Division of Labour in Society,* trans. W. D. Halls (London: Macmillan, 1984 [1893]), 360, he maintained that the "solidarity" generated by the division of labor in economically complex societies is insufficient, and hence leads to pathological states such as "anomie" (alienation).

26. A number of critics have remarked on the functionalist tendencies of Foucault's conception of power. Gilles Deleuze speaks of "this new functionalism" in *Fou-*

cault, ed. and trans. Sean Hand (Minneapolis: Minnesota University Press, 1988), 25; see also Gareth Stedman-Jones's important study, *Languages of Class*, 16. Fred Dallmayr has noted the similarities between Foucault's and Talcott Parsons's conceptions of power in *Polis and Praxis: Exercises in Contemporary Political Theory* (Cambridge: Massachusetts Institute of Technology Press, 1984), 85.

27. Harriot, *Briefe and True Report of the New Found Land of Virginia*, 27.

28. See Emile Durkheim, *Elementary Forms of Religious Life*, trans. Carol Cosman (Oxford: Oxford University Press, 2001 [1912]). Tom McAlindon disputes the accuracy of Greenblatt's summary of Niccolò Machiavelli in "Testing the New Historicism: 'Invisible Bullets' Reconsidered," *Studies in Philology* 92 (1995): 411–38, esp. 413–19.

29. See Harriot, *Briefe and True Report of the New Found Land of Virginia*, chapters 1–2.

30. In the wake of "Invisible Bullets," new historicists have repeatedly returned to *Henry V* and Hal in order to furnish exemplary instances of the subversion/containment model. See Leonard Tennenhouse, *Power on Display: The Politics of Shakespeare's Genres* (London: Methuen, 1986), 68–70; Steven Mullaney, *The Place of the Stage: License, Play, and Power in Renaissance England* (Chicago: University of Chicago Press, 1988), chapter 3; and Richard Helgerson, *Forms of Nationhood: The Elizabethan Writing of England* (Berkeley: University of California Press, 1992), chapter 5.

31. *Riverside Shakespeare*, ed. G. Blakemore Evans et al. (Boston: Houghton, 1974). See, for example, 3.1.38–43, 4.1.54–66, 4.5.62–66.

32. For a useful discussion of *Henry V*'s ideological project and its engagement with England's internal contradictions and conflicts (which it seeks unsuccessfully to efface), see Jonathan Dollimore and Alan Sinfield, "History and Ideology, Masculinity and Miscegenation: The Instance of *Henry V*," in Sinfield, *Faultlines*, 109–42. See also Graham Holderness, "'What Is My Nation': Shakespeare and National Identities," *Textual Practice* 5 (1991): 74–93.

7

New Historicizing the New Historicism; or, Did Stephen Greenblatt Watch the Evening News in Early 1968?

IVO KAMPS

> The journalists reorder the actuality of Vietnam into . . . isolated hard-news incidents for the benefit of their editors. The editors say that that's what the public wants, and, to a great extent, the editors are right about that. The public does indeed want and need hard news, something amid the chaos, something you can reach out to over the morning coffee and almost *touch*. . . .
> —Michael J. Arlen, *The Living Room War* (my emphasis)

> We wanted the *touch* of the real in a way that in an earlier period people wanted the touch of the transcendent.
> —Catherine Gallagher and Stephen Greenblatt,
> *Practicing New Historicism* (my emphasis)

"I WAS MORE PERSUADED BY THE TUBE. . . ."

On 1 February 1968, in the early hours of the North Vietnamese Tet Offensive, somewhere on the streets of Saigon, Brig. Gen. Nguyen Loan, chief of the South Vietnamese National Police, raised his right arm to within inches of the head of a man dressed in dark shorts and a checked shirt, and fired a single bullet. The man grimaced and then slumped to the pavement with a jet of blood splashing from a hole in the side of his head. In the chaos of Tet, this man was not the only suspected Vietcong (VC) sympathizer to be disposed of in this gruesome manner, without a trial or even as much as a hearing. What made this now infamous execution different was that it was caught on film by an NBC cameraman and broadcast the next day on the evening news into the living rooms of millions of Americans.[1]

For the Johnson administration, the broadcast of the execution came at a highly inopportune time, just as the administration was launching an intense public relations campaign to convince the press and the American people that the Vietcong's massive invasion of the South was really an act of desperation rather than a sign of its military strength. Following the onset of Tet, the White House had urged the commander of the U.S. forces in Vietnam, Gen. William C. Westmoreland, to explain to reporters that the Vietcong's military infiltration of Saigon and the U.S. Embassy itself were not significant militarily. Westmoreland met with reporters on the grounds of the newly liberated U.S. Embassy; the press dutifully filmed and recorded the general's statements of assurance. Westmoreland's words of assurance were reported on the front page of *The Washington Post* and the *New York Times* the next day, but they were completely overshadowed by sensational coverage of the execution of the suspected VC sympathizer by Loan.[2] On the same day, President Johnson met with ten reporters to do some more "convincin,'" and expressed "concern about the television reporting of the Tet Offensive and the *Pueblo* Affair."[3] Late that afternoon it was decided that Secretary of State Dean Rusk and Defense Secretary Robert McNamara would appear on a one-hour special edition of NBC's *Meet the Press* on 4 February to make the administration's case to the American people. It was that night that NBC's *Huntley-Brinkley Report* showed gruesome film of the Loan execution, editing the footage slightly to spare the viewing audience the fountain of blood splashing from the victim's head.[4] Anything the administration planned to say on Sunday morning about the progress of the war amid the terrible confusion of Tet was bound to be overwhelmed in the public mind by the brutal execution of this single individual. A few days later, Secretary Rusk would, in a "background session" before twenty-nine reporters, directly question the patriotism of the media: "Whose side are you on?"[5]

Although it is not my purpose to attempt to measure the impact on the American psyche of the broadcast of the execution[6]—an execution that in and of itself meant little or nothing to a war in which tens of thousands of Americans and untold numbers of Vietnamese lost their lives—it may be instructive to glance at a single example because it reaches into the White House itself. Harry McPherson, one of Johnson's speech writers and confidants, had the following response:

I watched the invasion of the American embassy compound, and the terrible sight of General Loan killing the Vietcong captive. You got a sense of the awfulness, the endlessness, of the war—and, though it sounds naïve, the unethical quality of the war in which a prisoner is shot at point-blank range. I put aside the confidential cables. I was more persuaded by the tube and by the newspapers. I was fed up with the optimism that seemed to flow without stopping from Saigon.[7]

Illustrative about McPherson's response is "the tube's" ability to affect the disposition of a man whose job it is to help craft the administration's very message about progress and success in Vietnam for the American people.

"FROM WHAT SOURCES SHOULD PEOPLE DO THIS?"

As a part a volume that seeks to *historicize* various literary theories, my essay attempts to link specific elements of new historicist criticism to the television coverage of the premier event in American life in the late 1960s, the Vietnam War. It is my hypothesis that the television coverage of the Tet Offensive of 1968 exercised an emotional as well as an intellectual influence on new historicism's eventual foregrounding of a structural tension between synchronic and diachronic history, its intense concern with the particular, its deployment of anecdotes, its distrust of official voices, and its ambivalent relationship to the historical "real." Stephen Greenblatt has written that his "own critical practice and that of many others associated with the new historicism was decisively shaped by the American 1960s and early '70s, and especially by the opposition to the Viet Nam War."[8] Obviously, the television coverage of the war is only one among many "social energies"[9] shaping new historicism, but the nightly dose of anecdotal and poorly contextualized images of bloodshed, suffering, and devastation that defined the evening news in early 1968 arguably anticipates the new historicism's penchant for essay-opening anecdotes detailing outlandish and sometimes violent occurrences[10]—and is thus too provocative to be ignored. We may recall here, for instance, the opening pages of one of Greenblatt's earliest new historicist essays (written ca. 1976), which take their cue to action from a merchant's account of the willful burning of a village on the West African coast by the English in 1586.[11] "What is most striking" about the anecdote detailing the village's destruction, Greenblatt writes, "is the casual, unexplained violence."[12] Part of what I hope to do in the pages that follow is to show that the evening news in 1968 presented its viewers, notwithstanding the efforts of correspondents and news anchors to the contrary, with a steady dose of "unexplained violence" that may well have shaped if not the fantasies then certainly the nightmares of a generation of future new historicists. The evening news, I suggest, is part of the "cognitive map" that is new historicism.[13]

In part my essay is born out of a mild frustration with Catherine Gallagher and Greenblatt's recent book *Practicing New Historicism* (2000), which, in my view, is neither personal nor (new) historical enough, especially when the authors attempt to construct an historical account of new historicism itself. Gallagher and Greenblatt observe that they "of all people should know something of the history and the principles of new historicism."[14] But in the pages that purport to deal with the "history and principles" of new historicism, we are given only an account of the intellectual influences of thinkers such as Clifford Geertz, Michel Foucault, Pierre Bourdieu, Friedrich Nietzsche, and the eighteenth-century German philosopher Johann Gottfried von Herder on the inception and evolution of new historicist thought that reads suspiciously like "old" historicism. We are told about an eclectic, interdisciplinary reading group at Berkeley whose members "eagerly read works of 'theory' emanating principally from Paris, Constance [Germany], Berlin, Frankfurt, Budapest, Tartu [Estonia], and Moscow, and met regularly . . . to argue about them" (2). Yet there are no significant insights into the dynamics of the group or the personal motivations and desires driving the various debates. From more than two decades of new historicist work, we know that new historicists have a predilection for tales of violence, sexual deviance, salutary anxiety, religious heresy, erotic dreams, and so forth, but Gallagher and Greenblatt opt for strictly academic language and concerns to describe their own motivations. They tell us that "Several of us particularly wanted to hold on to our aesthetic pleasures; our desire for critical innovation; our interest in contingency, spontaneity, improvisation; our urge to pick up a tangential fact and watch its circulation; our sense of history's unpredictable galvanic appearances and disappearances" (4). The members of the group, however, remain "nameless,"[15] their motives a secret, and their feelings unarticulated.

But if we remain committed to understanding something of the *history* of new historicism, we must ask why Greenblatt and other critics were so fascinated with Geertz, Foucault, Bourdieu, and other thinkers *in the first place*? What was going on *outside* these texts that made new historicists so interested in those texts? That is what a *new* historicist would want to know, right? Gallagher and Greenblatt quote Herder to make a claim about art that is seminal to new historicists: "The first questions to be asked about an art such as drama, Herder writes, are 'When? Where? Under what circumstances? From what sources should people do this?'" (7). To answer that question with regard to new historicism, one would have to look beyond the fact that Foucault, Geertz, and other critics were thinkers who elaborated in particularly searching and provocative ways on the question of art's embeddedness in social and psychological formations. One should have to answer under what circumstances and from what sources—cultural, personal, historical, intellectual, and so forth—do new historicists do this? Under what circumstances and from what sources should new historicism emerge? It is, in my view, not enough for Gallagher and Greenblatt to report that there were heated debates over Louis Althusser and Jacques Lacan; they would have to explore the *source* and *nature* of the heat, would they not? Should the new historicist critic not tease out for us the jealousies, the suppressed desires, the hidden anxieties, the movements of power, and the very *social energies* that circulate among and around the members of the reading group? Shouldn't we be curious about *friction*?[16] And beyond the group's immediate dynamics, should we not be concerned with an analysis of the rise of new historicism in the context of Berkeley campus politics, California social policy, the group's favorite television sitcoms, the Reagan phenomenon, Foucault's forays into San Francisco nightlife, and what have you?

To be fair, in the course of his immensely impressive career, Greenblatt has at times given us glimpses into the particular (personal) circumstances that shape his thought,[17] and it certainly would be awkward for any critic to breach academic decorum and truly bring the "personal" into the analysis of the "professional." And Greenblatt has acknowledged the influence of history on his personal style. But he then goes on to reject Jean Howard's call for a more overt self-consciousness of new historicist method on the grounds that the forces and values that have shaped him over the years are "pervasive . . . in the textual and visual traces [he] choose[s] to analyze, in the stories [he] choose[s] to tell, in the cultural conjunctions [he] attempt[s] to make, in my syntax, adjectives, pronouns."[18] Fair enough. Greenblatt should not be asked to do a history of Greenblatt just because he is the primary architect of a widely influential critical practice. That said, I do think that it is reasonable and even necessary to ask new historicists to turn their eyes more rigorously to the *broader* historical "circumstances" and "sources" of their own emergence.

THE PARTICULAR, THE ANECDOTE, AND THE "REAL"

New historicist critics, by their own admission, are an eclectic group, ideologically as well as methodologically. But if there is one thing that appears to connect new historicist critics to each other it is "a commitment to particularity."[19] "Particularity" here of course does not only mean "detail"; it also signals new historicism's fascination with the "peculiar" or the "singular," with that which doesn't fit, which never quite came into existence fully, or is suppressed by, or partially erased by a larger, more powerful cultural force that may or may not be in cahoots with state power. As Howard puts it, "instead of invoking a monolithic and repressive 'history,' one must acknowledge the existence of 'histories' produced by various subjects variously positioned. . . ."[20] The "particular" is generally considered and analyzed in the relatively narrow context of the moment of its existence (though the new historicist may associate any number of distantly located "particulars" via the "social energy"—as opposed to *material* reality—that connects them[21]), and comparatively little weight is given to its place in the diachronic historiographical narrative that is generally the purview of "old" historians, social historians, and Marxist historians.

As we have so often seen in the work of new historicist critics, this fascination with peculiarity and "histories" translates into the use of historical anecdotes as a corrective of, or supplement to, existing historical narratives. Historical narratives, we find, are almost always *organized* around a specific principle or set of principles that aims to demonstrate cause-and-effect sequences, origins, and developmental trajectories.[22] Without getting into the question of whether historical facts dictate the organizing principle or whether the organizing principle is imposed by the historian on those facts, I think we can reasonably assert that all historical narratives necessarily reveal a process of selection that judges some facts germane and others immaterial. Although this process of selection may not be driven overtly by politics, it is always ideological in the Althusserian sense, and inevitably crowds out or suppresses or omits portions of the past in a way that their very absence shapes our understanding of that past. The intense study of the anecdote, which Joel Fineman calls "the smallest minimal unit of the historiographic fact,"[23] is intended as an antidote or historiographic "counterhistory"[24] to monolithic or repressive historical narratives. The term "fact" is perhaps slightly misleading because anecdotes, even very brief ones, are hardly devoid of narrative, but the vital issue for new historicists is that the narrative and content of the anecdote endure in a relationship of palpable (or latent) tension with the dominant narrative mode of the culture in which it exists. This tension arises primarily from the uneasy relationship in social life between contingency and continuity, between the anomaly and the customary chain of events, for the latter is always seeking to suppress, erase, or discipline the former. The anecdote insists on the contingent, on "the sense if not of a break then at least of a swerve in the ordinary and well-understood succession of events,"[25] and does so by virtue of "a vehement and cryptic particularity that would make one pause or even stumble on the threshold of history."[26] Pausing or stumbling gives one the opportunity to contemplate ways in which these "little stories" interrupt the historiographical *grand récits* and how they "work against the historical grain."[27]

New historicists, however, do not merely analyze anecdotes to demonstrate that "history" is heterogeneous rather than monolithic; they also maintain, as Fineman does, that anecdotes possess the ability to create an "opening into the teleological . . . narrative" and produce "the effect of the real."[28] This is a potent claim in the poststructuralist age because it positions new historicism not merely as *another* way of constructing the past, but as a method that yields the lingering "traces" of that which other historicisms suppress in favor of metanarrative, namely the "real." At the same time, we should be clear that new historicism is hardly a throwback to old-fashioned positivism. The "effect of the real" or the "touch of the real" (as Greenblatt and Gallagher call it)[29] is not a promise that the study of anecdotes will yield unfettered access to historical reality—to the way it *really* was—but an assertion that the stories of the past that survive in literary texts, letters, legal records, medical records, church records, and so forth, ought not to be collapsed into the literary category called "textuality."[30] The text points to something that lies beyond itself but to which it is linked: "the real, the material, the realm of practice, pain, bodily pleasure, silence, or death—to which the text gestures as that which lies beyond the written word, outside of its textual mode of being."[31] The "real" itself, however, remains *un*available for scrutiny, and is only felt or glimpsed through the "traces"[32] or "effects" it has left in the textual or in other objects of the past.

WATCHING TV; OR "'VIGNETTE' JOURNALISM"[33]

But even if the anecdote cannot reveal to us the grand truth of an epoch or grant us unmediated access to the real, it clearly possesses the power to disrupt some of the most aggressively disseminated narratives of the day, namely those of the government. In his autobiography, General Westmoreland noted that there grew in the late 1960s "an unbridgeable chasm" between the government and the American people in part because the Johnson administration "failed to level with the American people about the extent and nature of the sacrifice that had to be made."[34] It was not so much the evening news' steady dose of images of carnage and death in a strange faraway land that downcast the American people as it was the fact that "the pictures did not match the optimistic chatter coming from the [Johnson] administration."[35] This so-called "credibility gap" between the government's version of the war and television's version of the same is important to my argument because it provides the basic conditions for what new historicists call "oppositional" history or "counternarrative."

The "credibility gap," however, clearly existed sometime before Westmoreland first discerned it, and, if we read Michael J. Arlen's brilliant essay collection *Living-Room War* (1966)[36] we get more than just a glimpse of television's instrumentality in directing the viewer's gaze. Arlen's mediations on television coverage of the Vietnam War are invariably thoughtful, full of passion, and frequently poetic. His subtle mind's eye, exploring the images that flicker by on the screen, is always searching to make sense of incongruencies and oddities, always striving to highlight and confront rather than to suppress the troublesome and the seemingly inexplicable. Watching television and writing about it for *The New Yorker* in the mid-1960s, Arlen of course does not avail himself of new historicist terminology, but he would have found in new historicism an investigative language well-suited to his efforts to understand more about the war in Vietnam from the anecdotal coverage offered on the nightly news. I will quote from *Living-Room War* at length.

> Vietnam is often referred to as "television's war," in the sense that this is the first war that has been brought to the people preponderantly by television. People indeed look at television. They really look at it. They look at Dick van Dyke and become his friend. They look at a new Pontiac commercial and go out and buy it. They look at thoughtful Chet Huntley and find him thoughtful, and at witty David Brinkley and find him witty. They look at Vietnam. They look at Vietnam, it seems, as a child kneeling in the corridor, his eye to the keyhole, looks at two grownups arguing in a locked room—the aperture of the keyhole small; the figures shadowy, mostly out of sight; the voices indistinct, isolated threats without meaning; isolated glimpses, part of an elbow, a man's jacket (who is the man?), part of a face, a woman's face. Ah, she is crying. One sees the tears. (The voices continue indistinctly.) One counts the tears. Two tears. Three tears. Two bombing raids. Four seek-and-destroy missions. Six administration pronouncements. Such a fine-looking woman. One searches in vain for the other grownup, but, ah, the keyhole is so small, he is somehow never in the line of sight. Look! There is General Ky. Look! There are some planes returning safely to the *Ticonderoga*. I wonder (sometimes) what it is that the people who run television think about the war, because *they* have given us this keyhole view; we have given them the airways, and now, at this critical time, they have given us this keyhole view—and I wonder if they truly think that those isolated glimpses of elbow, face, a swirl of dress (who *is* that other person, anyway?) are all we children can really stand to see of what is going on inside that room.
>
> Vo Huynh, admittedly, will show us as much of the larger truth of a small battle and of a wounded soldier as he is able to, and CBS, as it did some nights ago, will show us a half-hour special interview with Marine Corps General Walt, which is nice of CBS, but there are other things, it seems, that make up the Vietnam war, that intelligent men *know* make up the Vietnam war—factors of doubt, politics, propaganda, truth, untruth, of what we actually do and actually don't do, that aren't in most ways tangible, or certifiably right or wrong, or easily reducible to mathematics, but that, even so (and even now), exist as parts of this equation that we're supposedly trying so hard to solve—and almost none of them get mentioned.[37]

Tears, bombing raids, government, the swirl of a dress—seeming nonsequitors in a spectacle that remains fragmented and painfully incomplete. Our keyhole view of a war.

Arlen goes on to mention some of the things that don't get mentioned enough—doubts about the effectiveness of our search-and-destroy missions, the seeming inaccuracy of enemy casualty figures, questions about the (in)effectiveness of our bombing campaign, and the precise extent of our use of "anti-personal" weapons—but most striking in the context of our discussion is his almost poetic account of the *fragmentation* of the story of the Vietnam War on the news. Clearly, what Arlen desires is the truth and a compelling narrative of the war, but all he gets through the keyhole are bewildering fragments that don't fit together into a coherent whole. His desire for a comprehensive narrative may at first not appear particularly new historical, but what is new historical is Arlen's readiness to be *disturbed* by his keyhole view of the war. The fragments almost seem too small to serve as anecdotes, but for Arlen they do clearly function as what Greenblatt calls "disturbance, as that which requires explanation, contextualization, interpretation."[38] We see in Arlen's description the same "vehement and cryptic particularity"—tears, and elbow, a face, four bombing raids, six administration pronouncements—that Greenblatt and Gallagher look for to make us (and themselves) "stumble on the threshold of history."[39] A stumbling Arlen yearns for a way to put the pieces together into a context that makes sense, and it is not the Johnson administration's contextualization that satisfies this yearning (even though that government's grand narrative, which speaks of a significant but reasonable price we have to pay to stop the threat of communism and bring peace and democracy to East Asia, still had a ring of truth with many of the American people). As if on his knees on the threshold of history, Arlen's keyhole view of the war arrests and compels his attention with "flashes of an always inaccessible 'real.'"[40] But while the three-to four-to five-minute news films that show helicopter rescues, American soldiers firing their guns into the thick green jungle, Vietnamese refuges huddled by the roadside in the splashing rain, burning villages, and authoritative pronouncements by General Westmoreland and President Johnson, are enough to disturb, to raise questions, they do not provide meaningful answers. They challenge the government's narrative—history as usual—by signaling that "there is something—the 'real'—outside of the historical narrative,"[41] although they cannot (yet) offer a narrative to replace it.

Arlen implicitly blames the news media for not reporting the story in such a way that it *does* make sense. But Arlen is not one to blame this on bias among reporters. Rather, much like a new historicist might, he turns to the structural and institutional limitations of evening news programming to locate the culprit. "Television," he writes, "with all its technical resources, with all the possibilities of film and film-editing for revealing fluid motion, continues for the most part to report the war as a long, long narrative broken into two-minute, three-minute, or four-minute stretches of visual incident. . . ."[42] The problem is that the format of the news does not encourage the telling of a long and complex story, and that reporters therefore don't

> have either the time or the inclination to investigate the various parts of the
> Vietnam picture. . . . And, more important, when they do get hold of one of
> these parts, neither most of the newspapers nor most of television seems *to
> be able to do anything more with it than to treat it as an isolated piece of detail*—
> maybe an important piece of detail, maybe unimportant, but *isolated* in any
> case, cut off by the rigors and conventions of journalism from the events and
> forces that brought it into being, cut off, too, from the events and forces that
> it will in turn animate. (emphasis added)[43]

One might object here that the fragments yielded by Arlen's keyhole perspective—"those isolated glimpses of elbow, face, a swirl of dress"—are not sufficiently structured or "whole" to qualify as anecdotes. It is true that the anecdote of new historicist criticism possesses a "compact wholeness" and an
undeniably literary and narrative form[44] that Arlen's "isolated" details, "cut off"
from their context, seem to lack. But it is good to remember here that Greenblatt and Gallagher discern at least two stages in the development of the concept of the anecdote in Geertz's work. At first, Greenblatt and Gallagher
point out, Geertz describes a particular anecdote in his field diary as "quoted
raw, a note in a bottle," but then abandons this notion of the "raw" to convey
that the anecdote itself is a story told and shaped by an "informant" for the
benefit of the anthropologist.[45] The initial notion of "raw," Gallagher and
Greenblatt suggest, "is meant to convey the idea of the 'empirical' (as distinct
from the philosopher's 'artificial' stories) but also to arouse the bafflement, the
intense curiosity and interest, that necessitates the interpretation of cultures."
Now it is of course true that the television evening news performs the shaping function of Geertz's "informant," except that the news appears unable to
transform the bits and pieces it broadcasts into a story; restricted by the conventions of journalism, reporters appear unable "to do anything more with
[something important] than to treat it as an isolated piece of detail." What is
more, we can easily tell from Arlen's bewildered *response* to what he sees
through the television keyhole that the "isolated glimpses" before him retain
their rawness as well as their "empirical" properties. They gesture to that
which "lies beyond the written word": to "the real, the material, the realm of
practice, pain, pleasure, silence, or death."[46] So if Arlen's disjointed (but poetic)
account of what he watches on TV fails to take the shape of a fully formed
anecdote with narrative and all, this is so because, although Arlen is grappling
"toward textual constructions," these constructions are "presented as 'raw' data
or 'evidence,' which seem less purpose-built, more resistant to simple appropriation, and hence more nearly autonomous."[47] They "arouse" Arlen's "bafflement" and they necessitate the "interpretation of" the war (in American culture).[48] It is a story that one must tell, but one does not know how it should
be told. In the introduction to *Learning to Curse* (1992), Greenblatt writes that
"Anecdotes are the equivalents in the register of the real of what drew me to

the study of literature: the encounter with something that I could not stand not understanding, that I could not quite finish with or finish off, that I had to get out of my inner life where it had taken hold, that I could retell and contemplate and struggle with."[49] Is it possible that Geertz's formulations resonated with Greenblatt precisely because they gave academic expression to what it felt like to watch the war on TV in early 1968?

Arlen's dismay and bewilderment are shared not only by other television viewers but also by sometime-maverick reporter Morley Safer, who, as Arlen writes, through editorializing or by putting "a little edge in his voice" contextualizes the "bang-bang footage" required by news producers, and perhaps comes "a bit closer to the way things were."[50] More importantly, as the following account suggests, Safer's is the kind of report that sets powerful anecdotal images against government narratives and that could easily give rise to responses such as Arlen's and a new-historical utilization of anecdotal materials. The only significant difference between Arlen's response (as just documented) and Safer's is that the latter, in his role as professional journalist, tries to make sense of the events before him by elevating their anecdotal status in the Vietnam conflict to that of a "miniature" version of the entire war. Arlen points to the absence of any overarching narrative that links the anecdotal, while Safer offers the anecdotal (i.e., his reading thereof) as narrative.

In August of 1965, following the rapid U.S. military buildup in Vietnam, Safer filed a report for *CBS News* from the Vietnamese village of Cam Ne. We see an American soldier set fire to the roof of a Vietnamese hut. "This is what the war in Vietnam is all about," narrates Safer. An old man with clasped hands stands in front of the blazing structure; he talks agitatedly in the direction of Safer, who is only a few feet away. Is the hut his home? Perhaps moved by the old man's anguish, perhaps drawn by a reporter's instinct, Safer momentarily turns toward the man, microphone in hand, as if to record the man's lament. But almost in the same instant Safer turns away and back to the camera: after all, neither Safer nor most of the American television audience can understand a single word of what the Vietnamese man has to say. The scene dramatizes Safer's (and our) simultaneous identification with, and fundamental alienation from, the old man. We want to recognize this man as a fellow human being and help him, but we know that we do not know him (could he or his family be VC after all?) and have no way of coming to his aid.

A moment later, Safer speaks straight into the camera for a moment: "Marines have burned this old couple's cottage because [gun]fire was coming from here. Now you walk into the village and you see no young people at all. . . . [The sound of women crying is heard.] It's not really a village; it's a string of huts." We see two women trying to drag an object from the flames with a long stick. Safer continues: "It first appeared that marines had been sniped at and that a few houses were made to pay. Shortly after, an officer told me he had orders to go in and level the string of hamlets that surrounds Cam Ne village." The camera turns to a group of now homeless women and children, huddled together, crying. The CBS camera turns back to Safer, who finishes his report by summing up as follows:

> The day's operation burned down 150 houses, wounded three women, killed one baby, wounded one marine, and netted these four prisoners [we see film of four blindfolded men walking], four old men who could not answer questions put to them in English. . . . Today's operation is the frustration of Vietnam in miniature. There's little doubt that American firepower can win a military victory here, but to a Vietnamese peasant whose home means a lifetime of backbreaking labor, it will take more than presidential promises that we are on his side. . . ."[51]

Safer's report vividly presents his and our intense frustration with what seems arbitrary suffering in the war. He suggests that we destroyed a village in order to interrogate four old men who were unable to tell us anything. Safer even goes so far as to say that no amount of presidential rhetoric can convince the average Vietnamese that we are burning his country for his own good. But—and this is important—Safer states resolutely that "American firepower can win a military victory" pretty much anytime we want it to. In other words, while creating a great deal of sympathy for Vietnamese women and children who suffer the brunt of the war and for the Vietnamese peasants who cannot be made to understand that we are doing it all for them, Safer strongly implies that *we*—the American television viewers—*know* that President Johnson speaks the truth when he promises victory, and that we unequivocally accept the premise that we possess the military might to crush the enemy if and when we decide to do so. Both implications are significant because they show that despite a growing dissatisfaction with the progress of the war in Vietnam in 1965, the American people are presumed still to be in support of their president's efforts to halt the onslaught of communism and to give democracy a chance in Vietnam. More importantly, American citizens still are presumed to *trust* their president, even as Safer suggests it may be hard for a South Vietnamese peasant to understand why he should do likewise. But in the end Safer's assumption that, despite a number of doubts, Americans trust their president, allows the film anecdote about the village of Cam Ne to be folded back into the Johnson administration's grand narrative of superior U.S. military might, implying that there is a formula for success to dispose of this whole awful mess. Also noteworthy about Safer's report is that its conclusion is in no way suggested by the anecdotes presented to us on the television screen. The futile exercise of burning the village, killing a few people, and vainly interrogating four old men appears to suggest precisely the opposite conclusion: American military might is embarrassingly impotent in the Vietnam environment. But this is a conclusion that Safer is apparently unable or unwilling to draw in front of millions of American television viewers.

Therefore, despite Safer's daring editorializing or the "little edge in his voice," it is clear that his "subversive" acts remain too isolated and restrained (within the context of the network's "unbiased" reporting) to form a narrative of opposition. But they do contribute to a growing sense of public doubt and frustration for as "the detail accretes, day in, day out; paragraphs clatter out over the cable, film by the bagload heads home for processing, detail, detail, detail, and people back home, who have been fed more words and pictures on Vietnam than on any other event in the last twenty years, have the vague, unhappy feeling that they still haven't been told it straight."[52] Whether you read Arlen or watch Safer on television, you cannot help but feel that the Vietnam War is a war in search of a narrative, a narrative powerful enough to make sense of all those horrible bits and pieces and to refute the story put out by the government. As a result, Arlen writes, the American people do not "pay any rigorous attention to Vietnam. It obsesses people, certainly, but more as a neurosis. . . ."[53] They can't stop peering through the keyhole but they never know quite what they see.

THE TET OFFENSIVE, COUNTERNARRATIVE, AND NEW HISTORY

All this begins to change on 31 January 1968. On that day, the first of the Tet Lunar New Year, the North Vietnamese broke the cease-fire and launched a massive offensive along virtually the entire South Vietnamese border, attacking many of the South's urban centers. As the offensive unfolded, some television journalists began to construct a counternarrative, a narrative that took clear exception to the administration's narrative of progress. The counternarrative itself, however, was, although clearly energized by powerful anecdotal information, entirely inadequate as an historical narrative of the war in general. In the section that follows, therefore, I will try to show that a journalist like CBS news anchor Walter Cronkite may have been a source of inspiration as well as frustration to incipient new historicists.

On the day that the Tet Offensive erupted the *nature* of the war changed, or so Cronkite told the American audience that watched his 27 February television special on the state of the war in Vietnam.[54] Cronkite concluded his broadcast by declaring that he now thought the war unwinnable. President Johnson is reported to have said in response to the broadcast, "If I've lost Cronkite I've lost middle America."[55] For the first time, a "counternarrative" was voiced by one of the most trusted voices in America. Whether Johnson was correct is his assessment or whether Cronkite's words actually changed the views of a significant number of Americans is not my concern here.[56]

What is of concern here is that in the course of his half hour news special entitled "Who, What, When, Where, Why?" Cronkite put into a play a narrative
that openly defied the government's version of the war. Why Cronkite's narrative just now? Two things make his narrative possible: first, Cronkite is con-
vinced that Tet signals a significant shift in the *way* the war is fought, and,
second, there is a further widening of the credibility gap between the administration's rhetoric and what men such as Cronkite see with their own eyes in
Vietnam. First the credibility gap.

On 1 February, the *CBS Evenings News* showed film of street battles in
Saigon and chaotic scenes of people running from their homes for safety.
There was also film of a firefight in downtown Ha Trang, as well as the attack
on, and occupation of, the South Vietnamese-language radio station in
Saigon, and the surprise Vietcong attack on the U.S. Embassy. To appreciate
the impact of such footage, we have to remember that the "Pacification Program," which was to place U.S. soldiers in small South Vietnamese villages
and safeguard them against VC infiltration,[57] was thought to make it impossible for the enemy to gain the necessary strongholds in the countryside to
launch attacks on South Vietnam's population centers. However, street fighting in Saigon and footage (shown on *CBS News* on 2 February) of U.S. rock-
ets and shells pulverizing the VC-occupied city of Hue and its old Citadel
hardly gave the American public a sense that progress was being made in the
war. In fact, it suggested exactly the opposite.

Upon seeing the first bulletins on the Tet Offensive, Cronkite is supposed
to have exclaimed, "What the hell is going on, I thought we were winning the
war."[58] Not surprisingly, journalistic cynicism regarding the administration's
optimism is palpable in the first Tet bulletins, and especially during that first
makeshift press conference held by General Westmoreland on the grounds of
the U.S. Embassy in Saigon. Responding to the administration's sense of
urgency, Westmoreland appears before the cameras even before the dead bodies have been removed from the grounds. The general does his best to get the
administration's point of view out, but a reporter's voice added to the film
before its broadcast in the United States undermines Westmoreland's interview by listing all of the enemy's bold exploits, including the attack on the
U.S. Embassy. Then, just *before* Westmoreland starts speaking, the reporter's
voice announces with thinly veiled irony that according to the general "all this
represented a Vietcong defeat."[59] The general has been discredited before
uttering a single word. If this does not make the American television audience
doubt the general's veracity, an uncanny explosion that occurs just as Westmoreland begins to answer questions rudely adds force to the reporter's irony.
The general looks up distractedly for a moment, then returns to the interview
and says, with the outward calm of the consummate soldier, "that's EOD setting off a couple of M79 duds, I believe." He follows this pronouncement with

a forced smile that tells everyone not to worry. But the reporters clearly are worried. Are there still VC snipers in the area? Are they lobbing grenades? Westmoreland talks of Tet as merely a "diversionary" action, and of our "effective air strikes" that have delayed the enemy's main offensive against Quang Tri Province, but it is clear that the general isn't assuring anybody.

In retrospect, it is a bit of a mystery why a shrewd politician like Johnson stuck with his public relations "progress" campaign in light of so much bloodshed, chaos, and confusion on American television screens. The "progress" campaign had been intensified in the fall of 1967. Westmoreland had said in late 1967 that while victory was not yet in hand, "the end begins to come into view."[60] Johnson himself had set the tone during a press conference on 17 November 1967: "We are making progress. . . . We are inflicting greater losses than we are taking. . . . The fact that the population under free control has constantly risen . . . is a very encouraging sign . . . overall we are making progress."[61]

When these statements were made toward the end of 1967, there was, of course, uncertainty in the press as to their validity, but, "although they voiced misgivings, newsmen in Vietnam (or Washington) could not *prove* in 1967 that the Administration's professed optimism was overblown."[62] As the Tet Offensive unfolded and as the images of combat and chaos saturated network news programs, Johnson inexplicably "sought to repeat his 1967 public relations strategy, dominating the media with reassuring statements about Vietnam by subordinates."[63] During a press conference on 2 February 1968, Johnson declared the VC's military mission "a complete failure,"[64] and added that Gen. Maxwell Taylor, the Joint Chiefs of Staff, Secretary McNamara, and the Pentagon itself agreed with that assessment. The American people would come to share this view, he added, as soon as they learned "the facts." He also noted that as soon as the public would understand this, the Vietcong's second objective—to score a "psychological victory"—would also fail. But the press was not buying it.

Standing amid the rubble in a Saigon street, Cronkite begins his 27 February broadcast as follows:

> These ruins are in Saigon, capital of the largest city of South Vietnam. They were left here by an act of war, Vietnamese against Vietnamese. Hundreds died here. Here in these ruins can be seen physical evidence of the Vietcong's Tet Offensive, but far less tangible is what those ruins mean, and like everything else in this burned and blasted and weary land, they mean success or setback, victory or defeat, depending upon whom you talk to. . . . How many died and how much damage was done, however, still are but approximations, despite the official figures. The very preciseness of the figures brings them under suspicion. Anyone who has wandered through these ruins knows that an exact count is impossible. Why, just a short while ago a little old man

came and told us that two V.C. were buried in a hastily-dug grave up at the end of the block. Had they been counted? And what about these ruins? Have they gone through all of them for buried civilians and soldiers? And what about the 14 V.C. we found in the courtyard behind the post office at Hue? Had they been counted and tabulated. They certainly hadn't been buried.[65]

"We came to Vietnam to try to determine what all this means to the future of the war here," Cronkite continues, and it is clear that that meaning is indeterminate and that the anecdotal evidence gathered by Cronkite and his CBS team strongly suggests that we should not turn to the U.S. government for a straight answer. In the final paragraph of his report, Cronkite shockingly concludes, "To say that we are mired in stalemate seems the only realistic, yet unsatisfactory, conclusion."

For Cronkite, who was universally known as a cautious journalist not given to fanciful editorializing, a second factor that made him call for an honorable withdrawal from Vietnam was his belief that the *nature* of the war had changed. Till the onset of the Tet Offensive, most of the fighting had been limited to rural areas and the jungle, and the U.S. military's mission had been to pacify the countryside and prevent the spread of hostilities to urban centers. Successful pacification of the countryside also meant that, aside from the occasional and unpreventable terrorist attack, life in South Vietnamese cities could continue with a sense of normalcy, and that the people had no reason to abandon their trust in the shaky Nguyen Van Thieu government and to join the communists, which was a continuous fear. During Tet, however, the Vietcong launched surprise attacks against thirty-five cities in the South. No longer, Cronkite observes, are the American forces dealing with a series of seemingly isolated battles, skirmishes, and guerrilla raids in hamlets, the jungle, or countryside. Now they are dealing with what Cronkite names a "classic Western" style war, "large armies locked in combat, moving toward a decision on the battlefield." And this is the kind of war Cronkite, a veteran World War II reporter, thinks he knows something about. As Cronkite later wrote, it was not until about 1965 that he was "prepared to grasp the fact that Vietnam was no ordinary war as some of us senior correspondents had known it in World War II."[66] He felt sorry for government officials who had to brief the press corps about a war "that had no explanation."[67] Cronkite's recasting of the Vietnam conflict, however, from a series of baffling anecdotes into a "classic" war narrative allows him to forecast boldly the war's future:

This summer's almost certain standoff will either end in real give-and-take negotiations or terrible escalation; and for every means we have to escalate, the enemy can match us, and that applies to invasion of the North, the use of nuclear weapons, or the mere commitment of one hundred, or two hundred, or three hundred thousand more American troops to the battle.[68]

Cronkite's conclusion about the war in general is really an extrapolation of his assessment of the Tet Offensive itself: "The Vietcong did not win by a knockout, but neither did we. The referees of history may make it a draw." In many respects, Cronkite's report may have been inspirational to budding new historicists. Both the distrust of official voices and the use of "raw" anecdotal matter to challenge a government narrative are native to much new historicist work.

What is decidedly anti-new historical about Cronkite's "counterhistory" is the *kind* of narrative it employs to make sense of things. What is intriguing here is that Cronkite's fledgling "counterhistory" is not a new *kind* of historical narrative seeking to displace the old and flawed Johnson administration narrative. Nor is it a carefully woven narrative made up of all the accumulated anecdotes that just do not fit the administration's narrative. But neither is it Safer's narrative, which, despite chronicling subversive anecdotal information, could be folded back neatly into the official government narrative of superior military might. Instead, Cronkite's analysis resuscitates an *old* and *familiar* World War II narrative—a narrative about "classic Western" warfare—to counter the administration's position and to make sense of the whole depressing mess.[69] But this does not mean that Cronkite actually understands this new *kind* of war. The *new* war remains inexplicable; it's just that the CBS reporter "recognizes" a particular phase in that war and proceeds to cast the entire future of the war in a narrative of recognition. This is a classic instance of Hayden White's description of how traditional narrative historians practice their craft. The historian's imposition of a familiar story line on a set of events makes the events *seem* familiar and therefore *seemingly* comprehensible.

> The original strangeness, mystery, exoticism of the events is dispelled, and they take on familiar aspects, not in their details, but in their functions as elements of a familiar kind of configuration. They are rendered comprehensible by being subsumed under the categories of the plot structure in which they are encoded as a story of a particular kind. They are familiarized, not only because the reader now has more *information* about the events, but also because he has shown how the data conform to an *icon* of a comprehensible finished process, a plot structure with which he is familiar as a part of his cultural endowment.[70]

Notice that the "events" do not become more familiar "in their details"; that is, in their own right; events become more familiar only with regard to their *role* in the narrative. And this is precisely why Cronkite's counterhistory, while perhaps praiseworthy for its stance against the administration, is fundamentally not new historical; it abandons the details and the anecdotes in favor of the big, familiar story. By calling on a "classic" narrative to explain the war "that had no explanation," Cronkite favors a diachronic abstraction of the historical process over a synchronic approach to that process, which typifies new historicism.[71] It is true, of course, that Cronkite proclaims that the nature of the war has changed, but this is a forced observation that hardly follows from his description of the chaos and from his enumeration of uncertainties about casualties, damage, progress, and the future of the war. Cronkite may indeed *believe* that the Tet Offensive was a new combat development in the war, but he has no way of knowing whether the North's next move will be another such offensive or a return to guerrilla warfare.[72]

Bernard Kalb's 20 February report on the "Vietcong" for *CBS News*, which aired a week before Cronkite's "Who, What, When, Where, Why?" offers an even clearer picture of the tension between the power of the anecdote to grip one's attention and the desire to transcend the anecdote in favor of a familiar narrative. Kalb's report displays Arlen's fascination with all things disjointed and fragmented and anticipates Cronkite's reach for the big story. Furthermore, in contrast with Safer's report on Cam Ne (1965) in which he still expressed confidence in U.S. military power to produce a victory, Kalb's already adopts the "we're-not-going-to-win-this-one" stance evident in Cronkite's report of 27 February. Kalb speaks as follows:

> Saigon becomes the newest, most dramatic, most embarrassing casualty of the war. The Vietcong attack came at a time when Americans were saying that V.C. morale was low. The Vietcong had again turned their weapons on American and South Vietnamese optimism—against a city that had been luxuriating as though the war were taking place in another country. It was an unconventional attack that posed unconventional questions: Is the strategy of the revolutionary war more powerful than a B-52? Is the Vietcong more brilliant than the Pentagon?
>
> One of the most infuriating questions is the nature of the enemy himself, the most remarkable and faceless foe in history. Who is this man? This woman? This boy? What's in that basket? Behind those vegetables? Where does this man go when he leaves here? Enemies are usually instantly recognizable. And that is one of the reasons why the war in Vietnam is so maddening, so exasperating for Americans. World War II had Hitler and Tojo, the Swastika and the Rising Sun, and Americans knew them at a glance. But the enemy in Vietnam looks like the non-enemy.[73]

Several of Kalb's questions—Who is this man? This woman? This boy? What's in that basket?—clearly evoke Arlen's keyhole perspective, and, to a lesser degree, Cronkite's notion of a war "that had no explanation." But these questions are preceded by other questions that convey a sense of desperation if not outright defeat: "Is the Vietcong more brilliant than the Pentagon?" In 1965, Safer may have remained confident in U.S. firepower, but Kalb points out that the Vietcong, though they have no air force, no navy, and no helicopters to resist us, and "have been attacked, assaulted, ambushed, bombarded, rocketed, mortared," have "found a way of outwitting U.S. strategy." It is not that "the enemy can match us" in terms of equipment and numbers of combatants, as Cronkite would have us believe, but that the enemy is smarter than us.

Kalb's introduction of the World War II metaphor/narrative plainly anticipates Cronkite's opinion that Tet has developed "more along the classic Western fashion of war, large armies locked in combat, moving toward a decision on the battlefield," but it does so by *denying* its applicability. The point here is not to debate who is right—Kalb or Cronkite—but to note that Kalb and Cronkite both reach out for the "classic war" narrative—one by lamenting its absence, the other by "finding" it—because only that familiar narrative has *explanatory* power for them. One could argue that the succession of views on the war discussed in this essay—from Arlen to Safer to Kalb to Cronkite—unequivocally points us to the power of the anecdote, only to see that power severely moderated by Safer's, Kalb's, and Cronkite's reliance on old and familiar narratives. In this way, these accounts draw our attention to that which is disruptive and does not fit, to that which strikes us as inexplicable, but they also show us that the old narratives insufficiently describe the events in Vietnam and that an entirely new approach is required if the specificity and the power of these events is to be captured and properly contextualized in our histories of the Vietnam War.[74] In this instance, then, television coverage of the war dramatized (in reversed order) some of the key elements in new historicist practice. Safer, Kalb, and Cronkite collectively demonstrate both the vitality of the anecdote and its power to "puncture" the *grand récit*, but they also dramatize the inadequacy of available narratives and strongly suggest that new methods for dealing with anecdotes need to be developed. Both are potent reasons for the rise of a new historicist criticism.

"You Had to Be There"; Or the (Im)possibility of History

One could assess the television coverage of the Tet Offensive by focusing on Johnson's apparent belief that after Cronkite's special report of 27 February he had "lost middle America." Others, primarily proponents of the war, have subsequently lamented that media coverage of Vietnam hurt the U.S. military effort and may have contributed to our failure to produce a victory. Don Oberdorfer notes that there was a "a sudden jump in public hawkishness" right after the first Tet attacks, but this burst of outrage at the North Vietnamese offensive was at once succeeded by a "steep drop in approval of President Johnson's handling of the war."[75] In March, Johnson's approval rating dropped to an all-time low 36 percent (down from 48 percept just before Tet),[76] and on

31 March Johnson made the stunning announcement that he would not run for reelection in November. One might be tempted to argue that television coverage of the war had effectively countered the government's "progress" campaign, had forced a president out of office, and had changed the course of world history. Or, if we were to translate this into new historicist terms, we might say that the power of film anecdotes was so great that it created a crevice in the government's *grand récit* of the war, offered the American television viewer "a touch of the real" Vietnam, and produced a victory of new history over narrative history.

But while this may be an attractive scenario because it empowers the press and the people, it is also a gross oversimplification from both a practical and a theoretical vantage point. Speaking practically, there is overwhelming consensus among historians today that the Tet Offensive was indeed the military debacle for the North Vietnamese that the Johnson administration said it was at the time. As Peter Braestrup observes, the communists threw much of their military might into the Offensive. "They not only utilized their local force battalions, but also surfaced key Vietcong cadres, exposing experienced, hard-to-replace guerrillas to heavy losses. But to little effect. The communist commanders were unable to *exploit* either the surprise they achieved or local allied weakness (even at Hue). They failed to crack or cripple ARVN [Army of the Republic of (South) Vietnam], to hold the urban centers, or to shake apart the Thieu-Ky 'puppet regime.'"[77] In short, Johnson's statement that the communists' offensive was "a complete failure" was not that far-off the mark, and the film anecdotes of violence and bloodshed on the evening news that countered the government's "progress campaign" may have offered the television viewer a "touch of the real" but they certainly did not give us a realistic overview of the true state of the war. It has been asserted by historians of media coverage of the Vietnam War that the press virtually always lacked sufficient information to make accurate assessments about the war in general.[78] One could suggest that the power of the anecdote led to a *mis*understanding about the exact state of the war.

However, before we reverse the scenario and crown the Johnson administration as the purveyor of truth and the television news as disseminators of falsehood, we should realize that the Johnson administration was at best guessing (and at worst misleading the public) when it pronounced the Tet Offensive a U.S. victory as early as 2 February, long before the entire situation could be assessed with any certainty. Even Westmoreland, whose press conference on 31 January was designed to assure the press and the public, admitted in his memoirs that he did not know about the full magnitude of the communist offensive until he arrived at Ton Son Nhut airbase later that day.[79] It has been well-documented that the U.S. government was totally surprised by Tet. Despite an outwardly confident appearance, "the President was seeking reassurance to quiet his own fears and doubts,"[80] and although no one from the administration would say this on the record, "unofficially, off-the-record and between-us-over-the-back-fence, which is how the mood of the American capital is set and transmitted, the U.S. government had been shaken by the Communist offensive and was worried sick about what was coming next."[81] In short, neither the administration's version of events nor Cronkite's was firmly rooted in the "real," although the administration's version now appears to have been closer to the truth than the administration itself believed to be the case at the time. To this we can add one more complicating factor when we consider North Vietnam's Tet strategy.

When Cronkite labeled Tet a development that transformed the war from something that could not be explained into a classic Western war, he was not only jumping to a conclusion without being in possession of most of the facts, he was also making an implicit assumption about the North's intentions. Now, he pronounced, "large armies locked in combat, [are] moving toward a decision on the battlefield." That Cronkite believed that such a "decision" was not forthcoming is beside the point; he assumed that the war would continue along the lines inaugurated by the Tet Offensive. The Johnson administration, which fundamentally disagreed with Cronkite's assessment of U.S. prospects for the war, agreed, however that Hanoi had tried to force a *decision* on the battlefield. When the president judged Tet a communist failure, he was in sync with Westmoreland who portrayed "the Tet Blitzkrieg as a desperate 'go-for-broke' bid by the enemy to avert inevitable defeat—not unlike the Battle of the Bulge staged by the Germans during the final days of World War II."[82] North Vietnamese gen. Vo Nguyen Giap, the "principal architect of the campaign," however, claims that Tet was never meant to be a decisive military encounter but "one episode in a protracted war that might last 'five, ten, or twenty years.'"[83] And, as we know, the Tet Offensive was followed by countless instances of small exchanges that characterize guerrilla warfare, as well as by larger battles. The World War II scenario never materialized.

All this goes to show that for a nascent new historicist, the beginning of 1968 represented an unusually mirky, ambiguous, overdetermined, and fertile historical landscape. A landscape that presented some of the most urgent, violent, and depressing images on the small screen—gripping images that demanded the viewer's attention and emotional involvement—but that could not be adequately explained—or made familiar—by the narratives brought to bear on them by the government or the television media. As a result, I suggest, new historicist criticism as we know it today, celebrates the anecdote as the key to the "real"—or traces thereof—and rejects traditional narrative as an acceptable or productive mode of explanation.

Favoring the anecdote over narrative, however, has its own set of problems. For without narrative or a narrative context in which to place it, the anecdote can quickly become unintelligible. The recent controversy over former Nebraska sen. Bob Kerrey's service in Vietnam illustrates the point perfectly. In a *New York Times Magazine* article, Gerhard Klann, a member of then lieutenant Kerrey's Navy SEAL team, alleges that during a mission to capture a Vietcong police chief in February of 1969 Kerry gave the order to kill a group of unarmed civilians: an old man, a woman, and three young children.[84] The five people, he says, were dispensed of by knife. Klann claims that Kerrey took part in the killing himself; Kerrey insists that the five people were men and denies taking part personally, although he accepts responsibility because he was in charge. Later that night in the village of Thanh Phong, Klann claims, Kerrey gave orders to line up and execute at least thirteen unarmed women, children, and elderly at close range with automatic fire— "there was blood flying up, bits and pieces of flesh hitting us"[85]—for fear that they might give away to the Vietcong the whereabouts of Kerrey's squad. The village of Thanh Phong was located in a so-called "free-fire zone," which, as Westmoreland explains in his memoirs, meant that anyone found in the area (including civilians) could be treated as "an enemy combatant"[86] and killed at any American soldier's discretion. But Westmoreland also emphasizes that he did not want "one innocent civilian killed," and that he took great pains to indoctrinate his men on the "rules of engagement," which "reiterated the rules of the Geneva Convention in regard to prisoners."[87] Kerrey, however, does not call on his soldier's "discretion" in a free-fire zone to explain what happened. Instead, he admits that women and children were killed during the mission but insists that this occurred by mistake when his squad was fired upon and returned fire. No weapons were found with the dead, however, and although several members of the squad corroborate Kerrey's version, there is also a sixty-two-year-old Vietnamese women named Pham Tri Lanh who says she witnessed the incident and who, in an interview with Dan Rather, independently confirmed virtually every detail of Gerhard Klann's recollection of the event.[88]

What do we do with such irreconcilable accounts? Should there be a congressional investigation? How do we judge Kerrey? How do we write the history of Kerrey's mission? All but one of the U.S. senators who were asked the second question, responded with a resounding "no."[89] Republican Sen. Chuck Hagel of Nebraska, wonders, "what's the point" of such an investigation? Surely, he asks, we do not want to "to apply rules, text book rules of warfare in combat in the year 2001 to a situation 32 years ago, a confused chaotic war from start to finish. . . ."[90] Sen. John Kerry, Democrat of Massachusetts, responds to the question of irreconcilability as follows on CNN's *Late Edition with Wolf Blitzer:* "Well, you reconcile it, Wolf, by recognizing that in war, particularly in any kind of battle situation, people have different reactions to what they did or were asked to do. It is not uncommon for people in the same traumatic experience anywhere to have somehow a different memory of it.[91] Republican sen. John McCain addresses the question of how we judge Kerrey by saying that "Those who now judge him must follow the dictates of their conscience. But unless you, too, have been to war, please be careful not to form your judgment of him on your understanding of what constitutes a war hero. They are not the Hollywood copy you might expect."[92] Finally, Rather closes his *60 Minutes II* broadcast by assessing our ability to historicize the Kerrey controversy:

> What you have seen and heard tonight is some of what the Vietnam War was like, what it was REALLY like. Some of the war, but not all. Most Americans who served in Vietnam never did or saw anything remotely resembling what Bob Kerrey and Gerard Klann went through.
>
> Kerrey and Klann were young commandos, trained to do what the enemy had been doing for years: terrorize key people, kill them if necessary, in hopes of winning the war. They went into Thanh Phong that night in 1969 to do what they were ordered to do. Whatever the precise details—which we may never know for certain—it turned into a nightmare. Think of it what you will, but know this: it is what some of war is like, what it's really like . . . a nightmare of unimaginable horror and savagery . . . the full depths of which only those who live through it can know.

In short, Hagel says that we can't evaluate or investigate the Kerrey episode by discussing it in light on the rules of war; John Kerry says that you reconcile it by admitting that you can't reconcile the memories of eyewitnesses; McCain says that you can't understand Kerrey unless you went through a similar experience because the familiar Hollywood narratives through which we "know" war are woefully inadequate; and Rather, echoing McCain, proclaims that although we have just seen what some of the Vietnam War was "*really* like," we cannot understand what we have just seen because we didn't live through the nightmare ourselves. The truth lies in the experience itself, and unless you have lived the experience you cannot understand it. And even if you have lived the experience, you cannot narrate it in a way that will make it genuinely accessible to anyone else (apparently even to those who were there *with* you). Gerhard Klann, when prodded by Rather to describe the execution of the villagers for the television audience, says, "I relive it often enough but *I can't describe it.*"[93]

All this points to the impossibility of doing history, or at least of doing the kind of history that calls on anecdotes to rupture received grand narratives and facilitates "contact with the 'real'"[94]—or some trace thereof—in a way that can make us truly understand history. Epistemologically speaking, this is certainly a disappointment, but, strangely enough, it does not make the anecdote any less powerful in its ability to compel our attention. Both the powerful promise of authentic history in the anecdote and in the anecdote's *in*ability to speak for itself are evident on the opening page of Greenblatt's *Shakespearean Negotiations*. There Greenblatt writes, "I began with the desire to speak with the dead,"[95] which seems to be an expression of Greenblatt's desire for unmediated access to authentic experience—history itself, the historian's elixir. But he then goes on to say that he "never believed that the dead could hear" or that they could actually speak. So why then begin with a desire to speak with the dead, when you realize that in your "most intense moments of straining to listen all [you] could hear was [your] own voice"? Because, Greenblatt says, "my own voice was the voice of the dead, for the dead had contrived to leave textual traces of themselves, and those traces make themselves heard in the voices of the living." If we accept this answer as true—which it may well be—we have to admit that in its formulation subject and object, historian and history, present and past, become fused to the point that we can hardly tell them apart. This undermines any and all claims to the truth or to the real.

In this essay, I have made some historical claims about the development of new historicist criticism. This may seem odd in light of what I have just said about the impossibility of extrapolating history from anecdotes. I therefore readily admit that my hypothesis that watching the evening news in January and February of 1968 may well have contributed to the kind of historical criticism practiced by Greenblatt, Montrose, and others, could be no more than a case of a "new-historical reading into." But that of course is precisely what a new historical reading is: a reading into. It is an effort "to imagine what might have, but did not, actually happen."[96] Or, to put it slightly differently, the desire to unravel the anecdote or to speak with the dead necessitates the search for plausible narratives that make the anecdote accessible and the words of the dead familiar. White and Montrose have rightly observed that new historicism emphasizes the synchronic over the diachronic, the contemporaneously interconnected over the teleological, the specific over the thematic,[97] but we have to recognize that this emphasis is only possible if new historicism has at least an implied sense of the broader cultural context and the diachronic currents/narratives in Renaissance England—as it does. Likewise, a large part of why we still have not come to terms with the Vietnam War is because we did not have—and still do not have—a plausible narrative of Vietnam and its history. In the 1960s, most Americans knew nothing about Vietnam, its language, its culture, its heritage, and of its history of successful resistance against the West, principally the French, since the nineteenth century. We were told to think of Vietnam foremost as a place where we were going to check communist expansion, and that if we had to bomb this small and unsophisticated Third World country into submission to do this, so be it. We were told that we had the right ideology to frame the conflict and plenty of firepower to end it in our favor. And when we saw firsthand the images of warfare, carnage, and confusion on the evenings news, we expected to understand what we saw because, after all, the images' uncompromising nature gave us a sense of what it might be like to be there; and yet, as Arlen so eloquently put it, "those isolated glimpses of elbow, face, a swirl of dress" yielded by the "keyhole" perspective raised endless questions instead.

Did our experiences with the evening news in early 1968 show us that Cronkite, and his colleagues simply imposed the wrong narrative on the Vietnam conflict (suggesting that they might have seized upon the right narrative if they had been more perceptive or better informed), or did the anecdotal character of the news demonstrate the need for a truly new approach to history that we now call "new historicism"? The answer is neither. Clearly, in this case the enigmatic nature of the anecdote impresses upon us the need for narrative while revealing simultaneously the utter inadequacy of the then available World War II and Cold War narratives. Could the anecdotes themselves yield new narratives? Fineman argues that because of its "literary" quality and its rootedness in the real the anecdote possesses its own "peculiar and eventful narrative force."[98] He then sets this narrative quality of the anecdote *against* the "teleological, and therefore timeless, narration of beginning, middle, and end" that we associate with traditional historical narratives.[99] This appears to point to a genuine difference between the narrative structure of the anecdote and the narrative structure of the *grand récit,* but the difference should not be overstated. First, as White has demonstrated in most compelling fashion, even the smallest unit of historical data, the "fact"—which, by the way, is much smaller than Fineman's smallest unit of historiographical fact, the anecdote— can only be identified *as such* after a process of selection, exclusion, and definition that is itself rooted in a metaphoric or "preencoded" understanding of the world.[100] Second, the opposition that Fineman implies between narrative structure of traditional narrative and that of the anecdote seems overstated. When Fineman describes historical narrative as a "teleological, and therefore timeless, narration of beginning, middle, and end" he is describing something very much like providential historical narrative, which indeed is timeless in so far as it rejects all forms of contingency. But one can think of any number of historical narratives that are both teleological and tolerant of contingency. The works of social historians Christopher Hill and Lawrence Stone instantly come to mind, and while the arguments of these men may be too teleological and not receptive enough to the anecdotal for most new historians, we may have to admit that this is largely a matter of emphasis, as opposed to a matter of difference in kind.

The traditional historian emphasizes narrative and presses the anecdotal into its service; the new historian revels in the anecdotal but never to the point that narrative is entirely obliterated, for without it the anecdotal would become unintelligible. To return to this essay's second epigraph, we can say that Greenblatt and Gallagher may wish to shun the transcendent in favor of the real, but that narrative is essentially a transcendent mode necessary for understanding the anecdote and therefore both an approach to, and a swerving away from, the real.

NOTES

1. Don Oberdorfer, *Tet!* (Garden City, NY: Doubleday, 1971), 170.

2. Ibid., 164–66; see also Stanley Karnow, *Vietnam: A History* (New York: Viking, 1983), 529.

3. Oberdorfer, *Tet!,* 168–69.

4. Karnow, *Vietnam,* 529.

5. Oberdorfer, *Tet!,* 170.

6. But see ibid., 238–43.

7. Karnow, *Vietnam,* 548.

8. Stephen Greenblatt, *Learning to Curse: Essays in Early Modern Culture* (New York: Routledge, 1992), 166–67. I do not know whether Greenblatt or Louis Montrose or any other new historian was a regular watcher of the evening news during this period. But I do not think that this matters very much, for there are times, as Montrose has observed in a different context, when "topical connections must remain wholly conjectural" (Montrose, "'Shaping Fantasies'": Figurations of Gender and Power in Elizabethan Culture," in *Representing the Renaissance,* ed. Greenblatt [Berkeley: University of California Press, 1988], 31–64, esp. 32). Just as the guessed-at presence of Elizabeth I at a performance of *A Midsummer Night's Dream* is less consequential to Montrose than is the queen's "pervasive *cultural presence*" as a "condition of the play's imaginative possibility" (32), so it is my contention that the representation of the Vietnam War and the Tet Offensive on the evening new constituted such a "pervasive" "cultural presence" in American life in February of 1968 that it shaped not only the mood and outlook of a broad segment of the American population (of those for as well as for those against the war) but also the imaginative possibilities of those who became the new historicists. Oberdorfer reports that in early February 20.3 percent of television homes watched *CBS Evening News* and 18.8 percent watched NBC's *Huntley-Brinkley Report.* This means that at least 21.7 million homes (of the roughly 56 million homes at that time) were tuned into evening news coverage of the war (240).

9. Greenblatt uses this term to explain how works of art can contain traces of life (or the illusion of life) that have long been extinguished. Social energy is that which makes doing history (or the illusion of history) possible. See Greenblatt, *Shakespearean Negotiations: The Circulation of Social Energy in Renaissance England* (Chicago: University of Chicago Press, 1988), 1–20, esp. 5–8.

10. Catherine Gallagher and Greenblatt explain that such anecdotes served their aim to "interrupt the Big Stories" because they make the reader "pause or even stum-

ble on the threshold of history" (Gallagher and Greenblatt, *Practicing New Historicism* [Chicago: University of Chicago Press, 2000], 51).

11. Greenblatt, "Marlowe and Renaissance Self-Fashioning," in *Two Renaissance Mythmakers: Christopher Marlowe and Ben Jonson*, ed. Alvin Kernan (Baltimore: Johns Hopkins University Press, 1977), 41–69, esp. 41–42.

12. Ibid., 41.

13. Montrose uses the phrase "cognitive map" as follows: "Women's bodies—and, in particular, the Queen's two bodies—provide a cognitive map for Elizabethan culture, a veritable matrix for the Elizabethan forms of desire" (Montrose, "'Shaping Fantasies,'" 47).

14. Gallagher and Greenblatt, *Practicing New Historicism*, 1.

15. This is not actually true, the names are given in a footnote, but just as my own footnote diminishes the visibility of this fact, so Gallagher and Greenblatt's delegation of the names to a footnote downplays the importance of the identities of the group's members.

16. Greenblatt, *Shakespearean Negotiations*, 66–93.

17. See, for instance, Greenblatt, *Learning to Curse*, 1–9, 146–47; and the Epilogue to Greenblatt, *Renaissance Self-Fashioning* (Chicago: University of Chicago Press, 1980), 255–57. In his most recent book, *Hamlet in Purgatory* (Princeton: Princeton University Press, 2001), Greenblatt is unusually frank about the relationship between his study of Shakespeare and his personal life (5–9). In a moving story about his father, who had a complex relationship to death, Greenblatt tells us how his father left a sum of money in his will to an organization that would recite the Aramaic prayer for the dead for him for a period of eleven months because, apparently, he "did not trust either my brother or me to recite the prayer for him" (7). "The effect," Greenblatt says, "the bequest had on me, perhaps perversely, was to impel me to do so, as if in a blend of love and spite." A much later consequence of this moment is, of course, *Hamlet in Purgatory*, a book that concerns itself deeply with the one place—purgatory—in which the suffering of the dead might perhaps be alleviated by the prayers of the living. But as powerful and enlightening as this story is, I do not think that it marks the beginning of a systematic effort by Greenblatt to historicize either his work or his critical method.

18. Greenblatt, *Learning to Curse*, 167.

19. Gallagher and Greenblatt, *Practicing New Historicism*, 19.

20. Jean Howard, "The New Historicism in Renaissance Studies," in *Renaissance Historicism: Selections from English Literary Renaissance*, eds. Arthur F. Kinney and Dan S. Collins (Amherst: University of Massachusetts Press, 1987), 13.

21. Greenblatt, *Shakespearean Negotiations*, 1–20; for the association of two "particulars" at great geographic distance from each other, see Greenblatt, "Fiction and Friction," 66–93.

22. On this question, see Hayden White, *Tropics of Discourse: Essays in Cultural Criticism* (Baltimore: Johns Hopkins University Press, 1978), 81–100.

23. Joel Fineman, "The History of the Anecdote: Fiction and Fiction," in *The New Historicism,* ed. H. Aram Veeser (New York: Routledge), 49–76, esp. 57.

24. Gallagher and Greenblatt, *Practicing New Historicism,* 49–74, esp. 49–54.

25. Greenblatt, *Learning to Curse,* 5.

26. Gallagher and Greenblatt, *Practicing New Historicism,* 51.

27. Ibid. See also Greenblatt, *Learning to Curse,* 5–6.

28. Fineman, "History of the Anecdote," 61.

29. Gallagher and Greenblatt, *Practicing New Historicism,* 20–48.

30. Ibid., 23.

31. Ibid.

32. Greenblatt, *Shakespearean Negotiations,* chapter 1.

33. I borrow the term "vignette journalism" from Peter Braestrup, *Big Story: How the American Press and Television Reported and Interpreted the Crisis of Tet 1968 in Vietnam and Washington* (Garden City: Anchor Press, 1978), 22–23.

34. William C. Westmoreland, *A Soldier Reports* (Garden City: Doubleday, 1976), 411.

35. Joanna Neuman, *Lights, Camera, War. Is Media Technology Driving International Politics?* (New York: St. Martin's, 1996), 177.

36. Michael J. Arlen, *The Living-Room War* (1966) (New York: Viking, 1969).

37. Ibid., 83.

38. Greenblatt, *Learning to Curse,* 5.

39. Gallagher and Greenblatt, *Practicing New Historicism,* 51.

40. Ibid.

41. Gallagher and Greenblatt's paraphrase of Fineman, "History of the Anecdote" (see Gallagher and Greenblatt, *Practicing New Historicism,* 50).

42. Arlen, *Living-Room War,* 108–9.

43. Ibid., 109, see also 112–13.

44. Gallagher and Greenblatt, *Practicing New Historicism,* 50.

45. Ibid., 22.

46. Ibid., 23.

47. Ibid., 25.

48. Ibid., 23.

49. Greenblatt, *Learning to Curse,* 5.

50. Arlen, *Living-Room War,* 115, see also 64.

51. Morley Safer, "Burning Village of Cam Ne," in *The War in Vietnam: A Multi Media Chronicle* (New York: Macmillan Digital USA, 1995).

52. Arlen, *Living-Room War*, 117.

53. Ibid., 111.

54. Walter Cronkite, "Who, What, When, Where, Why?" Report from Vietnam. *CBS News Special*, 27 February 1968. See also Karnow, *Vietnam*, 523–24, 538–39.

55. Robert Buzzanco, "The Myth of Tet: American Failure and the Politics of War," in *The Tet Offensive*, eds. Marc Jason Gilbert and William Head (Westport, CT: Praeger, 1996), 231–57, esp. 231.

56. See Braestrup, xiii, 505–7; and Oberdorfer, *Tet!*, 239–51.

57. See Braestrup, 404–32.

58. Quoted in ibid., 49.

59. *CBS News*, 1 February 1968.

60. Karnow, *Vietnam*, 514.

61. Quoted in Braestrup, 49. Vice President Hubert Humphrey went on NBC's *Meet the Press* on 26 November to pitch in as well:

> I do think it is fair to say that there has been progress on every front in Vietnam; militarily, substantial progress, politically, very significant progress, with the Constitution and the freely elected government. Diplomatically, in terms of peace negotiations, that is the place where there has been the stalemate. There is no military stalemate. There is no pacification stalemate. (quoted in Braestrup, 51)

For good measure, Westmoreland visited the National Press Club on 21 November 1967 to reiterate that "We are making progress. We know you want an honorable and early transition to the fourth and last phase [when U.S. units can begin to phase down]. So do your sons and so do I. It lies within our grasp—the enemy's hopes are bankrupt. With your support we will give you a success that will impact not only South Vietnam but on every emerging nation in the world" (quoted in Braestrup, 51).

62. Ibid., 156.

63. Ibid., 468. General Westmoreland was sent the following message: "The President desires that you make brief personal comments to the press at least once each day during the current period of mounting VC/NVA activity. The purpose of such statements should be to convey to the American public your confidence in our capability to blunt these enemy moves, and to reassure the public here that you have the situation under control" (quoted in Braestrup, 468; see also Karnow, *Vietnam*, 547).

64. President Lyndon B. Johnson, Press conference, 2 February 1968; *War in Vietnam*.

65. Cronkite, "Who, What, When, Where, Why?"

66. Cronkite, *A Reporter's Life* (New York: Knopf, 1997), 252.

67. Ibid. That the Vietnam War remains in some sense inexplicable until today is exemplified by the recent controversy surrounding the actions of former U.S. sen. Bob Kerry of Nebraska during a military operation in Vietnam during which he allegedly

executed Vietnamese civilians. Those who spoke in Kerry's defense, including Massachusetts sen. John Kerry, constantly emphasized that the Vietnam War was like no other war (especially when compared to World War II) because of the so-called "free fire zones" and the inability to distinguish between Vietcong fighters and civilians.

68. Cronkite, "Who, What, When, Where, Why?"

69. I suppose that we might recall here Greenblatt and Gallagher's observation that "counterhistories" are at times borne from the "impulse to the discredit old narratives" rather than from an "impulse to synthesize new ones, and the 1960s and 1970s were such a time" (Gallagher and Greenblatt, *Practicing New Historicism,* 52–53).

70. See White, *Tropics of Discourse,* 86.

71. See White, "New Historicism: A Comment," in *The New Historicism,* ed. H. Aram Veeser (New York: Routledge, 1989), 293–302, esp. 301–2.

72. As Braestrup has pointed out with the benefit of hindsight, "the problem in February 1968 for all would-be news analysts was that the Tet battlefields provided an insufficient 'data base' from which to draw broad independent conclusions or to 'project the story' in many areas" (159). Furthermore, it appears that Cronkite came to the conclusion that the war was "a stalemate" sometime after 14 February. On that day he spoke of the Tet Offensive very much as a traumatic event in an ongoing war that could push the possibility for peace well into the future. In other words, on 14 February Tet was still part of a process, not evidence of a stalemate (*CBS Evening News,* 14 February 1968).

73. Bernard Kalb, "Vietcong," in *War in Vietnam.*

74. One may discern here the seeds of the rather severe subversion-containment model of Greenblatt's late Cold War writings (the years prior to the dissolution of the Soviet Union) by suggesting that American culture values and encourages a "free" press that challenges official narratives, only to find that the media are not free enough to imagine anything other than an old (official and quintessentially American) World War II narrative to frame their "dissent."

75. Oberdorfer, *Tet!,* 158–59.

76. Braestrup, 501.

77. Ibid., 119.

78. Braestrup, for instance, points out that to reporters "and their superiors, the inherent drama—and importance—of Saigon, Hue, and Khe Sanh were compelling, and obviously 'news.' And the concentration of journalistic manpower on these dramatic but *isolated* stories insured that they treated at home as the significant 'news'" (ibid., 158; my emphasis).

79. Westmoreland, *Soldier Reports,* 323–25; see also James J. Wirtz, *The Tet Offensive: Intelligence Failure in War* (Ithaca: Cornell University Press, 1991), 235.

80. Oberdorfer, *Tet!,* 162.

81. Ibid., 171.

82. Karnow, *Vietnam,* 535.

83. Ibid., 535, 536.

84. "Memories of a Massacre: Varying Accounts of a Night In 1969," *60 Minutes II,* CBS News, 1 May 2001.

85. Gerhard Klann's account in ibid.

86. Westmoreland, *Soldier Reports,* 285–86.

87. Ibid., 286.

88. "Memories of a Massacre."

89. *Late Edition with Wolf Blitzer,* "Evaluating Bush's First 100 Days; Did Kerrey Handle Vietnam," CNN, 29 April 2001. Only John McCain of Arizona told *ABC News,* "I don't feel that Bob or the members of his team would feel any discomfort associated with an investigation if particularly the American people feel that's necessary." CNN, "Former Colleagues Rally Around Embattled Kerrey," 29 April 2001.

90. *Late Edition with Wolf Blitzer,* 29 April 2001.

91. Ibid.

92. *CNN Live Today,* "Public Reacts to Cherry's Statements," 27 April 2001.

93. Klann goes to describe a scene of carnage, but clearly the account he gives does not satisfy his standards of adequate description.

94. Gallagher and Greenblatt, *Practicing New Historicism,* 54.

95. Greenblatt, *Shakespearean Negotiations,* 1.

96. Gallagher and Greenblatt, *Practicing New Historicism,* 54.

97. See White, "New Historicism" and Montrose, "Professing the Renaissance: The Poetics and Politics of Culture," in *The New Historicism,* ed. H. Aram Veeser (New York: Routledge, 1989), 15–36.

98. Fineman, "History of the Anecdote," 57.

99. Ibid., 61.

100. White, *Tropics of Discourse,* 90.

8

The End of Culture

LOREN GLASS

> To be is to do.
> —Plato

> To do is to be.
> —Jean-Paul Sartre

> Doobie doobie doobie do.
> —Frank Sinatra

Walter Benn Michaels' *Our America* (1995) works to expose uncomfortable connections between doing and being in American discourses of identity, arguing persuasively that if "culture" describes what we do, then "race"— whether we like it or not—describes who we are. Michaels performs this exposure by complicating the shift from racial essentialism to cultural pluralism in the early twentieth century. Whereas the standard logic has been that this was a good thing insofar as it worked toward purging American race relations of essentialist logics, Michaels, in a move now typical of him, argues that it was precisely the reverse:

> although the move from racial identity to cultural identity appears to replace essentialist criteria of identity (who we are) with performative criteria (what we do), the commitment to pluralism requires in fact that the question of who we are continue[s] to be understood as prior to questions about what we do.[1]

In other words, Michaels argues that culture didn't so much replace race as become an expression of it, since in order for any group to *have* a culture they must *be* some sort of identifiable population in the first place. Michaels' conclusion, then, revises the generally accepted emplotment of the rise of "culture," at least in the anthropological sense of the term: "The modern concept of culture is not, in other words, a critique of racism; it is a form of racism. And, in fact, as skepticism about the biology of race has increased, it has become—at least among intellectuals—the dominant form of racism" (129). So those of us "intellectuals" who thought we were doing culture have really been doing race. Or, more incendiary, those of us who think we are using the term "culture" to describe, evaluate, celebrate, and promote the practices of various populations have actually been racist in our very ascription of specific practices to identifiable populations. In fact, as far as Michaels is concerned, "there are no anti-essentialist accounts of identity," and therefore *any* work that attempts to link culture to identity is racist (181).

So, although Michaels' argument focuses most explicitly on the literature of early twentieth-century America, it also quite clearly condemns contemporary "identity politics" and disputes over multiculturalism, as well as most of what passes for "cultural studies" in the University. In other words, Michaels uses his critique of early twentieth-century American discourses of race to condemn later twentieth-century discourses of race, at least as they are practiced in the University. As a consequence of this oblique method of critique, *Our America*—and Michaels' work generally—tends to be somewhat coy about its own historical context.

Nevertheless, like the texts he so deftly analyzes, Michaels' own work is very much a product of its time. In this essay I will align Michaels' participation in the "Against Theory" debates with the rise of a correlative neo-conservative and xenophobic orthodoxy in American English departments. I will then connect Michaels' theorization of the ubiquity of capitalism in his first book, *The Gold Standard and the Logic of Naturalism* (1987), to America's incipient "victory" in the Cold War and the associated globalization of American free-market ideology. Finally, I will return to *Our America* as a complex allegory of these very historical developments, which symptomatically elides the very decade that formed Michaels' generation of literary critics. Thus I conclude that a consideration of the sixties is crucial to an understanding of the contemporary debates over "culture."

PRACTICING THE PROFESSION

Michaels is no stranger to academic controversy; he's been raining on a number of disciplinary parades for the last two decades. Before he put the term "culture" in his critical sights, he had been taking aim at "theory" for some time, and the moves he made with his Berkeley colleague Stephen Knapp in their high-profile pragmatist counterassault on the theory invasion in the pages of *Critical Inquiry* are a necessary archaeology of his agenda in *Our America*. Not only do the logic and rhetoric of "Against Theory" continue to inform Michaels' work, but a return to the moment of "Against Theory" supplies us with a now almost forgotten prehistory of our current practices of literary and cultural analysis. In other words, if a return to the moment of "Against Theory" helps illuminate the terms of Michaels' critique of "culture," it simultaneously helps us understand a particular culture based in *institutional*—as opposed to racial or ethnic—affiliation. Thus going back to one of the inaugural moments in Michaels' career is also a way of understanding a crucial aporia in that career, which is nothing other than the very institution—the prestigious University and, more specifically, the academic "Star System"—which made that career possible in the first place.

In order to explain what I mean here I would like to briefly rehearse the "Against Theory" debates, focusing less on their philosophical content than on their institutional and historical conditions of possibility. "Against Theory" hinges on an argument that is easily reducible to a single polemical claim: "what a text means and what its author intends it to mean are identical and . . . their identity robs intention of any theoretical interest."[2] The debate following on the publication of this article in 1982 continued on and off over the next decade, mostly in the pages of *Critical Inquiry*, as prominent American academics such as Stanley Fish, Richard Rorty, E. D. Hirsch, and Steven Mailloux—to name just a few—attempted to decide what theory was and whether or not they were "for" or "against" it. Like the John Searle-Jacques Derrida debates or the "Purloined Poe" discussion, "Against Theory" and its many responses cloaked a peculiar combination of pedagogy and publicity beneath an apparently "philosophical" agenda. Its underlying and primary function was to show us what theory was and who the theorists were, and only secondarily to advise us on how to interpret texts. But, rhetorically at least, the stakes of "Against Theory" were more dire, as Knapp and Michaels boldly claimed that "the whole enterprise of critical theory is misguided and should be abandoned" (12).

Of course this never happened, nor could Knapp and Michaels have possibly thought it would, and the fate of "Against Theory" ironically affirms the modest consequences of any "theoretical" intervention. The almost quaint character it takes on in retrospect only seems to affirm that the stakes were always only rhetorical. But high rhetorical stakes frequently mask lasting institutional consequences, and if Knapp and Michaels did not succeed in convincing anyone of the equation between meaning and intention, they did succeed in clarifying for many graduate students what they needed to know and do in order to get ahead in the profession.

I mention this in order to affirm two related points. First, as many critics immediately recognized, there was nothing very anti-theoretical about "Against Theory": it arose out of, and remained engaged with, the presence of "theory" in the American university. And second, these theory debates say at least as much about changes in the academic career structure as they do about the interpretation of literary texts. Or, rather, the entire debate indicates how the former came to dominate the latter. Both "theory" and the neo-pragmatist response to it were part of a larger process of professional transformation in the eighties whose terms I would like to begin to explore in Peggy Kamuf's review of *Against Theory* (1982).

It is the rhetorical idiom rather than the philosophical substance of Kamuf's review that concerns me here. She compares the response to "Against Theory" to "a crisis set off by a pair of tinkerers who were sure they knew what they were doing but who made a terrible mess of things. Experts are called in to turn the damned thing off but nothing, so far, seems to work."[3] Deciding to collapse Knapp and Michaels into one critic/cipher she calls "KaM," she further claims that "He resembles an entrepreneur dreaming about the profits to be had within the institutional order once he markets his self-destructing theory-gadget."[4] What is remarkable about these citations—aside from their condescending tone—is their only partly ironic use of the twin metaphors of the market and the machine. On the one hand, theory is represented as a technically complex mechanism (assumedly for the interpretation of texts), Knapp and Michaels as neophyte engineers, possibly good at "tinkering" but certainly not competent enough to understand the principles that make it run. For this, "experts" (presumably like Kamuf) are required. On the other hand, they are compared to an "entrepreneur" who wants to market a "gadget" for a profit, presumably to be reaped in the currency of reputation (if not notoriety). Although Kamuf is certainly intending to be tongue-in-cheek here, she also clearly feels that she has selected the most apt figures for representing the situation, figures that seem more related to engineering and business administration than they do to literature.

By now we're somewhat inured to such phrases as "the academic marketplace" or "the technology of interpretation"; in a very real sense, they're no longer figurative. In fact, Kamuf's review reveals the "Against Theory" moment as part of the process by which such metaphors became concretized, a powerful index of what John Guillory identifies as the transformation of literary study in the eighties into a version of "the technobureaucratic labor of the new professional-managerial class."[5] Guillory sees the moment of theory as a symptomatic reaction to the declining relevance of literary study in American universities and society at large. First of all, by questioning the very category of literature, theory was able to—at least theoretically—expand the relevance of the interpretive techniques learned in English departments to a much wider variety of "texts." Second, the exposure to theory became a definitive element of the graduate school experience and its mastery an indication of one's technical competence and marketability. Certainly "Against Theory" embraces the broadly philosophical pretensions of its apparent opponent; the scope of its examples and the breadth of its claims all but affirm that its argument is intended to apply to every conceivable communicative exchange between sentient beings. Correlatively, it lends its opponent texts the seductive allure of forbidden sin. Theory was required reading if you wanted to understand what "Against Theory" was telling you not to do. The entire debate, then, would seem to prove Paul de Man's contemporaneous claim that "nothing can overcome the resistance to theory since theory *is* itself this resistance."[6]

THEORY AMERICAN STYLE

However, if Knapp and Michaels' work, in theory, was not so different from the theory that surrounded it, it was not exactly the same either. The most interesting formulation of this difference, for me, appears in W. J. T. Mitchell's introduction to the *Against Theory* collection. Mitchell claims that, although Knapp and Michaels' work conceptually resembles the theory it renounces, it may nevertheless "produce a loosely defined 'school' of antagonists who will take up the challenge to formulate a pragmatic account of theory, one that would identify it as a genre of writing, a type of discourse."[7] Mitchell then supplies a small two-column chart that serves as a sort of rhetorical guide for differentiating what "theory is" from what "theory is not." The most interesting pair in Mitchell's list for me is the apparently opposed dyad, "deductive or inductive" versus "adductive." In response to Rorty, Mitchell was compelled in a footnote to clarify what he meant by these terms: "Deduction proceeds from generals to particulars; induction, from particulars to generals; and adduction from particulars to particulars" (6). Mitchell's illustration of the procedure is from the practice of law: "A lawyer adduces precedents (which are always particular cases and judgments) or evidence in support of the application of the law to a particular case" (6). But this doesn't describe the practice of law in general; it describes the Anglo-American system of common law, which can be serviceably contrasted to continental systems of Roman law that are based on principle, not precedent. In other words, although Mitchell didn't add "European" versus "Anglo-American" to his chart, it clearly would fit there without much artificial forcing.

This is not a terribly new point but it is worth reaffirming here as a prelude to a discussion of Michaels' other work, which has become increasingly preoccupied with "Americanness." "Against Theory" was part of a specifically

Anglo-American response to what was perceived by many to be a European incursion into American English departments. If Knapp and Michaels nowhere indicate this directly in their essay, they do suspiciously conclude that theory "is a name for all the ways people have tried to stand outside practice in order to govern practice from without" (30). Now whether or not one can "stand outside practice" is a perennial problem of politics and philosophy, but if we substitute something like "the nation" (or "the culture" or "the department") for the term "practice" we get a closer idea of what the combined cultural and institutional stakes might have appeared to be to the participants in the "Against Theory" debates. In fact, rereading "Against Theory" with such a substitution in mind makes its insistence on the proprietary purity of a text's meaning seem oddly xenophobic.

This is only confirmed by what Mitchell calls the essay's "spare, laconic" style, which can easily be characterized as a sort of populist "plain talk" which, again according to Mitchell, requires no "special expertise" to understand (3). The preference for monosyllabic words of Anglo-Saxon derivation over polysyllabic "jargon" of Latin derivation further indicates the "Against Theory" intervention as at least partly an Anglo-American response to the presence of continental thought. The essay, in this sense, partakes of the anti-imperialist rhetoric that Michaels so deftly analyzes in *Our America*. "Against Theory" asserts a cultural "style" as a quasi-nationalist defense of "English" as a language intelligible to all who speak it. We don't need foreigners to tell us what our texts mean.

In other words, Knapp and Michaels' stubborn insistence that a text can only mean what an author intends it to mean can look more like a juridical (as opposed to epistemological) and cultural (as opposed to ontological) claim if it is placed firmly in its historical and institutional moment. To say that the text only means what the author intends is another way of saying that the text *belongs* to the author in some inalienable way, and to assert this proprietary relation as absolute is to affirm a certain cultural way of organizing the relationship between texts and persons. It is this proprietary relationship, it seems to me, that Knapp and Michaels felt was being threatened by "outside" influences.

MARKET LOGICS

Michaels' first book, *The Gold Standard and the Logic of Naturalism* (1987), is in many ways an extended meditation on precisely this proprietary relationship. In the introduction to that book, Michaels discusses Charlotte Perkins Gilman's "Yellow Wallpaper" and evacuates it of the political significance it was assumed to have by both its author and its earlier critics, affirming instead that it "is a story of the origin of property and, by the same token, of the origin of the self."[9] Deliberately ignoring the feminist scholarship that led to the rediscovery of the text in the first place, Michaels claims that it is simply an allegory of the relation between the self and the marketplace. The essays that follow are then above all concerned with locating and determining this relation, and *The Gold Standard* tends to reduce all other possible concerns about the dispositions of persons and texts to its relentless logic. Michaels summarizes this relation in the following terms:

> Ownership . . . is thus an internal relation required by the impossibility of understanding the self as a single, undifferentiated entity . . . the discourse of naturalism . . . is above all obsessed with manifestations of internal difference or, what comes to the same thing, personhood. Continually imagining the possibility of identity without difference, it is provoked by its own images into ever more powerful imaginations of identity by way of difference. (22)

The Gold Standard, then, takes the loaded categories of "identity" and "difference" and claims that they are primarily intelligible—at least in turn of the century American culture—in terms of market logic.

Michaels' net was bigger than this, however, and *The Gold Standard* is partly framed as a polemic against those "oppositional" critics who claim that it is possible to explain or evaluate such problems on any other terms. In this text, then, Michaels introduces us to his signature outflanking procedure that supplements the "no outside practice" argument of "Against Theory" with what in that text remains only an implicit conclusion that we're all on the inside anyway. Michaels has become well-known for exposing apparently subversive positions as always necessarily co-opted by the system—usually capitalism in some form or another—they were purported to oppose, and his contention, in the introduction to *The Gold Standard,* that "the only relation literature as such has to culture as such is that it is a part of it," became one of the flash points for those who wanted to criticize his work as part of an expanding ethos of conservative quietism that was leaking into the academy during the Reagan years (27). His "no way out" theory of culture seemed to translate quickly and inevitably into acceptance of the status quo and Michaels, unlike others such as Fish or Barbara Hernstein Smith, did little to deny this accusation.

What is interesting and informative about *The Gold Standard,* however, is that it explicitly identifies the culture that we can't escape as constituted in and by capitalism, and this suspicious conflation comfortably orients his work in its historical context of Reagan era deregulation and free market frenzy. Contemplating why it was impossible for him to imagine "a Dreiser outside capitalism," Michaels decides that "the logic of capitalism produces objects of desire only insofar as it produces subjects"; it is therefore apparently impossible to evaluate either the subjects or the objects outside of the market terms that gave rise to them in the first place. In the following chapters Michaels takes this structure of "internal difference" that constitutes both subjects and objects in the market and uses it to perform that quintessentially New Historicist task of synthesizing a remarkably heterogeneous collection of literary and nonliterary works from the same historical period, and reducing them to an expression of a single "structure." The almost seamlessly deft manner in which Michaels is able to perform these syntheses is quite stunning, and *The Gold Standard* remains a tour de force of New Historicist interpretive practice.

Michaels' totalizing logic brought criticism from two fronts, both of which are significant for understanding the genesis of *Our America*. On the one hand, his reduction of all "identities" to one homologous structure of internal difference meant that he willfully neglected the many "external" differences that also determine the relationship between the self and the market. Clearly anyone concerned with issues of race, class, gender, or sexuality would find problems with this reduction. On the other hand, Michaels' insistence that there is "no outside" to consumer culture implies that dialectical criticism of the market is not possible. Anyone invested in "transcendence," in the critical possibility and crucial importance of envisioning alternatives—utopian or real—to capitalism, would also have something to say to this book.

It is not surprising, then, that *The Gold Standard* takes center stage in Fredric Jameson's discussion of "Immanence and the New Historicism" in his *Postmodernism* (1991). For Jameson, the New Historicism can be described as "a return to immanence and to a prolongation of the procedures of 'homology' which eschews homology's theory and abandons the concept of 'structure'"; *The Gold Standard* serves as a preeminent example of this "return."[10] Jameson specifies the move as a "return" since the practice of analyzing texts by way of homologies was a specifically structuralist methodology, and critics like Michaels seem to want to disavow many of the explicitly *post*structuralist claims that have intervened. On the other hand, Michaels' insistence on "immanence," on the "suppression of distance" and the "exclusion of self-consciousness or reflexivity," makes his work support Jameson's definition of postmodernity, if not poststructuralism.[11] For Jameson, then, Michaels is the postmodern critic par excellence, who is able to appropriate the methodologies of "modernist" literary and cultural criticism while abandoning its radical or transformative pretensions.

If Michaels' homologies troubled someone like Jameson because they signified an historically symptomatic failure to imagine "alternate systems," they also troubled those who felt that differences *within* the system were also being effaced.[12] Thus we find Brook Thomas contending that, insofar as Michaels "succumbs to the ideology of the bourgeois juridical system that treats all subjects equally under the law of capitalism, . . . we find him not only ignoring class but also paying little attention to questions of gender and race."[13] If Jameson criticizes Michaels for his inability to picture some different position *outside* capitalism, Thomas wants to criticize his apparent inability to acknowledge critical differences of position *inside* it. Possibly we are all constituted in and by the market, but are we all constituted in the same way? Clearly not, and it is this particular contention, that Michaels had not adequately considered differences of *collective* identity—differences of race, class, gender, ethnicity, and sexuality—which eventually resulted in *Our America*, in which Michaels discusses all these categories, though rarely in ways that would please those whose criticisms undoubtedly contributed to the conception of the book.

ACADEMIC AFFECTS

Michaels unveiled an early version of what would become his "Race into Culture" article for *Critical Inquiry* at the 1992 Modern Language Association (MLA) convention in San Francisco. He spoke last, after a series of critics had given their versions of the significance of "identity politics" for the University. Michaels then gave his talk, affirming what would later become the polemical thesis of *Our America:* "there are no anti-essentialist accounts of identity" (181). The ensuing discussion was certainly as close to high drama as an MLA panel is ever likely to get, and what was most interesting about it had less to do with the issues discussed than with the affects invested in those issues or, more specifically, the affects displaced from those issues onto the person of Walter Benn Michaels. The substance of the debate seemed almost completely effaced by the emotional response to Michaels' implicit—and, on some level, self-evident—accusation that many academic intellectuals are unwittingly "racist" in their claims about cultural identity.

Michaels' name tends to provoke such irritation and even outrage from many academics, as if his work constituted a personal insult. I am, of course, not concerned as to whether Michaels is a friendly person, nor even, at this point, whether or not his work is "correct" in its condemnation of much of the work that is being done in the University. Rather, I am interested in the affective response his presence in the academy tends to generate. The fact that he provokes such anger and resentment seems to me to signify that his work exposes ethical dilemmas that most academics are more comfortable repressing, that he somehow exposes the "bad faith" of the University.

Although Michaels pulls his punches somewhat in *Our America,* he is not always so gentle in his criticism, and a brief look at his review of Marianna Torgovnick's *Gone Primitive* (1990) and Cary Nelson's *Repression and Recovery*

(1989) can indicate how he can ruthlessly expose ethical incoherences and emotional displacements at the heart of much contemporary cultural studies. Here is Michaels' conclusion:

> if, after all, we can know what our interests our, then why can't we know other things as well, like what other people's interests were, or what the poems they wrote mean, or what their societies were like? Neither Nelson nor Torgovnick addresses this question; their only concern is to get morality to the center stage and keep it there. And, from this perspective, it is perhaps unfair to complain about the banality of Nelson's appreciative criticism or the emptiness of Torgovnick's intellectual history, not to mention the incoherence of both their theoretical approaches. For neither one is really much interested in saying something about poetry or history. They are interested instead in being good. And, judging by the evidence presented in these texts, they probably are good.[14]

I am not concerned here with defending Torgovnick and Nelson against these alarming accusations. Rather, I cite this review because it illustrates more directly than Michaels' other work the combined personal and professional stakes of that work. His clear desire to disillusion us of any moral high ground we may feel has been established in the last twenty years of work on "identity." Arguably such a tonic is necessary for some of what passes as "cultural studies" today, but Michaels' attack is aimed more centrally: it goes to the heart of the contemporary condition of the humanities in the American university.

When Michaels dismisses Nelson's "appreciative criticism" and Torgovnick's "intellectual history," he is not so subtly referencing what he thinks the humanities used to be in the university, and therefore negatively indexing what he thinks they have become. If, in the past, we thought that we really could establish legitimate aesthetic standards of evaluation and if, in the past, we felt that we really had a shot at figuring out what dead people were thinking from the books they wrote, now, according to Michaels, we have disavowed both those things for claims that we can further what we consider to be moral/political agendas through consideration of these texts.

If this sounds like another neo-conservative critique of the "politicizing" of the humanities, that's because it is, but Michaels is a far more savvy adversary in this battle than Allan Bloom or William Bennett. This is because Michaels is able to pinpoint the bad faith at the center of so much of what passes as "political" in the University, and to expose the deep incoherences at the center of many of its ethical imperatives. In other words, Michaels functions as a disciplinary bad conscience, reminding us of the embarrassing guilt that lies beneath so many postures of innocence, exposing the self-righteousness that is only dimly veiled beneath so many of our "humble" moral claims.

Michaels serves to remind us that, whatever progress we have made in the last twenty years, there is something wrong with what the "humanities" in the American university have become.

UNIVERSAL VALUES

If, however, Michaels is able to tell us what's wrong, he is far more cagey about what's right. If *Our America* is very clear in its exposure of the conceptual incoherences that undergird our understanding of "culture," it is less clear about its own position on the issues we have been trying to work through in deploying the term in the first place. Although Michaels is always straight to the point in his negative claims, he is notoriously evasive in his positive claims; for these one has to remain content with implication and innuendo. Thus, I would now like to look more closely at the argument that moves *Our America*.

As I've already implied, *Our America* can be seen as a response to both of the criticisms of *The Gold Standard* discussed above: it deals with those "identities" that were excluded from the latter text, and it is more careful not to subsume all its primary evidence in a single structural homology. *Our America* talks about the differences that were apparently occluded by *The Gold Standard*'s logic of the same. I have already established what Michaels' basic response is to the first criticism; *Our America* asserts in no uncertain terms that culture has operated for at least the last half century as a euphemism for race, and that all claims for identity are constitutively essentialist. I have not yet mentioned Michaels' response to Jameson's critique, to the problem of "homology."

If *The Gold Standard* seemed to reduce all its evidence to a single structure of "internal difference," *Our America* improves on this method by offering two structures, and thereby expanding the synchronic claims of the former text into a diachronic thesis. In other words, in *Our America,* things change, and the change that things undergo is Michaels' version of the inception of what he calls "nativist modernism." Michaels summarizes the basic structure of this change in the opening pages: "this rewriting of both race and nation as family corresponded to two important shifts in racial logic, one that emphasized not the inferiority of alien races but their 'difference,' and a second that began to represent difference in cultural instead of political (and in addition to) racial terms" (11). This is the hinge on which Michaels' history turns, a change from racial hierarchy to racial difference and a concomitant shift from the State to Culture as the arena in which racial difference is negotiated. *Our America* follows this shift through the work of many of the canonical American modernists—Hemingway, Faulkner, Fitzgerald, Cather, Hurston, Williams, Eliot, Toomer—and, true to Michaels' continued allegiance to New Historicism's methodological style, reads them over and against a selection of lesser-known contemporaneous texts.

Michaels' focus on the second half of this shift—on the rise of "nativist modernism"—somewhat occludes the telling ways in which he represents the prior Progressive era discourse of race. However, there are some key locations in which Michaels exposes what could be considered the contemporary stakes of his historical emplotment:

> Where the assertion of racial superiority requires a primary commitment to certain universal values (the ones according to which some races are deemed superior and some inferior) and thus a merely secondary commitment to whichever race happens to rank the highest, the denial of the relevance of superiority and inferiority makes race as such into the cathected object. (77)

Progressive era claims about racial hierarchy were apparently only racist in a "merely secondary" way; their primary commitment was to "certain universal values." On the other hand, the claims of "nativist modernism" were *essentially* racist insofar as their primary commitment was to cultural difference as such.

Michaels goes further, however, than this characteristic claim that what has normally been written as a laudable shift from racial essentialism to cultural pluralism is actually the reverse. In claiming that the shift was one from a "common scale" for measuring racial differences to "an unmeasurable and hence incomparable racial essence," Michaels also, at least implicitly, seems to be valuing, if not endorsing, the former over the latter (66). If both the Progressive era and the interwar years were fundamentally racist, the Progressive era had the benefit of being logically consistent and coherent in its claims, whereas in the twenties the discourse of race became mired in the logical contradictions of "cultural pluralism."

There is a discernible nostalgia for, if not adherence to, concepts like "universal values" and "the common scale" in *Our America,* and this somewhat uncomfortably orients his book in the institutional context that it nowhere acknowledges. For, in terms of the academic culture of which this book is a part, such criteria translate into the concept of "merit," that liberal ideal that at least rhetorically remains the grounding concept in the evaluative procedures that determine so much of our concrete experience as academics. One possible message to derive from Michaels' work concerns the degree to which we still have not worked our way out of the "meritocracy," if it ever was our intention to do so in the first place.

RADICAL ALLEGORIES

It is interesting to note, in this regard, that Michaels entirely neglects the humanist meaning of the term "culture," which, after all, used to undergird the evaluative procedures of English departments. Boasian anthropologists had to work hard and long to muscle out the Arnoldian resonances of the term. In fact, the pervasive Arnoldian association is purportedly what led Alfred L. Kroeber to call his influential article for *American Anthropologist* "The Super-organic," a term which, not surprisingly, has not survived. Kroeber later claimed that "he feared to be misunderstood outside of anthropology if he used the word 'culture.'"[15] Furthermore, in the very decades that make up the explicit focus of Michaels' study, African-American artists and intellectuals of the Harlem Renaissance were working toward W. E. B. Dubois's vision of becoming "a coworker in the Kingdom of culture."[16] The collective ethos of the class fragment that formed around DuBois's conception was clearly grounded in the cosmopolitan sense of culture for which Arnold was the most well known exponent. Black intellectuals such as Dubois, Alain Locke, and James Weldon Johnson—to name only the most well-known—were deeply invested in a humanistic sense of culture that transcended, as opposed to expressed, race. Certainly Michaels could not have been unaware of the persistence of this meaning of the term. After all, Lionel Trilling, the humanist literary critic who towered over Michaels' generation, proclaimed in the preface to his sixties opus *Beyond Culture*.

> everyone is conscious of at least two meanings of the word. One of them refers to that complex of activities which includes the practice of the arts and of certain intellectual disciplines . . . the other meaning is much more inclusive. It comprises a people's technology and organization, its systems of valuation, whether expressed or implicit.[17]

Why would Michaels deliberately occlude this crucial genealogical complexity?

In this day and age, in fact, it is easy to forget the Arnoldian extensions of the term "culture." One need look no further than Stephen Greenblatt's recent definition of the term, in a reference book significantly titled *Critical Terms for Literary Study* (1990), to index the degree to which the humanistic meaning has receded. Greenblatt (a colleague and cofounder of the New Historicism with Michaels at Berkeley in the early eighties) opens not with Arnold but with English anthropologist E. B. Tylor, and his entire discussion is oriented around the anthropological idea of culture as a "complex whole," in which literature simply operates as a privileged mode of transmission.[18] Literary studies, in other words, has almost fully abandoned any overt claim to humanistic culture, and has enthusiastically adopted anthropological culture. Even the recent vogue for the sociology of culture that has been so fruitfully pursued under the critical auspices of Pierre Bourdieu takes the evaluative significance of culture as an anthropological object, as opposed to a humanistic subject, of critical consideration.

Thus it should not surprise us that none of the many prominent intellectuals who take up Michaels' gauntlet bothers to resuscitate the humanistic meanings of culture by which our discipline used to justify itself. Rather, most critics assume the same anthropological definition of culture, and then turn to a political critique. Robyn Wiegman concedes that Michaels' conclusions are "logical," but claims they fail to help us "understand the histories, contexts, and rhetorical strategies at work in identity's deployment." Eric Lott offers that Michaels is "cunning, brilliant, acutely suggestive," but he condemns *Our America* as "devoid of political weight and dynamism." Carla Kaplan claims that Michaels makes a "compelling logical case," but only at the expense of the "political dimension of the imaginative and metaphoric work" of identity.[19] All of these reviewers concede the analytic field to Michaels, in order to conserve the political and moral field for themselves. They acknowledge that, on a purely logical level, Michaels' argument makes sense, but that its sense is at the expense of both politics and history.

However, a more evaluative, humanistic sense of culture does slip into many of these critiques, emerging symptomatically in terms of the adversarial extensions of literary modernism. Thus the scholars who participated in the *Modernism/Modernity* panel on *Our America*—Marjorie Perloff, Charles Altieri, and Robert von Hallberg—take Michaels to task not for his reduced definition of culture, but for his reduced definition of modernism. Perloff asserts that, for Michaels, modernism "is best described as modernism without the modernists," since he neglects to discuss so many of the expatriate figures who forged the modernist canon.[20] Altieri agrees that "it simply does not suffice to equate modernist styles with the purity of the signifier."[21] And von Hallberg affirms that "Michaels' nativist modernism is more nativist than modernist."[22]

The definition of modernism that Perloff, Altieri, and von Hallberg implicitly deploy, and that Michaels overlooks, can easily be traced to Trilling's foundational theorization of the "adversary culture":

> the art and thought of the modern period assume that it is possible for at least some persons to extricate themselves from the culture into which they were born. Any historian of the literature of the modern age will take virtually for granted the adversary intention, the actually subversive intention, that characterizes modern writing—he will perceive its clear purpose of detaching the reader from the habits of thought and feeling that the larger culture imposes, of giving him a ground and a vantage point from which to judge and condemn, and perhaps revise, the culture that produced him.[23]

Trilling's career should remind us that a clear genealogical line can be traced from the Arnoldian humanistic culture to the modernist adversary culture. As Michael Nowlin affirms: "one of Trilling's great insights was to see the 'adversary' culture as essentially the dark mirror image of a frustrated humanistic enterprise."[24]

This insight further illuminates the genealogical aporia that enables Michaels to appropriate the title of Waldo Frank's book of the same name. Frank, both a Marxist and a modernist, here becomes purely another figure in the transition from race into culture in America. By choosing this emphasis, what could possibly be examined as cultural radicalism becomes simply another form of cultural nationalism:

> There is an important sense . . . in which the claim that America now belongs to Frank's generation is less important than is the fact that what Frank wants to claim is "America." The opposition to the "world of commerce," in other words, is here represented as nationalist; the territory that the younger generation wishes to take from the older is a *nation*. (135)

That Frank asserts that it is America that gave birth to the "world of commerce" in the first place, and that therefore the opposition to this world would be more complex than a simple nationalism, is completely occluded by Michaels' unwillingness to acknowledge the dialectical work that culture has done for many American intellectuals over the course of the twentieth century. This is not to say that Frank's national or cultural allegiances were not problematic in any number of ways, but that our view of him (and of ourselves) becomes impoverished if we can't see the tensions within and between these allegiances.

This is not only a question of the meanings of "culture," however; it is also a question of the meanings of "generation," another term that is crucially reduced in Michaels' study. For Frank's "younger generation" is not the same as the "lost generation," upon which Michaels so cleverly puns. If, as Michaels convincingly argues, Hemingway and Fitzgerald tended to identify their "generation" with the infertility of a dying master race, Frank and his compatriots had something else in mind. For Frank's "generation" was not dying but just being born. For him, "America" belonged to the young, whose responsibility it was to transform it. After all, the last word of Frank's *Our America* is "Revolution."

Michaels came of age in the sixties, a member of the last generation for whom a "Revolution" seemed possible. In fact, one can understand the entire emplotment of *Our America* allegorically as a story of the "failure" of the sixties. Michaels narrates a shift from "universalist" claims about citizenship and political allegiance to "relativist" claims about national, ethnic, and cultural identity. Certainly this is one way to understand the mid-sixties shift from integrationist appeals to the federal government for civil rights to separatist proclamations to the media for cultural power. The era of student activism—which began with the humanist idealism of the *Port Huron Statement* and ended with the radical desperation of the Weatherman—produced Michaels' generation of literary and cultural critics. And that generation undoubtedly emerges from the growing skepticism that there were "human" concerns that transcended and informed the struggles of all oppressed populations; it is undeniable that today most cultural critics conform to the "incommensurability" that Michaels identifies with "cultural pluralism."

But the transformative events of the sixties are oddly absent from Michaels' work. His new project, *The Shape of the Signifier*, perpetuates this aporia. In this new work Michaels nostalgically laments the gradual substitution of a Cold War "conflict of ideologies" with a posthistorical "conflict of interests." Thus in "winning" the Cold War, we have moved "from the universalist logic of conflict as a difference of opinion to the posthistoricist logic of conflict as difference in subject position."[25]

Michaels appears to be offering us the allegorical key to his earlier study: the shift from ideology to interest figures as the late-twentieth-century "unconscious" of the early-twentieth-century story told in *Our America*. By simply importing the shift from one period to another, Michaels more explicitly confronts the political stakes of his work, but he also further undermines his methods. All of modern American history starts to seem like a repeating declension narrative. Which should lead us to consider the possibility that these seemingly exclusive logics have some more complex, dialectical relation. Michaels' methods force us to see universalist conflicts of ideology repeatedly being displaced by relativist conflicts of interest, but isn't it more accurate to see the engagement between these positions as one of the principle dialectical engines of American history? And isn't it possible that the sense of popular agency that characterized sixties activism emerged from a utopian glimmer that opinions and subject positions, far from being mutually exclusive, could be intelligibly, and politically, articulated?

Micheals's leapfrogging of the sixties, I believe, indicates why he seems so reluctant to interrogate the evaluative extensions of culture, to correlate some sort of vision to his criticism. For it is precisely in the dialectic between prescriptive and descriptive extensions of the term "culture" that we must face the difficult relation between opinions and subject positions, between what we believe should be and who we believe we are. This difficult relation would appear to be the challenge that *Our America*, somewhat unwittingly, bequeathes to the younger generation.

NOTES

1. Walter Benn Michaels, *Our America: Nativism, Modernism and Pluralism* (Durham: Duke University Press, 1995), 14. This is less a new argument for Michaels than it is a final synthesis of a number of high-profile discussions of race and classic American literature in the pages of *Critical Inquiry, American Literary History, English*

Literary History and a number of other journals and collections. *Our America* is essentially a bricolage of the following already published material: "American Modernism and the Poetics of Identity" *Modernism-Modernity* 1.1 (January 1994): 38–56; "Race into Culture: A Critical Genealogy of Cultural Identity" *Critical Inquiry* 18.4 (summer 1992): 655–85; "The New Modernism" *English Literary History* 59.1 (spring 1992): 257–67; "The Vanishing American" *American Literary History* 2.2 (summer 1990): 220–41; and "The Souls of White Folk" in *Literature and the Body: Essays on Populations and Persons,* ed. Elaine Scarry (Baltimore: Johns Hopkins University Press, 1988), 185–209.

2. Steven Knapp and Michaels, "Against Theory," in *Against Theory: Literary Studies and the New Pragmatism,* ed. W. J. T. Mitchell (Chicago: University of Chicago Press, 1982), 19. The article originally appeared in *Critical Inquiry* 8.4 (summer 1982): 723–42. The debate continued in the following issues of *Critical Inquiry* 9.4 (summer 1983): 725–800; 11.3 (spring 1985): 432–73; 14.1 (autumn 1987): 49–69; and 19.1 (autumn 1992): 164–93. See also Richard Shusterman, "Interpretation, Intention, and Truth," *Journal of Aesthetics and Art Criticism* 46.3 (spring 1988): 399–410; Alex Segal, "Theory and Intention in 'Against Theory,'" *Southern Review* 22.2 (July 1989): 184–95; and Knapp, "The Impossibility of Intentionless Meaning," in *Intention and Interpretation,* ed. Gary Iseminger (Philadelphia: Temple University Press, 1992), 51–64.

3. Peggy Kamuf, "Floating Authorship," *diacritics* 16.4 (winter 1986): 4.

4. Ibid., 4–5.

5. John Guillory, *Cultural Capital: The Problem of Literary Canon Formation* (Chicago: University of Chicago Press, 1993), 181. My argument here is deeply indebted to Guillory's brilliant discussion of "Literature after Theory."

6. Paul de Man, *The Resistance to Theory* (Minneapolis: University of Minnesota Press, 1986), 19. De Man is Guillory's principle example of the rise of the "techno-bureaucracy."

7. Mitchell, "Introduction: Pragmatic Theory," *Against Theory* 4.

8. Michael Rogin, *Ronald Reagan: The Movie, and other Episodes in Political Demonology* (Berkeley: University of California Press, 1987), xvii.

9. Michaels, *The Gold Standard and the Logic of Naturalism* (Berkeley: University of California Press, 1987), 10.

10. Fredric Jameson, *Postmodernism: or, The Cultural Logic of Late Capitalism* (Durham: Duke University Press, 1991), 188. It is worth noting that *Our America* came out in the same "Post-Contemporary Interventions" series as this study.

11. Ibid., 188–89.

12. Ibid., 207.

13. Brook Thomas, "Walter Benn Michaels and the New Historicism: Where's the Difference?" *boundary* 2 (spring 1991): 28.

14. Michaels, "The New Modernism," *English Literary History* 59 (1992): 257–67.

15. A. L. Kroeber and Clyde Kluckhohn, *Culture: A Critical Review of Concepts and Definitions* (New York: Vintage, 1963), 53.

16. W. E. B. DuBois, *The Souls of Black Folk* (New York: Vintage, 1986), 9.

17. Lionel Trilling, *Beyond Culture: Essays on Literature and Learning* (New York: Viking, 1965), xi.

18. Stephen Greenblatt, "Culture," in *Critical Terms for Literary Study*, eds. Frank Lentricchia and Thomas McLaughlin (Chicago: University of Chicago Press, 1990), 225.

19. Robyn Wiegman, Review of *Our America: Nativism, Modernism and Pluralism, American Literature*, 433; Eric Lott, "The New Cosmopolitanism," *Transition*, 72, 122, 125; Carla Kaplan, "On Modernism and Race," 4.1 *Modernism/Modernity* (1997): 161–62.

20. Marjorie Perloff, "Modernism Without Modernists: A Response to Walter Benn Michaels," 3.3 *Modernism/Modernity* (1996): 99–105.

21. Charles Altieri, "Whose America is *Our America:* On Walter Benn Michaels Characterizations of Modernity in America," *Modernism/Modernity* 3:3 (1996).

22. Robert von Hallberg, "Literature and History: Neat Fits," in ibid., 115–20.

23. Trilling, *Beyond Culture*, xii.

24. Michael Nowlin, "Lionel Trilling and the Institutionalization of Humanism," *Journal of American Studies* 25 (1991): 37.

25. Michaels, "The Shape of the Signifier," *Critical Inquiry* 27.2 (winter 2001): 278.

9

Literature, Incorporated

Harold Bloom, Theory, and the Canon

MARC REDFIELD

I am a comic critic, and all I get are serious reviews.
—Harold Bloom, interview by
Imre Salusinszky, *Criticism in Society*

What is there to say, at this late date, about Harold Bloom?[1] The polemics are over, history has moved on—yet was anything ever said in a timely fashion about him, even back in the distant seventies? Has it not always been too late or too early in the day to figure him out? Such questions no doubt risk sounding tendentious: surely Bloom has received more than his share of attention over the years. And though he likes to complain (as what author doesn't?) of the incomprehending attacks and "weak misreadings" his work receives, has he not also been granted careful professional scrutiny as well as remarkable professional success? No doubt—and yet, as the slender but persistent trickle of books and essays about him testifies, Bloom remains, if not quite a mystery, a nagging question and idiosyncratic figure within the American literary-critical institution. As young, iconoclastic romanticist, as mature anxiety-of-influence theorist, and as pugnacious and hyperprolific éminence grise—the "Yiddisher Dr. Johnson" whose books on Shakespeare and the Western canon show up in airports, and whose Chelsea House volumes fill thirty feet of shelf-space—in all these incarnations, Bloom has left his mark on literary culture, and always in a way that has about it a certain improbability, baroque excess, and irreducible singularity. Despite the shrewd critiques and careful evaluations that his work has at various times inspired, he remains a compellingly inexplicable figure, at once strange and overfamiliar, like a literary character about whom we will always be able to write again.

It is as a literary character, figuratively speaking, that Bloom will appear in the pages that follow: as, that is, a character who sees himself, and has often been seen by others, as representing to the point of embodying the "literary," particularly when the literary is understood as "the Canon." This role catapulted Bloom to national prominence in the early 1990s at the height of the so-called "canon wars," and may therefore be understood in relation to developments in the American culture and education industries that made the canon wars possible—a broad and ongoing defunding of the humanities within increasingly technologically oriented, corporate-controlled, and corporationlike universities; the emergence of "theory" as a glamour discipline, soon to be partly absorbed into and eclipsed by "cultural studies"; the diversification of university populations and the increasing prominence of themes of cultural diversity in classrooms and journals; the well-funded production, by mainstream media sources and neo-conservative foundations, of a specter of multicultural, anti-aesthetic anarchy from which the university and Shakespeare must be saved; and so on.[2] The relations among these various phenomena are not always self-evident, but critics who have tried to provide synthetic overviews of the contemporary state of the humanities have often found themselves speculating about a crisis within literature, a crisis that in some fashion underlies both the outbreak of the canon wars and the emergence of literary theory. "The canon debate," in John Guillory's influential analysis, "signifies nothing less than a crisis in the form of cultural capital we call literature," literature being understood to name "the cultural capital of the old bourgeoisie, a form of capital increasingly marginal to the social function of the present educational system" (vii, x). Having become largely irresponsive to the needs of a new professional-managerial class, literature has entered a public state of crisis, one symptom of which, according to Guillory, was the emergence of an alternative canon of texts labeled "theory" in the 1970s. Theory, personified above all by Paul de Man, sought to stave off literature's irrelevance by reimagining literature as "literariness" (Guillory, 180); in similar fashion, the culture wars— the aggressive rejection of the category of the aesthetic by advocates of "cultural studies"; the corresponding conservative backlash by middlebrow cultural journalists and academics like Bloom—act out, with varying degrees of self-consciousness, the crisis within literature as an institution or social form.

As I have argued at some length elsewhere, however, this account of theory and the canon wars fails to register the power and persistence of aesthetics within contemporary Western cultural institutions (a persistence visible in the name "cultural" studies itself, as well as in the rhetoric of Guillory's own critique), and also considerably underestimates the complexity of "theory" as an intellectual and institutional event.[3] And in this context we can learn a good deal from Bloom, who as I read him has not just served as a spokesperson for, and symbol of, high literary culture, but has also functioned as a minor lodestone for anxieties about literature and literary theory. He thus offers us a focal point that can help us take a small step or two toward an historical understanding of theory. Such an understanding is not easily had. It demands, in the first place, a theory of history powerful enough to comprehend theory's own attempts at self-understanding; and since in the pages that follow I make no sustained attempt to provide such a theory of history, this essay must be understood to remain underway, at best, toward an historical understanding of theory.[4] Bloom allows us, however, to register efficiently the mutual entanglement of questions of theory, literature, and media technology, and to speculate that the emergence of a specter called "theory" in the 1970s had more to do with the unsettling character of modern technics than with a desire to prop up the literary canon. Or rather, the case of Bloom allows us to see that the binary oppositions between literature and technics, and by extension between high and popular literature, or between literature and popular culture, are in some respects a distraction. These differences have played an important sociological role ever since our modern institution of "literature" took shape in the mid- to late eighteenth century, and obviously they have their truth; but it is also the case that certain aspects of "literariness" are best understood in concert rather than in simple contrast with the communicational and representational technologies that define our modernity and its culture industry. The compelling, hallucinatory irreality and fundamental writtenness of literature suggest an odd, subterranean kinship with the world of tele-technics in which literature seems (endlessly) to be dying; indeed, we might do well to think of postliterary culture as enabled, paradoxically, by a massive projection and proliferation of literary effects. And the discourse that has sought to attend to this anti-aesthetic element within aesthetics, or within literature as an aesthetic idea and institution, is what we call "theory": "high" theory, which is to say theory as deconstruction. I share Guillory's belief that de Man came to serve both the media and the academy as theory's figurative representative during the 1970s and 1980s ("The easy condemnation in the media of theory along with de Man," Guillory rightly notes of the wartime journalism uproar, "only confirmed a symbolic equation already present in the professional imaginary" [178]). Bloom represented himself in the 1970s and to some extent in the 1980s as de Man's loving but stern adversary, and subsequently came to represent for the American mass media the Western canon itself in its struggle with theory and multiculturalism. In consequence, he provides us with an occasion to examine at close range the workings of a rhetoric of personification that is seemingly bound up with theory and any history that might be told about theory. Bloom's writings, together with his theatrical performance of himself as "Bloom" in the media, allow the specter of literariness as theory to be aligned with the kind of self-dislocation that Walter Benjamin called the "shock experience" *(Chockerlebnis)*, an experience that the figure of personification repeats yet also to some extent wards off.

CANON AND CORPUS

We may begin by examining how the figure of Bloom as the canon incorporate has been taken up and disseminated by the American media. In the early to mid-1980s, as the so-called "canon wars" began to be fought (sometimes) on campuses and (more often) in the popular press, Harold Bloom underwent a public metamorphosis from "Yale critic" into "genius": the genius *of* the canon. Bloom's reputation first expanded beyond academic and *New York Review of Books* circles with the publication of *The Anxiety of Influence* in 1973; but only about a decade later, when he was awarded a MacArthur "genius" grant and began the massive Chelsea House publishing venture, did he become what he is today: not quite a public intellectual in the traditional sense—he is too eccentric and professorial for that—but a high to high-middlebrow public icon who stands for superhuman mastery of literary culture. If one had to date the beginning of this phenomenon, one could do worse than point to David Lehman's 1986 *Newsweek* article, "Yale's Insomniac Genius," the opening paragraph of which reads as follows:

> Harold Bloom looks a lot like Zero Mostel and sounds rather like a sorrowful dandy, a combination of an Old Testament prophet and Oscar Wilde. An indefatigable monologist in a rumpled suit, he reclines in his favorite armchair at the New Haven suite of offices he calls his "factory" for producing literary criticism. The term is apt: Bloom, a professor at Yale University, is editing and writing introductions for five series of critical anthologies comprising no less than 800 separate volumes. His subject—the whole of literature. His model—Samuel Johnson's "Lives of the Poets." The task might daunt a lesser mortal, but leaves Bloom unfazed and rather excited. This is, after all, a man who blithely claims he can read and absorb up to 1,000 pages an hour. A man whose memory is legendary: "I think I have by heart every line of poetry that I like that I've ever read," he says, offering to illustrate with swatches of "The Faerie Queene" and "Paradise Lost."[5]

Lehman dwells on the speed with which Bloom reads and writes, but like most journalists who interview Bloom—and for that matter, like most

of Bloom's teachers, colleagues, and students over the past half century—
he is particularly fascinated and awed by Bloom's preternatural memory:

> How does he manage to do it all? . . . Bloom's scandalously rapid reading rate
> helps, of course, and his memory serves as his touchstone: "I've always made
> it a principle that if I cannot remember it, I won't quote it." Yale colleagues
> confirm his astonishing powers of verbatim recall. "When I was a student,"
> he says, "I would get a bit drunk and recite Hart Crane's 'The Bridge' front-
> wards, then backwards, quite like a tape recorder running wild."

An accompanying photo shows Bloom surrounded by books, his arm draped
over a stack of Chelsea House volumes (see below).[6] Behind him, on the
shelves, sits "the whole of literature"; before him, substituting for his mid-sec-
tion and more or less rhyming with the mass of his head, are the shiny tokens
of mastery, the books about books that the genius's internalization of the
canon authorizes.

Neither Bloom's pose nor the visual puns it sets in motion are particularly surprising, of course; given the tenor of the article, it would be odd if Bloom were *not* being photographed with books. Yet in some magazine photos from the canon-wars era this is in fact what happens: the books drop into the background or even disappear, with the result that the teasing equivalence between Bloom's body and the canon becomes all the more emphatic—as though the books had been devoured literally enough to *become* the body. It has proved impossible to reproduce these photographs here, so readers not wishing to check the archive themselves will have to take my descriptions on faith. *Time* Magazine's 1994 report, for instance, on the publication of *The Western Canon* (1994) (entitled "Hurrah for Dead White Males!"), offers its readers a full-body shot of Bloom in his New York apartment: the critic's black-clad stomach anchors the composition; while his open thighs, spread arms, and weary eyes and mouth offer a vulnerable but imposing body to the camera's gaze.[7] In another article from this period, Adam Begley's "Colossus among Critics" in *The New York Times Magazine* (1994) the accompanying photos are head shots. The subtitle of Begley's piece reads "Everything about Him Is Outsized"; and indeed, one of the head shots is a full-page portrait; in both, Bloom is shown camping it up—holding his head in his hands or shading his eyes: the Western canon, beset by resentniks, is suffering a corporeal and theatrical headache. Such, in any case, is the interpretation with which Begley flirts as he begins his article:

> In early summer, I paid two visits to Harold Bloom, the eminent literary critic famous for his prodigious intellectual energy. On both occasions he seemed intent on staging a deathbed scene. Collapsed on a reclining armchair, brow furrowed, mouth sour, the 64–year-old Bloom looked worse than pained. "The battle is lost," he whispered. "These resentniks have destroyed the canon." Enfeebled despite his generous bulk, he summoned the stamina for some impressive elegiac flourishes. . . . Once with a tragic sigh, he breathed, "I am weary unto death."
>
> Literature is dying and so, ipso facto, is Harold Bloom. Or could it be the other way around?[8]

Goaded on by Bloom, Begley repeatedly toys with the extravagant, not-seriously-meant-of-course fantasy that the head shots encourage: Bloom, having internalized all of literature, has become literature's incorporate representative. Indeed, by 1994 Bloom had been playing this public role for sometime: readers of a 1990 issue of *New York* magazine had encountered a full-page, full-body shot by John Hamilton introducing John Taylor's post-*Book of J* profile of Bloom, "Bloom's Day: Hanging Out with the Reigning Genius of Literary Criticism."[9] Bloom is sprawled in his easy chair and the camera angle is strangely high. We look down on a book-surrounded body that Taylor's article describes as "massive and frail," uncertain whether Bloom is exhibiting himself or whether the camera is excavating him: his vulnerability is also an aggressive claim on our gaze. Scattered books rhyme with the body's sprawl, suggesting a potential for chaos, yet at the same time offering us the consoling pleasures of metaphor: to the degree that one can imagine the books and the body resembling each other, their scatteredness recomposes into a modest sort of aesthetic form. To judge from a recent (2002) feature on Bloom in *The New Yorker,* this fantasy about Bloom's body and the canon seems to have lost none of its appeal over the last twelve years. Larissa MacFarquhar's "Prophet of Decline," which comes graced with a luminous head shot of Bloom by Richard Avedon, vigorously recycles a decade's worth of journalistic commonplaces about the genius and his body:

> He has memorized a large proportion of canonical poetry written in English; once, when drunk, as an undergraduate at Cornell, he recited Hart Crane's long poem "The Bridge" backward, word by word. He claims that in his youth he read a thousand pages an hour. Bloom has had poems inside him for so long that he doesn't really read them anymore. They are not a series of lines following one after the other—they exist in him all at once. He has swallowed them whole.

A few sentences later the Bloomian body is savored as a grotesquely phallic anti-Petrarchan catalog ("Bloom's face is a cluster of big, swollen, sensing instruments: a heroic nose, nostrils dilating; plump, colossal lips; a giant's heavy eyes . . ."), one that crescendos, inevitably, toward the stomach and its canonical contents: "His stomach is prodigious, like a great cathedral, in which all the uncountable poems and plays that he has swallowed roil and commingle with his own passions."[10]

It is a sheerly contingent fact that a canon-obsessed literary critic with a phenomenal memory and a turn for hyperdramatic self-presentation should also possess what Bloom genially calls a "Falstaffian body"; but it is the function of ideologies to invest contingencies with significance, and I think we may take these photographs and articles as symptomatic expressions of the instabilities besetting our late-twentieth-century fantasy of the canon.[11] By the 1990s, Bloom was well-prepared for this role. He had played a similar one on a smaller stage for many years: his memory, scholarly energy, and commitment to aesthetic judgment all went into the shaping of his idiosyncratic academic career. It was as a "genius"—as the young self-proclaimed champion of romanticism who could "recite from memory the entire body of English romantic verse of the nineteenth century"—that he broke through the Yale English Department's anti-Semitic ceiling while doing battle—at least such is the Bloom myth, and it's not an entirely fanciful one—with the Donne-to-Eliot canon of Cleanth Brooks.[12] His prolific publications in the 1960s included active and continuous efforts to promote the twentieth-century American poets in whose work he believed (Stevens, Ashbery, Bishop; after an initial hesitation, Merrill); and his turn from apocalyptic-humanistic romanticism to a theory of the "anxiety of influence" in the 1970s only increased—if that were possible—his investment in the idea of a canon, and his interest in ways in which canons might be internalized. We shall come back to Bloom's theoretical reflections on influence and internalization. Here it will suffice to note that the eruption of the "canon wars" in the late 1980s and early 1990s produced a context in which an increasingly public personality called "Bloom"—the precipitate of three or four decades of scholarship, journalism, and academic anecdote—could become a visible token of canonical literary history. And it is precisely *because* the canon had become a questionable idea in the public discourse of the time that it elicited such figuration. To the extent that they playfully treat Bloom as an allegorical figure for the canon, these journalists emphasize the bodiliness of the critic's body—its size, its vulnerability, and its potential unruliness; and this is at least in part because the representation of canon as body is inseparable from a fantasy of the canon as bordered, wounded, and mortal. The body is a double and unstable—as well as ineradicable—trope in aesthetic discourse: if the image of the body is humanity's "principle of unity," as Jacques Lacan suggests, it is also the figure of this unity's disruption.[13] The canon submits to a fantasy of embodiment because it is being seen as an uncertain corpus, its edges crumbling off into the even more amorphous and unmanageably vast ocean of "all of literature" (and nothing makes this more obvious than when the canon is represented as a list, even or especially a list as capacious as the three-thousand title one offered as *The Western Canon*'s appendix).[14]

The delight with which these journalists write about or photograph Bloom, therefore, has about it the headiness but also the uncertainty and aggressivity of imaginary totalizations; and we may advance a little further in our interpretation of these scenes if we ask how they construct Bloom as the canon's "genius." As genius, Bloom has in principle read everything and, even more crucially, judged everything. The first of these feats is the most obviously impossible of the two, since even a Harold Bloom will never finish reading and internalizing the archive; the second is in fact the one that matters, since aesthetic judgment is what constitutes the canon. To memorize a poem is not necessarily to understand or appreciate it (indeed, according to Hegel, at least, "it is well known that one knows a text by heart only when one no longer associates any meaning with the words").[15] Bloom himself has an answer to that objection; as we shall review momentarily, he has labored throughout his career to assimilate reading to understanding and judgment; and in several of these interviews he finds occasion to insist on the "auditory and aesthetic" character of his memory: for instance, "I can recite Milton's *Paradise Lost* from beginning to end, like running off a tape, simply because it is for me a major aesthetic experience . . ." (Taylor, 55). The inscription of a text on the mind, in other words, occurs as the call of a voice. Texts are intuitively understood as voices that call and claim us with greater or lesser urgency: thus inscription, understanding, and judgment coalesce in the living power of poetic voice. For more than three decades Bloom has been writing about canon formation as a struggle of voice against voice; and the pathos, dark humanism, and polemical aestheticism of his criticism has helped make possible his canonization as the canon's representative.

Yet Bloom's considerable authority as judge tends rhetorically, in these articles, to refer itself to his sheer ability to read and remember. He is the genius as professor largely, it seems, because he is the genius as cyborg, being possessed of such an uncanny ability to scan and store data that only the tape recorder and the computer provide adequate metaphors.[16] Bloom himself favors the tape recorder: he frequently regales journalists with his reciting-Hart-Crane-backward story ("like a tape recorder running wild"), and turns to this metaphor even when, as in my citation from Taylor's article ("like running off a tape"), he is emphasizing his memory's aesthetic character.[17] It is this figure of the recording machine—aided and abetted by that of the high-speed scanner—that underwrites the fantasy of embodiment we have been examining. The canon gets "inside" Bloom's head as data gets placed on a hard drive: only on such a basis can the phantasmatics of embodiment erect themselves. The metaphor, however, is double-edged. The tape recorder preserves voice, but does so thanks to a process of inscription that breaks with the self-presence of voice and transforms voice into writing—or, better, exposes and exploits the "writing," the iterability and self-difference, which inheres in voice and makes it possible: as recorded voice, Hart Crane can always, in a moment of inebriation, be played backward, because his voice endures only in and as the possibility of being grafted, spliced, overdubbed, and played elsewhere. To judge from the insistence of this trope, a Derridean specter haunts the Bloomian embodiment of the canon. The possibility arises, in other words, that the canon-embodying aesthetic founds itself on a process of inscription conveyed—and thus to some extent controlled or domesticated—by the figure of a machine utterly indifferent, as all machines are, to the meaning or beauty of what it records. In this sense the metaphor of the tape recorder registers a certain *materiality* of aesthetic embodiment: a materiality irreducible to phenomenal apprehension, yet without which no text, psyche, body, or voice could exist. Derrida's famous figure for this peculiar kind of materiality—the event of difference and deferral—is "writing"; another powerful trope for it is "literature," if, like de Man in his review of *The Anxiety of Influence,* one conceives of literature as the pressure, within writing, of a "decentered otherness."[18] And if we submit Bloom's oeuvre to a high-speed scan (the only speed available in the present context) we shall see that it bears traces of a recording inaccessible to perception—of, that is, an exposure to literature as literariness, a delight and a danger that at a certain point in his career Bloom began to thematize, cherish, and expel as the specter of theory, personified as his colleague and friend Paul de Man.

INFLUENCE, ANXIETY, LITERATURE

De Man has remained a charged locus in Bloom's work since *A Map of Misreading* (1975)—since, that is, de Man interpreted Bloom's *Anxiety of Influence* (1973) in a 1974 review as a book covertly dealing "with the difficulty, or rather the impossibility, of reading and, by inference, with the indeterminacy of literary meaning" (273). *A Map of Misreading,* which is dedicated to de Man, announces the appearance of "a new mythic being—clearly implied by Paul de Man in particular—the reader as Overman, the *Überleser*";[19] in Bloom's 1977 book on Wallace Stevens, de Manian deconstruction reappears as "Over-Reading, or the reading of an Over-Man," and de Man obtains Bloom's "reverence" as an "advanced critical consciousness, the most rigorous and scrupulous in the field today."[20] In other words, for Bloom as for the American professoriat generally, de Man came to serve as a personification of theory during these years. In Bloom's case, his ascription of this allegorical role to de Man formed part of a deeply felt friendship, with the result that Bloom's anecdotes about de Man, as we shall see, are sometimes interestingly peculiar. For the moment, though, it will suffice simply to note how persistently de Man has continued to haunt Bloom. In the preface to the 1997 reissue of *The Anxiety of Influence,* Bloom invokes his "useful (for me) decades-long quarrel with Paul de Man, a radiant intelligence," and distinguishes once again de Man's insistence on the question of truth from his, Bloom's, belief that the general figurativeness of language annuls the deconstructive problematic.[21] This most recent salute to de Man, that is, provides the occasion for yet one more attempt on Bloom's part to say farewell to theory. In the seventies he had tried to build theoretical refutations of de Manian deconstruction by absorbing and psychologizing de Man's rhetorical idiom; in the eighties and nineties he settled for simpler valedictions, dramatized as dialogue: "there is no 'troot,' dear Paul."[22] "He insisted that an epistemological stance in regard to a literary work was the only way out of the tropological labyrinth, while I replied that such a stance was no more or less a trope than any other" (*Anxiety,* xix). Indeed, in the 1990s Bloom began emphasizing one thing above all else: the glory that is Shakespeare. "Shakespeare created us" (xxvii); Shakespeare created inwardness and the possibility of Freud, as well as all else under the humanist sun; he "thought all thoughts, for all of us"; on this topic, "hyperbole is not possible" (xxviii). Bloom no longer needs to struggle to tie language and the psyche together, and to subordinate the former to the latter: in a sense, all now becomes language, since Shakespeare is language; yet Shakespeare also provides an origin—the human form divine that has always been Bloom's creed, despair, and desire. Shakespeare represents, in other words, both the end and the end of the line for Bloom's theoretical writing, as the ambiguities of reading and identity cede to an act of personification self-parodic in its grandiosity.

Personification is an ambiguous trope. It must but cannot quite be believed in; it affirms personhood at the expense of rendering personhood fictional. The unsettling ambiguity of personification haunts Bloom's writing just as it does his half-serious, half-playful self-representations as the Canon Incorporate in the media. Critics have frequently observed that Bloom's entire theoretical project in the 1970s was designed to ward off the threat represented by "theory" in its continental, Derridean, or de Manian instantiation. Jonathan Culler, for instance, argues—rightly, I think—that "Bloom transforms intertextuality from an endless series of anonymous codes and citations to an oedipal confrontation, one of whose effects is to preserve the integrity of his poets as agents of the poetic process."[23] But my summary of Bloom's invocations of, and investment in, de Man intends to suggest that Bloom's writing has been inspired by the uncanny literariness against which he defends and defines himself. If one had to sum up Bloom's theoretical maneuvering in a phrase, one could say that he seeks endlessly to frame epistemological issues as performative ones, and to understand performance as the exercise of will. It is always possible to understand a constative statement ("the cat is black") as a tacit or disguised performative ("I assert that the cat is black"); the problem Bloom faces is that, as Derrida has shown, performative utterances depend upon iterability—upon the radical possibility of being cited, repeated, and displaced elsewhere—and thus exceed the parameters of voice and the fantasy of presence-to-self that figures of voice support.[24] Put in rhetorical terms, the voice threatens, under such circumstances, to become an ungrounded figure: the effect of processes of personification rather than the essence of a person. And the possibility of the voice's figurativeness murmurs through Bloom's oeuvre, shadowing the proliferation of proper names and vatic utterances, the rapid segues, the texts quoted from memory, the Gnostic speculations in (e.g.) *Omens of Millennium* (1996) on the anxious, thrilling possibility that "we are dreamed by others," even the more recent hyperbole that Shakespeare "invented us," to the extent that Bloom's Shakespeare is, as just noted, a grotesquely hyperbolic personification.[25] *A Map of Misreading* and *Poetry and Repression* (1976) are stocked with anxiously strident humanist affirmations ("The human writes, the human thinks" (*Map*, 60); "*we can* tell the dancer from the dance";[26] etc.) not just because de Man was on Bloom's horizon, but because *The Anxiety of Influence* is a darker, more uncanny text than its author may have been prepared to admit, toying as it does with the idea that influence contaminates the self at a fundamental level. Influence is "the sense—amazing, agonizing, delighting—of *other poets*, as felt in the depths of the all but perfect solipsist, the potentially strong poet" (*Anxiety*, 26). The precursor is thus "at once the Wholly Other yet also a possessing force" (101). And at one point in this vatic text, the power of influence infects the will itself, turning it ghostly or cloned: "what does the anxiety of influence concern but the energy, the force, the will? Are they one's own, or emanations from the other, from the precursor?" (52). If the will can be the will of the other, and if every precursor has a precursor, the canon threatens to become a play of rhetorical effects without ground or border. These anxious moments thread through the pathos and the intersubjective drama of Bloom's manifesto.

Self and text in Bloom thus always have looming over them the possibility of their own dispersal into the uncanny space of literature—the space which, in the 1990s Bloom aggressively idealized as the memorial pattern of the "canon," but that in texts such as *The Anxiety of Influence* is always ready to become immemorial and anonymous. On the one hand, a poet struggles with poets, and the dark Tennysonian glamour of that rivalry draws most of our (and Bloom's) attention ("Made weak by time and fate, but strong in will / To strive, to seek, to find, and not to yield");[27] but on the other hand, this polytropic Ulysses is wrestling a text or texts that itself or themselves wrestled with precursors, and the ghosts thus threaten to proliferate into a haunting more primal than the individual self. When Bloom, in a famous phrase—one which, significantly, I think, has few analogues in his later work—tells us that an ephebe can be chosen by a poem "even if the ephebe *never read* that poem" (*Anxiety*, 70, Bloom's emphasis), he no doubt in part intends to suggest a certain more-than-verbal force of personality communicating itself between precursor and latecomer, since "a poet's stance, his Word, his imaginative identity, his whole being, *must* be unique to him" (71, Bloom's emphasis). Yet the pathos of that italicized "must" derives precisely from the possibility that effects of haunting and repetition may have hollowed out Word and identity and being. What effects of echo, what nameless, groundless murmur, makes conceivable the "choosing" of an ephebe by an *unread* poem? What strange sort of possession would then lie at the origin of the poet as poet? Would not reading itself then need to be thought as a potentially figurative or ghostly event, capable of occurring in or as its own absence, in advance of its own ability to understand itself? In the form I give them here, these are not Bloomian questions—they are closer to the idiom of Maurice Blanchot—but Bloom's writing derives part of its urgency from them.[28] The pathos and the melodrama of his texts, including his famously, often irritatingly apodictic and proper-name-driven style, respond to, and defend against, a deeper, more uncanny literary imperative.[29] "It is a theory of literature that is literary to the core," Elizabeth Bruss concludes near the end of her elegant and unsparing study of Bloom.[30] She means this as a criticism—as a way of driving home "how fragile the theoretical impulse is" in Bloom (295): how erratic, unsystematic, and unargued his work can appear. Yet these qualities seem bound up with Bloom's willingness, particularly in the mid-seventies, to vacillate on the near side of a literariness that was warded off with an energy very much derived from ambivalence, as Bruss suggests:

> [F]or Bloom, certain errors are indispensable, worth any error to preserve, even if preserving them involves a confession of their unreality. Thus, in the process of saving the self, Bloom is willing to incur enormous losses. Self-knowledge and self-reliance are shored up, but at the cost of making them necessary fictions, repressions that conceal the real limits of the self to beget or even know itself. (328)

Bruss is right to pressure these moments, but the lesson she draws from them needs nuancing. Bloom's claim that "there are no texts but only relations between texts" communicates a double urgency that his work never resolves: a critical drive to refigure all origins as error or trope, and a countervailing desire to exorcise the specter of literariness by transmuting trope into will power, language into pathos, and poetry into agon. The latter urgency may have generated the main lines of Bloom's systematizing, but the system's repression of its uncertain (and deeply literary) origins is persistently legible, and accounts, I think, for whatever power his writing commands.[31]

Earlier we examined Bloom's oddly technical figures for his own memory—his own powers of canon-internalization—and we might ask at this point whether these tropes can tell us anything about the emphasis on catastrophe in Bloom's poetic theory. Poets become poets thanks to a "scene of instruction" that Bloom frequently aligns with the Freudian notion of a primal scene:

> Wittgenstein, who resented Freud, and who dismissed Freud as a mythologist, however powerful, probably was too annoyed with Freud to read him closely. This may explain Wittgenstein's curious mistake in believing that Freud had not distinguished between the Primal Scene and the Primal Scene fantasy. Freud's Primal Scene takes place in the beginning, when an infant sees his parents in the act of love, without in any way understanding that sight. Memory, according to Freud, holds on to the image of copulation until the child, between the ages of three and five, creates the Primal Scene fantasy, which is an Oedipal reverie. One of my former students, Cathy Caruth, caught me in making this same error, so that in my literary transformation of Freud into the Primal Scene of Instruction, I referred to such a Primal

Scene as being at once oral and written. I would clarify this now by saying that the "oral" scene is the topos or Primal Scene proper, the negative moment of being influenced, a perpetually lost origin, while the "written" scene is the trope or Primal Scene fantasy. This means, in my terms, that in a poem a topos or rhetorical commonplace is *where* something can be *known*, but a trope or inventive turning is *when* something is desired or *willed*. Poems, as I have written often, are verbal utterances that cannot be regarded as being simply linguistic entities, because they manifest their will to utter *within* traditions of uttering, and as soon as you will that "within," your mode is discursive and topological as well as linguistic and tropological. As a Primal Scene, the Scene of Instruction is a Scene of Voicing; only when fantasized or troped does it become a Scene of Writing.[32]

The Bloomian Primal Scene—the future poet's catastrophic yet productive encounter with a precursor or precursors (the "precursor" usually being a composite figure)—is "oral" because the will must be grounded in speech; writing comes later, as the Primal Scene fantasy, produced by the poet willing himself as poet. The oral Primal Scene, as opposed to the written Primal Scene fantasy, is "a perpetually lost origin." And it is the specter of perpetual loss that Bloom, here as elsewhere, both acknowledges and avoids, as Caruth notes in a dense commentary on this passage:

> The "lostness" of the scene, which is also its "primal" quality, is implicit in the radical negativity of the words "without *in any way* understanding." Such a seeing-without-knowing elides consciousness, as it were, in bypassing perception and imprinting itself on memory. This odd elision is the striking characteristic as well of Freud's early description of trauma. . . . The catastrophic nature of trauma (as discussed in the *Project*) is connected, as [Jean] Laplanche notes, with the impossibility of locating it historically.[33]

Teasing out similarities between Bloom's writing about catastrophe and Freud's writing about trauma, Caruth notes trauma's "odd temporal structure"—since the trauma's meaning cannot be located in either of its two constitutive moments, the moment of marking or the moment of return or remarking—and observes that Freud emphasizes "the non-perceptual nature of the first 'seeing' by the use of the term 'memory-trace'" (1294): "The priority of the first scene with regard to the second scene is not that of a perception with regard to its memory, but rather of a 'trace' with regard to a perception, the two having no simple temporal relation" (1295). When Bloom acknowledges the "primal scene of instruction" to be radically *lost*, the scene's orality becomes legible as a trope for an immemorial writing: for a death, as Caruth puts it, which can never be "our death." The Bloomian theory of creation through catastrophe thereby becomes an extended reiteration and disavowal of the nonphenomenal *inscription* of meaning—a gigantic, unacknowledged commentary, one could say, on the trope of Bloom-as-tape recorder that we examined earlier.

A distant echo of poetry's traumatic catastrophe is audible at the beginning of *The Western Canon* (1994), as Bloom offers us an account of his canon-possessed mind that is more seriously intended, or at least more high-cultural, than that provided by his informal or semiformal remarks about tape recorders; here the allusion is to an aspect of the ancient technic of rhetoric, rather than to a device of modern technology:

> The art of memory, with its rhetorical antecedents and its magical burgeonings, is very much an affair of imaginary places, or of real places transmuted into visual images. Since childhood, I have enjoyed an uncanny memory for literature, but that memory is purely verbal, without anything in the way of a visual component. Only recently, past the age of sixty, have I come to understand that my literary memory has relied upon the Canon as a memory system. If I am a special case, it is only in the sense that my experience is a more extreme version of what I believe to be the principal pragmatic function of the Canon: the remembering and ordering of a lifetime's reading. The greatest authors take over the role of "places" in the Canon's theater of memory, and their masterworks occupy the position filled by "images" in the art of memory.[34]

To have the canon in your head, internalized, present, and harmoniously ordered: who—what literature professor, at any rate—could want more? Yet, once again, there is a cybernetic touch to this self-portrait ("my literary memory has relied upon the Canon as a memory system"), as though Bloom were incapable of reflecting on his preternatural memory without drifting toward metaphors of inscription, of technical devices of storage and retrieval. Internalization, here, comes to resemble the kind of taking-in that psychoanalysts call incorporation: a "literal" ingestion in the sense that the incorporated other refuses symbolic substitutes, resists the work of mourning, and remains other—an encrypted alienness within.[35] Bloom's pathos-laden style is in fact, one may hypothesize, a denial or foreclosure of loss—loss as the traumatic inscription and internalization of literature. And that inscription may in turn be understood as a version of what Benjamin, historicizing and displacing Freud's theory of trauma, called the "shock experience": the impact, which Benjamin associates above all with modern technics and the modern city, of stimuli that inscribe themselves in, or as, memory precisely to the extent that they cannot be *experienced*.[36] When we read Bloom, we read a corpus haunted by an allegiance to literature that the Bloomian text both celebrates and disavows: most visibly in the peculiar theoretical work on the "anxiety of influence" that composes Bloom's own image, and guarantees his place, in literary criticism's *ars memoria*.

MY HEAD, HIS HANDS

This brief survey of Bloom's writing suggests that literature, passionately read and absorbed by a critic possessed of exemplary powers of intake and retention, leaves its most telling mark on the mind when it least resembles an aesthetic experience. The shock of the literary precedes or exceeds any experience to which we can lay claim as self-possessed subjects—as ephebes encountering ourselves in encountering the precursor, to use Bloom's idiom. Delight or melancholy can accompany this shock, the transformation of which into narratives of aesthetic or affective experience, however, requires an act of personification, a giving of voice and face to a linguistic event that can never be made fully present to itself. Literariness in this sense is very much at work in modern technics and tele-technologies. The powers of storage and retrieval unleashed by the invention of writing and, centuries later, the printing press have been gigantically extended over the last hundred and fifty years, but the form of domination that modern communicational and informational technologies provide is always double-edged, because it exploits and submits to the iterability of the mark: that which is recorded can be dubbed and spliced and counterfeited; the moment captured is captured as simulacrum, reproduced elsewhere, never quite "live." Theory's attention to literariness is an attention to what one might call "technicity," or "mediation." A genuinely historical approach to theory would need to understand itself as a version of the question concerning technology. We have not pretended here to have moved very far down the road toward an historical assessment of theory, but we have perhaps been able to suggest the degree to which fantasies of incorporation, personification, and control have conditioned our culture's reception of theory.[37]

But it is appropriate that a literary character like Bloom be allowed to inhabit a more exciting sort of story, or be allowed to tell one; so, by way of conclusion, let me draw attention to a strange moment in the Bloom corpus that occurs not in an essay but in an interview he accorded Imre Salusinszky in November, 1985. About halfway through the interview, Bloom launches into a polemic—yet once more—against critics who fault him for writing socially irrelevant criticism. He accuses his accusers of self-righteousness and *ressentiment,* and affirms the "solitary pleasure" of the act of criticism; at a certain point, however this solitary pleasure yields to an anecdote involving two critics and two bodies:

> The best critic and best human being I've known in my life was my dear friend Paul de Man. "The trouble with you, Harold," he would say with a smile, cupping my head in his hands, and looking at me with an affection that always made me want to weep, "is that you are crazy: you do not believe in the 'troot.'" I would look at him, shake my head sadly, and say:

"No, I do not believe in the 'troot' because there is no 'troot,' dear Paul.

"There is no method: there is only yourself, and you are highly idio-syncratic.

"And you clone, my dear: I dislike what you do as a teacher, because your students are as alike as two peas in a pod." (*Criticism in Society*, 67)

When I first read the second sentence of this extract, I blinked and read again to confirm that, yes, in this remarkable scene—all the more remarkable if you were a student at Yale in those days, and have memories of glimpsing from afar these august professors having a decorous coffee together on Chapel Street—yes, de Man is cupping *Bloom*'s head, not his own head, in his, de Man's hands.[38] The scene is bizarre, a little grotesque—and comic, and oddly sweet; and it spurs absurd questions: How are the rest of their bodies disposed? How long does the gesture last? Is de Man, for instance, still cupping the Bloomian head when it begins shaking sadly? During the Bloomian admonishment? Does the tender-ness of de Man's gaze ever waver; does his smile narrow or broaden as he under-goes Bloom's tender chastisement? The storyteller is having his fun, and, with flamboyant self-consciousness, has given his characters the identifying marks they sport in many another academic anecdote featuring de Man or Bloom ("the troot"; "my dear"). In that sense, like all good gossip, it is a highly encoded sub-literary story, and we may pause over it a moment longer.

As in a painting by Mark Tansey or a "Yale Critics for Beginners" comic, Bloom and de Man are wrestling. Theirs is a rigged match, of course, and at first glance the antithetical critic, the theorist of agon who is staging this agon for us and for his interlocutor, seems to hold all the cards. He rebukes the con-ceptual rhetorician—the "highly idiosyncratic" but sinful man who has fallen into the error of truth, and who, blind to his own idiosyncracy, destroys that of his students. The conceptual rhetorician "clones." With the arrival of this peculiar intransitive verb, de Man's affectionate gaze and head-cupping ges-ture become even more surreal: "the best critic and best human being I've known in my life" becomes a bit less of a sentimental man and more of a space alien. Are there only two figures, then, in this scene of instruction? Is Bloom actually wrestling with a de Manic multiplicity, whose name is legion? That would suit the pathos and self-aggrandizement of the narrative, to be sure—and yet this cloning power complicates the other's "idiosyncracy" and lovable humanity, troubles the scene's specular structure, and ironizes the Bloomian moral: what sort of idiosyncracy is de Man's, that it is cloneable? What does it mean to be "only yourself" if the self—the "best human being," at that—has such terrible powers of reproduction? And if de Man's students themselves have nothing but their idiosyncratic selves, through what process do they become pod people, "two peas in a pod"—a twoness at odds with the seem-ingly more stable twoness of de Man and Bloom with which we began?

Consider one other peculiarity in this little anecdote: the overbalanced, or underweighted, distribution of pathos. Under the affectionate gaze of the beloved other, Bloom wants to weep. He feels himself loved, overloved. Guillory has characterized de Manian charisma as the effect of a master's apparent indifference to the love his disciples offer him (176–265); here, the master gives love superabundantly—and receives a lesson to boot. Yet it is Bloom, the lesson-giver, who holds back tears. He is not the master's master after all. It is still de Man—Bloom's de Man, to be sure: the de Man of this little fantasy—who runs the show, because, reaching out to cup Bloom's head, he offers love without caring whether or not he is loved back. That is the excess of love that brings Bloom close to tears. He will never be able to repay this gift. Giving or withholding love, the master, de Man, retains the power of his indifference; this is to say that his selfhood, though ungovernably multiple in its self-replication, is also more singular and whole, more unified than Bloom's. It is Bloom who tells this story, who summons his friend from the grave, puts him right, and lays him to rest; yet Bloom's very need to perform such gestures makes him the needy one. He can never win.

And who would know this better than Bloom? "Wrestling Jacob could triumph, because his Adversary was the Everliving, but even the strongest poets must grapple with phantoms" (*Map,* 17). If Bloom can never win, he has nonetheless told a winning story that ironizes, even burlesques its own sentimentality, indulges in love, personifies and thus wards off a threat, while gently parodying the specular, agonistic, obsessed thematics of Bloom's own theoretical plot. The comic and erotic excesses of this fantasy, in other words, both undermine and reenact its announced moral. Selfhood turns uncertain, but the flamboyant storyteller reaffirms his identity through the very narrative overload that calls into question his authority. By calling up de Man and rendering him at once demonic and the source of love, Bloom both represents and domesticates a threat, savoring the frisson of momentary self-loss as well as the pleasures of self-assertion. The satisfactions of gloominess and aggressive burlesque are not dissimilar. And we may understand the pathos and the narrative and figurative excess of Bloom's theories of agon and influence as serving just such a double role—providing him, that is, with a way to evoke, enjoy, and contradict the anonymity, instability, and immemorial inscriptive force, of literary representation. Literariness in this sense came to bear the name of "theory," for Bloom as for us, in the 1970s, and the specter of theory's strange technic ("You clone, my dear") continues to haunt Bloom as it does us. From this point of view Bloom is our most truly *literary* critic; and perhaps that is one reason why it has always been too early or late to figure him out: he figures our implication in the catastrophe of modernity.

NOTES

1. A considerably earlier and shorter version of this essay is to appear as "Canonical Anxiety: Harold Bloom and the Embodiment of Literature," in *Harold Bloom*, ed. Roy Sellars (Cambridge: Salt, in press). I thank the editor and publisher for permission to revise and republish.

2. The literature on these varied developments is of course vast. I shall be citing phrases from John Guillory, *Cultural Capital: The Problem of Literary Canon Formation* (Chicago: University of Chicago Press, 1993); apart from Guillory's work, see, for a broad and broadly influential account of the transformation of the university within global capitalism, Bill Readings, *The University in Ruins* (Cambridge: Harvard University Press, 1996). On the rise of cultural studies at the expense of theory, see Tilottama Rajan, "The University in Crisis: Cultural Studies, Civil Society, and the Place of Theory," *Literary Research/Recherche littéraire* 18.35 (2001): 8–25. Aspects of my account of Bloom's representation in the American media will have superficial affinities with observations offered by David R. Shumway, "The Star System in Literary Studies," *PMLA* 112.1 (1997): 85–100.

3. See the introduction to Marc Redfield, *The Politics of Aesthetics: Nationalism, Gender, Romanticism* (Stanford: Stanford University Press, 2003), 1–42; I discuss related issues in a different context in Redfield, *Phantom Formations: Aesthetic Ideology and the Bildungsroman* (Ithaca: Cornell University Press, 1996), 1–37. See also my introduction to a special issue of *Diacritics* that I'm editing on "Theory, Globalization, and the Remains of the University." Guillory closes his book with an appeal for an "aestheticism unbound" (340): a Schillerian moment which, I argue, undergirds his discomfort with, and disapproval of, "theory."

4. But see, for attempts to limn an understanding of history in terms of an event in excess of the narrative understanding it enables, Redfield's *Phantom Formations*, chapter 6, 171–200, and Redfield, *The Politics of Aesthetics*, chapter 3, 95–124.

5. David Lehman, "Yale's Insomniac Genius," *Newsweek*, 18 August 1986, 56. Though Bloom appears very briefly in a *Newsweek* article from a few years earlier, "A New Look at Lit Crit," by Kenneth L. Woodward et al. (11 June 1981), that piece, focused on Derrida and the "Gang of Four" at Yale, barely mentions Bloom.

6. Because of copyright complications, I reproduce here not the photo by Bernard Gotfryd published in *Newsweek* but, with Gotfryd's kind permission, an essentially identical one from the same photo shoot. I am grateful to Peter C. Herman for obtaining this photograph and for permission to use it.

7. Paul Gray, "Hurrah for Dead White Males!" *Time*, 10 October 1994, 62–63; photo by Ted Thai. I am grateful to Paul Saint-Amour for drawing my attention to this article, and to Adam Begley's and John Taylor's articles.

8. Begley, "Colossus among Critics: Harold Bloom," *New York Times Magazine*, 25 September 1994; photos by Ken Shung and Luc Novovitch.

9. John Taylor, "Bloom's Day: Hanging Out with the Reigning Genius of Literary Criticism," *New York*, 5 November 1990. Photo by John Hamilton.

10. Larissa MacFarquhar, "The Prophet of Decline: Harold Bloom's Influential Anxieties," *New Yorker*, 30 September 2002, 88. Some of this appears even in Colin Campbell's "Tyranny of the Yale Critics," *New York Times Magazine*, 9 February 1986. Bloom, though not the sole focus of the article, is the "Yale Critic" whose body Campbell most vigorously associates with both physicality and writing: "He is large, shaggy-haired and courteous. His belly sags. His pants look as wide as two old shopping bags," etc. "Chuckling, he swims toward a sort of Danish Lazy Boy and stretches out, nearly supine. Instantly, he is thinking aloud, his large dark eyes gazing at the ceiling, his brow a wall of hieroglyphic runes."

11. Bloom, *Omens of Millennium: The Gnosis of Angels, Dreams and Resurrection* (New York: Riverhead Books, 1996), 133. One way to get a quick sense of the historical shape of the canon debate is to note that, in his time, Samuel Johnson rarely if ever elicited fantasies of literary incorporation comparable to those inspired by Bloom, though the conventions of Augustan satire certainly encouraged associations between, for instance, a critic's physical size and the voraciousness of his reading. Eighteenth-century British culture had no real equivalent for our anxious fantasy of the "canon." There is, of course, considerable literature on Johnson's appearance and habits (he may have suffered from Tourette's syndrome), but surprisingly few analogies between his body and the extent of his learning. (I am grateful to Robert Folkenflik and Helen Deutsch for their help with this question.) Like Bloom, however, Johnson excited comments on his ability to remember what he read, and the speed with which he could read. The somewhat uncanny figure of the scanner or tape recorder that one encounters repeatedly in discourse about Bloom—and which I shall be discussing in greater detail—may be taken as the postmodern twist on what Boswell tends to present as the *non*physical character of Johnson's reading style. Remarkably for his time, Johnson had no need to sound out words and could thus read faster than he could speak: "The adulatory biographer was eager to make Johnson an 'eye-reader' . . . by describing his reading as nonphysical . . . he implied that it was interior and intellectual in the highest degree." Robert DeMaria Jr., *Samuel Johnson and the Life of Reading* (Baltimore: Johns Hopkins University Press, 1997), 23.

12. The quote is from John Hersey, and the passage is worth quoting at length since it affords a glimpse of Bloom (unnamed but hyperrecognizable) at the time of the disturbances at Yale during the Black Panther trial in the spring of 1970 (Hersey was a master of one of Yale's undergraduate residential colleges):

> Shortly after Mayday I sat in a meeting of a faculty committee [Yale University president Kingman] Brewster had set up to give advice on admissions policy, and I heard a professor in the English department, a brilliant critic, a man of massive intellect who can, I am told, recite from memory the entire body of English romantic verse of the nineteenth century, ask in a trembling voice if the admissions people couldn't let in what he called a "buffer quota," a large number of obviously solid and talented students who would serve as insurance against the destructive radical rebelliousness of the underprivileged high-risk students everyone seemed to think the university was obliged by social necessity to admit in these times. (Hersey, *Letter to the Alumni* [New York: Knopf, 1970], 123–24)

Hersey's point here is partly to defend the necessity of Brewster's reforms, but also to emphasize that most college radicals came from "middle and upper middle class families" (125); "I have reason to think that the anxious professor on the faculty advisory committee was most clearly worried by the admission of high-risk blacks" (126). That's not a speculation I want to endorse; but I do wish to remark Bloom's opposition at Yale, and at Cornell a year previously, where he had been a fellow of the Society of the Humanities, to the student movements of "the Sixties." His identification with a threatened institution (and thus, by extension in subsequent years, a threatened "canon") constituted one of his few points of agreement with his undergraduate mentor, M. H. Abrams, and was perhaps the only way in which he played the role of assimilated Jew in these Ivy League institutions. Otherwise, according to copious report, Bloom flaunted his working-class and Jewish origins, eschewed the coat-and-tie code of '50s and '60s Yale, and generally, to the extent that it was possible to do so, seems to have forced Yale to accommodate him rather than the other way around. His achievement should not be underrated. When Bloom began graduate study in 1951, the Yale English Department was notorious for its genteel anti-Semitism: a decade earlier its grand old man, Chauncey Brewster Tinker, had blocked Lionel Trilling's nomination to a professorship on racial grounds; and not until Tinker's retirement in 1945 did the departmental door begin to open, slowly and reluctantly, to Jewish scholars. According to Dan Oren, "the first known Jew to hold a teaching position in English at Yale" was Charles Feidelson, who was appointed to an instructorship in 1947 (and tenured a decade later): see Oren, *Joining the Club: A History of Jews at Yale* (New Haven: Yale University Press, 1985), 260.

13. Jacques Lacan, *The Seminar of Jacques Lacan, vol. 2: The Ego in Freud's Theory and in the Technique of Psychoanalysis, 1954–55,* trans. Sylvana Tomaselli (New York: Norton, 1991), 166. For a more in-depth examination of the conflicted figure of the body in aesthetic discourse, see Redfield, *Politics of Aesthetics,* 74–92.

14. Bloom's much-publicized fascination with Falstaff, which recently took the form of reading the part of Falstaff in well-publicized public performances in Boston and New York in the fall and spring of 2000–2001 (the New York performance was at the Kaye Playhouse on 12 March), may be taken as a version of this fantasy, which hesitates, coyly, between playacting and seriousness. Bloom is not really Falstaff; he is just pretending—but not quite as an actor pretends: we are to take his identification with this literary character as a partial expression of his omnivorous incorporation of the literary.

15. G. W. F. Hegel, *Enzyklopädie der philosophischen Wissenschaften, vol. 3,* in *Werke,* eds. Eva Moldenhauer and Karl Markus Michel (Frankfurt am Main, Germany: Suhrkamp, 1986), x, 281 (par. 463).

16. The genius is never far from the monster in popular iconography (see n. 35), and the literature on Bloom includes some efforts to humanize his gifts: "It turns out the legend that Harold Bloom can read 1,000 pages an hour is simply not true," John Taylor assures us, Bloom having pointed out that "no human being" could accomplish such a feat ("You can't turn pages that quickly"). According to this account Bloom can read "a 400–page book in just about an hour," and retain from it what he wants.

17. Sometimes Bloom seems to have added a short demonstration to his Hart Crane anecdote, to judge from Martin Kihn's account in his scandal-mongering "Bloom in Love," *GQ* (November 1990): "Forty years ago when he was drunk and in college at Cornell, he would recite Hart Crane's *The Bridge* backward, like some satanic tape recorder: 'Return lark's the of precincts agile the . . .'" (151). When Bloom has his way, the tape recorder is the usual trope; we find him rejecting Taylor's suggestion that his memory is "photographic" ("I assumed Bloom had a photographic memory, that his brain took a picture of the page, stored it, and reproduced it on demand"), and turning to the tape recorder trope so as to insist that his memory is "auditory and aesthetic" ("I can recite Milton's *Paradise Lost* from beginning to end, like running off a tape . . ."). Charles McGrath, however, a former Yale graduate student turned cultural journalist, offers a more postmodern trope in his *New Yorker* review of *The Western Canon*, imagining a Bloom "beleaguered by his own influences and unable to turn off that flood of remembered text scrolling endlessly through his brain" (McGrath, "Loose Canon," *New Yorker*, 26 September 1994, 105). In her *New Yorker* profile, MacFarquhar, unable entirely to resist drifting toward cyborgian metaphor despite her hyperbolic emphasis on Bloom's body, contents herself with claiming that Bloom is "a vulnerably receptive instrument" (94).

18. Paul de Man, "Review of Harold Bloom's *Anxiety of Influence*," in *Blindness and Insight: Essays in the Rhetoric of Contemporary Criticism*, 2d ed. (Minneapolis: University of Minnesota Press, 1983), 267–76. The review was originally published in *Comparative Literature* 26.3 (1974): 269–75. For Jacques Derrida's classic discussion of writing see *Of Grammatology*, trans. Gayatri Chakravorty Spivak (Baltimore: Johns Hopkins University Press, 1976).

19. Bloom, *A Map of Misreading* (New York: Oxford University Press, 1975), 5.

20. Bloom, *Wallace Stevens: The Poems of Our Climate* (Ithaca: Cornell University Press, 1977), 386, 393. It is perhaps worth recalling here that *A Map of Misreading* responds overtly to de Man's extraordinary review of *The Anxiety of Influence: A Theory of Poetry* (1973; reprint, New York: Oxford University Press, 1997), in which de Man suggested that Bloom's esoterically named defenses against influence ("clinamen," "tessera," etc.) could be translated into rhetorical tropes (irony, synecdoche, etc.). Bloom's response was to incorporate de Man's suggestion while ignoring or contradicting its essential point (which concerned the priority of questions of figuration over questions of will and desire). Good summaries and analyses of Bloom's development as a "theorist" may be had in the several books that have been published on Bloom: Graham Allen, *Harold Bloom: A Poetics of Conflict* (Hertfordshire: Harvester, 1994); Peter de Bolla, *Harold Bloom: Toward Historical Rhetorics* (London: Routledge, 1988); and David Fite, *Harold Bloom: The Rhetoric of Romantic Vision* (Amherst: University of Massachusetts Press, 1985).

21. Bloom, *Anxiety of Influence*, xix.

22. This is Bloom simulating a dialogue with de Man, in the course of the interview he granted Imre Salusinszky; I examine this scene at the end of the present essay. See Salusinszky, *Criticism in Society: Interviews with Jacques Derrida, Northrop Frye, Harold Bloom, Geoffrey Hartman, Frank Kermode, Edward Said, Barbara Johnson, Frank Lentricchia, and J. Hillis Miller* (New York: Methuen, 1987), 67.

23. Jonathan Culler, "Presupposition and Intertexuality," in *The Pursuit of Signs: Semiotics, Literature, Deconstruction* (Ithaca: Cornell University Press, 1981), 111; originally published in *MLN* 91.6 (1976). Culler is drawing on Neil Hertz's classic discussion of "The Notion of Blockage in the Literature of the Sublime," in *Psychoanalysis and the Question of the Text*, ed. Geoffrey Hartman (Baltimore: Johns Hopkins University Press, 1978), an essay that may be taken as, among other things, an indirect critique of Bloom. See also Culler's sharp review of *A Map of Misreading*, "Reading and Misreading," *Yale Review* 65 (1975): 88–95. For another deconstructively oriented review of Bloom's work during this period see Joseph Riddel's review of *Kaballah and Criticism* and *Poetry and Repression* in the *Georgia Review* 30 (1976): 989–1006.

24. See Derrida, "Signature Event Context," in *Limited Inc*, ed. Gerald Graff (Evanston, IL: Northwestern University Press, 1988), 1–23.

25. *Omens*, 104, 122. On Shakespeare, see Bloom's recent book *Shakespeare: The Invention of the Human* (New York: Riverhead Books, 1998).

26. Bloom, *Poetry and Repression: Revisionism from Blake to Stevens* (New York: Oxford University Press, 1976), 270 (emphasis in original). Bloom is echoing and contradicting here Paul de Man's famous reading of Yeats' "Among School Children," which argues that the poem's concluding line ("How can we tell the dancer from the dance?") may be read either literally or rhetorically. See de Man, *Allegories of Reading: Figural Language in Rousseau, Nietzsche, Rilke, and Proust* (New Haven: Yale University Press, 1979), 11–12.

27. Alfred, Lord Tennyson, "Ulysses," ll. 69–70 (1842), cited from *Poetry of the Victorian Period*, eds. Jerome Hamilton Buckley and George Benjamin Woods (1955; reprint, Glenview, IL: Scott, Foresman, 1965), 44.

28. See Maurice Blanchot, *The Space of Literature*, trans. Ann Smock (Lincoln: University of Nebraska Press, 1982).

29. Bloom's evasive strategies are many. One is perhaps worth noting here: at times Bloom's writing indulges in gendered fantasies that seek to anchor extralinguistic reality in the body of the mother, positing in *A Map of Misreading*, for instance, a maternal and material "ocean of incarnation" from which "poets whose sexual natures manifest unusual complexity . . . never get far" (13). Literalizing appeals of this sort to normative sexuality are relatively rare in Bloom's oeuvre, but they follow from that oeuvre's tendency to invoke the "metaphoric consummation or spousal union of masculine mind and feminine nature" that Mary Jacobus identifies as the gender plot of "natural supernatualism" (Jacobus, *Romanticism, Writing, and Sexual Difference: Essays on* The Prelude [Oxford: Clarendon Press, 1989], 206) and that Bloom himself, in *Blake's Apocalypse: A Study in Poetic Argument* (Ithaca: Cornell University Press, 1963), offers as "anyone's best hint for reading William Blake: every female personage finally relates to, or is, a form of nature; every male at last represents humankind, both male and female" (119). Bloom's work, which began as mythopoeic readings of Percy Shelley and Blake, has always had ready to hand such a symbolic economy; and since nature, in this mythopoesis, is what Man or the Imagination is not, the misogynistic potential of this set of associations is acute: woman figures the imagination's death, whether as the natural world of sensuality and sexuality or as "the genuine obscenity of a vampire will,

natural and female" (Bloom, *Blake's Apocalypse,* 292); the "sinister manifestation of Nature-as-temptress" (Bloom, *The Visionary Company: A Reading of English Romantic Poetry* [1961; reprint, Ithaca: Cornell University Press, 1971], 144). Feminist critics have of course often criticized Bloom's patriarchal model of literary influence; and it is certainly the case that, whether or not Bloom's theory needs the language of oedipal strife, it turns to this language in order to generate the pathos and structure it requires. A naturalizing rhetoric of gender marks the history of modern aesthetics in part, I suggest, because aesthetics constantly confronts the unnatural power of signs: for arguments that seek to back up that assertion, see my *Phantom Formations* and *Politics of Aesthetics.*

30. Elizabeth Bruss, *Beautiful Theories: The Spectacle of Discourse in Contemporary Criticism* (Baltimore: Johns Hopkins University Press, 1982), 345.

31. Bruss's trenchant characterization of Bloom's 1970s style also nicely conveys a sense of its peculiar, perverse, half-confessed literariness:

> a continuous recirculation of swatches of Wittgenstein and Freud, Vico and Kenneth Burke, Nietzsche, de Man, and Derrida, that float, unmoored and anonymous, among Bloom's own recurrent pet phrases (antithetical, central man, severe, ephebe, covering cherub), which themselves turn out to be derived from Yeats, Blake, Emerson, and Stevens. So powerful is the effect of this transumptive operation, that when one comes across these fragments in their original setting, one does indeed have the uncanny impression that "the mighty dead return" in Bloom's own voice. . . . (355–56)

32. Bloom, *The Breaking of the Vessels* (Chicago: University of Chicago Press, 1982), 60–61 (italics in original).

33. Cathy Caruth, "Speculative Returns: Bloom's Recent Work," *MLN* 98.5 (1983): 1286–96, esp. 1294 (italics in original).

34. Bloom, *The Western Canon: The Book and School of the Ages* (New York: Harcourt, 1994), 39.

35. On incorporation and melancholia, see Nicolas Abraham and Maria Torok, *The Shell and the Kernel: Renewals of Psychoanalysis,* trans. Richard Rand (Chicago: University of Chicago Press, 1994). The classical art of memory, with its emphasis on spatial relationships and lurid (and thus memorable) figures, plays a weirdly prominent role in Thomas Harris's best-seller *Hannibal* (New York: Delacorte Press, 1999), in which much is made of the eponymous, monstrous cannibal-hero's mnemnotechnic; though one could hardly imagine two literary characters more different in most respects than Harold Bloom and Hannibal the Cannibal, Harris's gothic thriller nonetheless suggests that the fantasies that go into the making of "Bloom" as the canon incorporate also circulate more widely. Hannibal Lecter (the pun, of course, is intended) is a Renaissance man of superhuman—that is, monstrous—proportion: like Bloom he has internalized all of Western culture; and his memory is the ur-technic that makes this masterful, aesthetic internalization possible. Harris, like Bloom in this quotation, is explicitly indebted to Frances Yates's classic *The Art of Memory* (Chicago: University of Chicago Press, 1966).

36. Walter Benjamin, "On Some Motifs in Baudelaire," in *Illuminations,* trans. Harry Zohn (New York: Schocken, 1969), 155–200, see esp. 160–65. I offer a gloss of Benjamin's notion of the shock experience in Redfield, *Politics of Aesthetics,* which may help clarify the link between technics, writing, and shock: "Even the photograph taken yesterday, at my behest, captures me in ways irreducible to perception or recollection: it can circulate beyond my knowledge or lifespan and can be altered, spliced, remade: as in Ridley Scott's *Blade Runner,* it and the identity-narrative it generates can always possibly be fakes, because technical reproduction captures its referent thanks to procedures that are inherently and essentially iterable, alien to the identity they construct and document. An irreducible anonymity laces our technonarratives of self-formation; and the impact of this anonymity is precisely what Benjamin calls shock" (53). My proposal in the present essay is that our modern institution of literature, in its essential *writtenness,* can convey the shock of such anonymity.

37. I discuss the coimplications of aesthetics, theory, literature, and technics at some length in Redfield, *Politics of Aesthetics,* esp. 14–29; see also, for a wide-ranging treatment of these issues, Samuel Weber, *Mass Mediauras: Form, Technics, Media* (Stanford: Stanford University Press, 1996).

38. As a critic who knew de Man well has remarked to me, "the notion that Paul de Man ever cupped *any*one's face in his hands (excluding some close family members) seems really unlikely" (Neil Hertz, E-mail to author).

10

The Sixties, the New Left, and the Emergence of Cultural Studies in the United States

DAVID R. SHUMWAY

It is often assumed that Cultural Studies in the United States is the North American branch of the Birmingham Centre for Contemporary Cultural Studies. This judgment is hard to prove, because assumptions are usually left unstated and no one had argued the point in so many words. Others have noticed the same thing, however. For example, Richard Ohmann, writing in 1991, asserted that Cultural Studies "felt almost like a British export" at what we must now recognize as U.S. Cultural Studies's coming out party, the Urbana, Illinois conference, "Cultural Studies Now and in the Future."[1] The history and genealogy of Cultural Studies has yet to be written, so there is no story about the influence of the Birmingham school in print that I can dispute here. I will have to rely on ambiguous bits of evidence, such as the title of the introduction to Lawrence Grossberg's collection of essays on Cultural Studies, "'Birmingham' in America?"[2] Noting the double qualification of scare quotes and question mark, one might assume that this piece would not support my position. But Grossberg doesn't explain the typography, and he does describe his brief residency at the center in the 1960s as the basis for the work he would do in graduate school, and, by implication, ever since. "'Birmingham'" might be read as a figure for Grossberg himself, and that too would support my case, since he has been Cultural Studies's most prominent spokesperson on this side of the Atlantic.

It is as a developer seeking to build Cultural Studies in the United States that Grossberg has written about the intellectual history of the Birmingham Centre. His work shows deep ambivalence about the degree to which Birmingham should serve as a norm for the movement as a whole, but the question is always practical rather than properly historical. Writing in 1989, Grossberg can lament that

> Five years ago [Cultural Studies] functioned largely as a proper name, referring primarily to a specifically British tradition, extending from the work of Raymond Williams and Richard Hoggart, through the contributions of the various members of the Centre, . . . to the increasingly dispersed and institutionalized sites of its contemporary practitioners. . . . However, "Cultural Studies" is becoming one of the most ambiguous terms in contemporary theory. . . .[3]

In 1995, Grossberg cautioned, "while I might argue that the link between Cultural Studies (as a somewhat dispersed intellectual discourse) and British Cultural Studies should not be ignored, it cannot be essentialized as if it were the only way into the discourse, the only genealogy, of Cultural Studies."[4] Yet in his writing it functions as the only genealogy since, aside from the bare mention of what he calls the "Chicago school of social thought," he never discusses an alternative. Patrick Brantlinger does offer a broader genealogy, but his book seems rather more to support Birmingham's paternity than to question it. The book proceeds from discussing the "Humanities in Crisis" in the United States to a chapter on "Cultural Studies in Britain," which provides a potential solution.[5]

The task of this essay is to offer an alternative genealogy by arguing that Cultural Studies in Britain and the United States derive from differing New Left movements and their academic offshoots. In the United States, left-wing political movements of the 1960s produced, besides campus protests, changes in the knowledge taught and studied at universities. There are four of these that help account for the rise and particular character of American Cultural Studies: (1) the rise of mass culture as an object of academic study; (2) the widespread rejection of the belief that genuine knowledge is politically disinterested; (3) the rise of academic feminism and the development of women's studies; and (4) the growth of African-American studies and the recognition of racism as a pervasive cultural evil that universities should address. This essay will argue that these changes in the American academy fostered the emergence of Cultural Studies here, and that the influence of Birmingham, while certainly significant, came late and provided, in Ohmann's words, "a way of gathering and naming a so-far inchoate movement."[6]

In order to understand where U.S. Cultural Studies came from, we need to know what U.S. Cultural Studies is. There is nothing obvious about this question. What Ohmann said in 1991, remains true today: "Cultural Studies doesn't (yet) exist in the U.S. as a clearly demarcated effort expressed in central institutions and normative practices."[7] Given this, Cultural Studies can have no institutional history of its own on which to base a genealogy. Indeed, without institutions to serve as monuments, it is hard even to date the movement. However, the mid-1980s seems to be the moment of its emergence. When Grossberg wrote about Cultural Studies in a 1983 essay, he refers mainly to "cultural theory" rather than "Cultural Studies."[8] That same year, four scholars working in obscurity in Oxford, Ohio, wrote an essay on "The Need for Cultural Studies," an argument for creating an enterprise that did not then exist in the United States.[9] The name "Cultural Studies" was new to at least two of the four, who previously had called that sort of work "cultural criticism." Gayatri Chakravorty Spivak said in 1991 that "I find myself in Cultural Studies now because suddenly in the last five years, it has become an extremely important movement in the United States."[10] However, this was not how the late and inchoate emergence of Cultural Studies in the United States was viewed abroad. Already in 1988, Megan Morris could speak of a Cultural Studies "boom" in the United States.[11] At the conference "Cultural Studies Now and in the Future" in 1990, Stuart Hall expressed amazement at "the enormous explosion of Cultural Studies in the United States, its rapid professionalization and institutionalization."[12] This was a fundamental misunderstanding. There may have been an explosion of Cultural Studies scholarship, but there was, and there remains, a lack of departments or programs with dedicated faculty lines, the usual markers of professionalization and institutionalization. Grossberg himself would complain a few years later about the promiscuous use of the name "Cultural Studies."[13] The lack of a specific institutional formation meant that the name could be claimed by anyone since no group had a professionally recognized stake. Cultural Studies did not develop in the United States as a distinct or separate enterprise. It was nurtured in traditional departments where its adherents were most often employed, especially English departments.

Clearly, Morris and Hall were responding to something, however, and their words point to the period 1984 to 1991 as the moment of the emergence of Cultural Studies in the United States. Since neither programs nor departments emerged in significant numbers, we are left with scholarship itself. While there will be disagreements about what work qualifies as "the major scholarship," the books I will mention here have been widely influential and have been regularly identified with Cultural Studies. It is to the point, however, that none of them was produced by someone working in a department or program in Cultural Studies, or even self-consciously *as* Cultural Studies. Rather, each is a work that emerged from a particular discipline and was addressed primarily to those working in that discipline.

Let us begin by looking at three texts that reflect the variety of disciplines and objects characteristic of Cultural Studies at this time. Janice A. Radway's *Reading the Romance* (1984), might be the book from this period that is most clearly identified with Cultural Studies and most clearly distinguished from earlier work in established disciplines.[14] Its focus on formula fiction and its use of ethnographic methods were both groundbreaking. As Ohmann observes, "it is symptomatic that when we look for models . . . CS [Cultural Studies] people in this country revert again and again to . . . *Reading the Romance*."[15] Yet, Radway's book came out of American Studies, a field with which she continues to be affiliated. Her subsequent study of the Book of the Month Club is more traditionally historical, and has not been as strongly identified with Cultural Studies.[16] Moreover, *Reading the Romance* has not, *pace* Ohmann, in practice served as an exemplar for the movement, its method having been not much imitated.

Of course, Radway's more or less empirical approach is in many respects atypical. Spivak's *In Other Worlds* (1987) illustrates the opposing tendency and the influence of poststructuralist theory.[17] Spivak was first known for her translation of Jacques Derrida's *Of Grammatology* (1976) and for the extended introduction to that translation. *In Other Worlds* collected essays that had been published elsewhere or had been presented as lectures. The disciplinary context of these essays is literature, and the field to which they seem to point is not Cultural Studies per se, but postcolonial studies—perhaps a subdiscipline of Cultural Studies, but in practice usually regarded as distinct. Spivak herself seems to want to insist on a certain distance between her and the movement, asserting that "I came to Cultural Studies; I do not belong to its mainstream. . . . I cannot say I really know what Cultural Studies is or are; I find myself within it."[18] The sort of theoretical work that Spivak does has been more identified with literary studies than with Cultural Studies, where Spivak is often cited but not much imitated.

Donna Haraway's *Primate Visions* (1989) would seem to fall somewhere between Radway and Spivak on the empirical-theoretical scale.[19] Moreover, one cannot name a single traditional discipline to which this book belongs. However, it still cannot be understood as a product of Cultural Studies. Rather, its roots lie in anthropology and in the history of science, and its feminist stance comes from women's studies. Its major object is science, making the book a leading example of science studies, another sometime element of Cultural Studies. One of the things that links the book to Cultural Studies is its analysis of the way in which primatology and nonhuman primates have been portrayed in mass culture. Like the other two books mentioned, *Primate Visions* has not so far had many imitators.

A list of other important examples of American Cultural Studies published between 1984 and 1991 bear out the trends these three have illustrated:

Teresa de Lauretis, *Alice Doesn't* (1984); Eve Kosofsky Sedgwick, *Between Men* (1985); Tania Modeleski, ed., *Studies in Entertainment* (1986); James Clifford and George Marcus, eds., *Writing Culture* (1986); Henry Louis Gates Jr., *The Signifying Monkey* (1988); Cary Nelson and Grossberg, eds., *Marxism and the Interpretation of Culture* (1988); Houston Baker, *Blues, Ideology, and Afro-American Literature* (1989); Andrew Ross, *No Respect* (1989); Patrick Brantlinger, *Crusoe's Footprints* (1990); Judith Butler, *Gender Trouble* (1990); Cornell West, *The American Evasion of Philosophy* (1990); and Fredric Jameson, *Postmodernism, Or, the Cultural Logic of Late Capitalism* (1991).[20]

While this is obviously not an exhaustive list, and it is doubtless biased in favor of the disciplines with which I am most familiar, these are widely accepted examples of Cultural Studies. What does the list tell us? First, the only books on this list that might be said to have emerged primarily from Cultural Studies are those of Nelson and Grossberg, Ross, and Brantlinger, and even the Nelson and Grossberg collection is not a clear case. British Cultural Studies clearly influenced other authors here, but these other works owe their existence more to traditional disciplines such as English or philosophy or to more recently established Women's Studies and African-American Studies. Indeed, what is most striking about the list is the dominance of feminist work and the emergence of Gay and Lesbian Studies, itself a child of the New Left-related gay rights movement. Marxism is present as an influence in many of the texts, but it is dominant only in Nelson and Grossberg, and Jameson. Identity politics are thus at the center of the majority of this work, and traditional Marxist class politics is clearly more marginal. While not all of these books deal with mass culture (e.g., Sedgwick, West), most of them do, and many treat it either as politically positive or as source of cultural insight. The Frankfurt school condemnation of mass culture is rare if it is not excluded entirely.

Where did this movement come from? To understand why Great Britain is not a satisfactory answer, we need to look at the history of British Cultural Studies. As Grant Farred has noted, "the rise of Cultural Studies as an academic discipline" was an unexpected result of the political agenda of the British New Left.[21] Farred's argument is that the New Left is the point of emergence for identity politics. While that position is surely right, Farred overestimates the similarities between the British and American New Lefts. In particular, Farred's concern to link the New Left to identity politics leads him to discount the degree to which the British New Left remained strongly connected to Marxism and to its conception of class. In the United States, Marxism as a dominant influence and its class politics came late to the New Left, after race, age, and other identities had already served to define the movement. Indeed, identity was a personal and intellectual preoccupation characteristic of the American New Left, a movement where authenticity, an issue of self-identity, was a more important value than solidarity.[22]

The New Left in the United States was a movement made up mainly of undergraduate students and focused on activism. In the United Kingdom, the New Left was founded by academics—professors and would-be professors— and its major work was intellectual. It manifested itself first in two journals, the *Reasoner,* later, the *New Reasoner,* and *Universities and Left Review (ULR),* later, the *New Left Review.* The former emerged in the wake of Nikita Khrushchev's revelation of Stalin's crimes and the Soviet invasion of Hungary in 1956. It represented a critique of the British Communist Party by members and former members, most prominently historians, including Christopher Hill, E. J. Hobsbawm, and E. P. Thompson.[23] *Universities and Left Review* represented a younger generation who in the main had not been party members, and many of whom became politically active in response to the British role in the Suez Crisis.[24] According to Dennis L. Dworkin, "the British New Left was a heterogeneous group of ex-Communists, disaffected Labour supporters, and socialist students hopeful of renewing socialist theory and practice. . . . They never succeeded in creating a permanent organization, but they created a new political space on the left."[25] Stuart Hall, one of the founders of *ULR,* admits that the British New Left "had no organized mass base" and that although it "was not just composed of intellectuals . . . since the journal, *Universities and Left Review,* played the leading role, it was the intellectuals who took the lead."[26] Despite some efforts to reach beyond the academy, the British New Left was never a grassroots movement. After its brief flowering, from 1956 to 1962,[27] the British New Left left a legacy that was almost entirely academic.

According to Dworkin, "A founding principle of Cultural Studies was opposition to orthodox Marxism, and Marxism did not play a particularly significant role in the Centre [for Contemporary Cultural Studies]'s early years."[28] Still, Cultural Studies in Britain developed in relation to a strong Marxist political tradition, and the influence of Marxism is ubiquitous. The founding documents of British Cultural Studies are all fundamentally concerned with class. The title of E. P. Thompson's *Making of the English Working Class* (1966) makes this obvious, but it is no less true of Raymond Williams's *Culture and Society* (1958) or Richard Hoggart's *Uses of Literacy* (1957).[29] For purposes of comparison to U.S. Cultural Studies, the last of these texts is the most important for it is centrally concerned with mass culture. Hoggart's focus is on the way in which working-class men and women made use of the "culture" that capitalism gave them. While the fact that men and women lived to a large extent in separate spheres is well described in the text, gender is not addressed as a political category. Race is not an issue. In Britain of the 1950s, class was the major cultural and political divide, and there remained an active and significant organized Left defined by class politics. It was almost inevitable that, as Cultural Studies developed in Britain, class would be its major intellectual category and Marxism its dominant theoretical tradition. Hall describes the New Left as not being Marxist in the way that those schooled in the old Communist tradition were, but rather as "related to Marxism, but much more critical of it." Hall's claim that class "was never the only question" even at the beginning is undermined by his own account of the center's history.[30] In his "Theoretical Legacies" essay, he asserts that feminism and race came as "interruptions in the work of the Center for Contemporary Cultural Studies."[31] This strongly suggests that identity politics arrived after the British New Left had already passed its prime. Although the later cultural politics of typical Birmingham scholarship, such as Dick Hebdige's *Subculture* (1979), were certainly a departure from "reductionist" Marxism, they nevertheless remained rooted in the tradition of Marxist theory.[32] In these studies, identity and class politics are aligned, rather than opposed.

Conditions in the United States were radically different. The American New Left developed largely in the vacuum that resulted from the McCarthy era repression of the Old Left.[33] Its most direct influence was the civil rights movement that had begun to challenge successfully segregation and discrimination in the South in the 1950s. The leading New Left organization, Students for a Democratic Society (SDS), began as an offshoot of the League for Industrial Democracy (LID), an organization that traced its history to turn-of-the-century socialist Upton Sinclair, but that had become by the 1950s "a tax-exempt sinecure—a kind of retirement home for aging social democrats" (*DS*, 29). LID's virulent anticommunism would be the major cause of tension between the SDS and its sponsor, but not because SDS was itself communist. Rather, SDS was criticized by the LID leadership for being "soft" on communism, for example, for admitting a Party member as an observer at a convention (*DS*, 126–32). Unlike the British New Left, which clearly evolved out of the Old Left and continued to struggle with it intellectually, SDS simply rejected the Old Left and sought to put sectarian battles behind it.

Marxism was just one of the intellectual traditions that informed the early politics of SDS, and it was by no means the most important. The most important manifesto of the American New Left, SDS's *Port Huron Statement,* is rooted in the language and history of American democracy. Terry H. Anderson traces the movement's intellectual heritage most directly to a scattered group of 1950s intellectuals including Paul Goodman, William Whyte, Dwight Macdonald, John Kenneth Galbraith, William Appleman Williams, and C. Wright Mills.[34] Mills was certainly the presiding individual influence, and he regarded Marxism as a nineteenth-century relic. Some sense of SDS's intellectual influences can be gleaned from a reading list of thirty-eight texts distributed in 1961. It included Karl Marx's *Economic and Philosophic Manuscripts of 1844,* and Fidel Castro's "History Will Absolve Me," but it was heavily weighted toward American political discourse both intellectual and

practical, including the most recent Democratic Party Platform and a manifesto of the right-wing Young Americans for Freedom. There were also
works by John Dewey, Daniel Bell, Seymour Martin Lipset, and, of course,
Mills. That Fyodor Dostoyevsky's "Grand Inquisitor" appears there indicates
that philosophical as well as strictly political questions were on the group's
table. The listing of *Conviction* and *Out of Apathy*, two anthologies produced
by the British New Left, shows an awareness of this movement (*DS*, 78).

Tom Hayden, principal author of the *Statement*, read all of the titles on
the list, but he was apparently not influenced by the work of the British New
Left, and, according to Miller, he "found scant solace in most of what he read"
(*DS*, 78). The central concern of the *Statement* is "participatory democracy," a
term that Hayden had borrowed from Arnold Kaufman, a political scientist
with whom Hayden had studied at the University of Michigan. Though its
meaning was never precise in SDS usage, it did not necessarily refer to some
system other than representative democracy (*DS*, 142–43). The *Statement* is
above all a call to enact American democratic values that it sees as lost or
neglected, and "values" are its very specific concern. For example, it asserts that
"We regard *men* as infinitely precious and possessed of unfulfilled capacities
for reason, freedom, and love."[35] While the document criticizes the role of
anticommunism in American political life, it also states that "as democrats we
are in basic opposition to the communist system" and asserts that the "communist movement has failed, in every sense, to achieve its stated intention of
leading a worldwide movement for human emancipation" (*PHS*, 350–51). But
communism was not the only element of the Old Left that the *Statement* criticized. The labor movement in the United States is accused of failing to play
its historic role as the "'countervailing power' against the excesses of Big Business" and of giving up its "dream of 'organizing the unorganized'" (*PHS*, 343).

As should be clear from this analysis, the New Left in the United States
was not founded on class struggle. Instead, its adherents recognized themselves as children of privilege when they begin their "Agenda for a Generation" with "We are people of this generation, bred in at least modest comfort,
housed in universities, looking uncomfortably to the world we inherit" (*PHS*,
329). The importance of the term "generation" indicates the degree to which
this is already an identity politics. While it is highly critical of the apathy of
the majority of students and of the then current legal doctrine that defined the
universities' relations to their students as *in loco parentis*, the document concludes with an extended case for the university as the primary site for future
social change in America.[36]

> First, the university is located in a permanent position of social influ-
> ence. Its educational function makes it indispensable and automatically
> makes it a crucial institution in the formation of social attitudes. Second, in

an unbelievably complicated world, it is the central institution for organizing, evaluating, and transmitting knowledge. Third, the extent to which academic resources presently are used to buttress immoral social practice is revealed, first, by the extent to which defense contracts make the universities engineers of the arms race. Too, the use of modern social science as a manipulative tool reveals itself in the "human relations" consultants of modern corporations. . . . But these social uses of the universities' resources also demonstrate the unchangeable reliance by men of power on the men and store-houses of knowledge: this makes the university functionally tied to society in new ways, revealing new potentialities, new levers for change. Fourth, the university is the only mainstream institution open to participation by individuals of nearly any viewpoint. (*PHS*, 373)

These "facts," the *Statement* continues, "make the university a potential base and agency in a movement of social change." The vision of a New Left that the document proceeds to outline depends on the university as its base. Because this New Left will be "committed to deliberativeness, honesty, and reflection," the university, which "permits the political life as an adjunct to the academic one, and action to be informed by reason," is its natural home. Since a New Left must consist of and recruit "younger people who matured in the post-war world. . . . The university is an obvious beginning point" (*PHS*, 373). The university, it is argued, can bring together liberals and socialists, while political parties cannot, and, since "the ideal university is a community of controversy," it is the place from which the nation can be awakened from apathy. While the *Statement* admits that the university cannot succeed alone, "[t]he power of students and faculty together is not only potential; it has shown its actuality in the South, and in the reform movements of the North" (*PHS*, 374). What is notable about this treatment of the university is how removed it is from the professorial view of academic life. Far from being troubled by issues of objectivity and disinterested knowledge, SDS simply assumes that the university is a political institution whether it knows it or not.

Clearly, then, the SDS of the *Statement* did not understand the working class as the vanguard or perhaps even as a significant element of the struggle. While SDS did eventually adopt Marxist theory and rhetoric in which "class" was the privileged term, its appeal was never to the working class. Moreover, SDS was itself always to the left of the movement it was trying to lead. The most important issues of the American New Left as a whole—peace, equality, and freedom—were those of the children of the middle class, especially of the professional-managerial class, and African-Americans; the economic issues that had driven class politics in America since the Civil War were not significant in New Left practice even if they were acknowledged in theory.

Although the *Statement* is more a work of intellectual reflection than a program for action, the American New Left would be much more activist than intellectual. The one person who might have turned the intellectual groping of SDS into a coherent intellectual position was Mills, who died in March of 1962 and did not live long enough to produce significant new work in response to the movement that his earlier writings so heavily influenced. Perhaps the closest the New Left came to producing an American equivalent of the British academic circles that produced the *New Reasoner,* and *New Left Review* was the *Studies on the Left* group at the University of Wisconsin in Madison. But it is important to understand that these "Wisconsin Marxists" were always peripheral to the movement, being both more academic and more Old Left than the student activists. The presiding influence of the group was historian William Appleman Williams whose book, *The Contours of American History,* would influence the SDS strategy that sought to link the demands of the poor to an end to the arms race (*DS,* 170–72). Borrowing from the circle as a whole, SDS would adopt the term "corporate liberalism" to name the Kennedy administration's program of "tinkering with the corporate economy in order to maintain it."[37] Unlike the *Statement, Studies on the Left* explicitly questioned the value placed on dispassionate, nonpartisan scholarship. The journal argued that what is called "objectivity . . . is reducible to the weight of authority, the viewpoint of those who are in a position to enforce standards."[38] While this critique took some time to become influential and remains controversial, it is foundational to the project of Cultural Studies. Moreover, theoretical statements that questioned the assumed divide between the academy and politics helped to pave the way for the politically invested work of Women's and African-American studies.

New Left activism, however, was in the short run probably more influential than academic arguments in convincing professors of the political character of knowledge. The political climate on campus and across the nation opened the door to a significant intellectual shift in which knowledge came to be understood as politically invested to a much greater degree than previously allowed. While various kinds of theory would later be invoked to explain the point, for members of the Modern Language Association (MLA), the awareness of the connection between knowledge and power did not have to wait for Foucault. In 1968, several professors attending the MLA Convention in New York were arrested for attempting to put up antiwar posters in one of the convention hotels. The arrests led to protests and eventually to the election of two politically committed individuals, Louis Kampf and Florence Howe, to the office of president of the MLA.[39] While these events did not immediately change scholarship in the modern languages, such change did follow in their wake. Not only did the organization spawn radical allied organizations such as the Radical Caucus and the Marxist Literary Group, but it would eventually embrace the politicized knowledges of Women's and African-American studies, something that would have been less likely had belief in "disinterested" knowledge remained uncontested.

Another significant influence of the New Left on the academy can be seen in the way in which popular culture would be taken up as an object of study. To understand this point, it needs to be observed that the American New Left, especially as it grew in the wake of mass antiwar protests, was itself very much something that happened in the media. As a result, the New Left transcended the various organizations and factions that tried to lead the movement to include, as James Miller puts it, "hundreds of thousands of young people . . . [who] came to consider themselves radicals" (*DS,* 310). Even though SDS was the leading New Left organization in the United States, it would be wrong to understand the movement as limited to SDS. Rather, the New Left must be understood to include the black-power movement as represented by organizations such as the Student Nonviolent Coordinating Committee and the Black Panthers, the antiwar movement in general, and the beginnings of second-wave feminism. Moreover, the politics of the American New Left ranged from that of the left-liberal wing of the Democratic Party to the rigid Marxism (sometimes said to be "Maoism") of the Progressive Labor Party. Because of the broad impact of the three social movements mentioned and the lack of a dominant sectarian doctrine to limit membership or identification, the New Left became by 1968 a major force in the American political scene, "briefly affect[ing] the whole tone of political life in America" (*DS,* 320). While Eugene McCarthy and Robert Kennedy, who both challenged incumbent president Lyndon Johnson as antiwar candidates, cannot be regarded as New Lefties, many of their supporters could be. As a result of the breadth of its appeal and the media savvy of some of it leaders, the American New Left was constantly in the public eye.

But the New Left in the United States was a creature of mass culture even before it became mass culture. In Britain, the study of mass culture arose in response to the imperatives of New Left theory. In the United States, mass culture wasn't theorized by the New Left; rather mass cultural products provided the New Left with theories—or at least assumptions and rhetoric. Todd Gitlin explains how mass culture in late 1950s and early 1960s paved the way for the New Left: "Rock and roll and its dances were the opening wedge, hollowing out the cultural ground beneath the tranquilized center. Marlon Brando and James Dean embodied styles and gestures of disaffection. On the fringes, satirists of all kinds—*Mad,* Lenny Bruce, Mort Sahl, Chicago's Compass and Second City cabarets—ridiculed a host of pieties. TV's Steve Allen and Sid Caesar and their offshoots and imitators carried some of the rambunctious spirit into the mainstream."[40]

Gitlin is not the only scholar to have argued for such connections, though treatments of 1960s politics often do give short shrift to the culture that produced and accompanied the movement. Nick Bromell describes the typical student of the late 1960s as "living to music," a phrase he borrows from a contemporary writer, John Cunnick: "I wake up in the morning and do a Master's voice thing in front of the speakers for a while; *then* I go outside. Music defines a total environment. . . . Go to a house and someone hands you a joint in front of a record player and it's assumed . . . that you are going to sit for a couple of hours, not talking, hardly moving, *living* to music."[41] Bromell glosses "living to music" as "the existential and visionary side of the 1960s; more mundanely, the inside of the experience of listening to rock, hearing it as a spontaneous epic poem produced miraculously by your peers for immediate use."[42] Bromell's book is a sort of "report from the home-front" in which the meaning of popular culture is evoked in the context of the radical politics of the period.

Exactly how and why music could have had played such a large role in the making of the New Left is admittedly hard to explain. Gitlin emphasizes the importance of the initial emergence of rock and roll in the 1950s, which brought black R&B to white teenagers and produced Elvis Presley who became an unprecedented star. "For those of us who were ten or twelve when Elvis Presley came along, it was rock 'n' roll that named us a generation." It is no coincidence, in Gitlin's view, that the civil rights movement and rock emerge at about the same time.[43] Bromell depicts the Beatles as having an even larger impact than Elvis, since the Beatles' reach extended to college students. He quotes Griel Marcus on the transformation that *Meet the Beatles* produced, turning folkies on to rock: "This was something that never happened before."[44] Simon Frith concurs, holding that John Lennon in particular embodied the connections between music and the movement:

> It was Lennon who leapt more quickly (more desperately?) than the other Beatles at the unfolding possibilities of the 1960s rock and youth culture, and the importance of the Beatles in 1966–68 was not that they led any movement, but that they *joined in*. They became (John Lennon in particular), for all their established star status, comrades in the mid-sixties "liberation" of leisure. What's more, Lennon confirmed what I believed then and believe still—that it is not possible to separate the hippie aspects of 1960s youth culture, the drugs and mind-games and reconsiderations of sexuality, from the political process which fed the student movement, the anti-war movement, May 1968, the women's movement, gay liberation.[45]

Elsewhere, Frith argues that "Rock . . . is about difference and what distinguishes us from people with other tastes. It rests on an ideology of the *peer group* as both the ideal and reality of rock communion."[46] This suggests that rock was not only what defined a generation, but also what embodied its utopian communal vision, a point illustrated by one radical's deeply serious attempt to explain the political implications of the Beatles' song "Yellow Submarine" to a television reporter.[47]

Popular music helped create the conditions for the student movement, but, as Frith observed of John Lennon, it did not do this by leading youth to take particular positions. Indeed, the specific political positions articulated in rock usually followed their articulation in more traditional forms of political speech. Even Bob Dylan seems to have adopted politically oriented music because it was the coming thing in the folk music scene.[48] Yet, Dylan was enough ahead of the curve that he did function as an opinion maker. His lyrics would provide the American New Left with more of its rhetoric and slogans than all Marxist writing put together. Some of the major histories of the New Left reflect this by their use of Dylan's titles and lines to name chapters or gloss events.[49] Miller argues that by 1965 Dylan was "a central influence on SDS" (*DS*, 238). "'To understand *The Port Huron Statement*,'" Richard Flacks, one of the presidents of SDS, said "only half-joking, 'you have to understand Bob Dylan'" (quoted in *DS*, 161). Miller sees Dylan's development from the idealism of "Blowin' in the Wind" to the bitterness of "Like a Rolling Stone" as paralleling a similar development in SDS's outlook (*DS*, 254). Even as Dylan's songs became less political, they were still read politically by the New Left. Thus, a line from "Subterranean Homesick Blues," "you don't need a weatherman to know which way the wind blows" supplied the Weatherman faction with a name and a "strategy."

It is not surprising then that a generation that had treated rock stars as intellectuals, that is, serious contributors to public discourse, would think popular culture worthy of academic study. Thus, a second major change produced by the New Left in the American academy was that mass cultural objects for the first time were taken seriously. While the American Studies movement had begun this process starting in the late 1940s, by the 1960s it had largely disowned it. As a result, populist elements of the American Studies Association (ASA) founded the Popular Culture Association (PCA) in 1967. While it is safe to say that the PCA did not challenge the MLA or the ASA for prestige and influence, the very existence of the organization was a foot in the door. The PCA's populism, which opposed all distinctions as invidious, would keep it on the margins of the academy. There would be no departments of popular culture except the one at the PCA's home, Bowling Green State University in Ohio. Moreover, the older generation of populists who dominated the PCA would prevent it from endorsing Cultural Studies—for political judgments were seen to be just as invidious as aesthetic ones; their mission was to promote, not criticize, popular culture. Cultural Studies would have to await the next generation of scholars, who had learned from the political struggles of the 1960s to discriminate among mass cultural products, a project that would become a preoccupation of American Cultural

Studies. Still, such discrimination was not the total condemnation of mass culture one found in Max Horkheimer, Theodor Adorno, and the Frankfurt school.[50] American Cultural Studies began in part with the desire to endorse at least some expressions of mass culture in the face of the traditional dismissal of it by the academy.

If popular culture did not become a new academic discipline, the influence of the New Left did produce two of them, both major innovations in American higher education: Women's Studies and Black or Afro-American Studies. Both had become commonplace in American universities by the mid-1970s. The New Left had an impact on established disciplines, as I suggested in my discussion of the increased acceptance of the political character of knowledge. But it took much longer to effect general practice in these fields, an effect that has been in any case quite limited outside of the modern languages.

Both Women's Studies and Black Studies emerged as explicitly politicized fields, the first administratively recognized divisions of the university to be spawned by New Left activism. The connection of the women's liberation movement (now often called "second-wave feminism") to the New Left is well documented. Women, who were important participants in SDS and in other movement organizations from the beginning, experienced male dominance in them and learned how to fight it.[51] Moreover, it could be argued that the struggle for justice for the poor, for the Vietnamese, and for the young served as a model on which the struggle for women's equality might be understood. The first Women's Studies program began in 1970, and by the late 1990s there would be more than six hundred of them.[52] As Ellen Messer-Davidow shows, women's studies and other feminist scholarship is connected to 1960s movements in three ways. First, women who participated in the civil rights and New Left movements went on to be founders of feminist studies. Second, these activists created a vision of feminist studies as a project that would use the wherewithal of the academy to fuel the movement for social change, a vision that in Messer-Davidow's view has not been fulfilled. Last but not least, the feminist positions and theories assumed or advocated by feminist scholars often made their way from the movement into the academy.[53]

The relationship of Afro-American Studies to the civil rights, black power, and student movements is even more direct. The establishment of such programs was in many cases the response of a university to student protests or to the fear of them.[54] The agenda of Afro-American studies was always political, but perhaps not as explicitly transformative as that of Women's Studies. Even more than women, African-Americans believed that they had been excluded from the knowledge taught and studied at the university. The Black Nationalism of the black power movement was an important impetus for the shape that Afro-American studies took on many campuses.

Women's Studies and Afro-American Studies brought New Left identity politics into the academy, and not just into the courses in these still relatively marginal programs. Rather, women and African-Americans came increasingly to be taken seriously by traditional disciplines like English and history. Cultural Studies in the United States would inevitably draw both ideas and people from these new academic formations. This was truer of Women's Studies and the various feminisms that grew up elsewhere in the academy. One factor in this disparity is doubtless that there have been many more women than African-Americans in disciplines relevant to Cultural Studies. But another factor may derive from the New Left itself. While the civil rights movement was the most significant precursor of the New Left, by the end of the 1960s, the Black and White New Left organizations had almost entirely separated from each other. The Black Panthers served as a model for increasingly militant white New Leftists, but they remained organizationally separate. Similarly, while race was recognized as a central category of analysis in U.S. Cultural Studies, African-Americans were not in the main identified with Cultural Studies. Still, the dominance of the categories of race and gender in American Cultural Studies derives to a large extent from the existence of programs in Women's and Black Studies, and the lack of a successful "Working-Class Studies" movement.

Yet the growing importance of class in U.S. Cultural Studies may also be a legacy of the New Left, and its late impact in the former parallels its similarly late significance in the latter. Marxism was increasingly significant to the New Left as the decade developed. The explicitly Marxist-Leninist Progressive Labor (PL) Party began to influence and infiltrate SDS in 1965. By 1967, as Gitlin puts it, "PL and its principal opponents in the SDS leadership were building up their titles to the revolutionary future, lining up on behalf of their various Marxism-Leninisms."[55] By the time SDS disintegrated in 1969, the two leading factions, PL's Worker-Student Alliance and the Weathermen, were looking to the working class to continue what students had started. Moreover, while the Weathermen trumped PL by destroying SDS as an organization, the nerdy, shorthaired Maoists brought Marxist theory into the New Left. While most New Left decendents did not remain in PL's orbit—or, indeed, remain Marxist-Leninists of any stripe—Marxism would now be part of the New Left legacy to Cultural Studies.

Most of what distinguishes the practices that have come to be thought of as Cultural Studies from traditional disciplinary practices can be traced to the influence of the New Left: the focus on mass culture and its products; approaches based in feminist, African-Americanist, and Marxist politics; and the assumption that knowledge is political. The final difference, the influence of poststructuralism and other kinds of high theory, can only be indirectly related to the New Left, and it is also the most ambiguous difference given the influence of such theory on literary studies in the 1970s and 1980s. American Cultural Studies emerged out of American political and academic conditions, with Birmingham serving less as a parent than as a midwife. And, it was the legacy of the New Left that provided an opening for the influence of the Birmingham school.

If Cultural Studies "exploded" between 1984 and 1990, it was not because the Birmingham model became newly influential and suddenly transformed old-fashioned humanists into politically committed critics of mass culture. Rather, we need to understand the emergence of Cultural Studies in the United States as the coalescing of trends in progress since the late 1960s and early 1970s around a concept and name that gave them a specific identity and coherence. Besides the indigenous influences, poststructuralist theory had already had a major impact in the United States by the mid-1980s, which might explain Stuart Hall's "astonishment" at the "theoretical fluency" he discovered here.[56] This is not to say that Williams, Hall, and other Birmingham members were ignored, but it is to suggest that they need to be regarded as merely among the influences that have produced American Cultural Studies. The influence of British Cultural Studies has served to raise awareness of the category of class. The politics of gender and race remain dominant, however, and the influence of Birmingham has done little to move American Cultural Studies away from the interpretation of mass cultural texts—toward, say, the study of subcultures, the current political conjuncture, or other nontextual objects.

Of course, Cultural Studies in the United States has changed since the Urbana conference. The publication of Grossberg's *We Gotta Get Out of This Place* in 1992 represented an explicit attempt to do a Birmingham style analysis of the then current American political conjuncture.[57] Richard Ohmann's *Selling Culture* (1996) and Michael Denning's *Cultural Front* (1996) marked a new prominence for history and class in U.S. Cultural Studies.[58] Moreover, the study of mass culture grew seemingly exponentially, so that it is hard to name the books that were the most significant. What did not change was Cultural Studies' institutional status. The movement remains largely without its own programs or departments, and at this writing it still lacks a professional association.[59] Whether this status will allow Cultural Studies to avoid disciplinary limitations and change knowledge, or merely consign Cultural Studies to the margins of the academy remains to be seen.

NOTES

1. Richard Ohmann, "Thoughts on Cultural Studies in the United States," *Critical Studies* 3.1 (1991): 11.

2. Lawrence Grossberg, *Bringing It All Back Home: Essays on Cultural Studies* (Durham: Duke University Press, 1997).

3. Lawrence Grossberg, "The Formation(s) of Cultural Studies: An American in Birmingham," *Bringing it All Back Home,* 195.

4. Lawrence Grossberg, "Cultural Studies: What's in a Name? (One More Time)," *Bringing it All Back Home,* 247.

5. Patrick Brantlinger, *Crusoe's Footprints: Cultural Studies in Britain and America* (New York: Routledge, 1990), 1–67.

6. Ohmann, "Thoughts on Cultural Studies in the United States," 5.

7. Ibid.

8. Lawrence Grossberg, "Cultural Studies Revisited and Revised," *Bringing it All Back Home,* 141–73.

9. Henry Giroux, David R. Shumway, James J. Sosnoski, and Paul Smith, "The Need for Cultural Studies: Resisting Intellectuals and Oppositional Public Spheres," *Dalhousie Review* 64 (1984): 472–86.

10. Gayatri Chakravorty Spivak, "Reflections on Cultural Studies in the Post-Colonial Conjuncture: An Interview with the Guest Editor," *Critical Studies* 3.1 (1991): 64–78.

11. Megan Morris, *The Pirate's Fiancée: Feminism, Reading, Postmodernism* (London: Verso, 1988).

12. Stuart Hall, "Cultural Studies and its Theoretical Legacies," in *Cultural Studies,* eds. Lawrence Grossberg, Cary Nelson, and Paula Treichler (New York: Routledge, 1992), 285.

13. Grossberg, "Cultural Studies," 245–71.

14. Janice A. Radway, *Reading the Romance: Women, Patriarchy, and Popular Literature* (Chapel Hill: University of North Carolina Press, 1984).

15. Ohmann, "Thoughts on Cultural Studies in the United States," 10.

16. Janice A. Radway, *A Feeling for Books: The Book-of-the-Month Club, Literary Taste, and Middle-Class Desire* (Chapel Hill: University of North Carolina Press, 1997).

17. Gayatri Chakravorty Spivak, *In Other Worlds: Essays in Cultural Politics* (New York: Routledge, 1987).

18. Spivak, "Reflections on Cultural Studies in the Post-Colonial Conjuncture," 65.

19. Donna Haraway, *Primate Visions: Gender, Race, and Nature in Modern Science* (New York: Routledge, 1989).

20. All of these books are listed in the bibliography of Grossberg, Nelson, and Treichler, eds., *Cultural Studies,* except Butler's. Jameson's book came out too late to be included, but his *New Left Review* essay by the same title is present on the list. Teresa de Lauretis, *Alice Doesn't* (Bloomington: Indiana University Press, 1984); Eve Kosofsky Sedgwick, *Between Men: English Literature and Male Homosocial Desire* (New York:

Columbia University Press, 1985); Tania Modeleski, ed., *Studies in Entertainment* (Bloomington: Indiana University Press, 1986); James Clifford and George Marcus, eds., *Writing Culture: The Poetics and Politics of Ethnography* (Berkeley: University of California Press, 1986); Henry Louis Gates Jr., *The Signifying Monkey: A Theory of Afro-American Literary Criticism* (New York: Oxford University Press, 1988); Cary Nelson and Lawrence Grossberg, eds., *Marxism and the Interpretation of Culture* (Urbana: University of Illinois Press, 1988); Huston Baker, *Blues, Ideology, and Afro-American Literature* (Chicago: University of Chicago Press, 1989); Andrew Ross, *No Respect: Intellectuals and Popular Culture* (New York: Routledge, 1989); Brantlinger, *Crusoe's Footprints;* Judith Butler, *Gender Trouble: Feminism and the Subversion of Identity* (New York: Routledge, 1990); Cornell West, *The American Evasion of Philosophy* (Madison: University of Wisconsin Press, 1990); Fredric Jameson, *Postmodernism, Or, the Cultural Logic of Late Capitalism* (Durham: Duke University Press, 1991).

21. Grant Farred, "Endgame Identity? Mapping the New Left Roots of Identity Politics," *New Literary History* 31 (2000): 629.

22. James Miller, *Democracy in the Streets: From Port Huron to the Siege of Chicago* (New York: Simon & Shuster, 1987), 184–217. Subsequent references indicated in the text as *DS*.

23. Fred Inglis, *Raymond Williams* (London: Routledge, 1995), 152–53.

24. Stuart Hall, "The Formation of a Diasporic Intellectual: An Interview," by Kuan-Hsing Chen, in *Stuart Hall: Critical Dialogues in Cultural Studies,* eds. David Morley and Kuan-Hsing Chen (London: Routledge, 1996), 493; Dennis L. Dworkin, *Cultural Marxism in Postwar Britain: History, the New Left, and the Origins of Cultural Studies* (Durham: Duke University Press, 1997), 43.

25. Dworkin, *Cultural Marxism in Postwar Britain,* 45.

26. Hall, "Formation of a Diasporic Intellectual," 494.

27. Dworkin, *Cultural Marxism in Postwar Britain,* 77; Michael Kenny, *The First New Left: British Intellectuals after Stalin* (London: Lawrence & Wishart, 1995), 1.

28. Dworkin, *Cultural Marxism in Postwar Britain,* 141–42.

29. Raymond Williams, *Culture and Society 1780–1950* (London: Chatto, 1958); E. P. Thompson, *The Making of the English Working Class* (New York: Vintage, 1966); Richard Hoggart, *The Uses of Literacy* (London: Chatto, 1957).

30. Hall, "Formation of a Diasporic Intellectual," 496, 499.

31. Stuart Hall, "Cultural Studies and its Theoretical Legacies," 282.

32. Dick Hebdige, *Subculture: The Meaning of Style* (New York: Routledge, 1979).

33. Miller, *DS*, quotes Students for a Democratic Society (SDS) activist Paul Booth, "Unfortunately, the Old Left *didn't* influence us: we viewed them as intellectually bankrupt." See also Todd Gitlin, *The Sixties: Years of Hope, Days of Rage* (New York: Bantam, 1987), 66–77, on "Left Remnants," and Terry H. Anderson, *The Movement and the Sixties* (New York: Oxford University Press, 1995), 3–39, on "Cold War Culture."

34. Anderson, *The Movement and the Sixties*, 36–37.

35. SDS, *The Port Huron Statement*, appendix to Miller, *DS*, 332 (emphasis in original). Subsequent references indicated in the text as *PHS*.

36. Brantlinger, *Crusoe's Footprints*, 5–6, cites *The Port Huron Statement* as an early indication of the crisis in the humanities.

37. Gitlin, *Sixties*, 130.

38. "Statement of Purpose," *Studies on the Left* 1 (fall 1959): 2–4, reprinted in *The Times were a Changin': The Sixties Reader*, eds. Irvin Unger and Debi Unger (New York: Three Rivers, 1998), 65.

39. Richard Ohmann, *English in America: A Radical View of the Profession* (New York: Oxford University Press, 1976), 27–50.

40. Gitlin, *Sixties*, 29.

41. Nick Bromell, *Tomorrow Never Knows* (Chicago: University of Chicago Press, 2000), 1, quoting Cunnick.

42. Bromell, *Tomorrow Never Knows*, 5.

43. Gitlin, *Sixties*, 43, 39.

44. Bromell, *Tomorrow Never Knows*, 13.

45. Simon Frith, *Music for Pleasure: Essays in the Sociology of Pop* (New York: Routledge, 1988), 75.

46. Ibid., 213.

47. *Berkeley in the Sixties*, documentary film, Kitchell Films in association with P.O.V. Theatrical Films, released by California Newsreel, 1990.

48. David Haidu, *Positively Fourth Street: The Lives and Times of Joan Baez, Bob Dylan, Mimi Baez Fariña, and Richard Fariña* (New York: Farrar, 2001).

49. Gitlin, *Sixties*; Charles Kaiser, *1968 in America: Music, Politics, Chaos, Counterculture, and the Shaping of a Generation* (New York: Weidenfeld & Nicolson, 1988).

50. The key text is Max Horkheimer and Theodor W. Adorno, *Dialectic of Enlightenment*, trans. John Cumming (New York: Continuum, 1972).

51. Alice Echols, *Daring to Be Bad: Radical Feminism in America 1967–1975* (Minneapolis: University of Minnesota Press, 1989); Sarah Evans, *Personal Politics: The Roots of Women's Liberation in the Civil Rights Movement and the New Left* (New York: Random, 1980).

52. Marilyn Jacoby Boxer, *When Women Ask the Questions: Creating Women's Studies in America* (Baltimore: Johns Hopkins University Press, 1998), 1.

53. Ellen Messer-Davidow, *Disciplining Feminism: From Social Activism to Academic Discourse* (Durham: Duke University Press, 2002).

54. William H. Exum, *Paradoxes of Protest: Black Student Activism in a White University* (Philadelphia: Temple University Press, 1985).

55. Gitlin, *Sixties*, 240–41.

56. Hall, "Cultural Studies and its Theoretical Legacies," 286.

57. Grossberg, *We Gotta Get Out of This Place: Popular Conservatism and Postmodern Culture* (New York: Routledge, 1992).

58. Michael Denning, *The Cultural Front: The Laboring of American Culture in the Twentieth Century* (London and New York: Verso, 1996); Richard Ohmann, *Selling Culture: Magazines, Markets, and Class at the Turn of the Century* (London and New York: Verso, 1996).

59. This lack is in the process of being filled. The Cultural Studies Association (U.S.) held its founding conference in June 2003.

11

The Postcolonial Godfather

H. ARAM VEESER

One of Peter C. Herman's premises for this volume, *Historicizing Theory*, receives confirmation in postcolonial theory, since historical events patently inspired it. The other premise runs into some very particular difficulties. For while it is true, for the most part, that critics prefer to suppress their own historicity—who wouldn't, after all, rather be a cause than an effect?—the very name of postcolonial theory ties it to its historical origins, and its principle critics have had to acknowledge the historical preconditions of their thought. Of the holy trinity who preside in postcolonial studies, Gayatri Chakravorty Spivak has consistently grappled with her historical genesis as a privileged member of the Bengali upper middle class. And Edward W. Said has grappled with the genetic question in his book *Beginnings* (1975).[1] Unlike his fellow Trinitarians, he has written his memoirs and a great deal of other autobiographical work. He offers himself up as an exhibit in the annals of exile and dispossession. But it goes beyond that. Said's PLO involvement stands at the fountainhead of postcolonial theory, which would have had a far different shape had Said not struggled for, and within, the Palestinian liberation movement.

I begin in medias res with a rehearsal of his first major break with the PLO, an *al-Qabas* interview that led to angry exchanges between him and Yaser Abedrabbo, PLO spokesperson in Tunis. What might be read as merely an internecine spat instead throws off the sparks that ignite three key problematics of postcolonial theory. Lurking within these exchanges are the paradigmatic postcolonial questions about hybrid identity, geographic determination, and catachretic ruptures of Enlightenment-style reasoning. These three concepts loom large in postcolonial theory both in the Holy Trinity (Said, Spivak, and Homi K. Bhabha) and also across the postcolonial board. They stem from Said's efforts to force the PLO to adopt his own literary enthusiasm for permanent exile, unlocatability, and a complete break with the past.

> I am part of the PLO and I have taken part in this long struggle which led us to the Algiers Declaration [in which the Palestine National Council endorsed a two-state solution in historic Palestine in November of 1988]....
> My intention is to indulge in criticism from within, not from without. (Said, *Al-Qabas* [Kuwait], 6 October 1989)

With these words he opens an attack that ends only with his resignation from the Palestine National Council, terminating his fourteen-year tenure as an active member of that body. Up until 1989, Said had been more or less a loyal soldier, helping out with English translations and defending the Palestinian cause. He is of course known for bucking the majority. In *The Question of Palestine* he condemns what he calls "the conservative version of the Palestinian quest," by which he means the desire to push Israel into the sea and other such bluster. He dismisses as theological the position that demands a return of all land expropriated, bought, or abandoned in 1947–48. As Bruce Robbins once observed, Said's main point is the point of no return.[2]

His 1989 interview goes much further in attacking the PLO itself. The interview begins with Said demanding that we question Palestinian activity in America:

> Why has the United States become an arena where small Palestinian "stores" are vying for the spoils? . . . Why is it allowed that this should be an alternative to the formidable political and national task of representing the Palestinian cause in the United States in a clever and logical manner? Because at the end of the day we will succeed if we do this properly. (*Mideast Mirror,* 9 October 1989, 18)[3]

The petty, shopkeeper mentality connoted by "'stores' vying for spoils" was not the worst of it. He next called the PLO ignorant and charged that it had no idea about the way American society worked. He and Palestinians in the United States "feel utterly disgusted by the neglect, corruption and incompetence in the Palestinian performance in this country"(19). The PLO was guilty of "a tragic and stupid mistake"(18) when it approached the U.S. government through Israeli intermediaries. These dishonest intercessors had simply contrived to embarrass the Palestinians by making sure their visa requests were denied. It was "an unnecessary humiliation inflicted on our people"(18). He said that he had himself arranged such visas in the past and that the leadership should have asked him to step in.

"To go through this public comedy over whether he will get a visa or not," charged Said, "harms our people"(18). Said went on to berate other Palestinian leaders for their submissive and imploring style (18). Said is attempting to make Palestinians see the loss of self reliance as a literary event, as tragedy, as comedy, and as style, whereas they see it as the necessary wheeling and dealing of the political roughhouse.

Officials of the PLO predictably shrugged this off as the precious mutterings of an unworldly academic. Yasser Arafat should have seen it coming. Said's denunciation of the PLO in *Al-Qabas* was followed within a year by his resignation from the Palestine National Council. But the PLO could not understand why an acknowledged insider would act this way. The Arab press duly reported a "surprise criticism by an 'insider'" and a "surprise attack on the organization's [PLO's] performance in the United States." PLO officials made some polite gestures. Chair Arafat called Said and invited him to come to Tunis in order to discuss the criticisms. One of Said's intended targets, Hasan Rahman, the ranking PLO dignitary in the United States, was dispatched briefly to Canada, and a few other PLO officials were told that they might be reassigned. But for the most part nothing changed. Meanwhile, the PLO rebutted Said's criticism. "It is naïve to believe that Edward's personal role could have reversed this decision, as he said in his interview," observed Abedrabbo, a member of the PLO Executive Committee who headed the Palestinian team in the U.S.-PLO dialogue in Tunis (*Mideast Mirror*, 13 October 1989, 14).[4] The charge of naïveté must have stung, given Said's habit of proclaiming himself a worldly critic. As is clearly announced in the title of his 1983 theoretical volume, *The World, the Text, and the Critic* (1983), "worldliness" was becoming the principal tenet in Said's manifesto for a new criticism. Thus it must have been irksome to hear that he was speaking "with the mentality of an academic rather than a politician" (*Mideast Mirror*, 16 October 1989, 12).[5]

Abedrabbo denied the connection between power and knowledge. "The leaders of the PLO . . . are not sociologists specializing in the American social structure and its decision-making processes, neither are they required to be," he said, accusing Said of favoring technocrats and sociologists over war-hardened PLO negotiators. How ironic, he continued, that Said should join forces with those who "present the PLO as unqualified to hold a dialogue," Abedrabbo continued. He concluded by saying that the PLO leadership welcomes criticism—so long as the critic "avoids excessive subjectivity and veiled opportunism" (*Mideast Mirror*, 13 October 1989, 15). In saying that Palestinians can gain power in America without bothering to amass knowledge about America, the PLO spokesperson gave some hint of the abyss separating politics from postcolonial criticism. If there is one axiom that all postcolonial critics agree on, it's the dependency of power on knowledge and vice versa.

Said has himself been the most brilliant explicator of power/knowledge, beginning with his account of Napoleon's invasion of Egypt, where the scholars were sent in before the troops. After Michel Foucault's striking analyses of power and knowledge, it's difficult to hear Abedrabbo's words as more than stupidity or prejudice.[6] The charge that Said is too subjective is, by contrast, instantly recognizable. Said's most astute critics, James Clifford, Catherine Gallagher, and Dennis Porter all understand that he has become enmeshed in his own contradictions, and principally so in his incompatible beliefs in the irresistable force of faceless discourse and the unstoppable power of the individual.[7]

The most telling PLO counterblast, both in the power of its insight and the felicity of its language, was Abedrabbo's perfect metabole: "we need to 'Palestinize' the community in America, not to 'Americanize' the leadership in Tunis" (*Mideast Mirror,* 13 October 1989, 13). This pithy remark sums up many of the misgivings that literary critics have about Said. They are concerned that he overvalues individual will and power, and that he fails to escape the same ethnocentrism that he so carefully documents in others. Still, it's a bit unsettling to have to answer for your ethnocentrism to the PLO.

The PLO seems to have thought, in short, that Said was (1) too far away from the struggle; (2) too ready to believe that he personally could change the course of U.S. policy; (3) acting like an American, not like a Palestinian; and (4) acting like an academic, not like a worldly person. From the PLO's point of view, Said had a lot of chutzpah.

There are three issues that are forced upon Said by the PLO, and they are central to the later history of postcolonial criticism. The most obvious one is that of dual identity. Said must decide whether he is a Palestinian or an American. This is an impossible decision since, obviously, he is both. He was even born with an American passport—though he was born to Palestinian parents in Jerusalem. His duality links him to postcolonial critics from Spivak to Bhabha to Chandra Mohanty to Dipesh Chakrabarty and Abdul Jan Mohammed. Second, the gulf between Said and the PLO has a literal, geographic referent. The Tunis-based PLO leaders entrusted with persuading America have never been to America and do not speak English, nor had Said ever been to Gaza or Nablus.[8] The leaders respond that they cannot and do not wish to understand America. Understanding and persuading Americans is the job of the Palestinians who live in the United States. Said admits that he could never live in Palestine ("Perhaps I would find it hard to live there: exile seems to me a more liberated state"), even under the best, impossible circumstances. Finally, there is catachresis. The PLO and Said both identify a locus of power. But each locus is different. Said insists that the individual (in this case, himself) can be the agent and instigator of history. But in *Orientalism* he demonstrates that a great, impersonal "discourse," with its own immense institutional machinery and deep historical roots, governs Arab-European relations. The PLO by contrast asserts an almost Foucauldian view of historical determination. They have a humbly realistic sense of the limitations on personal initiative and power. Antinomies of the sort that emerge in the PLO-Said exchange color Said's book *Orientalism*. These contradictions are well-known and have provided many years of activity to Said's commentators and redactors. The general thrust may be seen in Samuel Weber's observation: "a social and historical critique which does not consider the conflictual structure of its own discursive operations will only reproduce the constraints it is seeking to displace."[9] The richest compendium of Said's self-contradictions can be found in Robert Young's essay, "Disorienting Orientalism." Among the difficulties that Young discerns are the following: Said fails to develop a mode of analysis that escapes the pitfalls that he himself is criticizing. Thus, when he criticizes the early Orientalists for imposing on the East a static vision rather than changing narratives, he almost immediately turns around to praise Erich Auerbach precisely for achieving "true vision" when he delivers his encompassing summa of Western literature in his totalizing tome, *Mimesis*. Said objects to stereotyping but himself energetically stereotypes "the French" and "the English" as epitomized by the Orientalists Louis Massignon and Sir Hamilton A. R. Gibb (Said, *Orientalism*, 259, 263).[10] Said argues that the Orient is a fiction and a representation, yet he contends that the study and construction of this fictional Orient provided the instrumental knowledge required for the actual conquest of territory.[11] Said asserts that Orientalism changed and yet he asserts that it stayed the same.[12] He denies that any actual Orient exists, yet contends that Western representations of this nonexistent entity are false. He lauds humanism unproblematically (45, 46, 246, 266, 267, 328) and castigates Orientalism as anti-human ("Orientalist reality is both antihuman and persistent" [266]) and yet is aware of the fact that high-humanist culture produced that same Orientalism. His deep involvement in Western culture and ideas—something noted wryly by the PLO in the *al-Qabas* exchanges—remains uninterrogated, and Said simply assumes that he is in a position to separate himself from those values at will. He contends that novels make a direct, instrumental contribution to the shoring up of state power. But he fails to acknowledge that they do so only by way of the state's educational institutions, and these he never discusses although such a discussion would make more sense than do his elaborate rereadings of classic English novels. He describes the impassive, relentless workings of discourse, with all its journals, publishing houses, conferences, links to the state, intellectual traditions, professorships, and momentum and yet posits a resistant individual who can stand outside that totality and successfully oppose it. This positing lacks coherence with statements such as "it is therefore correct that every European, in what he could say about the Orient, was consequently a racist, an imperialist, and almost totally ethnocentric" (204). That sort of thinking forces a reductive account of Marx, about whom Said concludes, "Yet in the end it is the Romantic Orientalist vision that wins out" (154). That judgment rests on a single citation from *Surveys from Exile* and suppresses all of Marx's ambivalence.[13] Above all, he preserves in his own thinking the outside/inside structure of Orientalism even while reserving for himself the heroic and romantic position of the intractable, uncompromising outsider. This is of course the contradiction that most exasperated the PLO.

Said's contradictions have been, however, anything but disabling. They have incited or inspired a rich succession of reconsiderations and corrections by scholars, including, indeed, Said himself. Thus these contradictions are more than contradictions, and they merit something more than accusations or excuses. Rather than hapless blunders, these contradictions are catachreses.

∽

Spivak has made several attempts to define catachresis, and while this is not the place to construct an itinerary of those attempts, a few of her examples will clarify its potential meanings. "Catechresis" is a word that she admits is "one of the worst offenders in the general crime of inaccessibility."[14] She calls it the abuse or perversion of a trope or a metaphor. But what does that mean? In the first instance, we find that a catachresis occurs when the supporting examples and the arguments they support fail to jibe. Spivak writes of such instances, "if read by way of the deconstructive theorizing of practice, this does not summon up excuses or accusation. This is how theory brings practice to crisis, and practice norms theory, and deviations constitute a forever precarious norm."[15] Conventional writers who observe Enlightenment norms have registered their frustration with Said's irreverence. One such writer, Gallagher, will stand for many, and I will discuss her argument in detail. But for the moment, suffice it to say that Said's catachreses have proven to be remarkably productive both for other scholars and for himself.[16]

Real disagreements over political praxis and the motor forces of history stand behind postcolonial issues like hybrid identity, locations of cultures, and abuses of Enlightenment rationality. If these issues are central to Said's debates with the PLO leadership, then they cannot be relegated to the politically pointless realm of pure textuality, as Timothy Brennan has suggested. I cannot do justice to all of the nuances of Brennan's complex argument, but in essence he says that Said's dislike of poststructural theory should be extended to postcolonial theory as well. Said has been opportunistically misread as a defender of non-Western identities, Brennan contends. *Orientalism* in particular has been taken up and proclaimed as a credo by the South Asian and other non-European scholars who now have so strong a presence in postcolonial studies. In short, "had there not been a transitory need within the academy for a curricular and discursive shift to account for the collapse of anticolonial liberation movements and the new demographics of American graduate schools—*Orientalism* would probably not have had the impact that it did."[17] But in fact, Brennan continues, Said's *Orientalism* really has very little to do with Arab or South Asian identities and everything to do with an indictment of American practices of literary criticism. At the heart of Brennan's argument is the notion that Said intends a homology between nineteenth-century English and French philology and late-twentieth-century literary theory. Just as philology had two paths from which to choose, one good and one evil, so too late-twentieth-century literary criticism can pick the road of virtue (with C. L. R. James, Raymond Williams, and empiricist-sociological Marxist criticism) or the satanic path of pure textuality. The bad philology, incidentally, stemmed from philologist Ernest Renan's decision to ally himself with race theorist Georges Curvier.

Brennan's extraordinary effort at reclamation involves, however, a playing-down of the debts to French theory that have given Said his redoubtable staying power on the contemporary critical scene. It is more accurate to say that by attacking deconstruction, Said has helped to perpetuate it. For postcolonial theory has revived deconstruction, which seemed to be losing force a decade back. Said's themes and methodologies are overwhelmingly more sophisticated than Brennan wishes to admit. Said's consistently resonant work on hybrid identities, his cubistic sense of space, and his knowingly self-contradictory argumentation connect him to the PLO/praxis and to poststructuralist theory. What is more, his insistence on every true critic's need to sustain absolute sovereign independence, his unwillingness to join any organized political group, and his occasional celebration of betrayal as a guarantee of critical honesty, all mark him as significantly different from more identifiably "Left" political intellectuals. In every respect Said is closer to Spivak and Bhabha than he is to James or Williams. Rather than say that Said abjures textuality, it would be more accurate to say that, after *Orientalism*, he textualizes himself. He himself becomes a signifier without a referent, a figure in whom syntax outweighs semantics, a complex figure who will not reveal the secret of its structure to the first comer, a catachretic figure destabilizing the critical field. Said came by his themes and ideas honestly, in the heat of political struggle. It is chiefly through his mediation that history had a shaping impact on postcolonial theory.

The counterarguments are interesting but mistaken. Brennan contends that Said is really a traditional class-struggle sort of Marxist, as is Brennan himself. This seems to be patently wrong, because Said openly disavows any criticism that goes underneath an ideological label such as Marxism:

> . . . criticism modified in advance by labels like "Marxism" or "liberalism" is, in my view, an oxymoron. The history of thought, to say nothing of political movements, is extravagantly illustrative of how the dictum "solidarity before criticism" means the end of criticism . . . even in the very midst of a battle in which one is unmistakably on one side against another, there should be criticism.[18]

It is also wrong because Said has a considerable antipathy to Marx based on the latter's prejudices against Asiatic societies and the Asiatic mode of production. He finds Williams to be fatally insular, party discipline obnoxious, and programmatic Marxism impossibly confining.

Another perhaps a more plausible genealogy of postcolonialism comes from Robert Young. Young considers poststructuralism the basis of postcolonialism. And he traces the origins of poststructuralism to Algeria. The founders of poststructuralism were French Algerians, such as Jacques Derrida and Hélène Cixous.

> If "so-called poststructualism" is the product of a single historical moment, then that moment is probably not May 1968 but rather the Algerian War of Independence . . . it is significant that [Jean-Paul] Sartre, [Louis] Althusser, Derrida and [Jean François] Lyotard, among others, were all either born in Algeria or personally involved with the events of the war. But let us begin instead with Helene Cixous's remarkable account. (Young, *White Mythologies*, 1)

Aside from the ironies that a brilliant poststructuralist like Young could embrace so simplistic a myth of origin, the relationship between poststructuralism and postcolonialism is by no means direct or unmediated. Said's case is rather different from Derrida's or Cixous's.[19] He was involved simultaneously with advanced theory and with militant struggle.

The more plausible case is that Said was both a poststructualist and the originator of postcolonial theory. Like Derrida, Cixous, and others of the poststructuralist avant-garde, Said participated in the theoretical revolution that succeeded French structuralism. Unlike them, and *pace* Young, he put himself from the first into a militant liberation movement, at great personal and professional risk. He is agreed, *pace* Brennan, to have played an important role in bringing the theoretical revolution home to the United States. "Said's importance was initially considered to derive from his mediation of certain kinds of French 'high theory' into the Anglo-American academic world of the 1970s," writes the best and most theoretical analyst of postcolonial criticism.[20] Although you would hardly know it after reading Brennan, Said has been accused by a respected Marxist critic of textualizing criticism and of confusing real activism with empty textual engagement.[21] His high-theory bona fides are intact. At the same time, he has been attached to the Palestine Liberation movement almost from its inception in 1968. He performed the duties of a translator for the leadership of that organization, and indeed translated its leader Yasser Arafat's speech to the United Nations in 1974. He was a member of the Palestinian National Committee (its "parliament in exile") from 1977 through 1990. Over the past thirty-four years he has given hundreds and perhaps thousands of addresses, participated in debates, written newspaper and magazine articles, and in every way agitated to advance the cause of Palestinian liberation. I can remember his addressing a tumultuous meeting of the Students for a Democratic Society, of which I was a member, and urging the rowdy, anti-war, anti-capitalist assemblage to take up the militant demands of Palestinian liberation seekers. Few other faculty members could have made such an appeal. And none did.

The Palestinian situation exerted pressure that required an immediate response. In this sense, Said's position was unlike that of intellectuals from the Indian subcontinent and elsewhere. He was summoned to participate. An older Palestinian, Ibrahim Abu-Lughod, who remembered him from Princeton, where they had met as students, asked Said to contribute an article to a volume about the 1967 war. The result was Said's first political piece, "The Arab Portrayed." Abu-Lughod was overwhelmed when he read the finished piece.[22] Thus Said became actively engaged in an anti-colonial movement.

Israel is pretty much a colonial operation. Even its defenders have to admit that. "Occupation" and "settlers" are colonial words, and they are in the lexicon that Israel uses to describe its own realities. Said has been a witness to the creation of Israel more or less from the beginning, either with his own eyes or through the lens of an aunt who was a sort of Mother Teresa to displaced Palestinians in Cairo. He saw in recent Palestinian history an epitome of every postcolonial situation. In the words of one Israeli historian,

> On November 29, 1947, the UN General Assembly voted to partition Palestine into two states, one Jewish and the other Arab. . . . Between November 29, 1947, and the Declaration of Independence on May 14, 1948, the country was swept by a wave of terror and bloodshed in which thousands lost their lives and hundreds of thousands (most of them Arabs) were forced to abandon their homes.[23]

The Jerusalem-born Edward Said was twelve years old. Through the following decades, he could precisely and at firsthand observe the whole imperialist process from initial conquest to securing the borders to expropriation of the natives to expansion into further occupied territories.

Admittedly, the Palestinian cause was a special case within the history of global decolonization. Israel in Palestine was unlike England in India and Egypt, France in Algeria and Vietnam, Belgium in the Congo, or the Boers in South Africa. The colonizers and settlers had, in this case, a remarkable historical grievance, the Jewish Holocaust. They were often themselves in flight. The international governing body, the UN, had approved the division of Palestine: it was not a rogue operation or a putsch. Yet it was nonetheless a classic instance of conquest-and-occupation, otherwise known as colonization. The New Historians in Israel have been forthright about this. Benny Morris and Tom Segev have searched the Israeli state archives, including the state papers and letters of founders such as David Ben-Gurion. What emerges is the wholesale expropriation of everything the Arabs had owned in Haifa, Tiberias, Safed, Acre, Jaffa, Ramlah, Lydda, Jerusalem, and indeed everywhere, a movement that was unambiguously devoted to the conquest of Palestinian lands, and the expropriation and replacement of the natives.

> And so tens of thousands of Israelis, soldiers and civilians, helped themselves to the spoils. One took an armchair, another a rug, a third took a sewing machine and a fourth—a combine; one took an apartment and another took a vineyard . . . more than half a million acres were thus expropriated from their owners. (Segev, "Dividing the Spoils," 79)[24]

Thus was Israel created in 1948. As a Palestinian living in Cairo, Said had a panoptic, fifty-yard-line seat from which to observe imperialism in action. Said was favorably placed to study the larger effects of colonialism and he was professionally situated to translate his observations into theory. Learning that his dinner companion of the night before had been assassinated by the Shin Bet, to pick one of many events, gave him a more immediate experience of struggle than was vouchsafed to those intellectuals who were attempting to recover a distant subaltern past. But it was not an attitude of passive observation that made Said the paradigmatic postcolonial intellectual.

How did the Israeli-Palestinian conflict give rise to the incipient postcolonial themes? Hybrid identity, geography as a mode of analysis, and catachresis or ruptures in logic and syntax—these significant areas of postcolonial literary theory gain their first mature expression in Said's work. Each fosters a spate of sequels, such as Homi K. Bhabha's many works about ambivalence and hybridity, Timothy Mitchell's analysis of North African spatiality in his book *Colonizing Egypt* (1988), and Spivak's use of catachresis and her warnings against repetition-in-rupture.[25]

Postcolonial perceptions of hybridity developed out of Modernist thoughts on exile. For example, the Palestinian situation made Said the very divided self that characterizes late colonial literature, psychology, and culture. Early on, Said wrote lyrically about exile. His first book about Polish exile Joseph Conrad turned on the latter's sense of himself as "a mental and moral outcast."[26] He favored texts about "orphans, outcasts, parvenus, emanations, solitaries, and deranged types whose background is either rejected, mysterious, or unknown."[27] He writes of himself, "I was a creature of exile, a fate I shared with more than fifty percent of my compatriots, most of whom live in Jordan, Syria, Lebanon, and, before the Gulf War, in the Gulf States."[28] It is "not that home and love of home are lost, but that loss is inherent in the existence of both."[29] This nostalgic note is familiar to every reader of literary modernism, and it resonates with nineteenth- and twentieth-century ideas about alienation and transcendental homelessness. Like the modernists, Said values exile because it is richer, was "a potent, even enriching motif of modern culture" (*ROE*, 173). Exile has even had political benefits: "The Palestinians also know that their own sense of national identity has been nourished in the exile milieu" (178). Said's essays on exile are lyrical and wide-ranging, moving through the rich traditions of exiles who have compensated for loss by creating new worlds. Thus he speaks of Odysseus and Dante, James Joyce and Joseph Conrad, of [Georg] Lukacs, Theodor Adorno, and [Erich] Auerbach (178–86). He prefers Jean Genet to George Orwell as a real to a faux exile: "Compare Genet with Orwell and the point is not even arguable . . . Orwell was . . . someone who very definitely felt, and really was, at home somewhere."[30] Genet is, by contrast, "a representative figure of the modern absolute renegades, deliberate violators of national boundaries, and who were always in search of turbulent states, in search of liberation."[31] The "utterly undomesticated sensibility" (*ROE*, 36), the ascetic code of willed homelessness, seemed very much worthy of imitation. (The attraction went both ways: Genet spent his final years among the Palestinian guerrillas in the Shouf above Beirut.)[32] Said has said that he feels intellectually rather strange and largely unacceptable, and that he still aspires to be marginal and as undomesticated as someone who is in real exile. These are unexpected words coming from a recent president of the thirty-odd thousand-member Modern Language Association. Similarly, he admires philosopher Adorno because "to follow Adorno is to stand away from 'home' in order to look at it with the exile's detachment" (*ROE*, 185).

Gradually this Modernist language of exile subsides and in its place arises the lexicon of the divided self. Self-division receives a precise articulation from Conrad in "The Secret Sharer," and even in the late-Victorians such as Robert Louis Stevenson and Oscar Wilde. A certain Jekyll-and-Hyde sensibility comes to inhabit Said's later writing. It is explained autobiographically as "my emerging consciousness of self as something altogether more complex and authentic than a colonial mimic."[33] Much of Said's memoir is organized around the idea of "the emergence of a second self buried for a very long time beneath a surface of often expertly acquired and wielded social characteristics" (*Out*, 217). In more global terms, this doubleness is defined as "the whole notion of crossing over, of moving from one identity to another."[34] He adds that his work began to bring the two identities closer together, that he "had at last managed to connect the part that was a professor of English and the part that lived, in a small way, the life of Palestine" (Conversation with Rushdie, 123). Elsewhere he introduces the word that has such purchase on postcolonial theory: "We are migrants and perhaps hybrids in, but not of, any situation."[35] The double subjectivity is beautifully explained in "Cairo Recalled," an essay in which we learn that the "Said" part of his name made him deplorable in the eyes of his European, British, and American schoolmasters, but that the "Edward" half of it meant he had in their eyes some hope of redemption. The divided self has another manifestation besides double subjectivity or splitness. This second feature is the exilic consciousness of two places, two cultures, two situations, the themes of cultural hybridity, postcolonial mimicry, the ambivalence of the colonized and colonizer, and the colonial as a single figure comprising both the colonizer and the colonized. Identity politics are often oversimplified and mindless when taken up by enthusiastic multiculturalists, and simultaneously by women, African-Americans, gays and lesbians, and so forth, as the celebration of an endangered identity, but identity is bisected in Said and by extension throughout the postcolonial movement that he founded. Not only is the postcolonial divided between two cultural traditions—in Said's case, the Anglo-American versus the Arab-Palestinian—but also, as mediated by Said, identity is split in its attitude toward nationhood and the politics of return. Because he rejected the idea of pushing Israel into the sea, and denied the possibility of a full Palestinian return, he had a much earlier awareness of the unrealities and fantasies of the more extreme identity politics. Identity concerns nations as well as individuals, and on that plane, too, the Palestinians "had in some very fundamental way unsettled Lebanon's identity."[36] The unsettled and fluctuating identity of the nation and the national have a central place in postcolonial theory. In this light, an apparently simple statement like "I am part of the PLO" initiates a maelstrom of contradiction and qualification.

Second, geography supplants temporality. Rupture and discontinuity had already become familiar ways of rethinking history, but only in temporal terms. Now the dislocation from one place to another could also precipitate epistemological rupture. Geography emerges as central in the Palestinian struggle, in Said's life and work, and in contemporary theory. Palestinian history since 1948 consists of a chain of displacements—they are chased from the land to the camps, from the camps to Amman, from Amman to Beirut, and from Beirut to Tunis. Said titles one book about them, *The Politics of Dispossession*. His own memoir bears the title *Out of Place* (1999). Radical geographers move onto Said's university reading lists: In his lectures and writings, Yves Lacoste, Foucault on geography, and Henri Lefebvre, all begin to crop up. Frantz Fanon's passages on the divided colonial city appear in Said's books, and Fanon receives praise for recognizing "the primacy of geography in history" (*ROE*, 446). The contraction and intensification of space summon his extended attention, as for example the way "the more significant and charged geography and atmosphere of Cairo were concentrated for us in Zamalek." His time in Jerusalem was also marked by spatial segregation: "Soon Said would need a pass to get from his home to his school [St. George's School]," according to one journalist. "The situation was dangerous and inconvenient."[37] Cairo was memorable for similar reasons: "Part of the city's hold over my memory was the clearness of its nearly incredible divisions" ("Cairo Recalled," 20). Organized, segmented, concentrated space will inevitably recall Foucault, and indeed, for Said, Foucault's view of things was spatial; in this Foucault radically parted ways with critics who discussed only "continuities, temporalities, and absences" (*ROE*, 239–40). The connection to Palestinians' contemporary predicament, with its green lines, its wire-enclosed refugee camps, and its omnipresent checkpoints, was readily evident. More subtle but as pervasive was its purchase on Said's literary theories. The geography of the divided city as explained in the memoir was displaced inward and reconfigured as a hopelessly irreconcilable splitness within. This insistent turn to space and away from time extends even to his book on music, that most temporally bound of the arts. "I shall briefly suggest an alternative [to Adorno's Hegelian, time-fixated model] based on a *geographical* or spatial idea that is truer to the diversity and spread of human activity" (*Musical Elaborations*, xviii). Said's geographic emphasis emerges in his article about "Aida," and spatiality becomes a powerful current in postcolonial history (as in Timothy Mitchell's *Colonizing Egypt* [1988]), and it also gives a physical and material anticipation of the splitness elaborated in Bhaba, Spivak, and in many others, with their favored themes of hybridity, ambivalence, and "third space."

Finally, catachresis or disrupted logic takes on unexpected importance. We know from Said's work on Jonathan Swift that he is not only unembarrassed about contradicting himself: he considers it a virtue. To those who, like Gallagher, would pin down the contradictions in his work, he points to Swift. "Too many claims are made for Swift as a moralist and thinker who peddled one or another final view of human nature, whereas not enough claims are made for Swift as a kind of local activist, a columnist, a pamphleteer, a caricaturist. . . ." It's not as if Swift wanted to be John Locke or Thomas Hobbes. Critics who suppose he wants that "pay too much attention to his ideas and not enough to the deployment and disposition of his energies, his local performances" (*The World, the Text, and the Critic* [1983], 82).

The usual response to catachretic disruption in Said is to consider it as bad argumentation. Such is particularly the case with critics as rigorously logical not to say Jesuitical as Gallagher:

> Edward Said has been writing himself into a dilemma that has ontological, epistemological, political, and literary-critical dimensions. He writes of

distortions of reality while denying the existence of a reality beneath the distortions. He notes that knowledge is always bounded by place but insists that there is an epistemologically privileged locus of displacement called exile. He champions the right of political self-determination for a people longing to end their exile but then appraises that exile as valuable in itself. He calls on the literary critic to be—in and through criticism—engaged in the world and simultaneously in permanent exile from any particular location.[38]

One recalls the voluminous commentary on Said that consists in nothing but excuses and accusations. The accusations (James Clifford, Dennis Porter, Arif Dirlik, and Gallagher) pinpoint contradictions in Said's work and demand to know why. The excuses (Paul Bové, Steven Mailloux, Timothy Brennan, and Aijaz Ahmad) resolve the contradictions in favor of one pole or the other—a most unsatisfactory exercise, since the "losing" pole undeniably survives. Gallagher's complaints provoke Steven Mailloux to say that

> By denying the existence of an "objective" Orient, Said does not make an idealist claim, nor in condemning Orientalist distortions does he make a realist claim. He takes no stand on epistemological issues at all . . . *Orientalism* is self-consciously an act of persuasion at the service of rhetorical interests opposed to those of Western Orientalism. Idealist and realist epistemologies remain completely irrelevant here. What remains relevant is the historical content of rhetorical power that Said describes and the cultural conversation in which *Orientalism* participates.[39]

This rejoinder has the unfortunate qualities associated with American pragmatism. Although Mailloux is right to note Said's lack of interest in refining a philosophically air-tight theory of knowledge, he proposes a sort of good opportunism that fails to address Said's own avowed high-minded devotion to principles. Said misses no occasion to pronounce himself wedded to universals such as justice, truth, and freedom. Indeed, it's precisely against people like Said that the pragmatically inclined Stanley Fish writes his book, *The Trouble with Principle* (1999).[40] Mailloux simply cannot explain Said as a principles-doubting pragmatist.

Said explains his own contradictions catachretically. Any rational observer must conclude that the Palestinians are a lost cause. Perhaps the situation really calls for "pessimism of the intellect and pessimism of the will," Said writes. "But most Palestinians would say in response: 'If those are the facts, then so much the worse for the facts'"(*POD*, 266). Said knowingly courts catachresis and contradiction. He must posit, for example, an all-encompassing dominative Orientalism in order to carve out a place for himself and for a few other powerful individual scholars whose counterwill disrupts Orientalism from outside. On some level he knows that such a polarity is nonsensical, that if Orientalism is really totalizing, then no corner remains for the heroically romantic resistance-scholar, whose very capacity to speak is created by the discourse he wishes to oppose. The absolute hegemony of Orientalist theory contradicts Said's absolute resistance to it. Said's very motto is catachretical: "Pessimism of the intellect, optimism of the will." Desire flies in the face of Enlightenment reason, and vice versa, as theory/intellect and practice/will interrupt each other.

But there is more to catachresis than mutually interruptive theory/practice. Naming and defining inevitably prove to be catachretic. Spivak's example is a definition that begins with a series of abdicatory gestures. The definition turns out to be a series of questions. Thus the word "definition" itself becomes catachrestic, because the thinker has given a "definition" that has not been nor can it be used.[41] A story is catachrestic because "there is no literal referent for the concept 'original Indian nation'" (*Critique*, 141). The most hegemonic identity will turn out to be catachrestic (143).

The postcolonial critic deploys Enlightenment concepts catachretically, then: in ways such that they must fail of their goals. In Spivak's words, "the (ab)-use of the Enlightenment in the interest of building a civil society brings the subaltern discursive formation into crisis, making it deconstruct" (*Critique*, 142 n.). This means that the benevolent Western bourgeois feminist saves her brown-skinned sister by destroying the latter's particularity. As does the well-meaning Indian civil servant who offers a friendly helping hand to the tribal protagonists in Mahasweta Devi's haunting novella, *Pterodactyl* (1995). The tribals' response is summed up toward the end of the story: "But I say to you in great humility, you can't do anything for us. We became unclean as soon as you entered our lives. No more roads, no more relief—what will you give to a people in exchange for the vanished land, home field, burial-ground?' Shankar comes up close and says, 'Can you move far away? Very far? Very, very far?'"[42] Critics begin to court self-contradiction. The theoretical self-contradictions that so many have noted in *Orientalism* resembled the split subjectivity that Said would later explain autobiographically in articles such as "Cairo Recalled," and in books such as *After the Last Sky* and in his memoir *Out of Place* (1999). But self-contradiction was also a chosen, cultivated intellectual style, and moreover a style for which Said has provided an historical genealogy. Swift was the first, and there follow a whole line of those whom Said refers to as "sports," namely figures like Wilde, Rudyard Kipling, and C. L. R. James, figures who abjure philosophical consistency and anarchically embrace whatever tactics fit the rhetorical demands of the moment—ideas that theory and practice interrupt each other and push each other to crisis; the willingness of critics to embrace contradictions themselves (now called "catachretic" or self-interruptive thought); the itinerary of silencing and the suggestions that postcolonials below a certain threshold cannot speak; the issue of double representation as on the one hand furthering forth and on the other hand displacing and replacing that which is represented; and finally the violent shuttling of the "Third World woman" caught between tradition (say, widow burning) and modernization.

Said's rich and passionate encounter with the Palestinians has shaped postcolonial studies. The obviously Palestinian-Israeli themes include split subjectivity, the marginality and double-consciousness of exiles, transcendental homelessness, nationalism-in-literature, definition of the self by means of excluding the Other, the theological and fantastic character of a dream of full return, the dubiousness of the primitive excitement of identification with one's own community, and the shuttling between humanist universals such as justice and the theoretical pessimism that annuls the category of the human. My contention is that few of these ideas, methods, and moves would be in place today had not the Palestinian-Israeli conflict developed as it has, and had not Said been writing about it constantly and trying to bring his resulting political insights into fruitful, shaping contact with his literary theories.

I have shown that Said's earliest writing about, and conflicts with, the Palestinians demonstrate the most important postcolonial motifs. Initially, we saw how Palestinian-Israeli history has shaped the humanism often noticed and criticized in Said's theory, forcing him to declare to the PLO leadership that the individual can make a difference, that ineptitude and corruption can be rooted out, that the United States can be changed, not just fatalistically accepted. His 1989 *al-Qabas* exchanges with the PLO dislodge the intuition that displays of nationalism and identity would be the heart of PLO propaganda and self-concept. Indeed, the exchanges show that the PLO has a more sophisticated view of human agency as something that is possible only collectively. The single human person is, to a mass movement like the PLO, more like Karl Marx's "divided and dislocated" subject, someone lost in the wilderness, or like Althusser's decentered subject held together by the illusion of free subjectivity—an illusion fostered by the interpellations of ideology.

Some of Said's concerns never make it into mainstream postcolonial theory. Outside of Said's work, we hear little about the conflict between solidarity and criticism. Postcolonial literary intellectuals rarely have anything to do with groups at all. But they certainly engage themselves in the issues of representation, and representation proved the crux of the dispute between Said and Tunis. Said claimed that the PLO was incompetent to represent itself. The PLO in turn sought to expose Said's residual Western humanism, universalism, and ethnocentrism. They charged him with a ridiculously inflated and hubristic belief that he alone could get visas approved. They balked at his implicit assumption that American ways of doing things were superior to the PLO's. They indicted him for having the mentality of an academic, for being naive and unworldly. They complained that he allowed his subjectivity to overrule solidarity. They objected to his presumption of his own intellectual spokesmanship. And they identified the central dilemmas of postcolonial theory. The militants in Tunis drew attention to the humanist and voluntarist leanings that sophisticated postmodern critics have also objected to. The dispute between Said and the PLO casts the sophisticated critic and the brutal PLO in roles just the opposite of those that one would expect. Said adopts the role of a nostalgic Auerbachian, Trilling-esque defender of the human, whereas the PLO takes the postmodern and poststructuralist view that humanism and Western normativity may potentially destroy Palestinian autonomy, integrity, and political force.

This odd exchange clarifies much about Said's own violent shuttling between humanism and poststructuralism. If modernism was a vortex, then postcolonialism is a whipsaw. Caught between the PLO and the academy, Said pulsates back and forth. It is this spasmodic shuddering, along with hybridity, ambivalence, and the "third space," which defines postcolonial theory. Commentators and critics who stand outside the postcolonial problematic see this shocked, jobbled, lurching jacitation. They call it "contradiction." Seen through the prism of Enlightenment rationality, the postcolonial perturbation cries out for correction or mitigation. A wiser reading would understand that the postcolonial critic is constitutively tossed and pitched, rocked and coggled, fluctuating between two worlds. Postcolonial theorists are perpetually caught in the act of crossing-over.

Nowhere has the violent shuttling been more palpable, more carefully explained than in Said's mediations of Israeli-Palestinian politics. The deconstructive excess of signification was visible in his very name, the "Edward"-English half being at odds with the Arab-"Said" half, the rift between self and origin literalized in his legal banishment from both of his natal places, Jerusalem and Egypt. Historical rupture became visible through him. His work made available the strange sensations of faltering, staggering, weltering, rolling, rocking, reeling, and thrashing, and these destabilizing perceptions have breathed their subtle influence into fields as diverse as queer theory, feminist theory, new historicism, and rhetoric and composition. The novel intellectual experiences of hybrid identity, geographic disorientation, and catechretic abuse have in the right hands reunited thought and emotion, repairing T. S. Eliot's lamented dissociation of sensibility. Not everyone aspires to the condition of Locke and David Hume. There can be "Pessimism of the intellect, optimism of the will." Wherever we encounter meditations on othering and sameness, exclusion and marginality, power and knowledge, body and nation, we can say: Palestine/Said was instrumental here.

NOTES

1. Edward Said, *Beginnings: Intention and Method* (New York: Basic, 1975).

2. Bruce Robbins, "Homelessness and Worldliness." *Diacritics* 13.3 (fall 1983): 69–77. Said, *The Question of Palestine* (New York: Times Books, 1979).

3. Said's interview was published simultaneously in the weekend edition of the Kuwaiti daily *al-Qabas* and in the Lebanese daily *as-Safir,* and then reported with commentary in *Mideast Mirror,* 9 October 1989, 17–20.

4. "Yaser Abedrabbo Replies to Edward Said," *Mideast Mirror,* 13 October 1989, 13–15.

5. "'Said Debate' Underlines Need for a Single Palestinian-American Lobby," *Mideast Mirror,* 16 October 1989, 11–12.

6. Michel Foucault, *Power/Knowledge,* ed. Colin Gordon (New York: Pantheon, 1980); Foucault, *Surveiller et punir* (Paris: Editions Gallimard, 1975), Foucault, *Discipline and Punish,* trans. Alan Sheridan (New York: Random House, 1979). In the context of the nation, see Foucault, "Governmentality," in *The Foucault Effect: Studies in Governmentality,* eds. Graham Burchell, Colin Gordon, and Peter Miller (Chicago: University of Chicago Press, 1991), 87–104. For a postcolonial reading see Spivak, "More on Power/Knowledge," in *The Spivak Reader,* eds. Donna Landry and Gerald MacLean (New York and London: Routledge, 1996), 141–74.

7. Many have faulted Said for his inconsistencies. See, for example, James Clifford, "On Orientalism," in *The Predicament of Culture: Twentieth Century Ethnography, Literature and Art* (Cambridge: Harvard University Press, 1988), 255–76; and Dennis Porter, "*Orientalism* and its Problems" (1983), rpt. in Patrick Williams and Laura Crisman, eds., *Colonial Discourse and Postcolonial Theory: A Reader* (Hemel Hempstead: Harvester Wheatsheaf, 1993), 150–61. Robert J. C. Young's deconstructive reading offers Said a way out of his double bind, but he describes Said's predicament as follows:

> It seems that, once again, he must have it both ways. In fact, however, the two, far from being opposed, are rather mirror images of each other: positing a hegemonic Orientalism as a totality which has no reference—for there is no object to which it corresponds—nor inner conflict, but solely an intention to dominate, Said must then demand a counterintention from outside the system for any resistance. This double bind, instead of being recognized as such, is given a theoretical corollary through an awkward meshing of Foucault's discursive system with Gramsci's organic intellectual, embodied in a methodological distinction between "strategic location"—the author's position in a text with regard to the material he writes about—and "strategic formation"—the relationship between texts and the way in which groups of texts acquire referential power. (Young, *White Mythologies: Writing History and the West* [New York and London: Routledge, 1990], 134–35)

8. This was at the time of the interview. In 1992, Said went to Gaza and the West Bank, for the first time since 1947. See Said, "Palestine, Then and Now," *Harper's,* December 1992, 47–55.

9. Samuel Weber, "The Intersection: Marxism and the Philosophy of Language," *Diacritics* 15.4 (1985): 111; quoted in Young, *White Mythologies,* 128.

10. Quoted in Young, *White Mythologies,* 128.

11. Said, *Orientalism* 5, 203; see Young, *White Mythologies,* 129.

12. Young, *White Mythologies,* 130.

13. Ibid., 138. Karl Marx, *Surveys from Exile,* ed. David Fernbach (London: Pelican Books, 1973), 306–7.

14. Spivak, *A Critique of Postcolonial Reason: Toward a History of the Vanishing Present* (Cambridge and London: Harvard University Press, 1999), 142n.

15. Spivak, "More on Power/Knowledge," 153–54.

16. Said, "Orientalism Reconsidered," *Race & Class* (autumn 1985), is an instance of Said taking cues from his own antinomies.

17. Timothy Brennan, "The Illusion of a Future: *Orientalism* as Traveling Theory," *Critical Inquiry* 26 (spring 2000): 583. See also Brennan's excellent "Places of Mind, Occupied Lands," in *Edward Said: A Critical Reader,* ed. Michael Sprinker (Oxford and Cambridge, MA: Blackwell), 74–95.

18. Said, *The World, the Text, and the Critic* (Cambridge: Harvard University Press, 1983), 29.

19. For discussions of Derrida in Algeria, see Young, "Subjectivity and History: Derrida in Algeria," in *Postcolonialism: An Historical Introduction* (Oxford and Malden, MA: Blackwell, 2001), 411–26; and, in the present volume, *Historicizing Theory,* Lee Morrisey, "'Nostalgeria' and Derrida's 'Strucure, Sign, and Play in the Human Sciences." For the impact of Algeria on French theory, see Jean-Francois Lyotard, *Political Writings,* trans. Bill Readings and Kevin Paul Geiman (Minneapolis: University of Minnesota Press, 1993). On Helene Cixous, see her essay, "My Algeriance, in Other Words: To Depart Not to Arrive from Algeria," in *Stigmata: Escaping Texts* (London: Routledge, 1998), 153–72.

20. Bart Moore-Gilbert, *Postcolonial Theory: Contexts, Practices, Politics* (London and New York: Verso, 1997), 34.

21. Aijaz Ahmad, *In Theory: Classes, Nations, Literatures* (London: Verso, 1992), 3.

22. Ibrahim Abu-Lughod, unpublished interview with H. Aram Veeser (1990).

23. Tom Segev, *1949, ha Yisre 'elim ha-rishonim* (1949: The first Israelis), trans. Arlen Neal Weinstein (New York: Henry Holt, 1998), xix.

24. Ibid., 79. The title of Segev's chapter, "Dividing the Spoils," tells a tale. See also, Norman G. Finkelstein, *Image and Reality of the Israel-Palestine Conflict* (London and New York: Verso, 1995); Benny Morris, The *Birth of the Palestinian Refugee Problem,* 1947–1949 (Cambridge and New York: Cambridge University Press, 1988); Morris, *Israel's Border Wars, 1949–1956* (Oxford: Clarendon Press, 1993); Morris, "The Eel and History," *Tikkun* (January-February 1990); and Morris, "The Origins of the

Palestinian Refugee Problem," *New Perspectives on Israeli History,* ed. Laurence J. Silberstein (New York: New York University Press, 1991), 42–55; Simha Flapan, *The Birth of Israel* (New York: Pantheon, 1987); Ilan Pappe, *Britain and the Arab-Israeli Conflict, 1948–'51* (New York: Macmillan, 1988); Avi Shlaim, *The Politics of Partition* (New York: Oxford University Press, 1988); and Said, *The Question of Palestine* (New York: Times Books, 1979).

25. Homi K. Bhabha, "The Postcolonial Critic," *Arena* 96 (1991): 47–63; Bhabha, *The Location of Culture* (New York and London: Routledge, 1994); Timothy Mitchell, *Colonizing Egypt* (Cambridge: Cambridge University Press, 1988); Gayatri Chakravorty Spivak, *Outside in the Teaching Machine* (New York and London: Routledge, 1993); and Spivak, *A Critique of Postcolonial Reason: Toward a History of the Vanishing Present* (Cambridge: Harvard University Press, 1999). See also, Bart Moore-Gilbert, "Gayatri Spivak: The Deconstructive Twist," in *Postcolonial Theory: Contexts, Practices, Politics* (London and New York: Verso, 1997); and Young, "India III: Hybridity and Subaltern Agency," *Postcolonialism: An Historical Introduction* (Oxford and Malden, MA: Blackwell, 2001).

26. Said, *Joseph Conrad and the Fiction of Autobiography* (Cambridge: Harvard University Press, 1966), 19

27. Said, *Beginnings,* 228.

28. Said, *The Politics of Dispossession: The Struggle for Palestinian Self-Determination 1969–1994* (New York: Random House, 1994), 186. Subsequent references indicated in the text as *POD.*

29. Said, "The Mind of Winter," *Harper's* (September 1984). Subsequent references indicated in the text as "Mind."

30. Said, *Reflections on Exile and Other Essays* (Cambridge: Harvard University Press, 2000), 95. Subsequent references indicated in the text as *ROE.*

31. Said, "On Jean Genet's Late Works," in *Imperialism and Theatre: Essays on World Theatre, Drama and Performance,* ed. Ellen Gainor (London: Routledge, 1995), 238.

32. See Genet, *Un captif amoureux* (Paris: Editions Gallimard, 1986), passim. Genet recounts his experiences among the Palestinian fedayeen, with whom intermittently he stayed in Jordan 1970–72. In '72 he was forced out of Jordan. During 16–18 September 1982 Palestinian refugees are massacred at Sabra and Shatila refugee camps in Beirut, Lebanon. Genet visits Shatila on 18 September and writes his impressions. These are published by the *Journal for Palestine Studies.*

33. Said, *Out of Place: A Memoir* (New York: Knopf, 1999), 198. Subsequent references indicated in the text as *Out.*

34. "On Palestinian Identity—A Conversation with Salman Rushdie," *New Left Review* 160 (1986), 123.

35. Said, *After the Last Sky: Palestinian Lives* (New York: Pantheon, 1985), 164.

36. *The Edward Said Reader,* eds. Moustafa Bayoumi and Andrew Rubin (New York: Vintage, 2000), 17.

37. Dinitia Smith, "Arafat's Man in New York," *New York Magazine,* 23 January 1989, 44.

38. Catherine Gallagher, "Politics, the Profession, and the Critic," *Diacritics* (summer 1985): 37.

39. Stephen Mailloux, *Rhetorical Power* (Ithaca: Cornell University Press, 1989), 147–48.

40. Stanley Fish, *The Trouble with Principle* (Cambridge: Harvard University Press, 1999).

41. Landry and MacLean, *Spivak Reader,* 153.

42. *Imaginary Maps: Three Stories by Mahasweta Devi,* trans. Gayatri Chakravorty Spivak (New York: Routledge and Calcutta: Thema, 1995), 120.

12

The Spectrality of the Sixties

BENJAMIN BERTRAM

> Alas! The time is coming when man will no more shoot the arrow of his longing out over mankind, and the string of his bow will have forgotten how to twang!
> —Friedrich Nietzsche, *Thus Spoke Zarathustra*

In an interview for the documentary *Berkeley in the Sixties,* activist Frank Bardacke reflects on the utopian aspirations of "People's Park":

> In a down to earth way we were showing in our very activity the image of a new society; our job is to form a counter culture, a more rural culture, a more decentralized culture, to develop counter values of cooperation, production for use rather than production for profit—develop that culture in hopes that that culture would be in revolutionary contradiction to bourgeois culture. And we should view ourselves as revolutionaries but really as mothers and fathers of this counter culture. I can almost convince myself of it now.

The utopian impulse contributed to social movements like People's Park, but it was also a "structure of feeling" that inspired critical theory from the sixties to the present day. Utopia was not always the lucid ideology exemplified by Bardacke's "image of a new society"; it also appeared as an unspecified desire or hope for major systemic change or what Raymond Williams calls "affective elements of consciousness."[1] The academics of the "next generation," who did not experience the euphoric and utopian moments of sixties activism in the United States, were nevertheless often trained or inspired by the theory-hope of baby boomers.[2] Much of the theoretical work in that decade was inspired by the utopian sense that anything is possible if not in genuine social or political change than surely in the way we interpret, shape, and think about reality. Indeed, many social and political concerns in contemporary theory today are based on the utopian view that radical systemic change is extremely desirable if not imminent. At the same time, utopian ideologies have become hard to maintain amid a crisis of representation.[3] In particular, socialist utopianism has been pushed further into the margins as perspectival or molecular formations have taken center stage.[4] Utopia may no longer be a structure of feeling or ideology as it was for progressives in the sixties, but I hope to show that Jacques Derrida's notion of the messianic in *Specters of Marx* (1994) is one important indication that utopia continues to have a shaping presence in critical theory. The juxtaposition of poststructuralism and Marxism will enable us to see a range of utopian inspirations that were so crucial to the historical emergence of theory. Utopia may be fragmented and uncertain in the post-Cold War global imaginary, but it still enjoys a strong presence in the Marxist tradition and critical theory in general.

Once regarded as the historical residue of the desire for the land of Cockaigne and other folktales of a land of plenty, utopia has more recently been attacked as an egregious totalizing discourse.[5] In the 1980s, for example, when irony and fragmentation stood as the pillars of American postmodernism, utopia looked politically bankrupt and outmoded. More ominously, a consensus was formed by many people that, as Jean Baudrillard put it, "the US is utopia achieved."[6] If utopia was almost abandoned by the Left, it was still available to serve other interests, including the Disney vision of the future or the "conservative revolution" of the early 1990s. When utopia no longer serves the interests of left-wing intellectuals, it remains a vital part of popular culture, politics, and artistic symbolism. In fact, as Fredric Jameson points out, utopian consciousness is part of class consciousness or rather the relational structure of collective group struggle. Thus utopia even plays a vital role in the right-wing culture of market economies. Because it grapples with the reality principle, utopia is more than a dream of Cockaigne, an affirmative map that eradicates the negative and social conflict.[7] Moreover, utopia transcends Cartesian representational consciousness by operating in unconscious libidinal desires and in the unconscious ideological positions of class conflict.

As Jameson's global perspective on the sixties suggests, the events of that decade called for totalizing or even revolutionary responses. Demonstrating that Third World revolutions can be understood in relation to structural changes and collective forms of praxis in the First World, in particular the United States and France, Jameson links the revolutionary cultural politics of the sixties to anti-colonial wars, the revolution in Cuba, and larger economic transformations around the globe.[8] Since the revolutions of that decade, we have witnessed an expansion of American hegemony globally—Third World nations no longer have the former Soviet Union as an alternative base of economic and political support. Postmodernism, as Jameson has shown, is the cultural manifestation or "logic" of this expansion of global capitalism.[9] As the social conditions of globalization change, dissatisfaction could grow into large-scale political movements based on the needs of workers in a mobile, transnational economic structure.[10] Furthermore, the cynical response to utopian thinking (which most of us are prone to more or less) has itself become an object of study involving self-reflection and ideological deprogramming of all kinds.[11] The most recent stage in the globalization of capitalism does not spell the end of utopian thinking or the "end of history." Although Jameson argues that it is important to consider the possibilities created by changes in communication networks and class formations, he also makes the sobering point that "to invoke the future in this way . . . is also unseasonable, in a situation in which postmodernity also means an imprisonment in the system of a present time from which the narrative categories of change seem excluded."[12]

Jameson's notion of totalization, which is vital to utopian theory, is based on an understanding of the workings of global capital itself. If representational thinking, a key requirement for grappling with a totality, is abandoned, we would have to surrender to the system that grows more totalizing every day. As we will see, Derrida's messianism, like Jameson's utopian dialectics, emphasizes historical motion, change, difference, and gaps in consciousness. Yet while utopia and messianism jolt us out of complacency, utopia is, as Jameson puts it, "a code word for the systemic transformation of contemporary society" and thus it has a political genealogy that links it to socialist movements of the past. Even as Derrida and other critical theorists have moved away from the socialist utopian politics of the sixties, they continue to be inspired by the sense that anything is possible.

I

The difficult position of utopian thought was clearly expressed long ago by Friedrich Engels, who pointed out that it attempts to solve problems without genuine social struggle. Utopia, in other words, remains caught in the web of ideology: "The solution of the social problems, which as yet lay hidden in undeveloped economic conditions, the Utopians attempted to evolve out of the human brain." Nevertheless, Engels finds an important place for utopian thinking: "We delight in the stupendously grand thoughts and germs of thought that everywhere break out through their phantastic covering."[13] From Engels to Jameson, the Marxist tradition sees utopia as a vital and productive contradiction. Located in the gap between consciousness and praxis, utopia is not just a luxurious daydream or blueprint for a rationally perfect society. Instead, it forges a crisis of representation that pushes us to think in terms of gaps, incongruities, and difference. Karl Mannheim, for example, suggests that utopia creates "an immediately perceptible picture" or "a directly intelligible set of meanings"; nevertheless, it is based on what he calls "incongruence"—it transcends our current, immediate situation by shattering the current order of things. Mannheim points out that "conservative mentality as such has no utopian mentality"; it has adjusted to a supposed natural world order and thus has no need for theorizing.[14] The death of utopia, he argues, comes with the end of a world picture.

In our time, poststructuralism has contributed to the destruction of the world picture that has been essential to utopian thinking in the past. This philosophical problem is, of course, part of a larger geopolitical shift: globalization and the end of the Cold War have had serious consequences for utopian thinking. In the sixties, it was easier for intellectuals to think they were challenging a larger cultural and economic system. But when the New Left and other movements eventually gave way to what are now called the "new social movements," the Jacobin imaginary was supplanted by a resistance to totalizing discourses. In fact, the term "revolution" was appropriated by Newt Gingrich and by the "conservative revolutionaries" in the 1990s while leftist activists looked back on the rhetoric of revolution in the sixties with a sense of regret or shame over their hubris. Of course, as Jameson points out, the "situation" of the sixties (the particular socioeconomic conditions of possibility for historical change) defies simple regret over "failures and missed opportunities."[15] Utopian ideology cannot be understood simply as the "determination in the last instance" by the economic base of capitalism in the sixties or seventies. Like revolution, utopia is a construct that relates to various semi-autonomous levels (politics, culture, and law).

Political movements in the sixties were often inspired by a widespread revolutionary, if not strictly utopian, structure of feeling. The Berkeley movement for a People's Park, for example, grew out of other movements that had revolutionary overtones, especially the Black Panthers and the Students for a Democratic Society (SDS). A local and eccentric protest by affluent college students, People's Park was nevertheless enmeshed in a larger struggle for social, economic, and racial justice. The anti-bourgeois ethos, more important to rebellious and privileged college students than the Black Panthers, gave the agrarian People's Park an affinity with the "end of alienation" movement. The SDS *Port Huron Statement* of 1962 combines the rhetoric of revolution, utopia, and anti-alienation:

> The decline of utopia and hope is in fact one of the defining features of social life today. The reasons are various: the dreams of the older left were

perverted by Stalinism and never recreated; the congressional stalemate makes men narrow their view of the possible; the specialization of human activity leaves little room for sweeping thought; the horrors of the twentieth century, symbolized in the gas-ovens and concentration camps and atom bombs, have blasted hopefulness. To be idealistic is to be considered apocalyptic, deluded. To have no serious aspirations, on the contrary, is to be "toughminded."[16]

Resisting the end of ideology thesis set forth by Daniel Bell in 1960, this document is framed by a deep humanistic desire for more participatory democracy. The New Left, unlike many postmodernists today, did not equate utopianism with Stalinism. Although such totalizing thinking was increasingly common, the intellectual seeds of its demise among intellectuals and academics had already been planted by structuralism in France and, by the late sixties, poststructuralism in the United States.

Jameson developed "cognitive mapping" in order to counter the debilitating effects of poststructuralist attacks on history, consciousness, and reason.[17] Since cognitive mapping was a common habit of thought for activists and intellectuals in the sixties, it did not have to be theorized in Jamesonian fashion.[18] On the political level, for example, many of the radical attacks on the system (as opposed to liberal reformism) came from the recognition that capitalism was a driving force in the horrors of Vietnam. In a speech a year before his assassination, the "Declaration of Independence from the War in Vietnam," Martin Luther King Jr. created a strong cognitive mapping of the interrelations between sociopolitical phenomena. King attempts to make as many connections as possible between race, imperialism, and economic oppression. Calling for a "true revolution of values," he argues that the system needs to be restructured to help poor people around the world. The war in Vietnam is only one part of a larger web of injustice that covers the globe: "A true revolution of values will lay hands on the world order and say of war: 'This way of settling differences is not just. . . . A nation that continues year after year to spend more money on military defense than on programs of social uplift is approaching spiritual death.'"[19]

It is important to note that this is a side of King that has not been championed by mainstream liberalism. As we might expect in the much more conservative political climate of our own day, people of many different political persuasions would rather forget that King laid out such a totalizing critique of imperialism and economic injustice. The Vietnam War was a moment of danger that inspired synoptic—as opposed to perspectival—political critiques of American materialism. Laying bare the interrelation between economic and racial injustice, King does a lot more than moralize against a lack of spiritual values: he demystifies the political rhetoric of American imperialism. According to

King's quasi-Marxist critique, American actions in Vietnam exposed America's domestic and international abandonment of its own democratic promise. The protest of the war in Vietnam cried out for King's cognitive map, the larger picture that put current affairs into moral and political focus.

Well before the Vietnam War, Frankfurt school philosophers created a totalizing, utopian theory that would spur political protests. Herbert Marcuse, doubtless the most important utopian philosopher of the fifties and sixties, fused Marx and Freud as he maintained a strong defiance of the dystopian effects of post-World War II prosperity. Marcuse's desire to overcome alienation through social change was contagious: artists, protesters, and intellectuals latched onto his humanistic goal of liberating eros and creativity. *The Port Huron Statement,* for example, tries to break down the limitations placed on human possibility by the reification of American social and cultural life. In *One-Dimensional Man* (1964), Marcuse argues that the oppositional status of the artist lies in the capacity to be alienated from the tough-minded positivism of the world of finance and its reality principle. The negative function of art is threatened by the prosperous, administered society that absorbs the erstwhile dissatisfied and desiring artist into its own desublimated logic of pleasure:

> Whether ritualized or not, art contains the rationality of negation. In its advanced positions, it is the great refusal—the protest against that which is. The modes in which man and things are made to appear, to sing and sound and speak, are modes of refuting, breaking, and recreating their factual existence. But these modes of negation pay tribute to the antagonistic society to which they are linked. Separated from the sphere of labor where society reproduces itself and its misery, the world of art which they created remains, with all its truth, a privilege and an illusion.[20]

Marcuse's "great refusal" modernizes a long-standing celebration of the transgressive function of art, including the festive, carnivalesque structures of mythical and literary constructs. In the complex, administered society of late capitalism, the opposition between the pleasures of Falstaff and the work ethic of postcarnivalesque Prince Hal disappears: "If all the year were playing holidays," Shakespeare's Hal points out, "To sport would be as tedious as to work" (1.2.199–200).[21]

Marcuse's "repressive desublimation" shows how the real killjoy is no longer the Lenten prince or puritan of yesteryear since the transgressive status of the *promesse de bonheur* is destroyed when all sexual liberation and expression is brought into the culture industry and mainstream entertainment. Like Shakespeare's *Henry IV,* Thomas More's *Utopia* (the book that inaugurated the genre of utopian literature), could not have existed without the aesthetic condition outlined by Marcuse. Social leveling, cultural experimentation, and festive license, the vital components of More's satire, were inherited from ancient saturnalia. More, like the Marxist utopians who so admired his work, built on the folk tradition of carnival saturnalia by incorporating a rational critique of structural economic injustice. Consequently, the imaginary society described by the traveler Hythloday in book two is deeply interwoven with the critique of socioeconomic change wrought by what Marx called "primitive accumulation." The ability and desire to criticize or denaturalize the current order of things, *Utopia* suggests, would not exist without the alternative futures mapped out by the imagination. Marcuse's great refusal—"the protest against that which is"— strengthens such logic in a more advanced stage of capitalism.

According to Marcuse's great refusal, if art is to maintain its utopian function it must resist the oppressive organization of labor that would defeat the freeplay of the imagination. If art is not entirely controlled by the dialectic of enlightenment, it can refuse "to forget what can be," and retain a critical function. Like many radical thinkers of his generation, Marcuse challenged the bourgeois notion of progress (the reality principle). The alienated condition of labor provided by this modern reality principle has placed pleasure and work into separate spheres of existence. In *Eros and Civilization* (1962), Marcuse points out that "the reconciliation between [the] pleasure and reality principle does not depend on the existence of abundance for all. The only pertinent question is whether a state of civilization can be reasonably envisaged in which human needs are fulfilled in such a manner and to such an extent that surplus-repression can be eliminated."[22]

Although the commodity culture of the present is an intensification of what Marcuse saw in the fifties and sixties, there are fewer intellectuals around who want to advocate resistance. Nevertheless, the Frankfurt school rethinking of German aesthetics (especially Sigmund Freud, Schiller, and Immanuel Kant) remains a vital part of utopian thinking, since many people still have trouble accepting the notion that capitalism offers us genuine freedom from necessity. As Frankfurt school critiques have fallen out of favor, denunciations of consumer culture are now made almost entirely on a moralistic level. While the children and grandchildren of baby boomers are increasingly interpellated by market rhetoric and a virtually unchallenged ethos of consumerism, few intellectuals remain who follow the Frankfurt school view of aesthetics. In other words, the reality principle of late capitalism no longer requires an identifiable ideology since commodification has been internalized and metastasized throughout every aspect of our cultural life.[23]

II

Looking to change the entire structure of society, the New Left in the United States and Europe strove for cultural as well as economic revolution. French radicals, who eschewed the Stalinist model of their predecessors, added diverse emancipatory goals to the long-standing utopian one of ending alienated labor. In France, unlike the United States, students and workers joined in widespread protests. While protesters in France created a general strike that virtually shut down the economy, protesters in the United States did not manage to incorporate blue-collar workers in any significant way. American student radicals searching for the end of alienation never posed a serious threat to the socioeconomic order. Nevertheless, protests in both places incorporated a redemptive, humanistic rhetoric attacking alienation and economic inequality. The hope was that a better society could replace the existing one.

In the United States, the desire for systemic transformation was a major part of the humanism of the Students for a Democratic Society and for Marcuse's philosophy. The utopian structure of feeling encompassed multivalent ideologies based on both liberal reform and leftist radicalism.[24] Utopian desire has a much more dubious role in the anti-humanist social movements of the present, however. Despite his claim that he was affirming the emancipatory spirit of Marxism, Derrida's entry into political theory in the nineties appeared to be another step away from the utopian projects of the sixties in France and the United States. In its American context (my focus throughout this essay), Derrida's work has been politically ambiguous: on the one hand, the basic terms of poststructuralist discourse—heterogeneity, difference, and textuality—call into question some of the utopian longings of the Left; on the other hand, poststructuralism frees us to develop new possibilities for the future by dismantling metaphysical visions that lock us into a rigid, supposedly natural world order. From its inception in the late sixties, poststructuralism carried this ambiguity: it contributed to the demise of humanism and its utopian aspirations in that decade while offering hope that there could be something new under the sun.

Since his early work in the sixties, Derrida has challenged what he characterizes as Western "phonocentrism" and "logocentrism." In deconstruction, representation enters a crisis when we encounter "the liberation of the signifier from its dependence or derivation with respect to the logos and the related concept of truth or the primary signified."[25] Derrida's project extends the anti-humanist positions of structuralism by launching a more thoroughgoing skepticism toward the basic ontological and epistemological traditions of philosophy. The utopian critique of liberal representative democracy, which is grounded on the notion that more collective participation would reach our human potential for fulfillment and a more gratifying life (i.e., "presence"), is one form of humanistic metaphysics that is easily deconstructed. By suggesting that there is no longer a presence to be re-presented, the notion of différence challenges the universalizing concept, the world picture of utopia. Thus the linguistic turn of poststructuralism can be used as a weapon not only against Marxist humanism but against utopian thinking in general, from the call for the end of alienation by the Students for a Democratic Society to the agrarian revolt of People's Park in Berkeley. If we follow poststructuralism, the synoptic world picture (playful or otherwise) of utopian theory must give way to perspectival conversation or textual difference. Theory becomes interpretation in a conversational mode of writing. In other words, deconstruction calls into question the referent of classical utopianism (the world picture and goal of an alternative reality) as well as its onto-theocentric humanism. For the formalism of poststructuralist discourse, jouissance in textuality takes the place of the historical referent of utopia.

In interviews of the late sixties, French theorists expressed concerns about Derrida's move away from history. Derrida went beyond Louis Althusser's rejection of "expressive causality" or "historicism" by using différence to call the metaphysics of history into question: "The metaphysical character of the concept of history is not only linked to linearity, but to an entire system of implications (teleology, eschatology, elevating and interiorizing accumulation of meaning, a certain type of traditionality, a certain concept of continuity, or truth, etc.)."[26] Rejecting the notion that history develops in an endogenous fashion (especially in the monist Hegelian conception of history), Derrida steers us toward heterogeneous, differentiated histories. If utopia is wrapped up in a metaphysical conception of history, then it too would have to be rejected.

Concerned with the blank spaces of representation, deconstruction calls into question any philosophy that builds a model of consciousness as presence. Richard Rorty makes a similar move when he examines how traditional philosophy has been shaped by the mirror of nature metaphor. The linguistic turn, he argues, entails moving away from the pursuit of an "accurate representation of the mind."[27] Thus it would appear that deconstruction eliminates the possibility of utopia's transcendence of the current situation, in effect wiping the entire temporal and spatial orientation of utopian thinking off the map. If the ocularcentric mapping of utopia as a world picture is now so highly problematic, we have to wonder what it means to tarry with the negative in the Frankfurt school sense of that Hegelian expression.

In *Specters of Marx* (1994), however, Derrida revives a kernel of Marxist utopian thinking by critiquing the systemic problems created by global capitalism and by making a clarion call for social justice. Taking note of the global economic situation after the fall of the Soviet Union, his critique goes against the grain of postmodernism by denouncing the abandonment of "great emancipatory discourses." Although he does not come out directly in favor of utopianism, Derrida's alternative notion of the messianic creates something comparable to the Marxist utopian imaginary. The messianic is not a theological concept. As a "messianic without messianism" it fits into his

long-standing account of différence as deferral and delay by functioning as a
philosophical and political aporia: "structural messianism" must have no content.[28] Hope and the acknowledgment of failure are both built into the system. The messianic without messianism emphasizes dislocation rather than
presence; it is a means of recuperating hope or expectation for justice without the use of traditional religious metaphysics. Like the notion of utopia, the
messianic places emphasis on the gaps and dislocations of our temporal experience in order to allow for the possibility of an alternative future. Unlike religious traditions, Derrida's quirky messianism grapples with the terrible "labor
of the negative," undermining onto-theological residues of humanistic
thought, and, in the process, evacuating the revolutionary impulse behind
utopian socialism.[29] Francis Fukuyama's pseudo-Hegelian philosophy of history, which hardly seems like a serious match for Derrida, takes on critical
importance for the political thinking in *Specters of Marx*. While he admits
that there is no empirical evidence for the final victory of liberalism around
the globe, Fukuyama argues that since other modes of production have simply failed, liberalism as a "regulative idea" cannot be surpassed.[30] Derrida
shrewdly deconstructs Fukuyama's evangelical rhetoric, the "good news" he
has brought to the world that the messiah has arrived in the form of neo-lib-
eralism. Derrida's suspicion of this pronouncement of the death of Marxism
and all revolutionary projects also enables him to produce an uncharacteris-
tically affirmative call for a "New International":

> For it must be cried out, at a time when some have the audacity to neo-evan-
> gelize in the name of the ideal of a liberal democracy that has finally realized
> itself as the ideal of human history: never have violence, inequality, exclusion,
> famine, and thus economic oppression affected as many human beings in the
> history of the earth and of humanity. Instead of singing the advent of the
> ideal of liberal democracy and of the capitalist market in the euphoria of the
> end of history, instead of celebrating the "end of ideologies" and the end of
> the great emancipatory discourses, let us never neglect this obvious macro-
> scopic fact, made up of innumerable singular sites of suffering: no degree of
> progress allows one to ignore that never before, in absolute figures, never
> have so many men, women, and children been subjugated, starved, or exter-
> minated on the earth.[31]

Although Fukuyama's *End of History and the Last Man* (1992) is at the center
of this critique, we find Derrida expanding his attack to the inverted millenarianism and complacency of those who would abandon the call for emancipation. This call is not totally surprising since it fits into a larger concern for
temporality in Derrida's work. In his usage, the millenarian is drained of metaphysical content (as far as that is possible). Unlike the language of the millennium in sixties discourse or in religious movements, the call for redemption

acknowledges its failure from the start; redemption must always be deferred. The emancipatory promise of a redemptive politics fits the deconstructive model because "the time is out of joint." We can trace Derrida's concern with temporality back to his reading of Martin Heidegger's translation of the word "dike" in the Anaximander fragment: joining, adjoining, adjustment, and articulation of accord or harmony. "Dike" is traditionally translated as "justice." As a call for vengeance in a time of disharmony, Hamlet's line—"the time is out of joint"—becomes a conceit for the presence of the ghost of Marx and for the importance of the call for justice. Derrida, like Marcuse and others in the Marxist tradition, wants to tarry with the negative as a means of challenging complacent affirmations of the present order of things.

As we might expect, the deconstruction of Fukuyama's notion that "the time is free" in a "new world order" is powerful. At the same time, it is hard to miss the peculiarity of Derrida's labor of the negative: the actual moment of joining is not only highly abstract but empty and exasperating. The New International, in Derrida's scheme, conjures up the ghost of Marx and posits a rejoining "without status, without title, and without name, barely public even if it is not clandestine, without contract, 'out of joint,' without coordination, without party, without country, without national community (International before, across, and beyond any national determination), without cocitizenship, without common belonging to a class."[32] Once the politics of redemption has been replaced by the ludic pleasure of différence, we can only accept an ironic view of a time that is proclaimed "free." Derrida's New International contributes to the new social movements that follow anti-essentialist democratic notions that "true" democracy or revolution are undesirable and even totalitarian. Since the sixties, the word "antagonism" has replaced "revolution," since the former maintains the playful openness of poststructuralism. Monist Hegelianism and Marxist endogenous history calling for the be-all-end-all of global oppression have been replaced by the multiple histories with no telos or center.[33]

Since the messianic abandons the quest for ultimate fulfillment or presence, Derrida holds onto the spirit of demystification and unmasking without supporting Marx's rationalism. While Derrida tries to deontologize Marxism, he does not attempt to escape ontology entirely; instead, he uses the form of the messianic without the content.[34] Eschewing messianic eschatology, Derrida maintains "a certain experience of the emancipatory promise" or "a structural messianism, a messianism without religion, even a messianic without messianism." The paradox here is meant to maintain an openness to heterogeneity and the coming of the other, a new geopolitical future (without the elimination of ghosts as a rationalist fulfillment of utopia or neo-Hegelian liberal democracy). At this point he is clearly playing with Walter Benjamin's theologico-materialist notion of "weak messianic time." Benjamin writes,

To articulate the past historically does not mean to recognize it "the way it really was" (Ranke). It means to seize hold of a memory as it flashes up at a moment of danger. Historical materialism wishes to retain that image of the past which unexpectedly appears to man singled out by history at a moment of danger. The danger affects both the content of the tradition and its receivers. The same threat hangs over both: that of becoming a tool of the ruling classes. In every era the attempt must be made anew to wrest tradition away from a conformism that is about to overpower it. The Messiah comes not only as the redeemer, he comes as the subduer of Antichrist.[35]

For Derrida, the moment of danger is the recent conformism of the celebratory anti-communism in Europe and America. Unlike religious messianism, which strives for a pure vision of the future, Derrida's messianic enjoys the impurity of the ghost and its indeterminate position. Thus Derrida captures the religious metaphors in Fukuyama's discourse by criticizing his spiritualized, teleological account of the success of capitalism (the "good news" is that all of history has led us up to the victory of liberal capitalism). Appropriating Benjamin's eclectic, theologico-materialist criticism of liberal economic progress, Derrida empties out metaphysical traditions and visions of history.

Unsurprisingly, the messianic quickly loses its theological grounding as it takes on intensely secular and profane meanings. In fact, Derrida argues, we have a lot to learn from Marx's combination of the psychological, biological, and cosmological traumas of Freud, Darwin, and Copernicus (respectively). All three intellectual revolutions decentered human beings. According to Derrida, Marx not only dismantled anthropocentrism, he combined these three traumas. While he might embrace such secular decentering, Derrida avoids any connection to the logocentric rationalism of Marx. More importantly, he wants to distinguish the messianic from metaphysical, teleological accounts of history, especially Fukuyama's pseudo-Hegelian philosophy. In *L'Autre Cap*, translated as "The other heading" (1992) Derrida puns on the word "cap" in order to question the various notions of a European cultural hegemony based on long-standing assumptions of the superiority of Western reason. The opposition to the "end" of history has to do with this fear of the notion that Europe is "heading" (cap) in a particular direction or leading history in a teleological fashion. Messianism is thus a punctual means of protesting such an end.[36]

As the title of Derrida's book suggests, specters hover everywhere in Marx's work. Given the widespread fascination with ghosts in the nineteenth century, it is not surprising that spectrality was one of Marx's favorite tropes. Why, then, does it become one of Derrida's major tropes? Poststructuralist debunking of the metaphysics of presence is symptomatic of a heavily mediated, spectral culture.[37] As our experience of space and time becomes more virtual, binary oppositions like presence and representation or even life and death become harder to sustain. Entering into the spirit of Marx's historicism, Derrida recognizes that material conditions have changed so we must address "the differantial deployment of tekhne, of techno-science or teletechnology." Marx developed his ontology well before such a world had emerged and was thus more likely to appropriate a Platonic metaphysics of image/reality or presence and its representation. Marxist categories like the international, value, or commodity fetishism were ripe for change given the radical ontological shift in the late twentieth century.

Skeptical of the search for realism in praxis ("work production, actualization, techniques"), Derrida takes Marx one step further in the process of undermining metaphysical constructions of subjectivity. In his critique of Max Stirner's metaphysical notion of the self, Marx develops the materialist conception of subjectivity that counters Stirner's more existential, phenomenological reduction. Derrida summarizes Marx on Stirner:

> The youth may indeed destroy his hallucinations or the phantomatic appearance of the bodies—of the Emperor, the State, the Fatherland. He does not actually (wirklich) destroy them. And if he stops relating to these realities through the prostheses of this representation and the "spectacles of his fantasy," if he stops transforming these realities into objects, objects of theoretical intuition, that is, into a spectacle, then he will have to take into account the "practical structure" of the world: Work production, actualization, techniques. Only this actuality . . . can get to the bottom of a purely imaginary or spectral flesh.[38]

Marx tracks down the ghosts in Stirner's representations by looking closely at his phenomenological reduction. In order to get closer to the reality of the body, Stirner makes it an egological representation. By referring to the anarchist Stirner as "Saint Max," Marx pokes fun at his claim that he alone seems to have a means of escaping the various religious abstractions of his day. Stirner focuses on his own body or ego as a means of escaping the abstract or, as Marx puts it, "the phantomatic appearance . . . of the Emperor, the State, the Fatherland." According to Marx, the way to challenge these institutions is to examine and criticize the "practical structure of the world." The focus on the individual ego only amounts to a narcissistic obsession with the body.

Unlike Marx, Derrida is happy to shatter the mystical shell without finding the kernel of reality or truth; he does not need to discover the reality behind phantasmal appearances. When this suspicion of realism leads Derrida to call into question the entire Marxist theory of praxis, we begin to wonder if he is committed to anything Marxist whatsoever. Without the fundamental notion that "the nature of individuals thus depends on the material conditions determining their production," Marxism has very little left to offer.[39] Derrida shifts the concern over the "mode of life" to the free play of language entirely removed from "practical reality" and history. As a result, Marx and Engels's distinction between utopia as an ideological fantasy and real, sensual human practice no longer makes any sense. Indeed, Derrida overturns Marx's famous thesis on Feuerbach: "The philosophers have only *interpreted* the world, in various ways; the point, however, is to *change* it."[40] For Derrida, the point is to change our interpretations of the world rather than change the real world.

To be sure, Derrida is not a supporter of socialist or humanistic utopian thinking, yet his work maintains the utopian sense that anything is possible. Like Marx, Derrida critiques long-standing traditions of subjectivity in the West such as liberal individualism. In the early critiques of phenomenology and structuralism, différence challenges the idea of the transcendent individual; indeed, from subjectivity we move into a new terrain of the "subjectivity effect."[41] There are political possibilities here since individualism has been central to so many forms of ideology (class politics but also race, gender, and sexuality). If différence calls into question naturalized forms of bourgeois subjectivity, we might think there are revolutionary possibilities for a new subject of history. Deconstruction enables us to entertain possibilities unimagined in traditions of liberal democracy, where the self is configured along the lines of private property.

The magnificence of Derrida's thoroughgoing critique of Western phonocentrism, the philosophy of consciousness, and the subject, is only matched by the disappointment left in its wake when no attractive alternative materializes. It is hard to imagine a revitalization of politics without an account of subjectivity to replace the metaphysics of presence. In Derrida's case, the challenge to bourgeois subjectivity remains precisely in the sphere Marx wanted to transform—philosophy. His critique of praxis dissolves any serious challenge to the material conditions that constitute subjectivity to begin with. Although Derrida has made a major contribution to the critique of neo-liberal ideas about a natural world order or the end of history, he is unwilling to set forth a clear agenda of what, if anything, might be be done to change the current state of affairs. In that case, he is hardly all that different from most critical theorists. As Hamlet says, "use every man after his desert, and who shall scape whipping?" (2.2.524–5). In our fragmented, dislocated postmodern climate, we cannot expect to find great utopian blueprints of a better society. Nevertheless, utopian thinking has been a shaping presence in critical theory, even if only in the form of the terrible labor of the negative.

III

Since the disastrous events of the twentieth century, utopias based on what Engels calls a "rational kernel" have increasingly seemed like dangerous ideological impositions of one group's conception of reason as a guide for all of humanity.[42] Nevertheless, utopia does not necessarily take the form of a static blueprint guided by an enlightenment conception of reason. Our new suspicion of such blueprints putting humans on the procrustean bed of utopia makes it necessary to rethink the relation of ideology and utopia. As Ernesto Laclau has suggested, ideology is the "will to totality," or the "non-recognition of the play of differences." Utopia, then, is ideological insofar as it provides a totalizing image of society. Laclau's anti-essentialism allows for utopia while deconstructing its positive will to totality. For Laclau, this paradoxical perspective is important to the pragmatic new social movements of the post-Cold War era. No longer striving for total systemic change, in other words, postmodernism recognizes the limits of modern rationalist dreams of the perfect society.[43]

In the sixties, utopianism was still part of the imaginary of the Left, which could think on a scale that today might counter the Disney dream of a privatized land of plenty.[44] The desire for systemic change in America had particular conditions of possibility in the revolutions around the globe. Although it is still possible for fragments of the utopian spirit of the sixties to be found in the new social movements of the present day, utopian thinking is less prominent. Derrida's messianic is itself a symptom of changes in the geopolitical situation that are having a profound impact on our work in the academy today. Consider, for example, the startling claims of Bill Readings in *The University in Ruins* (1996). Espousing an inverted millenarianism or dystopic nihilism, he argues that the modern university no longer functions as a privileged ideological space for the culture of the Nation-State. Instead, the university has become a techno-bureaucratic institution that celebrates the non-referential and empty term "excellence." This University of Excellence, he maintains, can no longer follow the narrative of liberal education with its heroic representatives of culture. Following a Derridean model of decentered subjectivity, Readings envisions "peripheral singularities" rather than "subjects" or "individuals" since "there is no ideal individual that might achieve either total self-consciousness or a harmonious, balanced relation to others and the world. Peripheral singularities do not stand at the center of culture."[45] Readings thus reconceives the university as a space of dissensus, differends, and aporia where we find customers rather than students, consumers rather than citizens. Furthermore, the radical theories people once believed might help generate revolutionary change are now part of the consumer culture of the university. Theory has thus been drained of its radical content. His book reminds us that we must rethink the role of theory given the new socioeconomic conditions of the university. If Readings is correct, the radical tradition of utopia is in big trouble, since peripheral singularities in the University of Excellence could hardly fight for such mighty theoretical concepts. According to such deconstructive thinking, utopianism would be logocentric baggage that preceded the crisis of representation and the University of Excellence.

Despite the hyperbolic nature of his claims, Readings correctly surmises that the utopian leftist imaginary has been weakened in the last two decades. The example of Disney should remind us, however, that utopian narratives of history remain ubiquitous even in the postmodern landscape. It is thus a serious error to consign utopia to the ash can of history or to link it strictly to what Derrida calls "metaphysical visions of history." Utopian desire can be found in larger historical projects of all kinds and hardly needs to take the form of monist Hegelian philosophy. Fukuyama, Derrida, Jameson, and others have taught us that the desire to grapple with large motions of historical change—the mode of production or the fundamental organizational structures of society—simply do not disappear. We have not yet become Nietzsche's "last men" who "have their little pleasures for the day, and their little pleasures for the night; but they are careful of their health," nor have we been completely ideologically programmed by the cynical reason of celebratory market rhetoric.[46] My final example of utopian thinking in the sixties, Thomas Pynchon's *Crying of Lot 49*, will illustrate the necessity of utopian thinking for our own day.

Published in 1965, Pynchon's novella was proleptic of the postmodern culture that followed years later. The novella shows how a tendency toward totalizing thinking (attempting to grasp the larger system controlling social relations) can be accompanied by a proliferation of microgroups or molecular, subterranean organizations. The protagonist, Oedipa Maas, tries to understand the legacy and meaning left behind by a real estate mogul named Pierce Inverarity. Her semiotic quest leads her to suspect that the legacy is America itself. She has come up empty-handed in her search for the ultimate Truth that links all the various tiny clues she has gathered. In a lonely, anxious state of mind, she wonders if the clues she has been investigating were in fact part of an elaborate plot by Inverarity to manipulate her from the grave.

In the novella's paranoid, alienated, and fragmented lifeworld, signifiers are detached from signifieds; people move in a spectral world with rhizomatic means of communication across nodal points. Micro-groups like *inamorati anonymous* participate in an alternative, underground mail system that enables them to take advantage of gaps in the larger system of representation—the postal system. As the "executrix" of Inverarity's will, Oedipa learns more about his economic past and soon finds herself enmeshed in a larger totality of relations. The printed circuit of a transistor radio serves as a metaphor for her position in the city of San Narciso: "Though she knew even less about radios than about Southern Californians, there were to both outward patterns a hieroglyph sense of concealed meanings, of an intent to communicate."[47] The world, for Oedipa, becomes a text. Her semiotic or hermeneutic dilemma suggests that there is no closure or final meaning to be discovered—it is essential that she engage in the project despite the fact that she will fail.

As Oedipa is abandoned by all the men in her life (who have gone insane), she becomes one of the "isolates" of *inamorati anonymous*. This atomization is dialectically linked to the transcendental signified of America—the meaning of Inverarity's legacy. Her cognitive mapping of America enables her to discover that a crucial aspect of the crisis of meaning lies in the nature of work, the social organization of labor. Pynchon's characters complain about their position vis-à-vis the new technologies and corporate control of human potential: the eventual founder of *inamorati anonymous,* an executive at Yoyodyne, plans to light himself on fire after learning he will be replaced by a computer; Stanley Koteks argues that corporate teamwork is part of the "gutlessness of the whole society" and Oedipa's husband, Mucho Maas, who has nightmarish visions of a sign reading "NADA" (an acronym for the National Automobile Dealer's Association), says that he could never find satisfaction in his work, particularly as a used car dealer. The refuse that Mucho finds in the cars is emblematic of the fallen world of consumerism:

> . . . when the cars were swept out you had to look at the actual residue of these lives, and there was no way of telling what things had been truly refused (when so little he supposed came by that out of fear most of it had to taken and kept) and what had simply (perhaps tragically) been lost: clipped coupons promising savings of 5 or 10 cents, trading stamps, pink flyers advertising specials at the markets, butts, tooth-shy combs, help-wanted ads, Yellow Pages torn from the phone book, rags of old underwear or dresses that already were period costumes, for wiping your own breath off the inside of a windshield with so you could see whatever it was, a movie, a woman or car you coveted, a cop who might pull you over just for drill, all the bits and pieces coated uniformly, like a salad of despair, in a gray dressing of ash, condensed exhaust, dust, bodily wastes—it made him sick to look , but he had to look.[48]

The "salad of despair," the fallen or degraded world of consumerism, defines the problem of history for all Americans: Oedipa's quest to understand the past takes her through an archaeology of human bones used as charcoal for cigarette filters, the San Narciso freeway paves over a cemetery and the remains are commodified as bone charcoal. Bits of trash in the cars and other signifiers of consumerism point to some higher, transcendental signified— the legacy of America. The challenge is to affirm the importance of memory in a reified and dislocated lifeworld in which automobiles become the metal extensions of people and human history is found in the Thing-world of consumerism. Trapped within the system, Oedipa struggles to map the totality and come to terms with her atomized position in a set of social relations seemingly beyond her cognitive grasp. The desire to find an alternative to the culture of Tupperware parties and "the greenish dead eye of the TV tube" remains essential to her existence.

The Crying of Lot 49 falls into the gap between sixties utopianism and the postmodern critique of the transcendental signified. The book has not abandoned humanistic concerns, but it has clearly set the stage for a radical skepticism toward Truth. Pynchon lifts the anchor and sails away from the modernist language of alienation, History, or Totality. Like the cognitive mapping of sixties utopianism, the fictive quest of Oedipa to find the legacy of America becomes hard to sustain after the linguistic turn. At the same time, Oedipa's quest exemplifies Jameson's point that the move toward the molecular in a great deal of postmodernism can only exist in relation to totality.[49] The experience of fragmentation, in other words, could not exist without a concept of unity and totality.

Oedipa's revelations, which often come from the most banal sources like a vast sprawl of tract homes, are like Derrida's "messianic without messianism" or even Marcuse's "great refusal." The moments of revelation serve to negate the nihilistic and hopeless world left behind by business moguls like Inverarity. Even if the legacy of America—utopia—may itself be impossible to find, it provides hope and a desire for transformation. Derrida's messianic, which arrived well after Pynchon's fictive lifeworld came to look like our postmodern experience, indicates that even though utopia hardly constitutes a structure of feeling today, it remains a shaping presence. Hence the reference to "spectrality" in my title: the legacy of the sixties is hard to interpret (like the ghost in *Hamlet*), but it "harrows [us] with fear and wonder." Much of the excitement surrounding critical theory has been generated by the utopian feeling that anything is possible. Whereas this feeling no longer seems prominent in the new social movements, it is still evident in some of the theory we engage today. While the next generation continues to engage critical theory, it has yet to come to terms with the legacy of utopian thinking that still interpellates many of us.

NOTES

1. Raymond Williams, *Marxism and Literature* (Oxford: Oxford University Press, 1977), 125.

2. In *Day Late, Dollar Short*, Peter C. Herman uses "next generation" to refer to assistant professors, recently tenured professors, and graduate students. I am using a more chronological sense of generation here, but I would also like to include people of all ages who have learned theory from those who were more cathected to events in the sixties and early seventies. See Herman, ed., *Day Late, Dollar Short* (Albany: State University of New York Press, 2000).

3. I am using the term "crisis of representation" to refer to the processes of differentiation that currently challenge logocentric discourses of all kinds. Art, politics, and social life have been profoundly altered by processes that call notions of mimesis, truth, and or totality into serious doubt. Thus the crisis of representation is, of course, also a crisis of legitimation.

4. I believe we may soon witness a renewed interest in concepts of utopia. For example, Russel Jacoby's recent book offers a sustained criticism of the current hostility to utopian thinking. See Jacoby, *The End of Utopia* (New York: Basic, 1999). Although I find that the analytic power of the book is vitiated by its cantankerous tone and glib denunciation of so much current intellectual discourse, I agree with many of its points. In particular, I share Jacoby's notion that utopia is not necessarily a dangerous totalitarianism; it can be a means of critiquing the present and thinking about a radically different future. Thus I agree with his claim that the Left suffers without utopia. In addition, the political efficacy of liberals is threatened when there is no leftist imaginary.

5. These two kinds of criticism capture the premodern mythical forms of utopia such as Ovid's "golden age" as well as rational and teleological modern forms. For an excellent discussion of the shift from mythical and festive forms to the literary genre or concept of utopia, see Robert C. Eliot, "Saturnalia, Satire, and Utopia," *Yale Review* 55 (1965): 521–36.

6. Jean Baudrillard, *America*, trans. Chris Turner (London: Verso, 1988), 77.

7. See Fredric Jameson, "The Dialectic of Utopia and Ideology," in *The Political Unconscious* (Ithaca: Cornell University Press, 1981), 281–300; and Jameson, "Utopia, Modernism, and Death," in *The Seeds of Time* (New York: Columbia University Press, 1994), 73–128.

8. See Jameson, "Periodizing the Sixties," in *The Ideologies of Theory, vol. 2* (Minneapolis: University of Minnesota Press, 1988), 178–208.

9. See Jameson, *Postmodernism, or, the Cultural Logic of Late Capitalism* (Durham: Duke University Press, 1991).

10. On the new political possibilities presented by transnational capitalism, see "The Multitude Against Empire," in *Empire*, Antonio Negri and Michael Hardt (Cambridge: Harvard University Press, 2000), 393–414.

11. The hostility to utopia as a totalizing discourse cannot be understood without confronting what Peter Sloterdijk has called "cynical reason," that pervasive mood or structure of feeling that has defined so much of the philosophical, political, and artistic thinking of the last quarter century in Europe and America. Sloterdijk defines cynicism as "enlightened false consciousness": "it is that modernized, unhappy consciousness, on which enlightenment has labored both successfully and in vain." The cynic, Sloterdijk tells us, "no longer feels affected by any critique of ideology; its falseness is already reflexively buffered." See Sloterdijk, *Critique of Cynical Reason*, trans. Michael Eldred (Minneapolis: University of Minnesota Press, 1987), 5. No longer accepting enlightenment rationality as the basis for grand political projects, the "chic bitterness" of the cynical mentality blocks the development of all great projects, especially utopian ones.

12. Jameson, "Actually Existing Marxism," *Polygraph* 6.7 (1993): 187.

13. Friedrich Engels, "Socialism: Utopian and Scientific," in *The Marx-Engels Reader*, ed. Robert C. Tucker (New York: Norton, 1978), 687–88.

14. Karl Mannheim, *Ideology and Utopia* (New York: Harcourt, 1968), 206.

15. Jameson, "Periodizing the Sixties," 178.

16. Students for a Democratic Society, *The Port Huron Statement* (Chicago, 1966), 6.

17. Jameson argues that cognitive mapping is an essential part of any socialist project, but he also makes an analogy to the mapping of urban space that extends the value of this notion into other areas. An imaginary map of a city can counter the experience of alienation in urban space. Jameson suggests that "mapping a totality" is similar. It enhances our ability to make connections between "levels" with respect to a "mode of production." In other words, it enables us to position our own subjective experience in the larger ideological imaginary of global capitalism. Jameson's notion of totality is thus indebted to Althusser's rethinking of the notions of ideology and base/superstructure. See Jameson, *Postmodernism*, 399–418.

18. In the introduction to his book on the sixties, Todd Gitlin points out how radically the configuration of the Left has changed:

> To invoke The Revolution was to claim title to the future; to see beyond raids and trials and wiretaps and empire and war and guilt; to justify the tedium of mimeographing one more leaflet, working out one more position, suffering through one more insufferable meeting. The Revolution: The name of our desire became firm and precise—never mind the absence of a vision of reconstruction—by dint of the definite article. . . . To invoke The Revolution was, in short, to acquire prepackaged identity, international sweep, and historical precedent for a breathtaking exercise of will. Black, white, male, female, democrats, antidemocrats, children of the suburbs and ghettos—if in all our diversity, all our conflicts of style and objective, we were destined in world-historical Hegelian fashion to live out fragments of the true and single revolution, then obstacles and even disasters could be seen as transitional, the errors and sins just friction in the machinery. (Gitlin, *The Sixties: Years of Hope, Days of Rage* [New York: Bantam, 1987], 345–47)

It is important to note the relation between such revolutionary goals and the inspiration of utopia. The structure of feeling is an important dimension of political praxis.

19. Martin Luther King Jr. "Declaration of Independence from the War in Vietnam," *Ramparts* (May 1967): 207. For a similar engagement with the problem of totality, see Maxine Hong Kingston, "The Brother in Vietnam," *Mother Jones* (June 1980). "The brother" believes that "in a country that operates on a war economy, there isn't much difference between being in the Navy and being a civilian." As consumers, "we were supporting the corporations that made tanks and bombers, napalm defoliants and bombs. Everything was connected to everything else and to war" (35).

20. Herbert Marcuse, *One-Dimensional Man* (Boston: Beacon, 1964), 63.

21. William Shakespeare, *Henry IV, Part 1,* Arden Edition, ed. A. R. Humphreys (London: Methuen, 1960).

22. Marcuse, *Eros and Civilization* (New York: Vintage Books, 1962), 137.

23. For an excellent recent view of sixties radicalism in relation to corporate culture, see Thomas Frank, *The Conquest of Cool* (Chicago: University of Chicago Press, 1997). Frank's book is a refreshing intervention in cultural studies since he focuses on the way in which the rebelliousness of the sixties became part of corporate planning itself. Unlike so many studies of consumerism, Frank does not focus on the supposedly "subversive" aspects of consumption. In fact, his analysis shows how much of the current populism in cultural studies may be seriously misguided.

24. In the last three decades, the political spectrum in the United States has changed remarkably. The culture wars between liberals and conservatives exclude the more lofty ambitions of sixties utopianism.

25. Jacques Derrida, *Of Grammatology,* trans. Gayatri Spivak (Baltimore: Johns Hopkins University Press, 1976), 19.

26. Derrida, *Positions,* trans. Alan Bass (Chicago: University of Chicago Press, 1981), 57.

27. Richard Rorty, *Philosophy and the Mirror of Nature* (Princeton: Princeton University Press, 1979). Rorty is very clear that his philosophy supports the basic liberal goals of American pragmatism. Derrida, on the other hand, has never wanted to be as direct about the political implications of his work.

28. Derrida, *Specters of Marx,* trans. Peggy Kamuf (New York: Routledge, 1994), 73.

29. The "negative" in deconstruction is, of course, nondialectical. Both Marxist and Hegelian philosophies of history work with "determinate negation," or forms of "contradiction," which help advance human knowledge and human freedom. For Deconstruction, on the other hand, negation is a means of coming up as empty-handed as possible. The expression, "the labour of the negative" is from Hegel's *Phenomenology of Spirit.*

30. See Francis Fukuyama, *The End of History and the Last Man* (New York: Free Press, 1992).

31. Derrida, *Specters of Marx,* 85.

32. Ibid.

33. The work of Laclau and Mouffe remains the most cogent anti-essentialist or post-Marxist appropriation of deconstruction for postmodern politics. Derrida mentions their work in a brief footnote. See Ernesto Laclau and Chantal Mouffe, *Hegemony and Socialist Strategy* (London: Verso, 1985).

34. Derrida was not the only one in the sixties and seventies to criticize the onto-theological grounding in notions of history. Foucault, for example, developed his Nietzschean notion of "genealogy," which demolishes teleological histories while exploring discontinuites and unstable relations of power.

35. Walter Benjamin, *Theses on the Philosophy of History* (New York: Schocken, 1968), 255.

36. Derrida, *The Other Heading: Reflections on Today's Europe,* trans. Pascale-Anne Brault and Michael B. Naas (Bloomington: Indiana University Press, 1992).

37. On the implications of the new media technologies for Marxism, see Mark Poster, *The Mode of Information* (Chicago: University of Chicago Press, 1990).

38. Derrida, *Specters of Marx,* 130.

39. Although Marx's realism is often incoherent, I think that Derrida loses the "spirit" of Marx when he fails to affirm the importance of Marx's theory of praxis. There have been much better critiques that do not give up on Marx. See, for example, the Wittgensteinian analysis by Gavin Kitching in *Karl Marx and the Philosophy of Praxis* (London: Routledge, 1988).

40. Marx, "Theses on Feuerbach," in *Marx-Engels Reader,* 145.

41. In an interview with Julia Kristeva published in 1968, he says, "Nothing—no present and in-diffferent being—thus precedes *différance* and spacing. There is no subject who is agent, author, and master of *différance,* who eventually and empirically would be overtaken by *différance.* Subjectivity—like objectivity—is an effect of *différance.*" Derrida, *Positions,* 28.

42. Engels uses the metaphor of the "rational kernel" to emphasize the importance of the early nineteenth-century utopians, Saint-Simon and Robert Owen.

43. Ernesto Laclau, *New Reflections on the Revolution of Our Time* (London: Verso, 1990), 92. Compare Paul Berman's argument that the liberal utopia of the sixties can now be found in Eastern European anti-communism and in such American movements as gay rights. The more radical (i.e., socialist) visions of sixties' utopianism should be placed in the ash can of history. See Berman, *A Tale of Two Utopias* (New York: Norton, 1996).

44. For a recent analysis of Disney "utopia," see *Inside the Mouse* (Durham: Duke University Press, 1995). The writers follow the Jamesonian model of looking for the utopian elements of mass culture. Their analysis shows, for example, how "the family" unit becomes the ideological model for utopia:

> The family enshrined by Disney and built into the park by his "imagineineers" is not in itself utopian. But a family's desire for togetherness can have utopian dimensions when it concretizes a response to the absence of available collectivity in society at large. This utopian aspect is, however, compromised by the fact that the notion of togetherness is imbricated with leisure time consumption. You have to pay—and pay a lot—in order to achieve the experience of collectivity. (51)

45. Bill Readings, *The University in Ruins* (Cambridge: Harvard University Press, 1996), 116.

46. Zarathustra also quotes the last men: "'We have discovered happiness,' say the Ultimate Men and blink." See Zarathustra's prologue in *Thus Spoke Zarathustra,* trans. R. J. Hollingdale (London: Penguin Books, 1961), 46–47.

47. Thomas Pynchon, *The Crying of Lot 49* (New York: Perennial Classics, 1999), 14.

48. Ibid., 4–5.

49. Jameson uses Deleuze as an example: "The value of the molecular in Deleuze, for instance, depends structurally on the preexisting molar or unifying impulse against which its truth is read" (Jameson, *Political Unconscious*, 53).

13

Afterword

Historicism and Its Limits

MORRIS DICKSTEIN

When I began teaching English at Columbia University in the fall of 1966, the campus atmosphere was alive with conflict but the revolution that would transform scholarship in the humanities was still in its infancy. National politics and the role of the university were the issues, not the methodology of any discipline. Every month brought demonstrations and teach-ins against the Vietnam War, the draft, the ROTC, and defense research, but the coming battle in literary and cultural studies was barely on the horizon. Caught up in the intense demands of my first weeks of full-time teaching, I missed the famous conference on structuralism at Johns Hopkins University in October at which Jacques Derrida's seminal paper "Structure, Sign, and Play in the Discourse of the Human Sciences"caused a sensation. Though no one knew it at the time, it marked the arrival of poststructuralism in this country. But the previous year as a graduate student I had helped Jacques Ehrmann organize a symposium at Yale that brought together some future stars of the theory firmament, including Paul de Man, Geoffrey Hartman, and J. Hillis Miller. These papers, most of which were later published in *Modern Language Notes,* showed how much theory there was before the official outbreak of Theory. They focused sympathetically on older European critics such as Georg Lukács, Erich Auerbach, Leo Spitzer, Georges Poulet, Ernst Robert Curtius, Maurice Blanchot, and Gaston Bachelard, some of whose major works had already appeared in English.[1] This initial phase of literary theory in America can be seen as a revolt of the younger comparative literature professors against the insular mind-set of postwar American criticism, which had settled into practical criticism—the methodical explication of texts and authors—as its primary goal. By contrast, the work of the European critics was closely allied with the history of ideas, including disciplines like philosophy, phenomenology, linguistics, and social history. Philologically trained critics like Spitzer and Auerbach and a phenomenologist like Poulet had taught here as émigré scholars and had already exerted some degree of influence. Their work had a range, erudition, and philosophical heft that was lacking in American criticism, but they did not pose as drastic a challenge to business as usual as their poststructuralist successors. Their work belonged to a long tradition of cosmopolitan scholarship and literary history, but it was not incompatible with prevailing academic techniques of close reading.

During that first year of teaching, as I struggled to keep up with the heavy reading for my courses, especially Columbia's famous survey of the Western tradition from Homer to Dostoevsky, I was trying to complete a thesis on the poetry of Keats.[2] With some effort, I could probably reconstruct the intellectual atmosphere in which this project originated. Clearly, it was stamped by the exegetical techniques of the New Critics yet also reflected a growing interest in Romanticism, which those critics had scorned. As an effort to penetrate the writer's inner life by following the shape and flow of the author's consciousness, it showed the impact of phenomenology, but as I can see today, it was also touched by the vitalism of young Nietzsche, William Blake, and Marcuse's *Eros and Civilization*. It brought to bear the early Romantic criticism of de Man and Hartman, still almost unknown, yet also the stoic and tragic perspective of Lionel Trilling, who had been my teacher when I was an undergraduate.[3] In this stew of influence, the strongest ingredient was probably the most idiosyncratic: the homegrown phenomenology of D. H. Lawrence's friend and rival John Middleton Murry, who had tried in numerous books and essays to convey the ripening of Keats's poetic imagination, to write a biography of the spirit from its traces in language.

These were intellectual influences—numerous, as in all apprentice works—the critical avant-garde of the moment combined with models all my own, such as Murry's incandescent identification with Keats's mind. Did the political upheavals of the period also act upon my little book, or did they belong to a different compartment of my life? Was my work on Keats merely simultaneous with the turmoil of the sixties or somehow conditioned by it? It would be hard to say, yet clearly the book belonged to its moment, however modestly. As an exploration of one writer's mental world, situating subjectivity at the heart of Romanticism, it was affected by the impassioned individualism that flourished in the early sixties—the utopian faith in personal liberation, the Freudian critique of repression, that Marcuse and Norman O. Brown preached and the nascent counterculture had already begun to practice. Keats had been there before them, projecting an erotic paradise with innumerable versions of Spenser's Bower of Bliss and delicious speculations about the passive flower and the active Bee ("and who shall say between Man and Woman which is the most delighted?"). With his celebrated ripe sensuousness and Shakespearean gusto, more and more colored by a tragic vision, Keats's poetry was the perfect vehicle for such an argument. A few months after finishing with Keats I began teaching a course on William Blake, whose early work, including his *Songs of Experience, The Marriage of Heaven and Hell, Visions of the Daughters of Albion,* and *America,* took both political *and* sexual revolution as their passionate cause. No one had to ask which side I was on.

But if my exploration of the inner world of Keats's poems and letters was an advance on the New Criticism for the mid-1960s, it must have looked hopelessly backward ten years later, when Derrida, Foucault, Barthes, and de Man had begun to deconstruct the human subject as an effect of language, of bourgeois ideology, of certain tropes and discursive practices, of the freeplay of difference. New Critical methods of close reading depended on establishing the structure of a work, including its patterns of metaphor, and connecting it to a recognizable human world. Derrida's paper at Johns Hopkins challenged the whole notion of a stable structure, a core of meaning that linked the text to the world around it. A structure, like a subject, required a center, but for Derrida the "center had no locus," for "it was not a fixed locus but a function" within a fluid system of sign-substitutions and differences. He connected the need for a fixed form with the need for stable foundations in metaphysics, and described it as a stay against anxiety, a fear of the free play of signifiers.[4] This playful application of linguistics to literary structure and meaning became a ticking bomb at the heart of all interpretation. Inspired by Derrida and Foucault, Eugenio Donato took this even further: "Interpretation is nothing but sedimenting one layer of language upon another to produce an illusory depth which gives us the temporary spectacle of things beyond words."[5] It followed that the critic could not approach what was real, could not excavate meaning, but could only examine the duplicities of language to determine how the illusion of depth and meaning was achieved. This robbed interpretation of its weight and power even as it made the *game* of interpretation more enticing. The theory years had begun, though the deepest inroads were at first limited to a few elite universities.

When I joined the doctoral faculty of the City University of New York in 1974, the courses were still parceled out in terms of conventional periods, genres, and major authors, with little attention paid to criticism itself or to literature published since 1945. But by 1980, many younger scholars had been trained in theory, and this curriculum was changing. Even departments far from the mainstream made room for black studies and women's studies. Some had already slotted in at least a single theorist, usually a deconstructionist, whose role was to play the young Turk, to shake up the department and give it a fresher look, an orientation toward the future. Like the Shakespearean Fool, exempt from the usual rules of decorum, the resident theorist was licensed to arraign his or her colleagues for their hidebound traditionalism. Gradually, however, as the next generation gained a tenuous, then a tenured foothold, theory became less a specialty of its own, more a radical critique of how the whole field of literary studies operated. Yet despite the sweeping, sometimes apocalyptic language, its radicalism never took a genuinely political form. As theory gained acceptance in the university and vast prestige in the profession, it never challenged institutional patterns of accreditation and authority already in place. Where the sixties generation had thrown itself into radical lifestyles, communal living, and alternate forms of education, the young theorists, facing tougher economic times, merely sought a place at the table, sometimes playing on liberal guilt as a way of gaining academic turf.

A new generation was asserting its identity, but in an ambiguous way. Earlier generations of literature professors had seen themselves as guardians of the language against the professional deformations of social scientists and academic Marxists. Now proponents of theory took a different turn. They tried to refashion the university into a radical enclave within a society of old-style liberals, new-style conservatives, and hip young professionals. Theory transformed the academic study of literature at the expense of its connections to the wider world. It turned its back on the kind of criticism that advances literacy, cherishes style, and honors clarity as it mediates between literature and its audience. As American politics gradually shifted to the right, theory turned inward, preaching to the choir and self-consciously polishing its own techniques. The success of the political Right in culture wars of the late 1980s and early 1990s, especially the battle over political correctness, was partly the result of theory's vulnerable position in the public sphere, its failure to cultivate a language in which it might defend itself in open debate. The new dispensation was mocked by traditionalists for its pseudosystematic ambitions, its paralyzing skepticism, its focus on method at the expense of other important issues (or at the expense of literature itself), its often impenetrable jargon, and the cults that surrounded its academic stars. This led eventually to a retreat from theory, a search for new ways of making literature meaningful, and a nostalgia for the kind of public intellectual, the accessible generalist, that theory had mocked and tried to supplant.

As we look back at the theory years today, now that the fierce polemical passions have waned, the transformation of literary studies in a single generation seems astonishing. Where did it come from? What kind of residue has it left? In a relatively short time, conventional scholarship and criticism focused on individual writers and their works were displaced by postmodern skepticism and the critique of ideology. Criticism shifted from a concentration on literature to an examination of the instruments of criticism itself, or the social or linguistic conditions that bring literature into being. The formalist emphasis on aesthetics, on the meaning and structure of the work itself, gave way to the contextual scholarship of the New Historicism, the political commitments of radical feminism and queer theory, and the ideological scrutiny that was the hallmark of cultural studies. Literature and history were denied their power to convey truth or depict the world, to achieve what Matthew Arnold quaintly called a "criticism of life." Instead they were seen as ideological formations and social or linguistic constructions.

In de Man's later work, wars and revolutions were reduced to rhetorical terms, that is, to the terms in which they had been interpreted, or represented in language; the periods and movements of standard literary histories became "rather crude metaphors for figural patterns rather than historical events or acts."[6] An iconoclastic exuberance lurks behind such dour, poker-faced pronouncements, a barely concealed delight in upsetting every applecart in sight. But the effect on the disciplines was not so amusing. The new history turned from sequential narratives that made causal connections toward excavations of deep-seated assumptions, projects of demystication designed to strike through the mask, to expose devices of control and representation. As one who remains at heart an old historicist, devoted to striking a balance between the social matrix of literature and the power that it achieves through language, voice, and formal expression, I am not the ideal person to explain this shift, though I'm fascinated by the suggestive answers proposed by the contributors to this volume, *Historicizing Theory*. In an ingenious twist, they search out the historical basis of theory itself by examining the circumstances that may have contributed to its genesis. But to the Jamesonian commandment "Always historicize" with which the editor begins his introduction, I'm tempted to respond, "Why historicize?"—especially when the theorists you're discussing have stubbornly resisted acknowledging the extra-literary influences that may have shaped their work. And why "always," when the evidence can be quite slim, when some historical explanations are more revealing than others, and when they can also differ so dramatically in their results, as this volume testifies? No interpretive project is self-justifying; we need to know why it should be pursued and to evaluate its claims at every turn.

Nowadays we tend too readily to think of the shift from historicism to formalism after 1945 as a function of the Cold War, a recoil from politics that can be observed not only in literary studies but in sociology, art criticism, analytic philosophy, and law. Historians turned their backs on the progressive traditions of Frederick Jackson Turner, Vernon Parrington, and Charles Beard, which put history at the service of populist or democratic values. Yet no one has shown convincingly how the Cold War *caused* any of these changes, though it may have coincided with them. Still, there was a remarkable consistency. The New Criticism in literature, functionalism in sociology, analytic philosophy, and the art criticism of Clement Greenberg were alike in turning their subjects into closed systems that left many important issues out-of-bounds, especially social questions about class and power that had dominated discussion before the war.

But even as we look to find some historical basis for this turn against history, it is worth recalling some weaknesses of the historical approach to literature that contributed to its decline. Modern poetry and painting could be exceptionally difficult. They broke sharply with nineteenth-century traditions of narration and representation. They took on forms of distortion or abstraction that seemed bent on effacing their origins. Historical criticism, on the other hand, except in the hands of exceptional critics like Meyer Schapiro or Edmund Wilson, seemed badly suited to the formal complexity and sheer bravado of modern art. Some leading historical critics like Georg Lukács and Van Wyck Brooks rejected modernism outright as a form of reactionary obscurantism. But even more sympathetic critics could be reductive or obtuse about art, just as some New Historicists who would later devalue aesthetics as a formation of middle-class ideology.

Other historically oriented critics failed to get deeply *into* the work or rise to its personal challenge. Marxist critics could betray their subject into predictable formulas. Some historical critics dissolved the work of art into its background, in much the same way that unimaginative New Critics reduced it to mechanical patterns of imagery, or the way psychoanalytic critics could reduce it to the neurotic conflicts of its author. As formal methods could be subtle but narrow, as if the critic were wearing blinders, the historical approach could be expansive but superficial, eschewing the close-up for the wide-angle view. Historical criticism supplied the big picture but often routinely, in terms of movements and periods that hardly accounted for what truly mattered in the work of individual artists. With some exceptions, like the writings of the Frankfurt school or of a few key art historians, it stood bewildered before the artistic revolutions of the twentieth century, with their premium on novelty, their demand for a radical transformation of consciousness. In the face of this challenge, many historical critics could offer little more than fierce resistance or soothing clichés about art movements, period styles, and social background.

Though it avoided many of the mistakes of its predecessors, the revived historical criticism after 1980 would not entirely escape such simplifications, despite its specialized academic audience. Often it relied on interesting but remote social anecdotes that could point up an arresting parallel to the literary work without convincing the reader that it was truly relevant or decisive. Sometimes it proposed what simply looked like an analogy between the text and its presumed context that was more formal than historical, an inferential pattern or structural resemblance rather than a source or point of origin. By avoiding the genetic, chronological approach of earlier historicists, it ran the risk of looking arbitrary or merely ingenious. The keys it found did not always fit the designated locks. Responding to approaches described by Stephen Greenblatt, Catherine Gallagher, and Joel Fineman, Ivo Kamps contrasts the new and old historicism very effectively in his essay, "New Historicizing the New Historicism." He shows how a synchronic narrative focused on small "particulars" has served as a counterweight (or "counterhistory") to the diachronic or sequential narratives favored by social historians, which claim access to the "real," to history as it actually happened. These traditional narratives have been pictured as repressive, teleological, and "pre-encoded" by the historian's own categories, as in part they no doubt were. But this is really a caricature of the older history, which was just as likely to be tentative and empirical. As Kamps points out, "one can think of any number of historical narratives that are both teleological and tolerant of contingency" (183). Narrative history is not simply a claim about how things happened but a method of interpretation, a way of shaping data and engaging the reader through story, identifying causes and effects, and weaving disparate strands together. At its best it remains open to correction by another account that will supersede it.

In recent years, Renaissance scholars and younger Americanists have done exciting work by recovering much that had been ignored or suppressed by conventional critics, including the viewpoints of outsiders—women, people of color, and colonial subjects—but they could not always convince us of its determining importance to our understanding of the literary work. Apart from their political motivation, the hint of special pleading, such oblique approaches were limited by their reliance on what was absent or unexpressed in the work itself. Examples of argument by inference and suggestion can be found in some very good essays in this volume. Derrida's emphasis on the break or rupture is traced to his own expulsion from school (and eventual departure from the country) as a young French Jew in Algeria; de Man's pessimism and sense of futility is linked to the sudden and catastrophic fall of Belgium to the Nazis; and Foucault's stress on totalitarian control within social institutions like the asylum and the prison is attributed to his own boyhood in Occupied France during World War II. Yet these men habitually avoided such connections and, indeed, strongly denied that their work was grounded in their personal histories. Since they argued that the individual subject was a social construction or a linguistic formation, they balked at seeing their ideas peeled back to their biographical roots, especially when, in de Man's case, they had much to conceal about their earlier lives.

As Peter C. Herman points out in his introduction, theorists may resist historicizing because it can be used to explode their work, as neoconservatives and hard leftists have sometimes done. They also do so because, despite their relativism or skepticism, they think their ideas are valid, or at least convincing, not simply contingent and generated by circumstance, and deserve to have a life of their own. We must also concede (as Herman notes) that all of us are badly positioned to contextualize our own lives, something only succeeding generations can do. For that reason, a collection like *Historicizing Theory* confirms the waning of theory since the eighties and mid-nineties, since it shows us a new generation sufficiently disengaged from theory to take the detached view of the landscape in which theory emerged.[7] For the Europeans, evidently, this background is dominated by World War II, a period of defeat, occupation, ruthless brutality, moral compromise, and near-total control. For American critics, there is a consensus that the sixties, the Vietnam War, and the New Left provided the political crucible from which theory emerged. Certainly the Left politics of most theorists seems to reflect the radicalism that dominated the earlier period. More broadly, the theorists' attacks on traditional forms of historiography and literary scholarship might owe something to the debunking spirit of the 1960s, its mockery of authority and disdain for tradition, including the liberal tradition. An astute critic of literary theory, Eugene Goodheart, gives us an incisive summary of this viewpoint in his recent memoir:

> The radical students who made careers in the academy sublimated their radicalism in the various disciplines they occupied, particularly in the humanities. Radicalism became theories of interpretation, its targets literary and philosophical texts and social and political institutions. Having failed to transform society, it also became disillusioned, and already, beginning in the seventies, the most radically skeptical of theories, deconstructionism, became the rage. Its aim was to unsettle our convictions about the possibility of objective truth, spiritual transcendence, authoritative discourse. It asserted a doctrine of uncertainty in the most certain of tones. Is it fortuitous that its originator was a French Jew, Jacques Derrida?[8]

In this partly ironic account, theory was both a product of radicalism and a marker of its defeat, which parallels the crushing sense of failure that Europeans experienced during World War II. Theory set out to revolutionize the academy in which it took refuge from an unsympathetic society. It sought a radical transformation of the interpretive disciplines only to saddle them with a methodology that stressed skepticism, disillusionment, and broken connections. During the backlash years of Nixonian demagoguery and Reaganite restoration, theory became catastrophe theory, a way of compensating for the sense of impotence, or of recouping failure by showing that it was inevitable. At the same time critics asserted a decisive power over the text, a refusal to be dominated by its structures, themes, or rhetorical strategies.

This linkage between literary theory and the 1960s is far more subtle than Allan Bloom's attacks on relativism in *The Closing of the American Mind*, which could be applied to virtually all modern thought since the Enlightenment, or the neoconservative argument that postmodernism and poststructuralism are simply revolutionary nihilism run amok. Neoconservatives always exaggerate the influence of the sixties as the source of all social and moral evil, including abuses that must be attributed to capitalism and the marketplace, such as the promotional uses of the counterculture. But even Goodheart's version, which is reminiscent of Hazlitt's witty argument that Wordsworth and Coleridge applied the leveling principles of the French Revolution to poetic diction and literary characters, raises some elusive historical issues. We can leave aside the objection that, to my knowledge, no major student radicals became literary theorists, and that those who gave theory its big push were generally older, far from political, and (both in Europe and America) began publishing their work well before the sixties revolution hit its stride in 1968. Foucault's *Les Mots et les choses* appeared in France in 1966; Derrida published three major books in 1967, including *De la grammatologie*. Unlike their more committed predecessor, Jean-Paul Sartre, they were not engaged in the uprising of students and workers the following year. Back in the United States, most of those who became theory stars in the 1970s, including de Man, Geoffrey Hartman, Harold Bloom, J. Hillis Miller, Edward Said, and Stanley Fish, had done their graduate work in the 1950s at Harvard or Yale. Their ambitions were academic and relatively traditional, and they were already becoming known for innovative work in their fields. None of them was especially political in the sixties. But we can partly discount this by arguing that it was not their own politics that linked theory to the sixties but the enthusiastic reception of their work among the foot soldiers of the younger generation.

Even so, serious problems remain in tracing the historical roots of theory to the 1960s. First of all, the politics of the sixties varied enormously through the course of the decade. In his concluding essay, "The Spectrality of the '60s," Benjamin Bertram performs a great service by reminding us of the redemptive utopian humanism of the early sixties, as represented by figures as different as Martin Luther King Jr., Herbert Marcuse, and the authors of *The Port Huron Statement*. Bertram recognizes that the "linguistic turn" of theory, as it developed from Derrida, became a weapon against utopian thinking, against humanism, against any totalizing or "monistic"conception of history. In the recent work of Derrida on Karl Marx, however, Bertram spies some survival of "the form of the messianic without the content," and he concludes, all too hopefully, that even at the present moment, "utopian thinking does not disappear with the decline of revolutionary politics but is reconfigured along new lines." Poststructuralist theory was nothing if not a drastic critique of Western humanism, including the existential humanism of the sixties, across which it cast a large epistemological shadow. The radical students I taught in the sixties were scarcely bent on deconstructing the residues of metaphysics in Western humanist texts. On the contrary, they responded with passion to the classics as subversive works whose humane promise remained unfulfilled. They connected with art and philosophy not because it was imposingly canonical but because it felt so fresh, so immediate—and so visionary. Blake, Dickens, Ruskin, and Lawrence felt like their contemporaries, not musty classics. Never had the Great Books seemed more relevant than when the whole direction of society was in play. The lineage of deconstruction takes us back not to the politics of the sixties but to its ultimate betrayal and blockage.

A better case for the roots of theory can be made from the sour political mood of the late sixties, when the smashed hopes of earlier years turned to anger, skepticism, and suspicion. As Kamps shows in his essay, Vietnam was "a war in search of a narrative," at least until the surprise Tet Offensive early in 1968, when media accounts of American embarrassment and failure overwhelmed the mundane facts of the defeat of the Vietcong on the ground. By then the triumphal claims of America's military and political leaders had been so discredited that no one believed them, even when they happened to be true. In the Tet Offensive the Vietcong had thrown everything they had into simultaneous strikes all around the country; their cadres were decimated, not to be rebuilt for many months, though few people knew this at the time. Yet in the other war, the battle for public opinion that was waged on television, America suffered a humiliating and finally decisive setback. Soon President Johnson and his advisors decided that the war could not be won. The antiwar movement gained its greatest victories in the media, not in the halls of Congress, the White House, or the voting booth. As the administration repeatedly lied to the people with optimistic predictions, phony successes, and exaggerated body counts, a vast reservoir of disbelief built up in American life, a deep distrust of official information, which could well have contributed to the later appeal of the "hermeneutics of suspicion" in interpretation. At the same time, as government pronouncements lost credibility, the virtual reality shaped by the media began to dominate public perception. In this sense, the rise of cultural studies might be linked to the darkening political climate of the late sixties, as both Ivo Kamps and David R. Shumway suggest.

Shumway argues convincingly in "The Sixties, the New Left, and the Emergence of Cultural Studies in the United States" that cultural studies in America was more closely tied to indigenous developments than to the Birmingham school of British cultural studies. The working-class consciousness of the Birmingham group and their Leavisite concern with separating authentic folkways from mass culture never took hold in America, though its later focus on ideology certainly did. Cultural studies in America descended from the American studies movement, which embraced popular culture along with the high arts, and it took off from the ever-expanding media scene. Its overweening interest in popular culture was licensed by the subtle and powerful pop culture of the sixties, especially the music, which made the hierarchical distinctions of the mass culture critics untenable. Cultural studies was also indebted to the rise of identity politics in the late sixties, beginning with black nationalism, feminism, and the gay pride movement. Rejecting the notion of a unified culture for an emphasis on diversity and difference, cultural studies was caught between an ethnically derived notion of group affirmation and a postmodern sense of fluid or constructed identity. For scholars who came of age in the sixties and seventies, issues of race and gender, like pop culture, were part of the air they breathed. Since this was also true for young writers, painters, and filmmakers, cultural studies developed in concert with an eclectic postmodernism in the arts, just as the earlier formalist criticism had responded to the strenuous innovations of modernism.

The pitfalls of historicizing are clear enough. Even when it has freed itself of Hegelian notions of the Zeitgeist or Marxist certitudes about historical inevitability, historical criticism is rarely as rigorous as formal analysis. As John Kerrigan wrote recently: "As the heat goes out of the theory wars, the literary critical mainstream has settled into a historicism that has never properly established which principles of relevance should apply."[9] Historicist readings may be idiosyncratic, empirically tenuous, or merely suggestive. According to Shumway, star careers have been made in recent decades with far-fetched readings that are more striking than convincing, interpretations that are widely discussed yet finally accepted by no one.[10] Once they are out there, students feel obliged to build on them or grapple with them; they become part of the conversation, which they help distract or derail. This is not limited to historicist readings. However, because they bring in social issues, historical interpretations are more likely to be predictable in their political sympathies. Eager to weigh in on the side of the insulted and the injured, they seem predetermined by their well-meaning political agendas. Yet compared to other kinds of reading, they call upon a larger knowledge of the world, and often do more to link literature or theory to the actual flow of human life.

The historical approach can be used polemically to diminish writers and movements by reducing them to their local circumstances. But it can also serve to enhance them by anchoring them in actuality. To be reminded of how the "shaping nightmare" of World War II might have affected the young Foucault, how the sudden "decapitation" of Belgium might have influenced de Man, or how the trauma of the Algerian War might play itself out in the work of Derrida can be a way of validating their abstractions, rightly or wrongly, by attaching them to great social movements and deeply felt personal experiences. Yet this leaves open the question of why such formative, perhaps traumatic events would take them in one direction rather than another. If

Foucault was so deeply affected by the totalitarian climate of the Nazi Occupation, why did he later apply this template almost exclusively to progressive institutions and liberal societies? There are diametrically opposed ways of reading the relationship between de Man's late work and his early collaborationist articles. Partisan scholars bring their own agendas to these issues. But no serious thinker can be reduced to his or her biography, no matter how much the life illuminates the work.

In the end, the justification for historical interpretation is that we must know everything, the life, the times, the intricate internal argument, the shape of the language. When a subject engages us, every detail is precious, every shred of evidence is worth considering. We want to know how life feeds into art, not simply how art feeds on itself. Thinkers or writers, like magicians, will never tell you how they learned their tricks, even if they imagine they know. The essays in this volume amplify our sense of the theory years by showing us that they were not inevitable; they were the work of specific people that unfolded in particular situations. They too now belong to history. The origin and reach of their work can be explained in different ways that vary here from chapter to chapter. Our obligation is to be as conscientious as possible in staking out the territory, to reach for a distinterestedness that may nevertheless escape us.

It's important that we bring to bear as much information and insight as possible, not just the curious sidelight or the odd, quirky, arresting analogy that gives one's account an unexpected turn. Professional historians, who often find the work of the New Historicism unconvincing, mostly remain committed to empirical canons of evidence, to sequential narratives that emphasize beginnings and endings, cause and effect. They feel obliged to weigh competing explanations, as the best interpretive work has always done. This does not mean that criticism must be confined to a dispassionate, elusive objectivity.

By the end of the 1950s, American academic criticism had fallen into a deadly and narrow common sense approach that was constrained not by a rigorous formalism but by a deep failure of imagination. Themes were summarized, characters characterized, images scrutinized, but the questions asked had grown less interesting. New Critical methods of close reading had contributed as much as they could but had reached a point of diminishing returns. They were being applied to the wrong texts or to texts that had already been exhaustively read. They were ferreting out subtexts where none needed to be found. They had grown mechanical and pedantic.

This is what made the essayistic approach of Blanchot, Barthes, and Benjamin seem so exciting at the time. Like the best critics of the past, they made arresting connections through paradoxical leaps of intuition and insight. They were essentially writers, not critics—writers whose aphoristic prose enforced a willing suspension of disbelief. They were as imaginative, as gifted, as much fun to read, as most of the writers they wrote about. They rose to the challenge of their subjects. This was what bold, unclassifiable American critics like Kenneth Burke and Alfred Kazin had been doing all along, but it hardly satisfied the demands of academic work as then construed. What these critics did could be emulated but not imitated: it offered no "method," and its effects could be disastrous in the hands of less agile practitioners. With such idiosyncratic critics, the reality check, the empirical constraints, came in the shock of recognition on the part of the reader, the shaft of illumination their essays provided.

Less gifted critics—we ourselves—can operate only through argument and evidence, the drama of persuasion and assent. Like other forms of criticism, historical interpretation can be well done or badly done, loopy or acute, ingenious or ingenuous. Yet setting things in context is always worth doing, and frequently revealing, as this volume repeatedly demonstrates. It helps us enlarge the picture. It peers behind the masks that writers or theorists put on to convince us they have given birth to themselves. There are always risks involved in searching out the figure in a carpet or shaping the multitude of possibilities into a single coherent narrative. The return of historical criticism was an invigorating breath of fresh air. It released a burst of interpretive energy beyond the limited horizon of formalism and deconstruction. At a moment of intellectual exhaustion, it offered provocative new readings for old. Drawn to political advocacy, to sitting in judgment on the power relationships it perceived in the past, it sometimes served as a vehicle for its own enlightened preconceptions. Yet finally, historical interpretation is an indispensable way of comprehending culture and shedding light on the theories and practices through which it has always tried to make sense of itself.

NOTES

The author is grateful to Mark Bauerlein and Peter C. Herman for their comments on an earlier version of this essay.

1. See *Modern Language Notes* 81.5 (December 1966): 527–94. The published papers include Paul de Man's essay on Georg Lukács's *Theory of the Novel,* later reprinted in his first book, *Blindness and Insight* (1971), and the title piece of Geoffrey Hartman's first collection, *Beyond Formalism and Other Essays* (1970), as well as essays on Erich Auerbach, Ernst Robert Curtius, and Gaston Bachelard, along with interesting afterthoughts by J. Hillis Miller, "The Antitheses of Criticism: Reflections on the Yale Colloquium," which mapped the conflict between older and newer forms of criticism. At that time in France the "new criticism," as represented by Roland Barthes, was under attack by Raymond Picard, an old-style literary scholar in the venerable historicist tradition of Gustave Lanson, which had decayed into anti-intellectualism.

2. In revised form it later appeared as a book, Morris Dickstein, *Keats and His Poetry: A Study in Development* (Chicago: University of Chicago Press, 1971).

3. Influential samples of new work on Romanticism affected by phenomenology can be found in *Romanticism and Consciousness,* ed. Harold Bloom (New York: Norton, 1970), including Paul de Man's "Intentional Structure of the Romantic Image" and Hartman's "Romanticism and 'Anti-Self-Consciousness.'" The new Romantic criticism would be a crucial matrix out of which theory in America would develop. This lineage can be traced in de Man's shift from phenomenology to rhetoric in *The Rhetoric of Romanticism* (New York: Columbia University Press, 1984) and in the manifesto of the so-called Yale School, *Deconstruction and Criticism* (New York: Seabury Press, 1979).

4. Jacques Derrida, "Structure, Sign, and Play in the Discourse of the Human Sciences," in *The Structuralist Controversy: The Languages of Criticism and the Sciences of Man,* eds. Richard Macksey and Eugenio Donato (Baltimore and London: Johns Hopkins University Press, 1972), 249.

5. Donato, "The Two Languages of Criticism," in ibid., 96.

6. De Man, *Rhetoric of Romanticism,* 254. Quoted by James J. Paxson in this volume, *Historicizing Theory,* 90, n. 2.

7. Jeffrey Williams and Peter C. Herman offer a valuable account of the younger generation in *Day Late, Dollar Short: The Next Generation and the New Academy,* ed. Peter Herman (Albany: State University of New York Press, 2000). They portray what Williams calls "the posttheory generation" not as a cohort of young scholars in rebellion against theory so much as one that grew up taking it too much for granted "as the lingua franca of literature programs" but is now raising serious questions about its received assumptions. Williams takes a broad overview of recent trends in criticism, including autobiographical criticism, public intellectual writing, and journalistic criticism, in "The New Belletrism," *Style* 33.3 (fall 1999): 414–42.

8. Eugene Goodheart, *Confessions of a Secular Jew: A Memoir* (Woodstock and New York: Overlook Press), 174.

9. John Kerrigan, review of Valentine Cunningham, *Reading After Theory,* London Review of Books (September 19, 2002).

10. Shumway illustrates his point by citing the work of the well-known Americanist Walter Benn Michaels: "He is a brilliant rhetorician, and his abilities as a writer certainly gain him an audience others cannot command. It would be hard, however, to name any argument by Michaels that has changed the profession's views of a text or a theoretical issue." "My point," he concludes, "is that in this scholarly economy it does not matter whether anyone will agree with it. All the critic has to do is to get people to notice it. . . . Performance has replaced persuasion as the standard by which scholarly practice is judged." Shumway, "The Star System Revisited," *minnesota review,* nos. 52–54 (fall 2001): 179–80. Of course, style, performance, and other attention-getting devices have always been a part of the critic's arsenal, but usually accompanied by a determined effort to influence opinion and to gain general agreement.

CONTRIBUTORS

BENJAMIN BERTRAM, an assistant professor at the University of Southern Maine, has also published "New Reflections on the Revolutionary Politics of Ernesto Laclau and Chantal Mouffe" (*boundary 2*, 22:3). He is currently completing a book on skepticism in early modern England.

EVAN CARTON, is Professor of English and Director of the Humanities Institute at the University of Texas. He is the author of *The Rhetoric of American Romance and The Marble Faun: Hawthorne's Transformations*, and the coauthor of *Poetry and Criticism, 1940–1995*, vol. 8 of *The Cambridge History of American Literature*. His essays on American literature, criticism, and culture have appeared in *American Scholar, Raritan, ESQ: A Journal of the American Renaissance*, and *American Literature*.

MORRIS DICKSTEIN is Distinguished Professor of English at the CUNY Graduate Center and Senior Fellow of the Center for the Humanities, which he founded in 1993. He is the author of *Keats and Poetry; Gates of Eden: American Culture in the Sixties; Double Agent: The Critic and Society;* and *Leopards in the Temple: The Transformation of American Fiction, 1945–1970*.

LOREN GLASS is Assistant Professor of American Literature and Cultural Studies at Towson State University. He is currently completing *More than Authors: Literary Celebrity in the Modern United States, 1880–1980*.

JONATHAN GIL HARRIS is Professor of English at George Washington University. He is the author of *Foreign Bodies and the Body Politic: Discourses of Social Pathology in Early Modern England* (1998) and coeditor, with Natasha Korda, of *Staged Properties in Early Modern English Drama* (2002). He has just completed *Etiologies of the Economy: Dramas of Mercantilism and Disease in Shakespeare's England*.

PETER C. HERMAN is Professor of English at San Diego State University. He is the author of *Squitter-wits and Muse-haters: Sidney, Spenser, Milton and Renaissance Antipoetic Sentiment* and he has edited *Rethinking the Henrician Era: Essays on Early Tudor Texts and Contexts* and *Day Late, Dollar Short: The Next Generation and the New Academy*. He has published essays on Milton, English historiography, Spenser, and Renaissance drama in *Renaissance Quarterly, Studies in English Literature, Exemplaria, Criticism, Texas Studies in Literature and Language,* and the *Journal of Medieval and Early Modern Studies*.

IVO KAMPS is Associate Professor of English at the University of Mississippi. He is the author of *Historiography and Ideology in Stuart Drama* (1996), and the series editor of Early Modern Cultural Studies, 1500–1700. He is a contributing editor to an anthology of Thomas Middleton's plays, and he is currently coediting, with Karen Raber, a contextual edition of *Measure for Measure*.

ANDREA LOSELLE is Associate Professor in the Department of French and Francophone Studies at the University of California at Los Angeles. She is the author of essays on travel and tourism, the compromised writers Louis-Ferdinand Céline and Paul Morand, French theory, and *History's Double: Cultural Tourism in Twentieth-Century French Writing* (1997).

LEE MORRISSEY is Associate Professor in English at Clemson University. He is currently completing *The Constitution of Literature: Literacy, Democracy, and Early Literary Criticism*.

JAMES J. PAXSON is Associate Professor of English at the University of Florida. He is the author of *The Poetics of Personification* (1994) and has coedited *Desiring Discourse: The Literature of Love, Ovid through Chaucer* (1998) and *The Performance of Middle English Culture: Essays on Chaucer and the Drama in Honor of Martin Stevens* (1998). He is an editor of *Exemplaria: A Journal of Theory in Medieval and Renaissance Studies*.

KAREN RABER is Associate Professor of English at the University of Mississippi. She is the author of essays on early modern English women writers, and *Dramatic Difference: Gender, Class and Genre in the Early Modern Closet Drama* (2001). She is currently coediting, with Ivo Kamps, a contextual edition of *Measure for Measure*.

MARC REDFIELD is Professor of English and holder of the John D. and Lillian Maguire Chair in the Humanities at Claremont Graduate University. He is the author of *Phantom Formations: Aesthetic Ideology and the Bildungsroman*

(1996) and *The Politics of Aesthetics: Nationalism, Gender, Romanticism* (2003). He has coedited, with Janet Brodie, *High Anxieties: Cultural Studies in Addiction* (2002).

DAVID R. SHUMWAY is Professor of English and Literary and Cultural Studies at Carnegie Mellon University and Director of its Center for Cultural Analysis. He is the author of *Michel Foucault* and *Creating American Civilization: A Genealogy of American Literature as an Academic Discipline*, and coeditor of *Knowledges: Critical and Historical Studies in Disciplinarity* and *Disciplining English*. He has just completed *Modern Love*, a study of the discourses of romance and intimacy in twentieth-century America, and he is completing *Classic Rockers*, a book on the cultural development of rock stars.

H. ARAM VEESER is Associate Professor of English at City College, CUNY. He is the coauthor of *Ken Aptekar: Painting between the Lines, 1990–2000* and editor of *The New Historicism, Confessions of the Critics*, and *The Stanley Fish Reader*. His articles have appeared in *The Nation, Minnesota Review, Armenian Forum*, and *Biblical Interpretation*.

INDEX